Territorial foundations of the Gulf states

The SOAS/GRC Geopolitics Series

Territorial foundations of the Gulf states
EDITED BY Richard Schofield

The boundaries of modern Iran
EDITED BY Keith McLachlan

The Horn of Africa
EDITED BY Charles Gurdon

The changing shape of the Balkans
EDITED BY Frank Carter & Harold Norris

Transcaucasian boundaries
EDITED BY John Wright, Richard Schofield, Suzanne Goldenberg

Territorial foundations of the Gulf states

Edited by

Richard Schofield

Geopolitics and International Boundaries Research Centre
School of Oriental and African Studies
University of London

UCL
PRESS

First published in 1994 by UCL Press.

UCL Press Limited
University College London
Gower Street
London WC1E 6BT

The name of University College London (UCL) is a registered
trade mark used by UCL Press with the consent of the owner.

ISBN:
1-85728-121-7 HB
1-85728-122-5 PB

A CIP catalogue record for this book
is available from the British Library.

Typeset in Palatino.
Printed and bound by
Biddles Ltd, Guildford and King's Lynn, England.

Contents

Preface   vi

Contributors   ix

Borders and territoriality in the Gulf and the Arabian peninsula
during the twentieth century *Richard Schofield*   1

Concepts of sovereignty in the Gulf region *George Joffé*   78

Britain's rôle in boundary drawing in Arabia: a synopsis
John C. Wilkinson   94

Practical problems of boundary delimitation in Arabia:
the case of the United Arab Emirates *Julian Walker*   109

Iraq's claim to sovereignty over Kuwait
Maurice Mendelson & Susan Hulton   117

The Kuwaiti islands of Warbah and Bubiyan, and Iraqi access
to the Gulf *Richard Schofield*   153

Maritime delimitation in the Gulf *Rodman R. Bundy*   176

Cross-border hydrocarbon reserves *David Pike*   187

Shared zones as a solution to problems of territorial sovereignty
in the Gulf states *Gerald Blake*   200

Contemporary oil exploration and development policies in
the Gulf region *Paul Stevens*   211

Hydrocarbons and Iranian policies towards the Gulf states:
confrontation and co-operation in island and continental shelf affairs
Keith McLachlan   223

Index   239

Preface

This volume has its origins in a one-day conference of the same name hosted by the Geopolitics and International Boundaries Research Centre at London University's School of Oriental and African Studies in May 1991. Then seemed a particularly timely occasion, following Iraq's brutal adventurism in Kuwait, to examine how the present framework of state territory in the Gulf region had been arrived at and whether the contradictions and vulnerabilities inherent in its origins had been ameliorated with time. Two years on, the reasons for undertaking such a review have, if anything, grown. In the aftermath of the Kuwait crisis it had been commonly assumed that states of the Gulf littoral would put a higher priority than before on respecting and maintaining territorial integrity. Yet a surprising number of new disputes have erupted, and dormant rather than previously resolved cyclical disputes have been resurrected. The United Nations' "final" settlement of the Iraq/Kuwait boundary is not without its problems, while Bahrain and Qatar are really no closer to solving their maritime disputes. A violent incident on the undemarcated Saudi/Qatar border during the autumn of 1992 and the flare-up of the previously controlled Irano–Arab dispute over the status of Abu Musa and the Tunb islands have overshadowed genuine strides made to finalize the political map of the Arabian peninsula in the last two years or so: the ratification and registration at appropriated international institutions of the March 1990 Saudi–Oman border agreement (May–July 1991); an agreement fixing the Oman–Yemen land boundary (October 1992); and the commencement of talks between Yemen and Saudi Arabia (July 1992) to arrive at a delimitation for the peninsula's last indeterminate frontier.

In a substantial introductory section, Richard Schofield traces in great detail the evolution of territorial limits within the peninsula and discusses their current status. For the sake of comprehensiveness, sizeable sections are included here on important contemporary disputes and issues, which have escaped detailed commentary in the remaining ten chapters of this volume: the UN settlement of the Iraq/Kuwait boundary; the Saudi–Yemen dispute over oil and borders; the Irano–Arab dispute over Abu Musa and the Tunbs; and, lastly, the Bahrain/Qatar dispute over the ownership of the Hawar islands and the Jaradah and Dibal shoals. George Joffé then reviews indigenous concepts of sovereignty in the Gulf region and their relation to the contemporary framework of territory. Britain's attitude to boundary-drawing within Arabia is tackled in general terms by John Wilkinson, focusing upon the long-running through ultimately fruitless Anglo–Saudi

negotiations towards establishing territorial limits in southern Arabia in the
1934–55 period, and in more geographically specific terms by Julian Walker,
who reviews his experience more than three decades ago of trying to arrive
at boundaries for the component shaikhdoms of the modern United Arab
Emirates. In the third section of the collection, Iraq's claim to the entirety
of Kuwait forms the subject of Maurice Mendelson's and Susan Hulton's
thorough legal review, while Iraq's constant quest to improve its access to
Gulf waters, generally at the expense of the Kuwaiti islands of Warbah and
Bubiyan, is addressed by Richard Schofield. Rodman Bundy begins the next
section on maritime and resource disputes with an analysis of the maritime
boundary delimitations that have been concluded to date in the Gulf. The
critically important subject of transboundary hydrocarbons disputes in the
region is then tackled by David Pike. This part of the book is rounded off
imaginatively by Gerald Blake, who asks whether there is not greater scope
for instituting shared political space in order to lessen the potential for
conflict of the region's most enduring territorial disputes. A final section
comprising chapters by Paul Stevens and Keith McLachlan discusses the oil
exploration and production policies of the states of the Gulf littoral and their
effect in promoting regional co-operation or, alternatively, conflict and
competition, the latter often manifesting itself in the outbreak of territorial
disputes.

A considerable effort has been made to ensure that this volume is as up to
date as possible. All developments up until the end of 1992 are covered,
where appropriate, in the text. Chapter 1 has been updated to August 1993.
An attempt has been made to employ familiar and simplified Arabic transliterations for placenames and real names on a consistent basis in the
following pages. Throughout this work, including in its title, the Persian
Gulf, a placename recognized by the UN and OPEC, is referred to as the Gulf.

It is now my pleasurable task to acknowledge those individuals and
institutions who have helped to ensure the success of the current project:
Natasha Beschorner for administering the original conference that inspired
the present publication; Patricia Toye, in-house editor at the Geopolitics and
International Boundaries Research Centre, for preparing the text for publication; Sebastian Ballard for his cartography; Roger Jones and Nick Esson
at UCL Press for publishing this collection, the first in the GRC's "Geopolitics Series" (Roger particularly for his constructive advice and patience); Liz
Paton for her fastidious copy-editing; and all those individuals who acted
as readers of the collection at an earlier stage for their helpful suggestions,
some of which, I hope, have been acted upon.

My thanks go to the following publishers and institutions: Archive
Editions, for allowing the appearance in Chapter 1 of a substantially revised,
amended and updated version of a piece that originally appeared as the
introduction to *Arabian boundary disputes*; I B Tauris, for permission to
include as Chapter 3 an updated and modified version of the prologue in

John Wilkinson's *Arabia's frontiers: the story of Britain's boundary drawing in the desert* (London, 1991); *Annuaire français de droit international*, for allowing a modified and updated English translation of a 1990 article by Maurice Mendelson and Susan Hulton to appear as Chapter 5; and the Middle East Programme at the Royal Institute of International Affairs, for permission to reproduce maps (in Figures 5.1, 5.2, 6.1 and 6.2) that originally appeared in the first edition of Richard Schofield's *Kuwait and Iraq: historical claims and territorial disputes* (London, 1991). The Arabic transliterations of the Foreign Office originals from which they were drawn have been kept in these four maps.

Richard Schofield
September 1993

Contributors

Gerald Blake is a Reader in Geography and the Director of the International Boundaries Research Unit at the University of Durham. He is co-author (with Alasdair Drysdale) of *The Middle East and North Africa: a political geography* (Oxford University Press, New York, 1985) and (with Peter Beaumont and Malcolm Wagstaff) of *The Middle East: a geographical study* (2nd ed., David Fulton, London, 1988) and co-editor (with Richard Schofield) of *Boundaries and state territory in the Middle East and North Africa* (Menas Press, Wisbech, 1987).

Rodman Bundy is a partner in the Paris office of Frere Cholmeley specializing in public and private international law. He has a BA from Yale University and a JD from Georgetown University Law Center. Mr Bundy acted as counsel in the Libya–Tunisia and Libya–Malta continental shelf cases, and has appeared as counsel and advocate before the International Court of Justice, the Court of Arbitration of the International Chamber of Commerce and the Iran–United States Claims Tribunal. He is also Legal Director at the Geopolitics and International Boundaries Research Centre, at London University's School of Oriental and African Studies (SOAS).

Susan Hulton is part-time lecturer in international law at University College London, and a practising lawyer. She is author (with Maurice Mendelson) of The Iraq–Kuwait boundary: legal aspects, *Revue Belge de Droit International* **23** (1990–2), 293.

George Joffé is a founder member and Vice-Director of the Geopolitics and International Boundaries Research Centre at SOAS and teaches courses in geography and international relations at SOAS and the universities of Southampton and Sussex. He is co-author (with Keith McLachlan) of *The Gulf War: a survey of political issues and economic consequences* (Economist Intelligence Unit, London, 1984), co-editor (with C. R. Pennell) of *Tribe and state: essays in honour of David Montgomery Hart* (Menas Press, Wisbech, 1991) and editor of *North Africa: nation, state and region* (Routledge, London, 1993).

Keith McLachlan is a Professor of Geography and the Director of the Geopolitics and International Boundaries Research Centre at SOAS. He is author of *The neglected garden: the politics and ecology of agriculture in Iran* (I B Tauris, London, 1988) and co-author (with George Joffé) of *Iran and Iraq: the next five years* (Economist Intelligence Unit, London, 1987) and (with Richard

Schofield) of *A bibliography of the Iran–Iraq borderland* (Menas Press, Wisbech, 1987).

Maurice Mendelson, Q.C., is Professor of International Law at University College London, and a practising barrister specializing in, amongst other things, international sovereignty and boundary disputes. He is the author of numerous articles on various aspects of international law, and is currently editing *Brierly's Law of Nations*.

David Pike is Middle East editor at the London based *Petroleum Argus* newsletter. He previously worked as a reporter in the Middle East before joining *Middle East Economic Digest* in 1988 to cover the Gulf and oil-related questions. He is author of "The Gulf: potential for economic cooperation" in Gerd Nonneman (ed.), *The Middle East and Europe: an integrated communities approach* (Federal Trust for Education and Research, London, 1992).

Richard Schofield is Deputy Director of the Geopolitics and International Boundaries Research Centre at SOAS and an Associate Fellow of the Middle East Programme at the Royal Institute of International Affairs. He is author of *Evolution of the Shatt al-Arab boundary dispute* (Menas Press, Wisbech, 1986), *Kuwait and Iraq: historical claims and territorial disputes* (Royal Institute of International Affairs, London, 1991: 2nd ed., 1993), *Unfinished business: Iran, the UAE, Abu Musa and the Tunbs* (Royal Institute of International Affairs, London, 1994 forthcoming) and editor of *Arabian boundary disputes* (Archive Editions, Farnham Common, 1992).

Paul Stevens is BP Professor of Petroleum Policy and Economics at the University of Dundee's Centre of Petroleum and Mineral Law and Policy. Formerly he was Senior Lecturer in Economics at the University of Surrey. He is the author of *Oil and politics: the post-war Gulf* (Royal Institute of International Affairs, London, 1992), "Practical record and prospects of privatisation programmes in the Arab World" in Tim Niblock and Emma Murphy (eds), *Economic and political liberalisation in the Middle East* (British Academic Press, London, 1993) and "Oil and energy cooperation" in Gerd Nonneman (ed.), *The Middle East and Europe: an integrated communities approach* (Federal Trust for Education and Research, London, 1992).

Julian Walker is an analyst in the Research and Analysis Department at the Foreign and Commonwealth Office. Throughout a long and busy diplomatic career he has maintained a close professional involvement in the shaping of many of the region's territorial limits, an involvement that continues to the present. He is author of "United Arab Emirates–Oman frontiers" in C. H. Schofield and R. N. Schofield (eds), *World boundaries: the Middle East and North Africa* (Routledge, London, 1994 forthcoming).

John Wilkinson is University Lecturer in the Geography of the Middle East at Oxford University and a Fellow of St Hugh's College. He is author of *Water and tribal settlement in south-east Arabia: a study of the aflaj of Oman* (Clarendon Press, Oxford, 1977), *The Imamate tradition of Oman* (Cambridge University Press, Cambridge, 1987) and *Arabia's frontiers: the story of Britain's boundary drawing in the desert* (I B Tauris, London, 1991).

CHAPTER ONE

Borders and territoriality in the Gulf and the Arabian peninsula during the twentieth century[1]

RICHARD SCHOFIELD

Introduction

During the 1980–8 Iran–Iraq war, the Gulf Cooperation Council (GCC) frequently articulated one of its most basic principles, that is, the territorial integrity of the eight riparian states of the Gulf was inviolable, a situation which was to be upheld at all costs.[2] The principle was, of course, shattered completely by the Iraqi invasion of Kuwait on 2 August 1990. Iraq's aggression posed a grave challenge to the very heart of the system of territorially-defined states established during Britain's stay as colonial power in the Gulf up until 1971. Immediately questions were raised about the origins of the tiny emirates of the western Gulf littoral. How had this territorial framework evolved? What was its *raison d'être*? How capable was this framework of withstanding serious internal and external challenges such as the Iraqi invasion? Iraqi President Saddam Husain's move on Kuwait also served as a potent reminder of the vulnerability of the smaller Gulf states to the territorial acquisitiveness of their larger, more powerful neighbours. This was no new phenomenon. Had it not been for Britain's decisive intervention at the turn of the 1920s at the height of the Jahrah crisis, Kuwait (or at least its southern reaches) would probably have been subsumed into Ibn Saud's expanding Najdi domain.

The determined and successful efforts of the international community to restore the independence and territorial integrity of Kuwait perhaps suggest that the current territorial definition of the Gulf states is likely to endure in the foreseeable future, certainly for as long as the West is prepared to guarantee their shapes and sizes. The bilateral defence pacts signed or currently being negotiated between the GCC states (not just Kuwait) of the western Gulf littoral and the United States, Britain and France (a process which began with the US–Kuwaiti agreement of autumn 1991) will only add to the security of these guarantees.[3]

1

On the face of it several moves seem currently to be being made that will further entrench the current framework of state territory in the Gulf region. In the late autumn of 1992 the Iraq/Kuwait land border was demarcated by permanent pillar[4] following the announcement of a detailed boundary delineation on 16 April 1992 by the United Nations team set up, during 1991, to dispose finally of this historically intransigent issue. The activities of the United Nations Iraq–Kuwait Boundary Demarcation Commission (UNIKBDC) formally effectively came to a close on 27 May 1993 with the passage by the Security Council of Resolution 833. By this, binding recognition was given to a set of coordinates nominated by UNIKBDC to constitute the final and unequivocal line of demarcation for the Iraq/Kuwait boundary. Furthermore, the UN guaranteed this line against the contingency of serious Iraqi encroachments in the future.[5] Progress has also been made towards finalizing the political map of southern Arabia (Fig. 1.3). Yemen and Oman have settled the course of their land border by treaty, details of the territorial agreements reached between Saudi Arabia and its neighbours in south-east Arabia have been made public, while talks aimed at settling Arabia's last indeterminate boundary are presently in motion between the Riyadh and San'a governments. It should also be noted that one of the most important principles embodied in the Damascus Declaration of 6 March 1991 (whose express purpose was to define a workable collective security structure involving the GCC states, Syria and Egypt) was the regulation of existing borders. Other principles enunciated in the declaration, that also work for the maintenance of the present territorial framework in the Gulf region are: the peaceful resolution of disputes; respect for international law; mutual non-interference and good neighbourliness.[6] The plans for a collective security structure envisaged in the Damascus Declaration may ultimately never see the light of day, but the document, recently ratified by the GCC states, remains an important statement of policy, principle and intent.

Yet there remain perhaps more border disputes and potential border disputes than one initially suspects amidst the framework of state territory that encompasses the Gulf and Arabian peninsula. This is partly explained by the origins of the region's boundaries themselves, which are surprisingly diverse, essentially the product of Britain's deliberations over the past century with the major regional powers in these parts – Persia, the Ottoman Empire and Saudi Arabia. Their unresolved legacy was certainly responsible to a large degree for the re-emergence of the classic, cyclical Irano–Arab dispute over the sovereignty of Abu Musa and the Tunb islands in 1992 and the outbreak of a violent incident at Khafus on the undemarcated Saudi/Qatar border later the same year. This overview seeks to outline the diversity of past and current disputes, explain why these have come about and consider whether they are likely to endure or disappear in the future. Should the current system and distribution of territorial states be regarded as a permanent feature of the political landscape?

The interplay of territorial disputes in the study area is often intriguing, demonstrating little respect for contemporary political and military alliances. One needs only to look at some of the ironies and contradictions thrown up immediately before and during the recent 1990–1 Gulf conflict.

Little more than two months before the Iraqi invasion of Kuwait, all of the Arab states present at the extraordinary Baghdad summit held late during May 1990 implicitly lent their full support to Iraq's claim to sovereignty over the whole of the Shatt al-Arab river.[7] Yet, by this stage, Saddam Husain and Iranian President Ali Akbar Hashemi Rafsanjani were already firmly embarked upon a dialogue which was hinting at greater Iraqi flexibility towards established Iranian conditions for a final, formal settlement of the 1980-8 Iran–Iraq war (see later section).

A GCC summit held in Dawhah during December 1990 was expected by many observers to result in a considered response being drawn up to the dire situation in the northern Gulf. Instead nearly all of the agenda was taken up by consideration of the Bahraini–Qatari dispute over the Hawar islands and the Dibal and Jaradah shoals.[8]

Finally, the first pieces of Kuwaiti territory liberated from Iraqi occupation by the allied forces during February 1991 were the islands of Qaru and Umm al Maradim. Yet Saudi Arabia maintains a partial territorial claim to these islands.[9]

Territorial disputes: roots, symptoms of or excuses for inter-state conflict?

The northern Gulf

Social scientists have long quibbled over whether there is any such thing as a good or bad boundary or whether dissatisfaction with boundaries *per se* is a root cause of instability between states. The renowned French political geographer Jacques Ancel commented during the mid-1930s that there were no problems of boundaries, only problems of nations.[10] Another geographical point of view contends that the shape and size of a state contained by its international boundaries can give rise to genuine geopolitical and strategic problems – most notably, problems of access and communications. One has only to look at the northern Gulf region in recent history to find evidence that apparently supports both contentions.

Let us first examine Ancel's viewpoint that serious boundary disputes are symptomatic only of the poor relations existing at any one time between the governments of neighbouring states. The long-standing dispute between Iran and Iraq over the Shatt al-Arab provides a case in point. In March 1975, on signing the Algiers Accord package of agreements with Iraq, Iran secured a *thalweg* boundary delimitation (the line of continuous deepest soundings) along the Shatt al-Arab to satisfy a long-standing positional demand (this had been prosecuted with some degree of consistency for nearly 50 years). In a period of 130 years (since the conclusion of the second Treaty of Erzurum in 1847 between the Ottoman Empire and Persia), the Shatt al-Arab had evolved from being an Ottoman river to being shared along the *thalweg* line between its riparians, as was customary in international law for a boundary along a navigable river following the Versailles treaties of 1919.[11] One of the most sophisticated river boundary treaties ever signed in international law, the Algiers Accord contained every conceivable safeguard against future dispute over the boundary. Yet less than six years later, after the first few months of the 1980–8 Iran–Iraq war, the Shatt al-Arab was blocked by the wreckage of burnt-out or abandoned vessels and Iraq was in effect landlocked. As a prelude to prosecuting war, Saddam Husain had unilaterally abrogated the river boundary agreement (in fact tearing his copy of the accord to pieces before an Iraqi television audience), sensing, perhaps (wrongly as it turned out) that in the aftermath of the Iranian revolution circumstances were favourable for the restoration of the Shatt to its "rightful owner". Iraq had felt obliged to make the territorial concession in 1975 to quell the Shah's support for the Kurdish rebellion in the north. It soon became apparent, however, that Saddam Husain had not been at all convinced of the territorial concession of 1975 on its own merits and had only concluded it as a last resort. There is perhaps no more graphic illustration that the status of an international boundary is subject to fluctuations in the relationship between the neighbouring states sharing that divide.[12] The fact that Iraq was prepared, two weeks into its occupation of Kuwait, to recognize once again a *thalweg* delimitation along the Shatt and once more because of factors extraneous to the dispute itself, seemingly reinforces the case for an Ancelian interpretation.

Ancel's observation makes no provision for the way in which the positioning of a state's boundaries can disadvantage it strategically. Iraq's southern boundaries provide a good example. Because of the proximity of Iraq's international boundaries with Kuwait to the south and Iran to the southeast, separated only by the largely undevelopable mud flat that is the Faw peninsula, access to the sea has been an overriding concern for successive Baghdad regimes. One has only to glance at a map to realize that Iraq, with its minuscule shoreline on the Gulf, can be classified as a geographically disadvantaged state. It has long perceived itself as "squeezed out" of the Gulf.[13] Traditionally, this consciousness has stiffened Iraq's resolve not to make territorial concessions to Iran over the Shatt al-Arab. The insecure status of the Shatt al-Arab boundary has, in turn, encouraged Iraq, from the late-1930s onwards, to seek alternative port facilities to Basrah, its principal dry-cargo port, at Umm Qasr on the Khawr Zubair

4

further west. In order to secure complete control over navigation in the Khawr Abdallah, the access channel that links this water inlet to the Gulf, Iraq has pressed, with remarkable consistency over the last half-century, for the cession or lease of the Kuwaiti islands of Warbah and Bubiyan.[14]

Though Umm Qasr port was finally developed by Iraq during the 1960s, Baghdad continued to insist that Kuwait make concessions over the islands question if it wanted Iraq to reciprocate by agreeing to the final delimitation and demarcation of the land boundary further west, a long-standing Kuwaiti objective. For well over 30 years up to the Iraqi invasion of Kuwait during early August 1990 and notwithstanding an agreement of October 1963 in which Iraq recognized an independent Kuwait and its boundaries, the Kuwait/Iraq border and islands question in effect remained deadlocked. Iraq would not agree to the demarcation of the land boundary unless Kuwait first showed some flexibility on the question of ceding or leasing Warbah and Bubiyan. Kuwait demanded the prerequisite of a fully demarcated land boundary in accordance with its description in existing official correspondence before any consideration of leasing Warbah would be entertained. In truth, Iraq's demand for some sort of control over the islands was less of a territorial dispute than a plea that the existing boundary be adjusted (or Kuwait's effective sovereignty over the islands be substantively reduced) so as to improve Iraq's access to the sea, in acknowledgement of its disadvantageous position at the head of the Gulf. Traditionally, over the last half-century or so, Iraq has pressed Kuwait on the islands question when its relationship with Iran has seriously deteriorated over the status of the Shatt al-Arab.[15] Successive Baghdad regimes have continually expected Kuwait to compensate Iraq for its geographic and strategic misfortune.[16]

Whether one accepts the thesis that dissatisfaction with existing boundaries is a genuine root of inter-state conflict, it is clear that, nominally at least, the status of the Shatt al-Arab boundary and Iraq's preoccupation with gaining rights over Warbah and Bubiyan were important factors in Saddam Husain's respective decisions to prosecute war against Iran during autumn 1980 and to annex Kuwait during the summer of 1990. The fact that United Nations peacekeeping forces have been stationed until recently (January 1991) along the Iran/Iraq border (United Nations Iran–Iraq Military Observer Group – UNIIMOG) and remain positioned along the Kuwait/Iraq border (United Nations Iraq–Kuwait Observation Mission – UNIKOM) only underlines the fact that the framework of state territory in the northern Gulf region remains highly unstable. This position holds true in spite of the current dormancy of the Shatt dispute and the UN's apparent success in finally settling the Iraq/Kuwait border. These issues are dealt with below.

Dormant but not yet settled: Iran-Iraq territorial disputes Saddam Husain's dramatic abandonment of territorial claims to the whole of the Shatt al-Arab river two weeks after Iraq's move on Kuwait surprised many observers and

5

understandably raised questions as to how, if at all, the two events were related. An earlier section of this chapter has already mentioned how an exchange of correspondence, beginning in April 1990, between the Iraqi President and Rafsanjani had been hinting at greater flexibility from the Baghdad government towards Iran's conditions for a final peace settlement. A number of sources have speculated that these exchanges were, by the end of May 1990, already pointing towards an Iraqi preparedness to recognize once again a *thalweg* delimitation along the Shatt, as had originally been prescribed by an Iran-Iraq agreement of 1975.[17] On the balance of available evidence it seems much more likely that Saddam Husain displayed no willingness to relax Iraqi claims to the Shatt until such time as the decision to invade Kuwait had been taken. That is, almost certainly, not before late July 1990. Although Saddam Husain suggested three days before his move on Kuwait that the Shatt dispute be submitted to arbitration, Iraq continued to reserve its position over the sovereignty of the river until 14 August 1990, when, two weeks into its occupation of the emirate, the Baghdad government accepted Iranian conditions for a peace settlement. By accepting that territorial settlement should be based upon the clauses of the 1975 Algiers Accord, which Saddam Husain himself had negotiated with the Shah one and a half decades earlier, Iraq had apparently dropped its claims and recognized a *thalweg* boundary along the Shatt al-Arab.[18]

The Iranian government wasted no time in acknowledging Saddam's strategically-motivated climbdown on the sovereignty of the Shatt al-Arab. Most observers calculated that this measure had been taken to neutralize Iran in the early days of the Kuwait crisis. Both Iran and Iraq soon registered the texts of the Husain-Rafsanjani correspondence (and most significantly Husain's all-important letter of 14 August 1990) with the United Nations.[19] Yet, despite brief efforts made during the late autumn of 1990 to follow up this development, there remains in the late summer of 1993 no evidence that Iran and Iraq have signed any document to formalize Saddam Husain's concession of August 1990.

Furthermore, the Iran/Iraq land boundary has continued to be a source of tension in the period that has followed Saddam's *volte-face* and the withdrawal of UN peacekeeping forces.[20] A crossing-point near Khosrovi, the last Iranian city to be vacated by Iraqi forces in November 1990, was the scene of a serious border incident in March 1991.[21] This was despite an announcement earlier in the year (January 1991) that the two sides had moved their border fences 1 km in from the boundary so as to leave a narrow (2 km), demilitarized buffer zone.[22] The huge post-Gulf war influx of Iraqi Kurds and Shi'ites across Iran's western borders exacerbated existing tensions to the degree that, early in April 1991, Iran announced that its western borders had been closed as all available resources for the absorption of these refugees had been exhausted.[23] At least in the south, the boundary has since been reopened on a more or less permanent basis.

UN attempts to finally settle the Iraq–Kuwait border question in the aftermath of the 1990–1 Iraqi invasion of Kuwait and the resultant Gulf war In accepting terms for the Gulf war ceasefire laid down in United Nations Resolution 687, passed in New York during the late afternoon of 3 April 1991, Iraq somewhat grudgingly committed itself to respect the inviolability of the existing boundary mentioned in the "Agreed Minutes regarding the Restoration of Friendly Relations, Recognition and Related Matters", signed between Iraq and Kuwait on 4 October 1963 and originally agreed upon some three decades earlier in diplomatic exchanges during the summer of 1932. With their acceptance of Resolution 687, in which the United Nations guaranteed the existing boundary, Kuwait and Iraq agreed to accept the advice and assistance of (former) Secretary-General Perez de Cuellar in demarcating their boundary in accordance with the 1963 agreement. On reporting back to the Security Council in early May 1991 with his proposals for the final demarcation of the Kuwait/Iraq boundary, de Cuellar announced the formation of a five-man boundary demarcation commission (UNIKBDC), comprising a neutral chairman, representatives from both the Kuwaiti and Iraqi governments and two neutral cartographers. After an opening session in New York during May 1991, the commission moved on to the border zone itself in June 1991.

By this stage the UNIKOM was firmly in place in a demilitarized zone along the border. This force had been instituted in early April 1991 to man the border zone and, in due course, oversee the land boundary which the United Nations team has only recently demarcated. UNIKOM's designated role is to monitor and observe developments along the entire length of the Kuwait/Iraq land boundary (around 160 km) and the 40 km of water boundary along the Khawr Abdallah.[24] This strategically-important waterway links Umm Qasr and the Khawr Zubair to the waters of the Gulf and separates the Kuwaiti islands of Warbah and Bubiyan from the Faw peninsula in Iraq. For the entire length of the land boundary the UNIKOM buffer zone extends 10 km into Iraqi territory and 5 km into Kuwaiti territory.[25]

It might reasonably be asked by reference to which boundary points the UNIKOM demilitarized zone had been defined? For the definition of the boundary contained within the spring 1932 exchange of correspondence between Kuwait and Iraq (the delimitation formula for the UN demarcation commission in their recent deliberations), which the two states had agreed to respect in 1963 and again confirmed with their acceptance of UN Resolution 687, is notoriously vague.[26] It embraces no more precise references to the boundary than "along the Batin (a dry wadi marking the north-west limits of Kuwait)" and "just south of Safwan". It took Britain until 1951 to come to a final conclusion about what delimitation the 1932 correspondence had meant to introduce.[27] Yet successive Iraqi governments have never formally accepted this interpretation – included in a proposal for the demarcation of the boundary – since it was submitted for their approval during late December 1951. On several occasions, however, Iraq had hinted that it would find its way to accept Britain's 1951 interpretation, if Kuwait was willing to surrender certain rights over Warbah and Bubiyan. Kuwait never proved willing and Iraq never accepted the demarcation proposal.

Yet there can be little doubt that Britain's 1951 demarcation proposal, which had stood for 40 years as the most detailed existing interpretation of the vaguely defined *de jure* Iraq/Kuwait boundary, informed the series of maps which the United Nations used to construct UNIKOM's demilitarized zone. These had been produced by the British Military Survey in 1990 and submitted by the British government in March 1991 as an "appropriate material" upon which the UN Secretary-General might draw when finalizing plans to settle the border question. The British Military Survey series had also utilized maps dating back to the mid-1930s and modern surveys necessarily limited to the Kuwaiti side of the *de facto* pre-1990 border. It represented the *de jure* border as the Military Survey was best able to depict it. The line it showed, despite clear disclaimers on the sheets of the 1990 series, was regarded by UNIKOM as the most authoritative interpretation of the *de jure* Iraq/Kuwait boundary until UNIKBDC announced its verdict on the course of the land boundary in the spring of 1992 (see below).[28] Iraq wasted no time in protesting against the United Nations' use of the 1990 British Military Survey map series. In a letter of 23 April 1991 to the UN Secretary-General, its Foreign Ministry characterized the UN action as a "unilateral imposition", which was "prejudging the delimitation of the boundary".[29] Nevertheless, a map showing the extent of UNIKOM's demilitarized zone, clearly based upon the provisional *de jure* line depicted on the 1990 British Military Survey map series, was published by the United Nations early during May 1991.[30] Despite its strong reservations concerning the UN's employment of the British map series and, more generally, the method by which the United Nations proposed to settle the border question, Iraq agreed unconditionally to accept the Secretary-General's proposals for demarcation in its Foreign Minister's letter of 23 April 1991. This was not before the point had been made that the final settlement of Iraq's southern border with Kuwait should properly be its own responsibility and not imposed from without.

By the autumn of 1991 it was evident that the neutral demarcation commissioners were experiencing great difficulties in getting the Kuwaiti and Iraqi delegates on the demarcation team to reach a mutually-acceptable interpretation of the boundary as defined by the 1932 diplomatic correspondence. The task of demarcation was, as a consequence, taking much longer than the United Nations had initially hoped. Iraq's less than wholehearted participation in the demarcation commission gave rise to accusations from Kuwait, articulated in a memorandum delivered to the Arab League in early September 1991, that it had not taken "any serious steps for the demarcation of official international borders with the state of Kuwait".[31] In late August 1991 the Kuwaiti media broadcast alarming reports of an armed Iraqi incursion on to Bubiyan island. Had these reports been true, UNIKOM would have been powerless to prevent such violations, possessing, as it did at this stage, a mandate only to observe developments in the demilitarized zone. Though the British Foreign Office and the US State Department initially appeared to uphold the Kuwaiti complaint, UNIKOM reports from the scene suggested that the Kuwaiti government's original account of the incident had been over-exaggerated.[32] The Bubiyan episode was to have two general but discernible detrimental consequences for Kuwait. Firstly, the Kuwaiti government would claim privately in the period following the incident that the West did not treat seriously enough reports of future Iraqi incursions. Secondly, the Western and Middle Eastern media would treat future Kuwaiti pronouncements both on border incidents and the issue of the UN demarcation itself much more cautiously and critically – Iraq's case would get a greater representation than previously.[33]

On 16 April 1992, after almost one year of careful deliberation, the boundary demarcation commission (UNIKBDC) announced its final interpretation of where, precisely, the historically-problematic Iraq/Kuwait land boundary should run.[34] This is the line that the UN demarcated in November 1992 with its erection of permanent boundary pillars along the entire course of the land border. UNIKBDC's sixth session, held in New York during July 1992 (at which the Iraqi delegate was not present, Iraq having withdrawn from the activities of the commission during late June/early July), had resulted in a restatement of the 16 April 1992 announcement for a delimitation of the boundary, couched in slightly defensive terms, following widespread criticism of the April 1992 delimitation in the Western and Arab media.[35] UNIKBDC's April 1992 line was presented (in an interim report) by UN Secretary-General Boutros Boutros-Ghali to the Security Council on 19 August 1992. Within one week UN Resolution 773 had been passed, welcoming the UN verdict on the course of the Iraq/Kuwait land boundary and urging UNIKBDC to go on and finally settle water boundaries farther east between the two states.[36]

Included within UNIKBDC's July 1992 interim report was a map plotting (in approximate terms) their recently announced line against the line depicted on the 1990 British Military Survey map series (which had up until this point been regarded as the operational boundary by the UN). The lines, both ostensibly showing the *de jure* Iraq/Kuwait boundary, coincided in places – such as the point where the land boundary terminated on the Khawr Zubair south of pre-1961 Umm Qasr, but diverged in others, such as the Safwan and Rumailah areas, where the UNIKBDC limit ran roughly parallel to but north of the 1990 Military Survey approximation.[37] In its various publications, UNIKBDC has to date failed to explain fully why the 1990 approximation and its own April 1992 verdict diverged in these critical regions along the border. The explanation offered seems almost too simple. The 1990 British Military Survey approximation was based upon existing but inadequate information, or so it is maintained, where as the UNIKBDC verdict was the result of the first joint survey of the border zone, after which the line of delimitation just happened to be confirmed as lying further north. The *de jure* boundary had not been moved northwards. It had merely been accurately established for the first time. Whatever the explanation, UNIKOM's demilitarized zone, previously centred upon the British Military Survey's 1990 interpretation of the *de jure* boundary, now had to be realigned to correspond with the UNIKBDC line. Authority had been given to take just such a measure in UN Resolution 773 of 26 August 1992, though no action in this respect was ultimately taken until January 1993.[38]

Contentiously, UNIKBDC insists that it has demarcated an existing boundary delimitation. Yet, as we have seen, its delimitation formula was notoriously vague and has remained unaltered since 1913 when it first appeared in an Anglo–Ottoman settlement of Persian Gulf questions. UNIKBDC can hardly deny that most of their time since the spring of 1991 has been spent trying to arrive at a much more detailed boundary delimitation, that could then be demarcated. By no stretch of the imagination can UNIKBDC truthfully claim that it has demarcated an existing water boundary. The delimitation that has recently been demarcated (that is the line defined by an old, imperial agreement of 1913, by exchanges of correspondence of 1923 and 1932 and which was referred to in the Iraq–Kuwait agreement of 1963) says nothing about any boundary along the Khawr Abdallah. UNIKBDC's eventual conclusion that a delimitation existed along the water inlet which could then be demarcated was the most contentious aspect of its entire operation.

Following the passage of UN Resolution 833 on 27 May 1993, the Iraq/Kuwait border question is finally and unequivocally settled, certainly as far as the United Nations is concerned. Yet Iraq's attitudes to the pronouncements of UNIKBDC from April 1992 onwards, ranging from denunciation to virtual rejection, should guard against any cosy assumptions that the last has been heard of a territorial dispute which had simmered for well over half a century before Iraq made its disastrous attempt to annex Kuwait during August 1990. Until Iraq withdrew from the activities of the commission in the summer of 1992, its delegate, Ambassador Riyadh al-Qaisi, largely went through the motions, not even bothering to cast a vote against the delimitation announced on 16 April 1992. It seems that Iraq accepted, albeit unwillingly, the existence, aims and mandate of UNIKBDC but cannot live with its findings. For the Iraqi government all but rejected the 16 April 1992 line, its National Assembly issuing a strongly worded denunciation on 17 May 1992, followed soon afterwards by an extraordinarily long letter of protest to the United Nations Security Council.[39] Perhaps more significantly, prominent Iraqi opposition groups in exile – the very groups which the

West would supposedly rather see ruling in Baghdad in one combination or another – have also rejected the April 1992 delimitation.[40]

Clearly there are awkward questions to be addressed when it comes to the United Nations imposing territorial settlement. Can a boundary be finally settled without the full consent of one of the countries sharing that territorial limit? It remains to be seen in the post-Cold War era whether international law will come to respect an increasingly powerful and interventionist United Nations imposing a final settlement on long-standing, seemingly intractable territorial disputes. Will the United Nations deliberations over the Iraq/Kuwait border set a precedent or simply be regarded as a justifiable exception in future years? For, ultimately, final agreement in international law to a boundary delimitation is usually achieved only by bilateral sanction. Even if the recent UNIKBDC demarcation has disposed of the legal issues surrounding the border question, and there have been some doubts expressed as to whether it has,[41] the geostrategic predicament of Iraq remains.

Certainly Kuwait is taking no chances with respect to its border defences. Demarcation, of course, in no way materially enhances the security of a boundary, especially in this instance, with pillars having been emplaced during November 1992 only every 2 km along the UNIKBDC line.[42] Specialized foreign contractors (primarily from Germany and Japan) are attending to Kuwait's reported requests for sophisticated and effective border defences to guard against any future moves from the north and west.[43] There were reports at one stage that Kuwait desired an impregnable 15 foot high security fence. After all of its recent tribulations, perhaps Kuwait, quite understandably, is adopting something of an ostrich mentality. As far as Iraq is concerned in the future: out of sight, out of mind! Iraqi incursions into the Kuwaiti side of UNIKOM's demilitarized zone in early 1993 only accelerated Kuwaiti plans for an elaborate border defence system. The Iraqi breaches of the border and the heavy-handedness of their retrieval operations during this period contributed significantly to the West renewing its bombing of southern Iraq, albeit in a more limited form than previously, on 13 January 1993.[44] By early May 1993 the Kuwaiti Cabinet had finally plumped for an arrangement which will see a 3 m deep ditch dug along the entire length of the land border. The ditch will be 5 m across and sealed on its southern bank by the construction of sand hills to a height of 4 m.[45]

It is instructive to briefly review the UNIKBDC announcement of spring 1992 on the course of the land boundary. Close inspection reveals a marked similarity to Britain's 1951 demarcation proposal, previously the most detailed existing clarification of the vague boundary established by the 1932 exchange of notes. The boundary "along the Batin" follows the *thalweg* of this feature (even though it has always been a dry wadi in recent times), as had originally been suggested by C. J. Edmonds as long ago as 1937 and as was embodied in the 1951 interpretation. Arrangements for the eastern terminus of the land boundary on the Khawr Zubair south of Umm Qasr

11

also seem consistent with Britain's 1951 delimitation proposal, though the Iraqi port has crept considerably farther south to a point well below this limit in the past 40 years. There had been some expectation, certainly from the Kuwaitis, that the land border announced on 16 April 1992 would take a slightly different course in this area.[46] While the 1951 interpretation ran in a straight line from the point south of Safwan to the tri-junction of the Khawr Zubair, Khawr Sabiya and Khawr Shetana, but deviated in such a way as to leave the whole of the former water inlet to Iraq, the 1992 United Nations version was widely tipped to follow the same straight line without any deviation, thereby placing part of the lower course of the Khawr Zubair within Kuwait. In the end the April announcement, confirmed in July, followed the 1951 interpretation unaltered, suggesting that there may have been a split vote between the commission's members on the issue. This actually was the case, the only occasion upon which the Kuwaiti representative on UNIKBDC voted against the commission's nomination for the boundary. It will be recalled that Iraq decided not to take part in these votes. The 16 April 1992 announcement of the delimitation decided upon by the United Nations team gives a definition for the point south of Safwan which, if anything, is slightly more beneficial to Iraq than Britain's interpretation of 1951. Whereas Britain had specified 40 years ago that the nodal point south of Safwan should be fixed arbitrarily at 1000 metres, the 16 April 1992 statement read: "the boundary south of Safwan shall be located at the distance of 1430 metres from the south-west extremity of the compound wall of the old customs post along the old road from Safwan to Kuwait".[47]

The northwards migration of Kuwait's boundaries? Periodically throughout the first half of 1992, but especially during late February/early March, Western broadsheets carried front-page headlines to the effect that Kuwait's borders were about to migrate northwards as a result of the preliminary findings of UNIKBDC. Such reports were originally informed by the rather tactless comments of Ambassador Tariq A. Razouki, the Kuwaiti representative on the demarcation team, that "the demarcation of borders in 1992 will be totally different than 60 years ago".[48] It was certainly never the intention of the United Nations team to draw a new boundary. The delineation it arrived at can most accurately be described as a tighter version of Britain's interpretation of 1951.

The evident media confusion of early 1992 probably came about because for nearly 30 years, following the settlement of the "first" 1961 Kuwait crisis, Iraq had extended its administration up to the Arab League line, a track that ran roughly parallel to but south of the notional international boundary (Britain's interpretation of 1951). At their closest point the two limits were 350 m apart, at their farthest, some 2 km. The Arab League line was a track probably laid down by the British forces stationed to defend Kuwait during the 1961 crisis. It was then used by the Arab League Force, who took over responsibility for the defence of Kuwait on Britain's departure later that year, staying until a conducive change of regime in Baghdad of early 1963. On its departure Iraq extended its administration south to the Arab League line. During the 1960s and 1970s wells were sunk by Iraq at the southern tip of the super-giant Rumailah oilfield directly above this *de facto* territorial limit (and farther south still), while the modern port of Umm Qasr expanded across the notional boundary to the very same Arab League line. Urban sprawl continued unchecked farther south of the extended Iraqi port and across the Arab League line to its west during the late 1970s as Saddam Husain strove to change the political geography of the border zone. Kuwait, not generally in much of a position to protest, turned a blind eye to such developments. With the UN more or less confirming Britain's 1951 interpretation of the land boundary in its announcements of 16 April 1992 and 24 July 1992 and the demarcation of this line in November 1992, Iraq has been required to abandon all infrastructure south of what the United Nations maintains is the *de jure* boundary.

United Nations resolutions of 1991 compelled the Iraq/Kuwait Boundary Demarcation Commission to finalize the existing boundary in law as defined by previous diplomatic correspondence (1932 and 1963) and, by extension, to ignore any temporary or *de facto* lines. As such the criticism that was levelled at the United Nations team early in 1992 seemed a little misplaced. For UNIKBDC was only carrying out its mandate.[49] The only fault that might have existed lay in the United Nations resolutions passed in 1991. Admittedly these were of necessity put together in great haste while border matters in the immediate aftermath of the conflict were probably not a top priority. Yet there were no criticisms of inadequate territorial directives in the broadsheets of spring 1991. During the spring of 1992 there were many articulate and intelligent calls by respected and experienced observers both of the northern Gulf region and of the United Nations for the Iraq–Kuwait demarcation team to show more flexibility in the execution of their tasks, to come up with a line that was "politically defensible" rather than one that was valid from a strict technical and historical perspective. It was suggested that this "politically defensible" line might extend southwards of the *de jure* line at Umm Qasr and Rumailah to the level of the pre-August 1990 *de facto* line so that Iraq need not abandon its oil wells and infrastructural development. Yet surely these are, like longer-established suggestions that Iraq be given more beneficial access to the waters of the Gulf along the water channels that surround Warbah and Bubiyan, concessions that only Kuwait, rather than the United Nations, can make. They are concessions which remain more unlikely than ever to be granted following Kuwait's recent tribulations and Iraq's less than enthusiastic participation in the UN sponsored border demarcation.

It is by no means exceptional for the resolution of a major international conflict or crisis to fail to address many of the underlying tensions that had contributed to its incidence in the first place. Even had the UNIKBDC been empowered to confirm the existing *de facto* Iraq/Kuwait boundary along the Arab League line and farther south still, Iraq would still, in the words of a prominent Kuwaiti minister during the early 1970s, resemble a "big garage with a very small door".[50] With the tiny strip of territory involved, Iraqi access to the Gulf would, in any case, hardly be improved in any material way. As has already been intimated, Iraq's borders have been so problematic historically only because of the proximity of the boundary to the east with Iran, because Iraq has failed to exert sole control over either of its two main arteries to the Gulf flanking the Faw Peninsula, the Khawr Zubair–Khawr Abdallah link in the west and the Shatt al-Arab less than 20 miles to the east.

Iraq's dissatisfaction with both of its boundaries in this part of the world was undeniably an important factor in Saddam's decisions to wage war against Iran in 1980 and to invade Kuwait 10 years later. Peace has been bought along both these border zones in the last half-decade only through the efforts of the United Nations. The presence of United Nations peace-keeping forces in the borderlands has been necessary to keep the peace. Indeed it is a combination of external factors (the allied campaign to oust the Iraqi occupying force from Kuwait, the peacekeeping operations of the United Nations, the United Nations-sponsored demarcation of the Iraq/Kuwait boundary and the conclusion of bilateral security pacts with Western powers) that has ensured that Kuwait continues to exist as an independent entity within its present borders and which guarantee that this state of affairs will prevail for the foreseeable future.

Clearly, claims that all territorial questions separating Iraq and Kuwait have been answered with the UN demarcation need to be treated with caution. For the future territorial stability and general peace of the northern Gulf it is vital, in the medium to long-term, that Iraq no longer perceives itself as "squeezed out" of this water body. This is clearly going to be no easy task. Especially so, when one considers that, nine decades ago, Lord Curzon and the Government of India, when actively supporting the Ruler of Kuwait's claim to Bubiyan and indeed encouraging him to claim Warbah during the first decade of this century, were motivated above all by a desire to prevent the Ottoman Empire from having any developable coastline on the Gulf, that is to ensure that the Porte was genuinely "squeezed out" of the Gulf.[51] In many ways the proof of their success is the instability that this geostrategic fact has fostered in the decades that have followed. Just how Iraq's deeply entrenched consciousness of being "squeezed" out of the Gulf (whether or not this presents it with genuine problems) might best be addressed without compromising the legitimate concerns of Kuwait and Iran is the question that remains to be answered, notwithstanding the recent efforts of UNIKBDC.

The framework of state territory within the Gulf and Arabian peninsula: imposed but here to stay?

Several attempts have been made to categorize land boundary types over the years. Those made by two American geographers, Stephen Whittemore Boggs (1940) and Richard Hartshorne (1936), have proved the more enduring.[52] Boggs produced a scheme that stressed the physical characteristics of a boundary or the landscape through which it had been drawn. Examples of each of his four categories of boundary (physiographic, geometric, anthropogeographic and complex) can be found, albeit sometimes only partially, in the territorial landscape under review in this overview. Conversely, Hartshorne devised a classification that defined a boundary in relation to the cultural landscape through which it had been drawn. As most of the *de facto* and *de jure* land boundaries in the Arabian peninsula traverse areas of extremely low population density it might be expected that to attempt any application of Hartshorne's five categories (pioneer, antecedent, subsequent, superimposed and relict) to the region would be only partially successful at best. Nevertheless it will be suggested that his superimposed and antecedent boundary classifications hold relevance for the area under review.[53]

Natural or physiographic boundaries and physically defined states: Kuwait, Iraq and Qatar

Physiographic boundaries follow physical features such as rivers or pronounced upland ridges. The dearth of prominent natural features in the desert interior of the northern Arabian peninsula presented British officials, generally employees of the Government of India (which administered the Gulf up until Indian independence in 1947) or the Colonial Office in the case of Iraq, with problems when drawing up northern limits to Ibn Saud's Najdi state in the early 1920s. For at this stage conventional wisdom dictated that a natural boundary should be adopted wherever possible.[54] Two of the Government of India's most famous administrators, Lord Curzon of Kedleston (Viceroy of India at the turn of the century) and Colonel Thomas Holdich (who headed the Indo–Persian Boundary Demarcation Commission in the mid-1890s) had publicly championed natural boundaries and conditioned the attitudes of their subordinates. Proudly reflecting upon his Indo–Persian delimitation some years later, Holdich wrote in 1916 that no more perfect boundary could be devised than that of mountains and rivers combined.[55] His views, with those of Curzon, have subsequently been discredited yet were enormously influential at the time. As a result natural features, despite their scarcity, were adopted where possible to delimit boundaries in the northern Arabian peninsula in the early 1920s. In the July 1913 Anglo– Ottoman Convention, the outer limit of influence of the autonomous Ottoman *qadha* of Kuwait was defined in the northwest as running along the Batin, a low-lying depression running southwest to northeast (Fig. 1.1).[56] The Batin has been confirmed as forming the Kuwait/Iraq boundary in all subsequent correspondence that has defined this limit (Fig. 1.2, exchanges of correspondence of 1923 and 1932, the Kuwait–Iraq agreement of October 1963, and, most recently, both sides' acceptance of United Nations Security Council Resolution 687 during April 1991), though there was still some confusion as to where, exactly, the line should run along the feature in the deliberations that culminated in the United Nations demarcation team's decision of 16 April 1992. It will be recalled that the boundary was confirmed as running along the *thalweg*. Not far to the south, Major Percy Cox, then British High Commissioner in Baghdad, utilized another shallow depression (al-Shaq) to delimit the western boundary of the Najdi–Kuwaiti Neutral Zone at Uqair during December 1922, though the British official concerned was under the mistaken impression that the feature was a low, mountainous ridge, as evidenced by the text of the Uqair Protocol.[57]

In most cases, however, boundaries in this region had to be drawn through desert terrain that possessed no distinctive features. The long-running, intermittent but ultimately fruitless Anglo–Saudi negotiations towards southern and southeastern limits for Saudi Arabia will be returned to in due course. Suffice it to say here that the most generous offer the British government made to Saudi Arabia for territorial limits in southern Arabia – the Riyadh line, rejected by Saudi Arabia in November 1935 and unilaterally declared (in a slightly modified form) by Britain 20 years later following the breakdown of the Buraimi arbitration proceedings – was based upon a natural feature, the southern rim of the Rub al-Khali. North of the Hadhramawt this line was deliberately defined to cut 20 or 30 miles into the Rub al-Khali, so as to provide a defensive buffer for the Aden Protectorate (Fig 1.1).[58] The Iraq/Saudi Arabia boundary, originally justified, like other territorial limits in the northern peninsula, on the rather vague and questionable affiliations of nomadic tribes, was essentially defined in the Uqair Protocol of 1922 by a series of straight-line segments linking notable natural features such as wadis or rocky outcrops.[59] Other boundary definitions in the area make no reference to natural features whatsoever, and in physical terms, are clearly artificial. The northern stretch of the Kuwait/Iraq border from the Batin to the Khawr Zubair is defined only as passing to the south of a series of small settlements and watering holes at Safwan, Jabal Sanam and Umm Qasr respectively. Yet, when it came to demarcating the Kuwait/Iraq boundary or to proposals for its demarcation, natural features were employed. Major John More, Political Agent in Kuwait, placed a notice-board south of Safwan in 1923 to mark the boundary after pacing out 1050 yards from the most southerly date palm at the oasis.[60] From the mid-1930s onwards, the British authorities at Kuwait and Baghdad drew up proposals for the demarcation of the boundary (these were never accepted by Iraq) that made reference to natural features in an effort to clarify the vague delimitation. The considerable difficulties experienced in arriving at these proposals only underline the problems of trying to demarcate an artificial boundary by reference to natural features.[61]

Qatar's southern land boundaries can hardly be classified as physiographic. Yet the territory of the state has been defined in strictly physical terms as, stretching over the whole of the Qatar peninsula (but not the Hawar group islands, lying off its west coast, which Britain awarded to Bahrain in 1939, a decision that may well be contested in the international courts in the next year or so). It was the grant of the Qatar mainland oil concession to the Anglo–Iranian Oil Company in 1935 that had the effect of defining the state territorially, rather than the conclusion of any boundary treaty. For in return for granting the concession to a British company, the Ruler of Qatar secured a pledge from the British government to guarantee the territorial integrity of the concession area, which covered the whole of the peninsula.[62] Up until this time, the British authorities in the Gulf had maintained somewhat theoretically that the territory of the al-Thani state stretched over the Qatar peninsula but acknowledged, in practice, that his authority did not.[63]

For the rest of the 1930s the existence of two territorial disputes over Jabal Naksh and the Khawr al-Udaid at the southwest and southeast extremes of the Qatar peninsula worked against any progress that might have been made in the Anglo–Saudi frontier negotiations. The dispute over Jabal Naksh, which was claimed by Saudi Arabia on historical grounds dating back to the first decade of the century and claimed by Britain on behalf of Qatar on the simple grounds that it lay within the concession area, was accentuated by rumours that sizeable oil deposits lay under the border zone in these parts. These proved false and the Saudi claim lapsed after the Second World War. The Saudi claim to the Khawr al-Udaid was fuelled by the strategic imperative of gaining a corridor to Gulf waters south of the Qatar peninsula, a move the British authorities in the Gulf were very keen to forestall. It was justified on the premise that tribes frequenting the area owed allegiance to Ibn Saud. As early as 1881 Britain recognized the water inlet as belonging to the Ruler of Abu Dhabi. His direct administration of the area proved short-lived, however, and lapsed following Ottoman encroachments down the Gulf littoral in the late 19th century. From 1906 onwards, while still continuing to uphold its claim, the Government of India recommended that Abu Dhabi should make no moves to reoccupy the locality in the interests of maintaining the local peace.[64] The Ruler of Qatar recognized the area in the mid-1930s as a sort of no-mans land in which only Ibn Saud was powerful enough to exert any authority.[65]

By a boundary agreement of December 1965, Saudi Arabia and Qatar agreed that the southern limits of the al-Thani shaikhdom marched with Saudi territory only, from Duhat as-Salwah in the west to the Khawr al-

Udaid on the Gulf in the east. Britain would not recognize the legality of this agreement for a long time since it maintained that long-standing and recognized Abu Dhabi claims to the Khawr al-Udaid had been completely ignored. Up until the recent political difficulties between Riyadh and Dawhah following the Khafus border post incident of 30 September 1992, the text of the 1965 agreement had never been released.[66] However, it was known that the 1965 line approximated closely to the territorial limit claimed by Britain on behalf of the Ruler of Qatar at the Anglo–Saudi Dammam Conference during February 1952. Until 1992 there were few, if any, indications that either side was dissatisfied with the 1965 delimitation, which has remained undemarcated. Atlases and maps produced recently in both states show this same line,[67] as do contemporary British operational and tactical pilotage navigation charts.

Yet early during 1992, problems surfaced with Saudi Arabia's closure of a key access route at the base of the Qatar peninsula.[68] Worse, of course, was to come with the serious border clash at Khafus on 30 September 1992, which resulted in three fatalities. The incident quickly resulted in Qatar formally severing the 1965 agreement, though, as it explained only a few days later, this action had the effect of suspending the agreement rather than abrogating it permanently.[69] Though one clearly should not underplay the serious nature of recent strains between Riyadh and Dawhah, it was always a fair presumption that difficulties over the border would be transitory, since there seemed to be no real difficulty with the boundary line itself. Recent tensions were more political than anything else. It always seemed likely that the two sides, once they had begun to redress the damage done by the Khafus incident, would take the fairly obvious step of demarcating the 1965 delimitation so as to insure against any future dispute over its precise course. This happened during late December 1992 on the occasion of Egyptian President Hosni Mubarak's visit to Qatar and Saudi Arabia.[70] Just how far the two states have moved towards implementing their agreement to demarcate is difficult to establish in the late summer of 1993.

To return once more to the Khawr al-Udaid question. Britain continued to uphold the claims of Abu Dhabi to the inlet until 1974, when, by an unpublished agreement, the dominant state of the recently constituted United Arab Emirates finally relented to Saudi pressure for an outlet to the Gulf south of the Qatar peninsula, apparently recognizing its sovereign rights to a 25 km stretch of coastline from the Khawr al-Udaid to the Sabkhat Matti in return for a substantial relaxation of the previously maintained Saudi claim in the Buraimi–al-Ain region.[71]

In truth the Jabal Naksh dispute of the late 1930s was conducted more between Britain and Ibn Saud than anyone else, while the Khawr al-Udaid dispute, in practice, concerned only Saudi Arabia and Abu Dhabi. The chief problems faced by the Ruler of Qatar following his grant of the 1935 oil concession, whose area defined the state territorially, were those of extending his authority over the whole of the peninsula, protected as it now was against attack by land from the south. The issue of national integration will be returned to presently.

Geometric or straight-line boundaries:
Anglo–Ottoman spheres of influence, Anglo–Saudi claims
in the southern peninsula, the Iraq/Saudi Arabia border
and the indeterminate Saudi/Yemen boundary

Geometric boundaries, Boggs' second category, are usually formed by a series of straight line segments linking fixed boundary points, or, alternatively, are based squarely upon lines of longitude and latitude. The best examples of the latter in the Arabian peninsula are the "Blue" and "Violet" lines, agreed between Britain and the Ottoman Empire to separate spheres of influence during 1913–14 (Fig. 1.1). These are not international boundaries as such but have proved critical to the territorial evolution of Arabia in the years since. Neither have the various lines that Saudi Arabia and Britain (on behalf of its protégés in southern and southeastern Arabia) have claimed as limits to territory in the southern peninsula been accepted as international boundaries, yet these remain alive to varying degrees. They are also fine examples of geometric delimitations.

As part of the July 1913 Anglo–Ottoman settlement of outstanding Gulf questions, an arbitrary eastern limit to Ottoman influence in Arabia (subsequently referred to as the Blue line) was drawn up running due south from Zakhnuniyah island, lying some distance west of the Qatar peninsula and terminating in the desert wastes of the Rub al-Khali.[72] During March 1914 the so-called Violet line was defined to link up the southern terminus of the Blue line with the Anglo–Ottoman boundary in southwest Arabia, delimited during 1903–5 to separate the *wilayat* of Yemen from the nine cantons of the loosely federated Aden Protectorate.[73] The Violet line ran at an angle of 45° from Wadi Bana in the southwest in a straight line until it met the Blue line.[74] The prevailing social and spatial organization of territory in southern Arabia played no part in Britain's decision to draw these lines.

Following the dissolution of the Ottoman Empire, these lines remained discarded relics of the past until Britain hit upon the idea of confronting Ibn Saud with the argument that these limits were binding on account of the Saudi Kingdom's position as successor state to the Ottoman Empire in these parts.[75] Even though this idea was being sounded out in interdepartmental meetings as early as 1926, there was no mention of the Anglo–Ottoman lines in the Anglo–Najdi Treaty of 1927 or in the earlier treaty of 1915. Indeed, it was specified in the 1915 treaty that the limits of the Najdi state with its neighbours on the western Gulf littoral and Arabian Sea would "hereafter be determined".[76] Yet, for over 20 years from the onset of the Anglo–Saudi negotiations in late 1934 until their breakdown in the autumn of 1955, the British government maintained that the Blue and Violet lines were the legal basis of its territorial claims (on behalf of its protégés – Qatar, Abu Dhabi, Muscat and Oman, Aden Protectorate). This was despite its own legal advisers having cautioned, as early as August 1934, that the stance on the Anglo–Ottoman lines would simply not stand up in international law.[77] Suffice it to say that Saudi Arabia never once accepted the British argument before the acrimonious breakdown of the Buraimi Arbitration Tribunal in Geneva during 1955. Despite all of this, the 1914 Violet line is shown on many contemporary Western maps as comprising a significant portion of the Saudi/Yemeni border – specifically, it is shown as forming the western stretch of Saudi Arabia's borders with what was the People's Democratic Republic of Yemen until Yemeni unification in May 1990. At independence in 1967 South Yemen inherited from the Aden Protectorate a *de facto* border (certainly this was Britain's opinion) often known as its "independence line" (Fig. 1.1). As outlined above, South Yemen's independence line incorporated the 1914 Violet line in its western reaches but in the east utilized another territorial limit proposed by Britain – the 1935 Riyadh line, the most generous concession on the Violet line Britain ever offered officially to Saudi Arabia in the course of the inconclusive 1934–55 frontier negotiations. The independence line had first been officially declared by Britain to constitute the Aden Protectorate's northern territorial limits with its unilateral statement of August 1955 concerning the borders of protégé states in the southern peninsula.[78] Following the conclusion of the 1990 Saudi/Oman border agreement and its ratification during the following year,[79] the Saudi/Yemen boundary apparently remains the only indeterminate territorial limit in southern Arabia. That is, except for its western reaches from the Red Sea to the oasis of Najran, a stretch of border delimited and demarcated after the Taif Treaty of 1934. As will be seen later in this review, however, there remains some problems with the stretch of border introduced by the 1934 treaty.

The 1935 Riyadh line with its modification of 1937,[80] which was unilaterally declared with the 1914 Violet line with Britain to constitute borders in southern Arabia during the autumn of 1955 (see above), are amongst the best examples of geometric delimitations formed by straight-line segments linking fixed boundary points (Fig. 1.1). Yet the boundary points specified possessed no great geographic logic. The co-ordinates in question in these claims were often every bit as arbitrary as the interconnecting straight-line segments themselves, frequently failing to coincide with prominent natural features. As already mentioned, the Riyadh line was the largest departure from the Anglo–Ottoman lines ever offered by the British government to Saudi Arabia. Before deciding to declare the modified Riyadh line as its (or more accurately its protégés,) boundary in southern Arabia following inter-departmental consultations at the end of 1954,[81] Britain had been uncertain about how far north to set the borders of the Aden Protectorate. Having been asked during late 1936 to consider additional concessions to the Riyadh line that might move along the frontier negotiations, the Aden government indicated, albeit grudgingly, during March 1937 that it would be prepared in the last resort to accept a northern boundary running along the southern edge of the Rub al-Khali, that is some 20–30 miles south of the Riyadh line (Fig. 1.1). The Foreign Office was convinced that such a concession would not be enough seriously to interest Ibn Saud and the proposal was never broached to the Saudi king.[82]

During 1949 and then again in 1954, the Aden government, backed by the Colonial Office, called for the recognition of a line (often referred to as the "median line") running from Jabal Raiyan to Umm al-Samim as its northern boundary.[83] The proposed delimitation ran north of the Riyadh line and, in its westernmost reaches, north of the Violet line (Fig. 1.1). Ultimately the British government decided against supporting the Governor of Aden since it was considered that to argue for an adjustment of the boundary on tribal grounds (this was the *raison d'etre* of the Umm al-Samim/Raiyan line – at least in its western reaches) would play into Saudi hands elsewhere along the border zone and weaken Britain's defence of the Blue and Violet lines at the Buraimi Arbitration Tribunal.[84] Also, with effective occupancy now the yardstick of international law by which any territorial claims were substantiated, it was realized that to show proof of the exercise of sovereignty as far north as the Riyadh line would be problematic enough, never mind the Umm al-Samim/Raiyan line, below which, in any case, ARAMCO (Saudi) survey teams were already operating.[85] Until the mid-1930s, garrisons of the Hadhrami Bedouin Legion had rarely ventured as far north as the locally important watering holes of Thanaw and Sanaw, which lay roughly equidistant between (to the north) Britain's November 1935 Riyadh line and (to the south) Saudi Arabia's Hamzah line of April 1935.[86]

Six months before Britain's offer and Saudi Arabia's rejection of the Riyadh line, the Saudi Foreign Ministry presented during April 1935 what it maintained was its absolute minimum claim to territory in the southern peninsula.[87] Its maximum claim had been articulated during late June 1934, also by Fuad Bey Hamzah, evidently put on the defensive by Britain's confirmation earlier that month that it would employ the 1913–14 Anglo–Ottoman Blue and Violet lines in forthcoming frontier negotiations with the Saudi government. Fuad Bey stated that "all the tribes living between the coastal towns of Qatar and the coast of Oman and the Hadhramaut belong to the Saudi Arab Kingdom, are entirely submissive to the laws of that country, pay *zakat* and are obedient to the calls of government in the time of war (Jihad) etc.".[88]

Ostensibly, the 1935 Hamzah or Red line, as it was variously known, enclosed (albeit very approximately) the tribal grazing grounds (*dira*) of various nomadic tribes under the sway of the Saudi king. Up until October

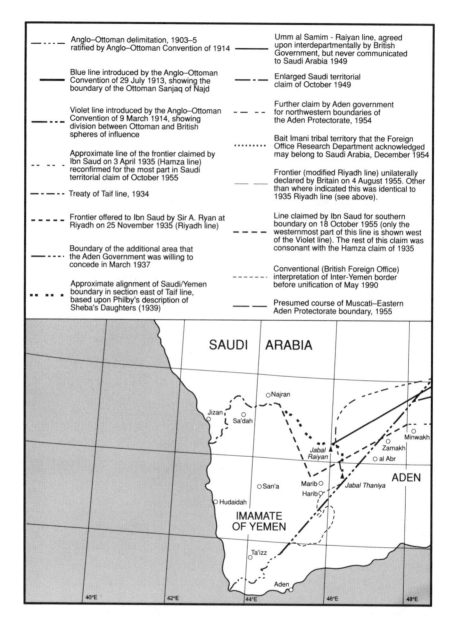

Figure 1.1 Evolution of territorial limits and claims in southern and south-eastern Arabia, 1903–1955. (This page and opposite.)

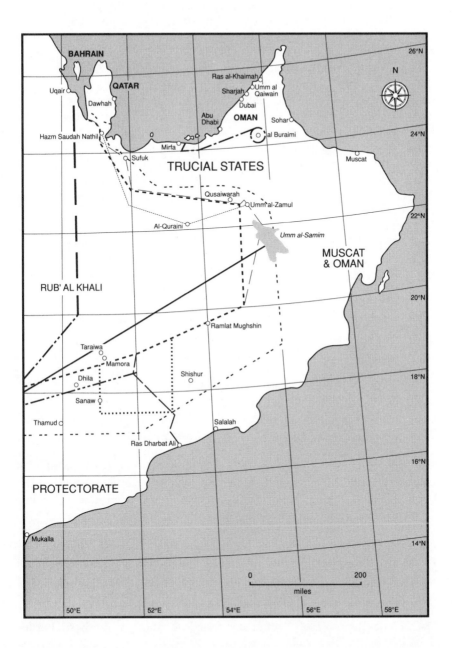

1949, when its territorial claim was enlarged to include the Buraimi oasis in the northeast, the Saudi government rested its case on the Hamzah line, consistently underlining that this was a straightforward expression of effective territorial control as it existed in 1935.[89] For the southern peninsula and, more specifically, the border zone north of the Hadhramawt, since the Saudi/Yemen boundary today remains indeterminate and a potential source of dispute, the Saudi government announced during 1949 merely that its claims were under investigation.[90] The statement issued by the Saudi Foreign Ministry on 18 October 1955 confirmed existing territorial claims (the enlarged demands of 1949 to territory as far east as the Buraimi oasis in the eastern peninsula and the 1935 Hamzah line for the area south and southwest of Abu Dhabi) but also introduced a new claim to territory that had traditionally been regarded as the preserve of the Imam of Yemen for the stretch between Najran (near the eastern terminus of the 1934 Treaty of Taif line) and Jabal Raiyan to the southeast (Fig. 1.1).[91] Despite the tribal basis of the Saudi lines of 1935 and 1955, no great efforts were made to incorporate precisely the *dira* of allegiant tribes in these delimitations. Both the Hamzah line and the October 1955 Saudi claim line were, like the British Riyadh line, geometric delimitations comprising straight-line segments that linked fixed boundary points.

When diplomatic relations were broken off following the Buraimi episode during autumn 1955, Britain and Saudi Arabia were really no closer to reconciling their original (1935) interpretations of where their boundaries should lie in this region. Until 1986 there was no evidence to show that Saudi Arabia had ever publicly retracted its claim of 18 October 1955 to territory in southern Arabia as far as it affected the borders of Yemen. Official and unofficial Saudi maps produced up to this point – for example, those produced by the Ministry of Petroleum and Mineral Resources during 1963 (already referred to in note 91), and Hussein Bindagji in 1984 – show this claim line. The appearance of the Saudi military survey map of 1986 saw its October 1955 claim upheld for the most part (certainly as far as the borders of the People's Democratic Republic of Yemen were concerned) but a greater area of the Yemeni *mashriq* attributed to the Saudi state (Fig. 1.3).

The map also witnessed the abandonment of traditional Saudi claims on the Oman border, recognition apparently being given to long-standing British and Muscati claims in southeast Arabia a full four years before Saudi Arabia and Oman finally agreed a boundary fully consonant with the modified Riyadh line.[92] For the period up until its unification with the Yemen Arab Republic in May 1990, maps produced by the People's Democratic Republic of Yemen continued to show a northern border delimited by the 1914 Violet line and the 1935 Riyadh line. These limits are, not surprisingly, also generally shown on British maps of the region.

Clearly, if, as a consequence of the bilateral talks inaugurated during the summer of 1992, any boundary agreement is ultimately negotiated between

Saudi Arabia and the recently unified Republic of Yemen for the stretch of the border zone between Najran and of Oman, then either one or both parties will have to relax their hitherto widely divergent territorial claims in the region. If and when a negotiated settlement is reached – talks were held as early as 1982 towards this end without success[93] – there is clearly little likelihood of a boundary being agreed that closely resembles the 1935 Hamzah line in the southern peninsula. For Yemen has for some time now extended effective occupation some way north of this limit.

From the mid-1950s onwards there is reasonable evidence to suggest that the Aden Protectorate and (since 1967) South Yemen have extended an effective administrative presence in the northwest up to the 1914 Violet line. Though Saudi Arabia has never formally accepted the Violet line as constituting what was the former northwestern boundary of South Yemen, there is a case for maintaining that serious border incidents have occurred only when South Yemeni forces crossed the Anglo/Ottoman limit, most notably at al-Wadi'ah during 1969.[94] It is perhaps not unreasonable to suggest that for the northwestern stretch of the former Saudi/South Yemeni border, the Saudi government has respected the 1914 Violet line on a *de facto* basis. Saudi sensitivities may have been alerted during the past two years or so when it realized that the northern tip of the Yemeni al-Jana block oil concession possibly transgressed the 1914 Violet line.[95] Yet curiously the northern tip of this oil concession extends into an area apparently not claimed by Saudi Arabia, that is if its 18 October 1955 claim and its slight modification in the 1986 Saudi military survey map still hold good. There is, therefore, apparently a small wedge of territory, possibly incorporating some of the tribal territories of the Saiar tribe, that has apparently not been formally claimed by either Saudi Arabia or Yemen. During the past couple of years, the Saudi Economic and Development Company (SEDCO–later recognized and registered during 1991 as the Nimr Petroleum Company in the Cayman islands), a subsidiary of the National Commercial Bank of Saudi Arabia (owned by the Bin Mahfouz family, coincidentally of Saiar origin), has bought into Yemeni concession areas close to but significantly, south of the al-Jana block. Following intermittent and inconsequential consultations with Riyadh on the border issue in the two years preceding Yemeni unification, Yemeni President Ali Abdallah Salih launched a new initiative on Yemeni television during September 1991. He called for the final settlement of the state's northern and eastern borders with Saudi Arabia and Oman "with no reservations and in the context of the legal and historical rights of the parties concerned". Salih, who displayed a particular anxiety to settle territorial disputes with Saudi Arabia, also announced the formation of a Yemeni Boundary Demarcation Committee.[96]

The winter of 1991–2 witnessed informal exchanges between the Saudis and Yemenis on the border question, but procedural difficulties, principally concerning irreconcilable interpretations of various articles of the 1934 Taif

Treaty, soon bogged these down. The stakes appeared to be raised when in March 1992 the Saudi government addressed letters to foreign oil companies operating in concessions in northern Yemen, advising that these were areas claimed by Saudi Arabia and that operations should therefore be ceased henceforth (see Chapter 8 for texts). American companies were addressed through a memorandum despatched to the United States State Department. Both the Yemeni and US governments advised the oil concessionaires to continue their operations and ignore the content of the Saudi letter. The State Department took a fairly uncompromising line on the whole issue, advising the Saudi government that its claims in the disputed border zone were not recognized and urging the peaceful resolution of any disputes, a stance welcomed by the Yemeni government.[97] At the end of 1992 it certainly seemed that the State Department's prudent words were being heeded. Following a preparatory meeting in Geneva during late July 1992, Saudi Arabia and Yemen met subsequently on three further occasions during 1992, ostensibly to discuss technical issues. Even in the late summer of 1993 they remain a long way short of getting past the procedural stage.[98] August 1993 witnessed the despatch of a further series of letters from the Saudi government to foreign oil companies operating Yemeni oil concessions claimed to lie within the territory of the kingdom. The companies concerned appear not to have acted upon their receipt.

Whereas for decades now Yemen (or the Aden Protectorate and the People's Democratic Republic of Yemen before it) has effectively exercised authority up to or beyond the Violet line to the northwest of the Hadhramawt, the extension of administrative control to the northeast has been much more gradual. This is the stretch of border where the divergence in Saudi and British/Yemeni claims has traditionally been greatest (Fig. 1.1). Most detailed maps of the region suggest that while Yemen has established effective occupancy in virtually all areas north of the Saudi Hamzah line of 1935, Yemeni infrastructural development is often not extended on any consistent basis as far north as the 1935 Riyadh line. Roads, for example, stop some distance south of this line. It might perhaps be argued, therefore, that there is, in effect, a desert zone stretching north from the northernmost limit effectively occupied by Yemen across the Riyadh line and into the Rub al-Khali to the southernmost limit effectively occupied by Saudi Arabia. It is possible that any boundary ultimately negotiated will fall within this zone. Alternatively, the two states may arrive in time at an accommodation whereby the area in question is jointly managed as some sort of common zone.[99] The division of territory by geometric lines within the Arabian peninsula has not been confined to straight-line delimitations and segments. The Anglo–Ottoman Convention of July 1913 defined a semi-circle (marked by a red line on the map accompanying the original text of the settlement) within which the complete autonomy of the Ruler of Kuwait was to be recognized by the Ottoman Empire (Fig. 1.2). The semi-circle was 80 miles in diameter and centred upon Kuwait port.[100] The southern half of the Red line of 1913 was recognized in the 1922 Uqair Protocol (concluded between Ibn Saud and the British authorities responsible for the foreign affairs of Iraq and Kuwait to delimit the emergent Najdi state's limits to territory in northeast Arabia) as forming Kuwait's southern boundaries with Najd and the Najd–Kuwait Neutral Zone.[101]

The Iraq/Saudi Arabia boundary has already been mentioned as a territorial limit consisting of, for the most part, straight-line segments connecting hill tops, dry wadis and other natural features. The delimitation fixed by the 1922 Uqair Protocol contained some rather jagged straight-line sections halfway along its course, west of the Saudi–Iraq Neutral Zone, which had been defined by the same treaty to lie at the eastern terminus of the boundary. During 1975 Iraq and Saudi Arabia agreed to partition their rhomboid-shaped neutral zone (baklawah), a division formalized by a boundary agreement of 1981.[102] Besides dividing the neutral zone, the 1981 agreement also smoothed and straightened the whole of the land boundary farther west (Fig. 1.2). Although the modified 1981 delimitation is shown on contemporary Iraqi and Saudi maps, precise details of the co-ordinates of its seven straight-line segments were released only very recently.[103] Although the exchange of ratifications of the 26 December 1981 Iraq/Saudi Arabia border treaty took place in February 1982, it took until the summer of 1991 for the text of the treaty (with the border co-ordinates) to be registered with the United Nations, and even then, this was done unilaterally by Saudi Arabia. The feeling persists that Saudi Arabia would not have bothered to make this move were it not for the action, in January 1991, of the Iraqi Revolutionary Command Council in cancelling all charters and agreements signed with the Riyadh government since 1968.[104]

Anthropogeographic and complex boundaries: Oman/United Arab Emirates and the Iran/Iraq boundary

Anthropogeographic boundaries follow manmade features such as roads, railways and canals or, alternatively, follow tribal, ethnic or religious divisions. Only the latter group of anthropogeographic boundaries holds any relevance for the Arabian peninsula. Throughout the late 1950s the British authorities in the Gulf and most notably Julian Walker, then a Political Officer in the Trucial Coast, made stringent efforts to delimit the respective tribal territories of the Trucial Coast shaikhs in an attempt to bring greater stability to this area following the breakdown of the Anglo–Saudi frontier negotiations and to obviate future war between the ruling families of the Trucial shaikhdoms – Abu Dhabi and Dubai had fought out a brief war, for instance, during 1945.[105] Britain's efforts to delimit international boundaries on a tribal basis contrasted with its efforts to impose largely arbitrary limits elsewhere in the peninsula. It should be noted, however, that what was being attempted here was to delimit, for the first time, land boundaries between Britain's protégé states along the Gulf coast. Saudi Arabia and other states whose foreign affairs Britain did not control were not involved in these calculations and it was therefore considered that there was no risk in adopting major tribal divisions as international boundaries. The boundary-makers' task was complicated as the territory through which limits had to be drawn was the inhabited highlands lying south of the Musandam peninsula (Ru'us al-Jibal) and not the largely featureless desert terrain through which most of the region's other boundaries had been plotted. The patchwork of tribal territories arrived at by Britain for the Trucial Coast shaikhdoms will be examined briefly in a later section of this overview.

Throughout late 1959 and early 1960 Julian Walker managed to induce the agreement of all but the Qasimi shaikhs of Sharjah and Ras al-Khaimah to boundary agreements with the Sultanate of Muscat and Oman.[106] What resulted was a punctuated boundary and Oman being split into three parts by the newly defined tribal territories of the Trucial Coast shaikhdoms. Following the federation of the Trucial Coast shaikhdoms into the United Arab Emirates during 1971, Oman remains the only non-contiguous, land-based state territory in the peninsula. Through its control of the Musandam peninsula, Oman shares the strategically vital Strait of Hormuz with Iran. Long-standing enmity between the Sultan of Muscat and the Qawasim tribal confederation had worked against any chances there may have been during the late 1950s of territorial limits being defined between the Sultanate and the shaikhdoms of Sharjah and Ras al-Khaimah. The Ruler of Sharjah claimed historic title to Dhank, lying 40 miles south of Buraimi, while the topography of the high mountains of the Ru'us al-Jibal south of the Musandam peninsula made the task of finalizing Ras al-Khaimah's northern boundaries all the more problematic.[107] Ultimately, at some point during the mid-1960s, the Qasimi shaikhs and Oman were able to reconcile their territorial grievances. A neutral zone was defined between Oman and Sharjah west of the Hajar range of mountains.[108] A neutral zone was also defined along the Wadi Hadf to solve an Ajman–Oman dispute that had hitherto proved incapable of settlement.[109] According to one recent source and contributor to this volume, Omani officials were present at the negotiations that led to Saudi Arabia and Abu Dhabi reaching their secret territorial understanding of 1974, giving the Wahhabi state access to the Gulf south of the Qatar peninsula.[110] Periodic though minor disputes occurred during the 1970s over Umm al-Zamul, which the Sultan of Muscat had recognized as belonging to Abu Dhabi in 1959, but which he had claimed publicly on several occasions before this date.[111] Apparently Abu Dhabi and Oman agreed to renegotiate the section of the boundary near Umm al-Zamul during the mid-1970s but no details were made public of what progress these achieved.[112] It was recently announced (April 1993) that all

UAE–Oman territorial disputes had been settled by agreement (see later in this chapter).

Some boundaries in the region comprise physiographic, geometric and anthropogeographic sections along the various stages of their course. The Iran/Iraq boundary provides a good example of this *complex* category of boundary.[113] In its lowest stages, the boundary follows the Shatt al-Arab. The delimitation then leaves the river and runs due north across a broad plain until it reaches the Zagros foothills. The boundary then runs due west, north again and northeast in a series of geometric straight-line segments until the 15th boundary pillar of the demarcated boundary is reached. Running north from this point until it reaches the tripoint with Turkey at Kuh-e Dalanper, the boundary assumes a course along the western foothills of the Zagros and then utilizes high drainage divides in Kurdistan.[114] One source has argued that the boundary, in its various stages, as originally delimited and demarcated during 1914 by the Turco–Persian boundary commission (on which the Ottoman Empire, Persia and the arbitrating powers of Britain and Russia were represented), also tried to separate territory on religious, linguistic and ethnic grounds. In its northern reaches an attempt had been made to leave Shi'i Kurds in Persia, while the central stretch of the boundary around Pusht-i-Kuh had supposedly been delimited in such a manner so as to separate Persian from Arabic dialects. Farther south in the lowland plains west of the Zagros, it was argued that the delimitation had endeavoured to separate Lurs from Arabs.[115]

The imposition of linear boundaries: an alien concept?

No attempt will be made here to join the established debate over whether the system of state territories established by Britain along the western littoral of the Gulf is necessarily the most suitable mode of social and spatial organization for the peninsula. The fact remains that it is here and, if the recent efforts of the international community to restore Kuwaiti independence are anything to go by, it is unlikely to be changed, except perhaps from within the Gulf Co-operation Council states themselves.

The chief objection to linear boundaries has traditionally been that they are a European concept that has been *superimposed* (one of Hartshorne's five categories of cultural boundary) upon a cultural landscape for which they hold no relevance. Conventional wisdom maintains that the predominant notion of territoriality in the Arabian desert was tribal and impermanent. The tribal *dar* would contract and expand with the resource base upon which (in the pre-hydrocarbons era) nomadic tribesmen were dependent for their livelihood. The huge size of many tribal *dira* in southern, central Arabia only underlined the resource-poor nature of the region. As a recent source has highlighted: "the extreme aridity of the region is indicated by the smallness of tribes and their extraordinary range. In traditional geopolitics, the poorer the resource base, the larger the tribal *dar*."[116] As late as 1946 the Murra tribe, on whose domination of the Rub al-Khali Saudi territorial claims in the southern peninsula were primarily based, numbered only 5000–10,000, yet could claim a territory in excess of 500,000 km^2.[117]

It has been suggested that a sedentary tribesman's territorial loyalty, so far as it was developed, might be to his house, wells and date gardens.[118] Yet even in predominantly sedentary areas, such as the Yemeni *mashriq*, tribal boundaries are, to this day, known and strictly respected by native inhabitants. When trying to finalize international limits to territory for the two Yemens (up until May 1990) in the indeterminate areas east of the *mashriq* and northwest of the Hadhramawt, the British and Yemeni authorities have traditionally experienced difficulties in getting these tribesmen to represent these areas of influence accurately on a map, even in those cases where they are well known on the ground.[119] The characteristic marginality of these tribes and their territories to central authority in both San'a and Aden, but especially the former, has only exacerbated these problems.

A frequently articulated complaint is that the advent of international boundaries created barriers across long-established desert trade routes. Throughout the mid-1930s, reaching its peak at the time of the *majlis* movement in Kuwait during 1938, Iraq insisted that Kuwait take more effective measures to counter the widespread prevalence of smuggling across its borders. This presented Kuwait's beleaguered ruler, Shaikh Ahmad, with problems, for to take draconian measures to outlaw what was a vital and long-established component of Kuwait's economy would certainly have alienated the emirate's influential merchant community.[120]

Previous sections have already outlined how Britain was loath to put tribal considerations to the fore when negotiating limits to territory in southern Arabia during the 20-year period from 1935. Britain's attempts to define territorial limits on a tribal basis in the mountainous terrain south of the Musandam peninsula have already been examined in so far as the Oman/United Arab Emirates boundary was concerned. The patchwork of small, frequently non-contiguous territories that were defined for the Trucial shaikhdoms at around the same time is sometimes cited as evidence that linear boundaries determined on a tribal basis simply do not work for Arabia (Fig. 9.3). This view probably arises, as much as anything else, from the cluttered appearance on a map of the shaikhdoms' boundaries. The European administrator has always had a predilection for neat and tidy boundaries. Any insuperable problems of national integration, which would certainly have arisen had the shaikhdoms tried to co-exist as independent states, were ameliorated by their federation in 1971 into the United Arab Emirates. Confederation has also minimized the upheaval caused by boundary disputes. Since 1971 only minor changes have needed to be made to the boundaries established primarily by Julian Walker in the late 1950s/early 1960s, including a small revision in the course of the Abu Dhabi/Dubai delimitation. There seems to be no little justice in Walker's own view that "the Trucial states have probably been able to relate to each other in a way that would not have developed if there had been no agreed frontiers between them and territorial disputes had proliferated".[121]

Of course, territorial limits were in existence in the region under review long before Britain arrived on the scene. While the creation of the Gulf emirates as territorial states chiefly resulted from Britain's presence in the Gulf and its determination that Saudi Arabia should not control territory up to the coastal ports of Dawhah, Abu Dhabi and Kuwait, different factors were responsible for the initial development of other interfaces, most notably the Iran/Iraq boundary. Imperial conflict over the Mesopotamian plain and the Zagros mountains dates back to pre-Islamic times and became most intense from the early sixteenth century onwards, as the Sunni Ottoman Empire and the Shi'i Persian Safavid Dynasty clashed repeatedly in their efforts to impose their respective creeds of Islam upon the region.[122] The 1639 "Treaty of peace and demarcation of frontiers (Zohab)" was, along with all similar accords signed before the early 1840s (the treaties of Hamadan, 1729, Kerden, 1746, and Erzurum, 1823)[123], when Britain and Russia intervened to stabilize territorial control, little more than a momentary truce in a long religious war between the two great empires. It in effect established a wide strip of territory in which the authority of both Sultan and Shah was weak and disputed.[124] Though this zone remained indeterminate for the next two centuries, the Zohab Treaty remains (certainly in name) the earliest explicitly territorial instrument signed between two Middle Eastern states.

Whatever the debate about the suitability of the present framework of state territory for Arabia, many authorities suggest that there are good reasons for thinking that it will endure for some time into the future. After all, the constitution of the Arab League explicitly pledges to uphold each member state's independence and sovereignty.[125] As Drysdale & Blake comment:

> The political spheres they [international boundaries] define have acquired a seeming permanence, and the state constitutes as basic, legitimate and universal a unit of political geographic organization in the Middle East and North Africa as elsewhere.[126]

Antecedent boundaries – nation-building within fixed territorial limits: the case of Qatar

Most of Hartshorne's classifications of boundary types really possess any validity only when applied to a cultural landscape that is fully developed, such as North America and Europe. There might, however, be a case for reviewing the applicability of his *antecedent* category (a boundary that is drawn prior to the development of the surrounding cultural landscape) when looking at Qatar. For the state of Qatar was granted fixed territorial limits covering the whole of the peninsula before state authority had even begun to expand on any consistent or effective basis beyond its northeast coastline. The task faced by the al-Thani ruling family in the years since was to establish authority and legitimacy where previously there had been none.

As already discussed, the territory of Qatar was determined during 1935 by the area of the oil concession granted to the Anglo–Iranian Oil Company during that year. This extended over the whole of the Qatar peninsula. In return for the Qatari ruler granting his oil concession to a British company, the British government promised guarantees against land attack from the south (that is, against attack from Ibn Saud), yet, in practice, al-Thani authority in the mid-1930s rarely stretched beyond the confines of Daw-hah.[127] The 1913 Anglo–Ottoman settlement of Gulf questions and the 1916 Anglo–Qatari Treaty had successfully disposed of the al-Khalifah threat to incorporate the Qatar peninsula into the Bahraini state, providing, as they did, guarantees against attack from the sea.[128] Yet, from the early 1920s onwards, the chief threat posed to the survival of al-Thani rule was from the expanding Najdi state to the south. For the 1916 Treaty provided no guarantees against attack by land. The Qatari rulers were therefore forced into a dialogue with Ibn Saud, who wielded much more authority over the desert interior of the Qatar peninsula than did Shaikh Abdallah al-Thani.[129] A *modus vivendi* was arrived at that reflected the unequal balance of power between the Wahhabi leader and the al-Thani shaikh. So long as Abdallah paid his annual *lakh* of rupees and did nothing overtly to antagonize Ibn Saud, the right claimed by the Saudi leader to call upon the allegiance of all the tribes in the Qatar desert remained a latent threat.[130] As late as January 1934, Hajji Abdallah Williamson, a charismatic English Muslim employee of the Anglo–Persian Oil Company, commented that:

Ibn Thani, other than the sixty-odd members of his own family, has no tribe which he can claim as his own in Qatar. There are a few scattered semi-nomads of the Naim tribe on the peninsula dating back to the time of Bini Muslim who were the rulers in Qatar before the Thani family. Ibn Thani depends for his fighting force on men drawn from the Bini Hajar and the Bini Murra, two of the three tribes pasturing along the border of Qatar. The third tribe is al-Manasir.

Ibn Thani is definitely dependent on the goodwill of Ibn Saud and his Hassa Governor, Ibn Jalloui: for the safety of his lands from the raids of the Nejd tribes, especially from the Manasir.[131]

The east coast peninsula towns of Wakrah, Dawhah, Dha'ain and Khawr al Mahadnadah fell within the al-Thani orbit but not the northern coastal settlements of Ru'us Abu Adh Dhuhif and Ashairij.[132]

In the years following Britain's territorial guarantee of 1935, the Qatari ruler found the task of consolidating al-Thani control over the whole of the area that had been defined for the Qatari state troublesome. Until the effects of oil wealth began to make themselves felt during the 1950s, centrifugal forces worked against any moves towards national integration. The post-Second World War slump in pearling,[133] which had dominated the traditional economy of the Gulf, resulted in large-scale tribal migrations from the Qatar peninsula to the surrounding states of Bahrain and Saudi Arabia, relatively much more affluent since the benefits of oil had been felt at an earlier stage. An already weak population base was further depleted. Political regionalism continued to have its effect within the peninsula. Sizeable pockets of the west coast population of Qatar, especially the Na'im tribe, still professed some sort of allegiance to the al-Khalifah ruling family of Bahrain.[134] It is possible that the Qatari ruling family's failure to exercise authority over much of the northern and western peninsula contributed towards Britain's decision to recognize the Hawar group of islands as belonging to Bahrain during 1939. The centripetal forces that the al-Thani rulers were able to generate were severely limited by the very nature of their shaikhly authority, derived, as it was, more from control of access to coastal resources than from influence over other prominent families in the peninsula.[135]

Importantly, however, from the early 1940s onwards, the relationship between Saudi Arabia and Qatar continued to improve. Though the al-Thani were technically prevented from maintaining a personal dialogue with the Saudi ruler because of Qatar's treaty commitments to Britain, the Foreign Office suspected that the two states had reached an understanding on their boundary a full 20 years before the boundary treaty of 1965 was concluded. It is possible that at some time during the early 1940s Ibn Saud agreed to stop claiming Jabal Naksh (the locality having been discovered by this stage to overlie no substantial oil deposits), in return for a recognition from the al-Thani ruler that Saudi Arabia was free to do as it pleased in the Khawr al-Udaid.

If Qatar remains perhaps the best example in the peninsula of a state that was given territory before it possessed legitimacy or authority, there were notable cases, for example in southern Arabia, of Britain having to bolster the authority of its protégé states in order to justify the extent of territory being claimed in frontier negotiations with the Saudis. Britain's attempts to establish effective occupancy on behalf of the Aden Protectorate in the steppeland and sands north of the Hadhramawt have already been examined. Qatar, the United Arab Emirates and Kuwait (before 1922) have all experienced some problems in extending effective jurisdiction over the territories allotted to them this century. Unity problems for the Gulf emirates have been ameliorated considerably by oil wealth. A recent source concludes optimistically that "national identities are being forged and territorial allegiances taking root, even in countries that once seemed hopelessly artificial".[136]

International relations, Arabian boundaries and territorial disputes

It is instructive to summarize briefly the sets of relationships that have been responsible for the present framework of state territory in the Gulf region and many of the disputes that were alive to varying degrees at the end of 1992. This involves not only land boundaries but awards made on the sovereignty of various Gulf islands. Five roughly chronological categories are readily identifiable: Anglo–Persian, Anglo–Ottoman, Anglo–Saudi, British (territorial awards involving neighbouring states under Britain's protection), and bilateral agreements reached independently between Saudi Arabia and its neighbours (the Arab shaikhdoms of the Gulf, Iran, Iraq and the Yemen). The legacy of boundaries and territorial disputes left by each of these sets of relationships is briefly reviewed below.

Anglo–Persian relations

Following the Great War of 1914–18, the strategic threats to Britain's omnipotent position in the Gulf had all but disappeared. Gone were the Ottoman Empire and Imperial Russia, while Germany was hardly in any position to reassert itself in the region. In this essentially pre-hydrocarbons era Britain sought to preserve the *status quo* and to do so needed only to come to an accommodation with Persia. The chief bones of contention that prevented Britain (on behalf of its protégés along the western Gulf littoral) from concluding a broad package of agreements during the 1920s and 1930s with Persia on outstanding Gulf issues[137] were the latter's claims to the islands of Abu Musa and Greater and Lesser Tunb and to the island state of Bahrain.[138]

Abu Musa and the Tunbs. Abu Musa, a well watered island with a population of around 600 people (whose civil population is Arab), lies on the Arab side of a median line drawn northwest to southeast through the Gulf, while the Greater and Lesser Tunbs lie closer to the Iranian coast. Rival claims by the Persian/Iranian state and the Qasimi shaikhdoms of Sharjah and Ras al-Khaimah (or Britain on their behalf) have been established for over a century now and maintained with great consistency. Let us now say a few words in turn about the origins and bases of rival claims to the islands, possible ways out of the dispute that have been suggested over the years, Iran's move on the islands after Britain's withdrawal during late 1971 and, finally, the resurrection of the dispute during 1992.

The Persian/Iranian claim to the islands has traditionally been based upon its boast to have owned the islands before Britain temporarily occupied them in the 1820s, apparently in the interests of maintaining security in the face of widespread piracy along the southern Gulf littoral, much of it considered as originating from the Qasimi stronghold of Sharjah.[139]

Evidence for ownership of the islands, certainly the Tunbs, for the period before the nineteenth century is far from conclusive. From the 1720s the Qasimi tribes of the southern Gulf littoral but especially Ras al-Khaimah had been active on the Persian coast, seizing Basidu in 1727. Territorial and political control at this time were marked by fluidity and it was no surprise when Persia avenged these earlier Qasimi attacks by taking Ras al-Khaimah (or Qasimi positions approximating to the modern geographical definition of the shaikhdom in 1992) in 1737, apparently obtaining the submission of its rulers. This hold did not last for long either.

During the mid-1840s the Persian Foreign Minister, Hajji Mirza Aghassi, claimed all of the waters and the islands of the Gulf as Persian. According to the British records, it was not until 1877 that a Persian claim to the Tunbs was first formally entered and not until 1888 that Tehran did the same, though informally, for Abu Musa. Up until 1873 the British Residency at Bushire had generally believed that the Tunbs belonged to Persia, because of these islands' close connection with the southern Persian, though Qasimi-controlled, port of Lingeh. But by 1882 Britain was apparently of the opinion that the Qasimi shaikh of Ras al-Khaimah held title over the Tunbs, after the receipt of original documents from the rulers of the southern Gulf littoral.[140]

Persian/Iranian claims rely strongly on the assertion that for 10 years during the late nineteenth century Abu Musa and the Tunbs were administered by a section of the Arab Qasimi tribe that had migrated to the Persian coast near Lingeh during the mid-eighteenth century. For at least 10 years up until 1887 Persia claimed that taxes were collected from the islanders of Simi and Tunb on behalf of the Qasimi headman of Lingeh. Importantly, Iran was to claim that the Qasimi shaikh of Lingeh and his followers had acquired the status of Persian subjects before beginning their loose administration of the islands. British records appear to confirm the latter contention, suggesting that, during the 1880s certainly, the Arab shaikhs of Lingeh had fallen under the increasing influence of central government in Tehran and paid tribute on request to the Persian Governor-General of Fars province.[141]

Iran has also laid great stress historically on a British War Office map produced in 1886 in which Abu Musa and the Tunbs are shown clearly in Iranian colours. This was presented to the Shah as a gift by the British Minister in Tehran during the summer of 1888 on the instructions of British Foreign Secretary Lord Salisbury. In 1887 the Persian government forced the Qasimi authorities at Lingeh to return to the southern Gulf littoral and also annexed the island of Sirri, a move in effect acquiesced in by Britain since no great objections were voiced either at the time or thereafter. Threats made at the same time to annex the Tunbs were not acted upon until 1904, by which time flags of the Qawasim flew on both Greater Tunb (though apparently not Lesser Tunb) and Abu Musa.[142]

Iranian claims have been justified above all on the strategic imperative of guarding the entrance to the Strait of Hormuz in the interests of national security, an argument that was supported most notably by senior United States government officials in 1971 as new regional security arrangements were being drawn up to fill the vacuum left by Britain's withdrawal from the Gulf.[143]

Qasimi claims to Abu Musa are based ostensibly upon the uninterrupted possession of the island by the ruling family of Sharjah over a long and continuous period. Sovereignty was gained, it is claimed, by a process of historical consolidation. Sharjah has pointed to historical documents collected at the British Bushire Residency as evidence that Britain recognized its hereditary estate over and exclusive right to Abu Musa from the end of the eighteenth century. Moreover, it points out that Britain actively defended its claims to the island from the early 1870s. It therefore claims prescriptive title dating back to 1872. While admitting that the administration of the Tunbs was in effect shared between the Qawasim shaikhs of Lingeh and Ras al-Khaimah during the 1878–87 period, Sharjah's rulers have denied that Abu Musa was anything other than directly administered from Sharjah itself. It is also claimed that pearlers and fishermen paid annual dues to the Ruler of Sharjah for the period from 1863 onwards.[144]

Sharjah and Ras al-Khaimah have also stressed that the Qawasim at Lingeh were acting on their own behalf rather than as Iranian subjects when administering the islands, if they did so at all, for a decade during the late nineteenth century. In any case, they continue to argue that Qasimi control of the southern Gulf and islands had been established before the breakaway section of the Arab tribe settled on the Persian coast at Lingeh during the mid-eighteenth century.[145]

As has been stated, Britain first formally recognized Qasimi ownership of Abu Musa during the 1870s and the Tunbs a decade later. The maintenance of Persian claims to the islands during the 1890s, by which time Britain had signed protectorate-style treaties with the rulers of the southern Gulf littoral and, more specifically, the announcement of proposals by a merchant shipping line to call at Abu Musa rather than Lingeh in the southern Gulf, led Britain, during 1903, to advise the Qasimi chiefs to place their flags on the islands, which was promptly done. At this stage, with Lord Curzon as Indian Viceroy, the Government of India (responsible for the administration of Britain's treaty relations with the Arab shaikhdoms of the southern Gulf until 1947) was taking all possible measures to preserve British omnipotency in the Gulf. Attempts were being made to support the claims of Britain's protégés to any territory, such as Abu Musa and the Tunbs, that was judged as possessing a strategic or commercial value that might attract the attention of rival imperial powers. In the event, the flags placed by the Qawasim on the islands were soon removed by Belgian employees of the Persian customs authorities. They simultaneously hoisted the Persian flag during the spring of 1904. Uncompromising British diplomacy in Tehran, which warned that naval action would be taken unless Persia backed down, resulted in the speedy evacuation of the islands two months later (June 1904), while the construction during the First World War of a lighthouse on Greater Tunb (not actually operational until a few years afterwards) provided further evidence of Britain's determination to see Qasimi claims to the islands substantiated.[146]

The early to mid-1920s saw Persia suggest that the disputes over Bahrain, Abu Musa and the Tunbs be referred to the League of Nations (1923) and also saw Persian efforts to interfere with customs at Abu Musa meet with little resistance from the British (1925). It was the Persian seizure of an Arab dhow near Greater Tunb in 1928, however, that had the effect of reopening the dispute in the inter-war years.[147]

For just over a century until its departure from the Gulf in 1971 Britain guaranteed and oversaw Qasimi control of the islands. Yet for much of the early part of this century the Iranian claim to the Tunbs if not, admittedly, to Abu Musa was sometimes maintained with greater force and consistency. On several occasions during the 1920s and 1930s the Iranian Foreign Ministry offered to drop its claim to Bahrain if Britain was prepared to recognize its sovereignty over the disputed islands in the lower central Gulf.[148]

The efforts made by Britain to uphold Ras al-Khaimah's claim to the Tunbs were not always helped over the years by the inconsistent attitude of its ruler towards maintaining effective sovereignty over the islands. The British authorities in the Gulf were deeply embarrassed during December 1934 when the Ruler of Ras al-Khaimah actually withdrew the Qasimi flag from Greater Tunb, an action that coincided with staunch British efforts to rebut Persian claims to the Tunbs and Abu Musa during the Anglo–Persian general treaty negotiations. There are two rival views of why such an action was taken, illustrating perfectly the frequently inconclusive nature of archival sources as hard and fast evidence for territorial claims. One stated that Ras al-Khaimah had lowered its flag as the result of an exchange of correspondence entered into directly with the Persian/Iranian government. Before Britain eventually persuaded the Ras al-Khaimah shaikh to reassert sovereignty over the island during the late spring of 1935, its diplomats in Tehran had practically resigned themselves to aiming for a compromise that would see Persian claims to the Tunbs admitted in return for recognition of Qasimi claims over Abu Musa. The other explanation for Ras al-Khaimah's action went as follows: the shaikh had taken this action to draw attention to the fact that no rent was received from the British for their use of the lighthouse at Tunb. Not surprisingly, Britain made some money available once Qasimi sovereignty had been reasserted in 1935.[149]

On other occasions Britain toyed with the idea of leasing Abu Musa and/or the Tunbs to Persia in a final bid to move along the stalled general treaty negotiations.[150] Sharjah steadfastly resisted any suggestions that Abu Musa should form part of these plans, however. Informally, Persia, or at least its Minister of Court, Monsieur Taimourtache, forwarded its own scheme, whereby Iran would renounce its claims to Abu Musa in return for Ras al-Khaimah dropping its claims to and administration of the Tunbs. Taimourtache had first raised such a possibility in 1930 and five years later, in 1935, added that Iran would also be prepared to consider granting leasehold rights to Ras al-Khaimah over the Tunbs.[151] All of these potential trade-offs, though evidently much discussed, never saw the light of day.

During 1955, with access to maritime oil deposits now a critical factor in the offshore political geography of the Gulf, Britain tried to sponsor an agreement whereby Sharjah would recognize Iranian sovereignty over Sirri, Iran would recognize Sharjah's ownership of Abu Musa and Ras al-Khaimah would be willing to sell the Tunbs to Iran. Though the Trucial Coast rulers were apparently ready to agree to such a scheme, Iran proved unwilling to sacrifice its claims to Abu Musa. That at least is the British version of events.

The Abu Musa/Tunbs dispute burst into international prominence on the last day of November 1971, when Iran stationed troops on Abu Musa (by prior agreement with Sharjah) but forcibly occupied the Tunbs after Britain departed the Gulf. Iran took this action on the day before Britain terminated its treaty relations with the rulers of the southern Gulf littoral (1 December 1971) and two days before the official proclamation of the United Arab Emirates (2 December 1971). The Iranian action provoked sufficient anger in the Arab world for the issue to be brought before the United Nations Security Council.[152]

On 29 November 1971 the Ruler of Sharjah announced that he had arrived voluntarily if reluctantly, at an agreement with Iran over Abu Musa by which each state would maintain its sovereign claims to the feature. This was in the face of a clear threat that the island would be taken forcibly by Iran should he not comply. No such arrangements had been made with respect to the Tunbs with the result that the islands were captured by Iran on 30 November 1971. The Ras al-Khaimah ruler had failed to accede to Iranian demands for a peaceful transfer of sovereignty. Though one source claims rather sensationally that 120 Qasimi inhabitants of Greater Tunb were expelled from the island to the Ras al-Khaimah mainland,[153] more accurate reports testify that the Tunbs were uninhabited in the period preceding Iran's move but that three officials from Ras al-Khaimah were stationed on the larger of the two islands immediately before Britain's vacation of the Gulf. Of these, one was killed and two wounded.

A protagonist in Iran's consultations with each of the Qasimi shaikhdoms during the period up until the Iranian occupation has actually revealed the type of understanding that was on the cards for the Tunbs between Iran and Ras al-Khaimah. It is clear that Ras al-Khaimah was given no option but to accede to Iranian demands for recognition of its full sovereignty over the two islands. Iran was apparently prepared to supply the shaikhdom with military and humanitarian support by way of compensation. Though the Ruler of Ras al-Khaimah initially seemed disposed to accept Iran's offer of Western-built guns and armoured vehicles plus the unspecified "humanitarian" component, he apparently later changed his mind, demanding a significant sum of money instead. Iran continues to maintain that it could not possibly have entertained paying a huge amount of money for features that possessed no economic value. The value of the Tunbs was and remains purely strategic to Iran.[154]

The 29 November 1971 Sharjah–Iran Memorandum of Understanding on Abu Musa was negotiated by Sir William Luce, Britain's last Political Resident in the Gulf, following consultations with the Iranian government in Tehran. Britain had endeavoured throughout 1971 to broker settlements for the Qasimi shaikhdoms in its negotiations with Tehran. However, as its Permanent Representative was later to claim in the proceedings before the United Nations Security Council during December 1971, Britain had never been anything less than honest about its inability to protect Abu Musa and the Tunbs against Iranian actions should no arrangements have been arrived at by the time it vacated the Gulf. Britain stated officially at the same forum that it was satisfied with the Memorandum of Understanding.[155] Perhaps this was a little surprising, given Britain's previous resolve to see Sharjah's claims to full sovereignty to the island substantiated and upheld. Yet surely this was a classic case of *realpolitik*. Iran had already been entrusted with the role of "Gulf policeman" in the so-called "twin pillar" policy for regional security following Britain's withdrawal from the Gulf.

The essentially pragmatic Memorandum of Understanding was most notable for the way in which it accommodated the claims of both Sharjah and Iran to Abu Musa. Its first clause read as follows: "Neither Iran nor Sharjah will give up its claim to Abu Musa nor recognize the other's claim."[156] By this agreement Iranian forces positioned themselves in key strategic areas (basically the range of hills in the north of the island) defined on a map attached to the text of the Memorandum of Understanding. Within this designated area Iran possessed full jurisdiction, but outside it fell to Sharjah as before. Iran and Sharjah each recognized a territorial sea for the island with a breadth of 12 nautical miles in which nationals of both parties possessed equal fishing rights. The Buttes Oil Company would continue to exploit hydrocarbon reserves under the conditions specified in its concession agreement with the Ruler of Sharjah (for so long as these were acceptable to Iran), though revenue would now be shared on an equal basis. Lastly, Iran was to give Sharjah £1.5 million annually in aid until such time as its oil revenue reached £3 million a year.[157]

Given the previous impasse in this dispute, an arrangement that allowed for the flying of each party's flag seemed, on the face of it, a fairly sustainable compromise. The 1971 Memorandum of Understanding withstood several challenges in the following two decades. On announcing his decision to prosecute war against Iran during September 1980, Saddam Husain declared the restoration of Abu Musa and the Tunbs to the Arab homeland as a prime territorial goal.[158] During 1987 the regime for Abu Musa set up by the Memorandum of Understanding was seriously infringed with an Iranian move into the southern Sharjah-controlled part of the island at the time of a rumoured Qasimi coup in Sharjah. By the time that Iran realized this had coup been aborted, the Iranian military had already lowered the Sharjah flag. They then hurriedly rehoisted it and returned to their allotted positions. Iranian infringements of the 1971 Memorandum of Understanding and Iranian patrols into the south of the island had become an increasingly regular feature since 1983 in point of fact.

In the late summer of 1993, as we have seen, that other serious Irano/-Arab faultline – the Shatt al-Arab dispute – lies dormant but essentially unsettled. Until the spring of 1992 the status of the Abu Musa dispute seemed very similar: all was quiet though far from being finally settled. Of course, the 1971 Memorandum of Understanding was a settlement – a pragmatic accommodation that may yet prove sustainable in the coming decades. It still falls some way short, however, of constituting a permanent settlement of the dispute over Abu Musa's sovereignty.

Perhaps the visit during February 1992 of Iranian state President Ali Akbar Hashemi Rafsanjani to Abu Musa and other lower Gulf islands (most of which are indisputably Iranian) had signalled a change in Iranian policy towards Gulf territorial issues. Yet well before this time, during the 1980–8 Iran–Iraq war, Iran had expressed misgivings with the security situation on Abu Musa, claiming that its own encroachments from 1983 onwards were a response to the increasing visits by non-Sharjah nationals to the island. Iran's seizure and arrest of a Dutch sailor, "armed" with a flaregun, during the third quarter of 1991 led to the intensification of protests that too many unknown third-party nationals were going back and forth between Sharjah and Abu Musa. In January 1992 Iran suggested that it should issue security passes to non-nationals visiting the island from Sharjah.

It seemed for a while during the autumn of 1992 that the well publicized incidents of April and August 1992, in which foreign nationals employed by the Sharjah state (Asian labourers and technicians and non-UAE Arab teachers) were denied entry to the island by the Iranian authorities, had, at worst, rendered the 1971 Memorandum of Understanding unworkable, or, at best, suggested that it needed renegotiating.[159]

Attempts to resolve the resurrected dispute over Abu Musa by bilateral negotiations in Abu Dhabi between delegations of the Iranian and United Arab Emirates governments during late September 1992 soon broke down when the UAE delegation demanded at the outset that Iran immediately end its military occupation of the Tunb islands.[160] Since then, Iran has tended to maintain a "crisis, what crisis?" line over Abu Musa in the face of an intermittent barrage of criticism from a hostile Arab media.[161] With the flare-up of a border dispute between Qatar and Saudi Arabia and Iran's admission of at least some responsibility for the incidents at Abu Musa,[162] tensions between Tehran and the Arab states of the lower Gulf seemed to ease in the last two months of 1992. They were certainly rekindled in late December 1992 with the issue in Abu Dhabi of the closing statement of the 13th Gulf Co-operation Council (GCC) summit. While this was arguably most notable for its hard and united line against Iraq,[163] its uncompromising sections dealing with the Abu Musa dispute provoked a fierce response from Tehran.[164] Certainly, if the GCC communique released at Abu Dhabi is taken at face value, then there must be considerable doubt concerning the position of the UAE federal government vis-à-vis the 1971 Memorandum of Understanding.[165]

Despite all of this it is difficult, realistically, to envisage an arrangement that improves on the 1971 Memorandum of Understanding's pragmatic accommodation of rival Iranian and Qasimi claims to the sovereignty of Abu Musa. It is similarly difficult to envisage Iran ever relaxing its present hold over the Tunbs. All would appear normal on the islands in the late summer of 1993, but in the late summer the GCC reiterated its statement of December 1992. Disputes over the islands are likely to remain wars of words although they are an important channel for the articulation of Irano-Arab rivalries.

Persian/Iranian claims to Bahrain. Iranian claims to the island of Bahrain were maintained, with varying degrees of conviction and intensity, from the mid-1840s, when, as has been mentioned, the Persian Prime Minister Hajji Mirza Aghassi claimed that the whole of the Gulf and its islands belonged to the Qajar state,[166] until 1969, when Shah Muhammad Reza Pahlavi announced that the inhabitants of the islands were free to decide their own fate. The finding of United Nations representative Vittorio Guicciardi that the vast majority of Bahrainis wished to retain independence from Iran was unanimously endorsed by the Security Council. When the endorsement was ratified by the Iranian *majlis* the dispute was in effect closed.[167] Reports that the dispute was reopened by revolutionary Iran in late 1979 have to be treated with some scepticism. Although one of the leading clergy, Ayatollah Rouhani, allegedly referred to Bahrain as Iranian during September 1979, the Iranian Foreign Ministry quickly denied that it had any territorial pretensions towards the island. Nevertheless, Iranian involvement in an unsuccessful Bahraini coup of December 1981 was widely suspected.[168]

Anglo–Ottoman relations

The central importance of the Anglo–Ottoman Blue and Violet lines of 1913–14 to Britain's defence of territorial claims within the peninsula has already been amply illustrated. Statements made only a year or so ago by the Yemeni President (September 1991) also suggest that the Violet line may still be considered to form part of the Republic's northern border with Saudi Arabia.[169] The Violet line was an arbitrary straight-line extension of the Anglo/Ottoman boundary delimited between 1903 and 1905 basically to separate the *wilayat* of Yemen from the nine loosely federated cantons of the Aden Protectorate. The 1903–5 limit, the first international boundary to be delimited in the Arabian peninsula, disappeared only recently with the unification of the two Yemens on 22 May 1990.

The Iraq/Kuwait boundary. The determination of the Indian Viceroy, Lord Curzon, to preserve the Gulf as a British lake clear of imperial rivals at the turn of the century contributed significantly to Britain's decision to recognize Warbah and Bubiyan as Kuwaiti islands. The Government of India openly admitted in 1906 that recent attempts to consolidate British influence at Kuwait and to support the Ruler of Kuwait's claims to Bubiyan had been made only "in anticipation of the day when the port of a transcontinental railway system should be located in the neighbourhood".[170]

As early as 1866 the British authorities in the Gulf had noted promising natural anchorage facilities on the Khawr Zubair at the site of the modern port of Umm Qasr, which it was considered, even then, might prove a useful location for a railway terminus.[171] It was the perceived threat of this very development – an Ottoman railhead brokered by either Germany or Russia, Britain's principal European rivals in the northern Gulf at this stage – that encouraged the Government of India to support the Shaikh of Kuwait's claim to Bubiyan (based upon the periodic use of the feature by fishermen of the Awazim tribe) and indeed to encourage him to claim the tiny island of Warbah to its immediate north. Warbah was recognized as belonging to Kuwait in the 1913 Anglo–Ottoman settlement despite no convincing evidence having been forwarded by Shaikh Mubarak to support such a claim. This is not to suggest that Ottoman claims to Warbah had any validity of their own, for, in truth, the island, with its surrounding water channels, was something of a no-man's land.[172] Originally the Foreign Office had doubted whether the Ottoman Empire's deployment of troops on Bubiyan island in early 1902 could be viewed as an infringement of the territory Britain had agreed to protect for the Ruler of Kuwait in earlier agreements reached with Shaikh Mubarak and the Ottomans themselves (the 1899 Anglo–Kuwaiti Secret Bond and the 1901 Anglo–Ottoman *status quo* agreement). By arguing that the network of water channels in the northwest extremes of the Persian Gulf (the Khawr Zubair and the northern shores of Khawr Bubiyan on Warbah island) was every bit as developable for use as a railway head as the shores of Kuwait Bay themselves, the Government of India convinced the Foreign Office that it should recognize Kuwaiti territory as extending far beyond the limits of Kuwait Bay. For the British authorities in the Gulf (employees of the Government of India) calculated that the Khawr Zubair could not be successfully developed by the Ottoman Empire if another power (Kuwait under Britain's protection) held sovereignty over these islands. This contention has, of course, been fully borne out in the years that have followed. Britain's ultimately successful attempts to "squeeze out" the Ottomans from the Gulf in the first decade or so of this century have resulted in Iraq feeling squeezed out ever since.

As has already been indicated, the inner and outer zones of diminishing Kuwaiti authority (the Red and Green lines) defined by the July 1913 Anglo–Ottoman Convention were each employed, though not in so many words, to delimit the boundaries of Kuwait in the early 1920s. The 1922 Uqair Protocol recognized the inner limit (Red line) as forming Kuwait's southern boundaries with Saudi Arabia and the Najdi–Kuwait Neutral Zone. A diplomatic exchange of spring 1923 recognized the outer limit (Green line) as delimiting Kuwait's northern boundaries with Iraq (Fig. 1.2).

Qaru and Umm al Maradim. The only contemporary dispute arising from territorial understandings reached between Britain and the Ottoman Empire (if one accepts that Iraq's consistent pleas for greater access to the sea are requests for the modification of the existing boundary with Kuwait rather than a genuine claim to sovereignty over Warbah and Bubiyan), is that currently being engaged in between Kuwait and Saudi Arabia over the sovereign status of the islands of Qaru and Umm al Maradim. In the fifth article of the Anglo–Ottoman Convention of 1913 these islands were stated to belong to the Kuwaiti ruler in full sovereignty, along with the other islands of Warbah, Bubiyan, Mashjan, Failakah, Awhah and Kubr. Yet Qaru and Umm al Maradim lay adjacent to the outer zone of Kuwaiti authority rather than, like the other islands, the inner, semi-circular area contained by the Red line. On the map annexed to the treaty they were therefore shown in a different colour from the other Kuwaiti islands. This was later to become important, for Saudi Arabia still claims that the islands should, at the very least, have been placed under the same conditions as the Kuwaiti–Najdi Neutral Zone, when Kuwait's southern borders were in effect foreshortened to the 1913 Red line by the 1922 Uqair Protocol.[173] The Uqair Protocol made no mention of the status of Qaru and Umm al Maradim. Kuwait has in the past awarded oil concessions to cover the two islands and their territorial waters though these have never been operated fully, possibly out of sensitivity to the Saudi claim.[174] Kuwait still claims full sovereignty over Qaru and Umm al Maradim.

Anglo–Saudi relations

The limits to the Saudi state in the northern Arabian peninsula set by Britain during conferences of the early to mid-1920s have survived, more or less, to the present day. Each of the limits with Jordan, Iraq and Kuwait has been modified in some small way (Fig. 1.2). However, considering the time and energy put in by both Britain and Saudi Arabia, the intermittent frontier negotiations conducted during the 20-year period from the mid-1930s were surprisingly unproductive. Only Qatar's southern boundaries can be said to have been effectively defined (on a *de facto* basis) during the period of negotiations, and this was an indirect development resulting from Britain's decision of 1935 to guarantee the area of the Qatar oil concession against land attack from the south. Britain's action during the autumn of 1955 physically to remove Saudi forces from Buraimi to positions behind the boundary line it had only recently declared unilaterally for its protégés in southern and southeastern Arabia (the modified Riyadh line), following the acrimonious breakdown of the Buraimi arbitration proceedings in Geneva, at least had the effect of ensuring that the United Arab Emirates and Oman would share a boundary in the hinterland to the southwest of the Buraimi oasis in succeeding years. There would be no salient of Saudi territory. Saudi Arabia's full claim to sovereignty over the oasis was in effect relinquished by the 1974 agreement with Abu Dhabi.

Saudi preference for informal territorial arrangements. Britain's urgency to forge limits to the expanding Najdi state in the early 1920s derived chiefly from the Ikhwan threat from the south. Had it not been for the British intervention at the height of the Jahrah (a settlement at the western end of Kuwait Bay) crisis, Ibn Saud might well have annexed Kuwait to his expanding Arabian domain.[175] Before Britain informed the Saudi leader that he would be allowed to control no territory south of Kuwait Bay beyond the inner limit (Red line) of Najdi authority defined by the July 1913 Anglo–Ottoman Convention,[176] Ibn Saud claimed to recognize al-Sabah authority as extending nowhere beyond the city walls of Kuwait port.[177] As late as the mid-1930s Ibn Saud took a similar line with Shaikh Abdallah of Qatar. Early during 1934, perhaps in an effort to persuade the Qatari ruler to grant his oil concession to the Standard Oil Company of California, which had acquired the Saudi oil concession during the previous year, Ibn Saud had informed Abdallah that he considered only Dawhah as belonging to the al-Thani family and the rest of the Qatar peninsula as belonging to him.[178] The maximum territorial claim that Saudi Arabia made later that year as a prelude to the Anglo–Saudi frontier negotiations, which has been outlined earlier in this article, recognized Kuwait, Dawhah and Abu Dhabi only as coastal enclaves in a broad sweep of Saudi territory. However, Ibn Saud was nothing if not a pragmatist and, once Britain had agreed to defend the Qatar peninsula against land attack, no further threats were made to call upon the allegiance of tribes bestriding the Qatar desert.

Neutral zones and the 1922 Uqair Protocol. The Uqair Protocol of late 1922 saw Kuwait's southern boundaries foreshortened to the Red line of the 1913

Anglo–Ottoman Convention (Fig. 1.2). Though the famous former Political Agent in Kuwait, Harold Dickson, later argued that this action had been taken to compensate Ibn Saud for territory lost to the newly defined state territory of Iraq to the west in the same agreement,[179] the new delimitation also certainly reflected a considerable diminution of al-Sabah control to the south of Kuwait Bay since the heady days of Shaikh Mubarak.[180] The Uqair Protocol also saw the appearance, for the first time in Arabia, of that strange feature in the territorial landscape – the "neutral zone". These are usually agreed upon when territorial disputes between neighbouring states reach deadlock and generally involve a partial surrender of sovereignty over the area in question.[181] In this case both the Iraq–Saudi and the Kuwait–Saudi Neutral Zones were decided upon unilaterally by Sir Percy Cox, then High Commissioner in Baghdad. He instituted the former zone in an attempt to minimize the problems caused by uncertain tribal allegiance and the latter, zone because reports were circulating that oil had been found in the vicinity of Khawr Maqtah. In each instance, tribes from both states enjoyed equal rights to water and pasture in these demilitarized zones. As has already been mentioned, the Iraq–Saudi Neutral Zone was partitioned by agreements of 1975 and 1981 after no oil had been found there.[182] The decision to divide the Kuwait–Saudi Neutral Zone into equal shares was taken in principle as early as 1960. After the July 1965 Partition Agreement had provided for the annexation of the two equal shares of the neutral zones into the Saudi and Kuwaiti states, the modified Kuwait/Saudi boundary was finally delimited in great detail by a further accord of 1969.[183]

Saudi–Jordanian land-swap of 1965. An imaginative modification of the Saudi/Jordanian boundary in 1965 is particularly noteworthy (Fig. 1.2). The original boundary delimitation, introduced, for the main part, by the Hadda Agreement of 1925, was altered in such a way by the 1965 Treaty of Amman that Jordan's narrow coastline on the Gulf of Aqabah was lengthened to the southeast of the port.[184] In return Saudi Arabia was granted a substantial area of inland desert.[185] There were unconfirmed reports during the 1980s that Iraq had suggested a similar scheme to Kuwait, whereby Warbah and Khawr Bubiyan to its south might be ceded or leased by Kuwait in return for unspecified inland Iraqi desert areas west of the Batin.[186] Clearly, for the foreseeable future, these are concessions that Kuwait is more unlikely than ever to consider after its recent disastrous experience at Iraqi hands. In the long term, however, with adequate safeguards and guarantees, they might be worth another look.

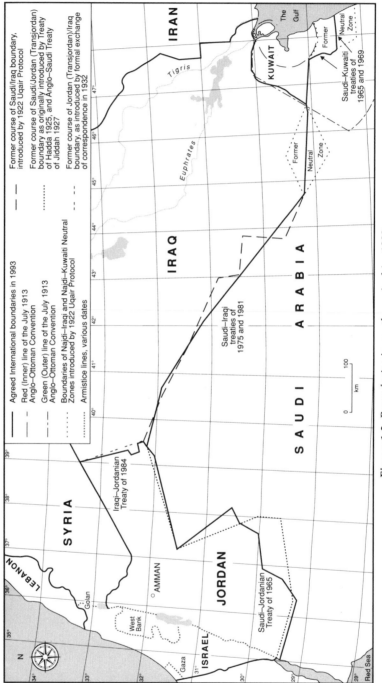

Figure 1.2 Boundaries in northern Arabia, 1993.

Rival views of the inconclusive Anglo–Saudi frontier negotiations, 1934–55. It was the award to the Standard Oil Company of California (SOCAL), the American oil giant, of the Hasa mainland concession by Ibn Saud during 1933 that opened the question of the kingdom's southern and eastern limits in Arabia. The stances maintained by both Saudi Arabia and Britain during 20 years of intermittent and ultimately fruitless negotiations and the territorial claims forwarded by each side have already been dealt with at length in this article. A new landmark work by John Wilkinson provides a fairly radical reinterpretation of Britain's policy towards territorial issues within Arabia this century.[187] He suggests that, during the frontier talks with Saudi Arabia, Britain knowingly maintained a seriously flawed negotiating position (that is, its defence of the Anglo–Ottoman Blue and Violet lines of 1913–14, which its own legal advisers had dismissed as inadmissible in international law as early as autumn 1934) in an effort to try and bluff the Saudi government into accepting Britain's territorial scheme for the peninsula (Fig. 9.4). When it seemed that the Buraimi arbitration might give a verdict that was unfavourable to the British position, Wilkinson argues that Britain unilaterally declared a boundary, which it could get the Saudis to respect only through the use of force.[188] Earlier English-language works[189] had generally expressed much more sympathy with Britain's contention that the conduct of Saudi representatives on the Arbitration Tribunal and Saudi government officials in the disputed Buraimi zone itself (charges of bribery were levelled by the British government) had prevented any chance there might originally have been of the arbitration reaching a fair verdict.

Territorial awards made by Britain
involving neighbouring states under its protection

Julian Walker, a prominent British boundary-maker in the southern Gulf region casts interesting light later in this volume (Ch. 4) upon the tendency of the British government to do little to solve territorial disputes between neighbouring shaikhdoms under its protection unless it was absolutely necessary.

> One problem faced over frontier settlement was that posed by the British official who believed that if a frontier was causing no problem it should be left well alone, at least while he had responsibility for the area. The last thing to be done was to create work and friction, and sleeping dogs should be left to lie.[190]

The Hawar islands and the Dibal and Jaradah shoals. Walker's own efforts to settle the boundaries south of the Musandam peninsula between Oman and the United Arab Emirates (and those between its component shaikhdoms) have already been reviewed. Perhaps the most serious and certainly the most enduring dispute arising from the set of decisions focused upon in this subsection is that over the sovereignty of the Hawar islands, lying off the west coast of the Qatar peninsula. Britain's 1939 award of the island group to Bahrain[191] (except for Janan in the south, which was later recognized during 1947 as belonging to Qatar) has been challenged by Qatar ever since. The Hawar dispute has been cited by more than one source as the principal reason why Qatar and Bahrain failed to join (along with the seven shaikhdoms that currently comprise the United Arab Emirates) a nine-state Federation of Arab Emirates, the institution of which had seemed more likely than not for most of the 1968–71 period.[192]

When Britain left the Gulf in 1971, Saudi Arabia accepted responsibility for mediation of the Hawar dispute. Saudi mediation efforts have been channelled through the offices of the Gulf Co-operation Council since its inception in early 1981, though successes in the period thereafter were in controlling the dispute rather than making any great strides towards solving it. During March 1982 a meeting of the GCC Council of Ministers reviewed the Hawar dispute after conspicuous muscle-flexing in Dawhah and Manamah. At this Bahrain and Qatar agreed to "freeze the situation and not to cause an escalation of the dispute".[193] After years in which Qatar and Bahrain had both kept themselves busy preparing defences of their claims to Hawar in anticipation of the dispute being referred to international arbitration, a committee sat during late December 1990 at the annual GCC summit (Dawhah) and apparently stipulated that, should no out of court settlement be attainable within six months, then the Hawar case should be forwarded to the International Court of Justice (ICJ) in The Hague for a ruling.[194]

So, on 8 July 1991, with Qatar evidently believing that the six-month deadline had passed without the requisite progress having been made, the Dawhah government referred the dispute to the International Court of Justice. The reference was to remain unilateral, however, for Bahrain contested the basis of jurisdiction invoked by Qatar in letters addressed to the ICJ of July and August 1991. Since then, the international courts have been considering whether Qatar was acting within its rights when unilaterally referring the case to them for a decision. Bahrain continued to claim in 1992 that a renewed joint application should have been made. In July 1992 Qatar reportedly rejected its initiative whereby a new joint reference would be made in which all possible items of dispute (probably including Bahrain's shadowy if deeply felt claim to extraterritorial rights in Zubarah – see below) would be placed on the agenda for treatment by the ICJ.[195]

The disputed status of Hawar is only part of the problem for Bahrain and Qatar, for the whole of their seabed boundary remains to be settled. In late 1947, with access to offshore oil reserves now a critical factor in the maritime political geography of the Gulf, Britain had also ruled on the division of the seabed between Bahrain and Qatar.[196] Its verdict was accepted by neither

Bahrain nor Qatar, the former objecting on the grounds that its authority should properly extend over all and not just part of the seabed area (including intervening reefs and shoals) lying to the west and northwest of the Qatar peninsula, the latter on the grounds that two low-tide elevations, the Dibal and Jaradah shoals, had been recognized as Bahraini enclaves within the seabed area provisionally allotted to Qatar.[197]

The disputed status of the shoals burst into the media headlines during the spring of 1986. Qatar's capture of Fasht al-Dibal (up until this point occupied by Bahrain) and its arrest of 30 contractors engaged in the construction of a Bahraini "coastguard station" – possibly a GCC project that Qatar had not approved – resulted in Bahrain strengthening its military garrison on Hawar. Qatar then declared Dibal and Jaradah, along with Hawar, as military zones and mobilized its considerably superior firepower. Conflict was averted after the decisive intervention of Saudi Arabia and other GCC states, which brokered a settlement whereby the two states would return the situation on the shoals to the *status quo ante*. After the GCC had set up a monitoring group to ensure that the two sides implemented the agreement, Qatar evacuated Dibal in early June 1986.[198] Until the Khafus border post incident of early autumn 1992, the incident constituted perhaps the greatest internal challenge to have confronted the Gulf Co-operation Council and its settlement one of the institution's notable successes. Preserving the peace is quite different from resolving the root problem, however, which remains to this day. Although Bahrain and Qatar may yet submit to an opinion of the international courts on the status of Hawar and the Fashts, tensions persist while reports of incidents continue. During 19 September 1991 the Qatari Foreign Ministry protested against Bahraini gunboats opening fire on Qatari vessels, a charge denied by the Bahrain government.[199] The issue on 16 April 1992 by the Qatar government of a decree extending territorial waters to 12 nautical miles and claiming a further adjacent area of 12 miles outside territorial waters "over which the state shall exercise all the rights provided for in the provisions of international law",[200] has not soothed Bahraini sensibilities. Early in 1993 Bahrain issued equivalent legislation of its own.

The issue of the ownership of the Hawar islands essentially arose early in 1936 when both the Bahrain Petroleum Company (a British-registered but essentially American oil company) and Petroleum Concessions Limited (a British consortium), which respectively held the Bahrain and Qatar mainland concessions, entered negotiations with the al-Khalifah shaikh to secure rights over the seabed area, variously called the Bahrain Additional Area or the Unallotted Zone, lying between Bahrain and the Qatari mainland.[201] The Ruler of Bahrain, backed by the energetic BAPCO and a knowledgeable British Adviser (a luxury not enjoyed by Qatar until the 1950s), seemed well aware that, to maximize the concession area to be offered to these oil companies, Bahrain would have to provide evidence of ownership of all the islands, shoals and reefs lying west of the Qatar peninsula. Therefore a military garrison was stationed upon the biggest island in the Hawar group in 1936,[202] while beacons in the red and white colours of Bahrain were placed on all the important low-tide elevations lying west of Qatar.[203] All these actions had been taken by the time (May 1938) the British authorities in the Gulf made their first detailed investigation of the maritime area to confirm what physical indicators of sovereignty existed there.[204]

Bahrain's active attempts to assert sovereignty were backed up by detailed claims, intelligently articulated by Sir Charles Belgrave, Adviser to the Bahraini ruler. Conversely the Qatari ruler had no idea that the ownership of the islands was disputed until 1938. Bahrain's claims rested on the permanent occupation of four of the islands in the Hawar group by Dawasir fishermen, who, it was alleged, paid tribute to the al-Khalifah rulers. Also the fishtraps periodically stationed at or around the island group had been sold or registered in Bahrain.[205] The Qatari ruler maintained that the islands should be recognized as belonging to the al-Thani state squarely on their propinquity to the Qatar peninsula.[206] After all, the state territory of Qatar had been defined in purely geographical terms. Bahrain's effective occupation or utilization of Hawar, Fasht al-Dibal and Qit'at al-Jaradah, no matter how recent in origin, proved decisive in Britain's awards of 1939 and 1947, a reminder of the old adage that possession is nine-tenths of the law.

The ICJ was originally scheduled to rule on whether it possessed jurisdiction to deal with the territorial disputes in the early spring of 1993. A backlog of cases in the Hague now means that this decision will not be reached until 1994. If the finer legal minutiae of the case are put to one side, it might be as well to consider what political objections Bahrain has to seeing the disputes go to the courts for a decision. For the island state, in the opinion of some observers, has been dragging its feet since 1991. Perhaps the most obvious observation is that Bahrain has virtually everything to lose. If and when the ICJ finally gets round to dealing with the territorial dispute itself rather than preliminary procedural matters, it will rule on the ownership of three features – the Hawar island group and the Dibal and Jaradah shoals – which are currently occupied by Bahrain and which Britain, as we have seen, has recognized previously as belonging to the island state.

Zubarah. The curious dispute over Zubarah, a seemingly worthless ruin lying on the northwest coast of the Qatar peninsula, has also greatly embittered Bahrain–Qatar relations over the years. Yet this unpromising locality (the land here is barren, salty and waterless) has retained an enduring symbolic significance for the al-Khalifah in Bahrain to reflect its position as their ancestral home – their first ruler was buried here. From the 1870s onwards, Bahrain has claimed rather ill-defined rights to Zubarah, ranging from full sovereignty to jurisdiction over Bahraini subjects (Na'im tribesmen of northwestern Qatar were claimed as Bahraini) in Qatar territory. The al-Thani ruling family's seriously underdeveloped authority in the northwestern Qatar peninsula during the mid-1930s has already been referred to. In his autobiography, Belgrave confesses to being continually surprised by the intense reaction a mere mention of Zubarah would engender in the al-Khalifah:

> When Shaikh Hamad died in 1942, I remembered the words which were attributed to Queen Mary Tudor: When I am dead . . . you shall find Calais lying on my heart, but in this case the word would have been Zubara.[207]

After years in which the British Gulf authorities had tried to persuade the Ruler of Qatar to allow Bahrain special facilities in Zubarah, Political Resident Sir Bernard Burrows finally ruled, during August 1957, after the al-Khalifah state had apparently resurrected a claim to the sovereignty of the locality, that Bahrain should entertain no further hopes of being granted any extraterritorial privileges at Zubarah. The ruined settlement remained every bit as integral a part of the state of Qatar as anywhere else along its shoreline.[208] Much less has been heard of the dispute since, yet it will be surprising if Bahrain does not invoke the historical claim to Zubarah in some form in the event of the Hawar dispute reaching international arbitration.

Halul island. Britain's decision to recognize Halul island as belonging to Qatar in the early spring of 1962 provides an interesting counterweight to the Hawar award of 1939. For the period up until the 1950s, Britain's conviction that the island belonged to Abu Dhabi had gradually hardened. Throughout this time, however, the sovereignty of the island had not been a burning issue and, as such, the British authorities in the Gulf had not felt any great need to make a definitive ruling. The position changed during the mid-1950s as Britain was faced with the prospect of having to rule on the respective extents of the Qatar and Abu Dhabi seabed areas that might be offered to the oil companies operating these offshore concessions. The sovereignty of the island was now hotly disputed, with Qatar articulating detailed claims for the first time. In May 1954, Political Resident Sir Bernard Burrows suggested that a final decision on the ownership of Halul could no longer be postponed. Following a more detailed review of the evidence pertaining to the dispute during 1955, the Foreign Office concluded that Qatar's claim to Halul could not be rejected out of hand.[209] So, for the next three years until 1958, Britain pursued the possibility of referring the dispute to arbitration or, at the very least, collecting sufficient evidence for a judgment to be made on the question of ownership.[210] These efforts met with failure, however, since the rulers of both Qatar and Abu Dhabi refused point-blank to acknowledge the need to present evidence of ownership of a feature each regarded as indisputably theirs. Shaikh Shakhbut of Abu Dhabi did not help his case by treating the Halul question as part and parcel

51

of his much larger and fanciful claim to Umm Said and the southeast coast of Qatar.[211] By the autumn of 1958, the Foreign Office was of the opinion that, while "nothing should be done for the time being", it "should deal with the situation on the basis, which we shall not necessarily declare, that Halul is neutral".[212]

By 1960 the pressure for the British government to make a definitive ruling on the sovereignty of Halul and seabed limits for Qatar and Abu Dhabi had become intense. The Shell Oil Company of Qatar, which had operated off Halul as early as 1955, struck oil in the eastern half of its seabed area. Since Halul lay significantly closer to Qatar than to Abu Dhabi, a maritime boundary award that recognized the latter's sovereignty over the feature would probably have been extremely untidy. For, if Abu Dhabi's sovereignty over the island were confirmed, Halul would in effect be no more than an enclave lying on the Qatar seabed. As early as 1952 Shell had been advised of its safe operating limits east of the Qatar peninsula. Halul island lay well within these limits.[213] Understandably weary of its continuing failure to fix the Bahrain/Qatar seabed limit (a task complicated considerably by Britain's previous rulings that Hawar and the Dibal and Jaradah shoals belonged to Bahrain despite lying closer to Qatar), a duplication of problems in the seabed area to the east of the Qatar peninsula was the last thing Britain wanted. So there may have been an element of pragmatism in Britain's decision to find in favour of Qatar's claim to Halul, based upon recent usage and propinquity, rather than Abu Dhabi's, based, above all, on Britain's previous, if only partial, recognition of its claim.[214] So while propinquity had seemingly been dismissed as a factor in the Hawar award of 1939, the principle had clearly been an important determinant in the Halul award of 1962. Some seven years later, the March 1969 Qatar–Abu Dhabi maritime boundary agreement resolved the dispute over the offshore Bunduq field in an imaginative manner. Terminal point B on the maritime boundary was offset slightly from the true equidistance line between the Qatar and Abu Dhabi coasts to coincide directly with the location of the oilfield (Fig. 9.5). For practical reasons it was specified that only one concessionaire (representing Abu Dhabi) be allowed to develop the field, though, importantly, all revenue from Bunduq was to be shared in perpetuity.[215]

Bilateral agreements reached independently between Saudi Arabia and its neighbours (the Arab shaikhdoms of the Gulf, Iran, Iraq and Yemen)
Early informal understandings reached with Kuwait and Qatar. Ever since the early 1920s the Saudi state has shown a marked preference for coming to private territorial arrangements with its neighbours in the Gulf and the southern Arabian peninsula (precise details of which have often remained elusive) rather than negotiating explicit boundary agreements and register-

ing their texts at the United Nations or other appropriate international institutions. The earliest example of this predilection came during March 1921, when Shaikh Ahmad succeeded his uncle Salim to commence his long rule of Kuwait. During the previous autumn, at the height of the Jahrah crisis, Ibn Saud stated that he recognized Kuwait as extending only as far as the walls of the port. Following bilateral discussions with Kuwait's new ruler, however, the Najdi emir announced that there were no longer any problems between him and the al-Sabah rulers and that, consequently, there was no need to fix a boundary between the two states.[216] By this stage the British authorities had already informed the Najdi leader that they would allow no territorial diminution of the al-Sabah state beyond the inner, semi-circular limit (Red line) of the 1913 Anglo–Ottoman Convention. As has already been mentioned, this limit more or less became the Kuwait/Najdi boundary awarded by Britain at Uqair in late 1922.

In Article Six of the 1927 Anglo–Najdi Treaty of Jiddah, Ibn Saud had agreed, following the conclusion of the Uqair Protocol, to respect the territorial integrity of Kuwait but only to maintain friendly and peaceful relations with the Ruler of Qatar.[217] Hence Saudi Arabia prefaced the Anglo–Saudi frontier negotiations during June 1934 with its maximum territorial claim (already referred to), which recognized the al-Thani state as limited to a small coastal strip around Dawhah. Before the award of the Qatar oil concession in 1935 and Britain's pledge to guarantee its extent against aggression from the south, Ibn Saud held back his latent claim to the Qatar peninsula (based upon the allegiance of tribes roaming the Qatari desert) until those few occasions when Shaikh Abdallah looked like stepping out of line. So long as the Qatari ruler continued to pay his secret annual subsidy – this was estimated at 100,000 rupees in 1930,[218] Ibn Saud saw no strong reasons for fixing precise limits to territory in and around the Qatar peninsula. This situation changed with the episode of the Qatar oil concession. Though this was given to a British company in return for British defence guarantees in 1935, Ibn Saud had earlier made efforts to ensure that Shaikh Abdallah would grant the option to SOCAL, the same American company that held the Hasa concession. There is evidence that Ibn Saud would have been prepared himself to recognize an al-Thani state extending over much of the peninsula if Shaikh Abdallah had acted accordingly. There were reports that the two leaders had come close to reaching an informal, bilateral agreement on this basis.[219] Concerns that the extension of the SOCAL concession over the Qatar peninsula would result in the effective annexation of the Qatari state by Saudi Arabia were primarily responsible for Britain's decisive intervention of 1935.[220]

The Saudi–Yemeni 1934 Treaty of Taif. During the inter-war years Britain was responsible for the foreign affairs and defence of all Saudi Arabia's neighbours in the peninsula except for one, the Imamate of Yemen. As a consequence Britain had little to do with the evolution of the boundary between Saudi Arabia and the Imamate, which was defined in its western reaches (from near Midi on the Red Sea to Najran) by the May 1934 Treaty of Taif (Fig. 1.3).[221] That the modern state territories of Saudi Arabia and Yemen march together on the eastern shores of the Red Sea is only as a result of a series of agreements reached between Ibn Saud and the Idrisi of Asir during the 1920s. An agreement of 1920 had seen the northeastern half of Asir, formerly an Ottoman administrative unit linked indirectly to the *wilayat* of Yemen, incorporated into the expanding Najdi state,[222] later to become the Saudi province of Asir Surat. Saudi–Idrisi agreements of 1926 and 1930[223] saw Ibn Saud extend protectorate facilities over and then formally annex the remaining portions of the Idrisi's territory (to become Tihamat Asir), including the Farasan archipelago. In the early 1920s the Idrisi had administered the coastal Tihamah plain as far south as Hudaidah, which had previously been regarded as an integral part of Yemen. The Zaidi Imam recaptured the Tihamah plain during the mid-1920s and advanced as far north as Saudi forces would permit. By 1927 a territorial equilibrium of sorts had been reached.[224] According to the Saudis at least, it was this *de facto* 1927 line that was formally recognized as the Saudi/Yemen boundary by the ratified Taif Treaty of May 1934, but not before Saudi forces had overrun the Tihamah, again as far south as Hudaidah, during the brief Saudi–Zaidi war fought out earlier that year. For the next two years, boundary commissions from each side co-operated in the final delimitation and demarcation of the Taif line.[225]

In signing the Taif Treaty Yemen ostensibly dropped its claims to the "Greater Yemen" of the seventeenth century, which embraced most of southwest Arabia from the mountains of northern Asir on the Red Sea in the northwest to the Dhufar coast of the Arabian Sea to the southeast.[226] The recapture of these "lost" territories has long remained a goal of Yemeni national sentiment, however. The "Treaty of Islamic Friendship and Brotherhood", to use the Taif Treaty's correct name, was far more than a border treaty *per se*. Interestingly, articles of the treaty called for renewal every 20 years. During the mid-1950s this was done,[227] but two decades later renewal of at least those articles dealing with territorial definition was seemingly obviated by the issue on 17 March 1973 of a joint communique by the Saudi Foreign Ministry and Abdallah al-Hajri, Prime Minister of the Yemen Arab Republic, during the latter's tour of Saudi Arabia and the Gulf states. The boundary established by the 1934 treaty was described in this rather obscure communique as "permanent and final".[228] To link al-Hajri's assassination during July 1977 in London to this commitment, uncharitably characterized by many Yemenis in the intervening period as the "surrender" of the "lost provinces" of Asir and Najran, is to underplay the complexities of Yemeni politics. Yet the enduring sensitivity of the issue is evidenced by the fact that no Yemeni leader since has ever felt able to ratify the March

1973 communique. As one astute observer of contemporary Saudi–Yemeni relations summises: "Though the [Taif] treaty remains in effect, no Yemeni government has been willing to publicly agree that the borders are final and permanent."[229] Yemeni unification on 22 May 1990 resulted only in more frequent calls from the media and public for the newly constituted republic to resurrect claims to Asir and Najran. During mid-April of 1991 Saudi Arabia denied reports that its troops had occupied the Yemeni border post at Buq'ah lying just to the east of the stretch of the boundary delimited by the 1934 Taif Treaty.[230] The latest word on the issue of the 1934 Taif line came from Yemeni Foreign Minister Abdul Karim al-Iryani in a press conference held in San'a on 30 July 1992. Following the promising Saudi–Yemeni talks initiated in Geneva during July 1992, al-Iryani stated that:

> the Taif agreement is a fact. It was signed and ratified by King 'Abd al-'Aziz and Imam Yahya. A border demarcation committee was established and delineated the border from north of Midi to the Thar mountains. A demarcation committee prepared a memorandum which was handed to King 'Abd al-'Aziz and Imam Yahya and they both ratified it.[231]

Bahrain–Saudi seabed boundary agreement, 1958. During early 1958 Saudi Arabia and Bahrain agreed the first maritime boundary delimitation in the Gulf,[232] the second of the Saudi state's international borders to be finalized by bilateral negotiations.[233] This had largely caught Britain, responsible for the foreign affairs of the al-Khalifah shaikhdom, unawares, for Ibn Saud had stated during the early 1950s that no agreement (with Britain on Bahrain's behalf) on the seabed boundary could be signed until the Buraimi dispute had first been disposed of.[234] Britain was worried that any bilateral agreement reached might be based on principles detrimental to itself and its protégés elsewhere in the Gulf. In the event the British government need not have worried. The boundary agreement recognized a simple median-line delimitation that in effect disregarded all interlying high- and low-tide elevations (the status of the Bainah islands had been disputed previously) (Fig. 9.4). This had been one of several possible boundaries mooted in the Anglo–Saudi negotiations convened in London during August 1951 to discuss the seabed question.[235] The main problem to be sorted out in the years since these negotiations was the northern terminus of the Saudi/Bahrain maritime boundary in the vicinity of the Bu Saafah shoal, the disputed status of which was accentuated by the presence of an oilfield underlying the structure. Instead of opting to share ownership of the feature by instituting a neutral zone, the 1958 agreement provided that Bu Saafah be ceded to Saudi Arabia but specified that in future Bahrain would receive half of the revenue accruing from the exploitation of the associated oil-field.[236] As recently as 30 December 1992, Ibrahim Abdul Karim, Bahrain's Minister of Finance and National Economy, announced that Saudi Arabia had agreed to allow Bahrain to increase its share of the output from the Bu Saafah field from 70,000 to 100,000 barrels per day (b/d) (that is, from a 50 per cent share to a 71.4 per cent share of the average total daily production figure of 140,000 b/d).[237]

Finalization of Saudi Arabia's boundaries in southern Arabia. The Saudi–Qatar boundary agreement of 1965 has already been commented upon, as has the modification to the Saudi/Jordan boundary agreed during the same year to afford the Hashimite state greater access to the Gulf of Aqabah. Following Britain's departure from the Gulf in 1971, Saudi Arabia negotiated an agreement with Abu Dhabi in 1974 that recognized a strategic Saudi corridor of territory to the Gulf south of the Qatar peninsula. This agreement, too, or as much as is known about it, has already been reviewed. Saudi Arabia made fleeting efforts to settle its southern boundary with the People's Democratic Republic of Yemen during 1982 but these came to nothing.

Most recently, during March 1990, Saudi Arabia and Oman announced the conclusion of a boundary agreement, which was ratified during May 1991.[238] Until October 1992, when Oman publicly released the text of this agreement and the co-ordinates it introduced, no-one could be absolutely sure about what had been decided. As mentioned earlier, however, there were reports that the instrument had previously been registered by the Saudi government with the League of Arab States in Cairo. It was fairly common knowledge, however, that Saudi Arabia had agreed a delimitation synonymous with that (following the modified Riyadh line) imposed by Britain during the autumn of 1955 on the Sultanate's behalf; that is, it had agreed to recognize long-standing Omani territorial claims.[239] Previously, right up until the 1980s, both Saudi Arabia and Oman had maintained different claims to territory in the southeast peninsula, which related closely to the Saudi and British claims of the 1950s. Oman's development of fields close to the Saudi border zone,[240] notably Lekhwair close to Umm al-Zamul, clearly heightened the need for clarification of where their limits to territory lay.[241] While King Fahd and Sultan Qabus signed the border agreement at Hafr al-Batin on 21 March 1990, their interior ministers concluded two supplementary accords concerning the organization of the boundary, addressing specifically such issues as the nomination of crossing-points and rights of access of border tribes to pasturage and water.[242] Progress made towards the finalization of the framework of state territory in southern Arabia in the past couple of years is, almost certainly, not unconnected with Saudi Arabia's current exploration drive for oil in its border regions (see Chapter 8). These moves finally to settle the Oman/Saudi boundary seem to have given fresh impetus to efforts to finalize the Oman/United Arab Emirates delimitation. For in May 1991 the two governments set up a joint committee to discuss bilateral issues including the border.[243] Their efforts culminated, almost two years later, in the statement on 9 April 1993 by Omani Foreign Minister Yusuf bin Alawi bin Abdullah that "the frontier dispute is completely settled", following the signature of a "lasting agreement" between the two states.[244]

The co-ordinates of the delimitation Saudi Arabia agreed with Abu Dhabi in 1974 have not been released, though they are clearly depicted on tactical pilotage charts produced in Britain. The texts of those agreed upon with Qatar in 1965 and Oman in 1990 were released only in late 1992, as a result of the Saudi–Qatar crisis over Khafus and Oman's simultaneous action of publishing details of all of its recently agreed land boundaries (Fig. 1.3). Before these recent disclosures, therefore, Saudi Arabia seemed, in a sense, to have returned to negotiating the informal territorial understandings that it has traditionally favoured and that it tried to implement with Kuwait and Qatar in the years before the British government guaranteed the integrity of these states. Until these recent developments, the less than complete nature of Saudi Arabia's recent territorial arrangements in the southern peninsula led one recent commentator, a contributor to this volume, to suggest that the boundaries cannot be regarded as finally settled in international law: "they [Saudi Arabia] are reluctant to finalize their agreements according to those international rules which would entitle them to consider that their arrangements constituted a permanent feature of the political map."[245] This perhaps hinted that they might be more susceptible to a deterioration in Saudi Arabia's political relationships with its southern neighbours. Yet even the 1974 Saudi/Abu Dhabi delimitation is, for the most part, demarcated. A German firm has recently or is currently demarcating the border delimitation signed by Saudi Arabia and Oman in March 1990. In modern times, demarcation, of course, gives a boundary line tangibility and permanence.

What of the future?

Boundary disputes have recently played a significant part in the regional geopolitics of the Gulf and the Arabian peninsula. The outbreak of serious if transitory disputes such as that between Saudi Arabia and Qatar following the Khafus border post incident has to be measured against strides that have undoubtedly been made towards finalizing the framework of state territory in the region: the United Nations' demarcation of the Iraq/Kuwait land boundary (though this is a double-edged sword as we have seen); the final settlement of the Oman/Yemen boundary; the release of previously withheld details of Saudi Arabia's recent boundary agreements with Qatar and Oman – apparently adding to the formality of these agreements; and the onset of talks between Saudi Arabia and Yemen, which share Arabia's last indeterminate territorial limit.

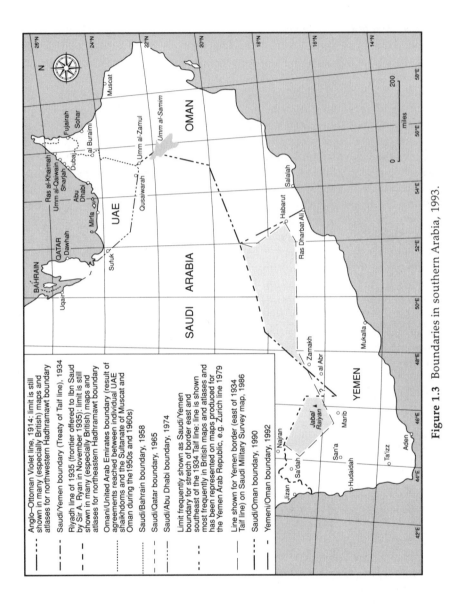

Figure 1.3 Boundaries in southern Arabia, 1993.

Yet several boundary disputes remain deeply entrenched and seemingly as resistant to final settlement as they have ever been. Disputes between Bahrain and Qatar, Iran and the Emirates (Abu Musa and the Tunbs), Iran and Iraq and Iraq and Kuwait have proved intransigent historically and will probably not prove capable of straightforward or satisfactory settlement in the coming decades (Iraq and Kuwait included – not withstanding the apparent successes of the UN).

At worst, territorial disputes between Bahrain and Qatar will probably continue to be controlled rather than solved as they have been during the past decade. Saudi Arabia's mediating role may continue to be crucial. Even should the international courts conclude in 1994 that they do not possess jurisdiction to rule on the Hawar dispute, the actions of a Saudi-dominated Gulf Co-operation Council seem certain to ensure that it never rages totally out of control in the future.

Clearly territorial instability characterizes the northern Gulf. United Nations peacekeeping forces have until only very recently manned two disputed international boundaries, dispute over which was, nominally at least, an important factor in Iraq's decision to prosecute war with Iran during 1980 and its decision to annex Kuwait 10 years later. While UNIIMOG left the Iran/Iraq border in early 1991, satisfied that it had fulfilled its mandate, UNIKOM has continued to be kept busy by Iraqi incursions into the demilitarized zone along the Iraq/Kuwait border, particularly in early 1993 as an apparent escalation of these raids contributed significantly to the resumption of military strikes by the West on Iraqi territory.

Territorial stability will probably come to this part of the world only when Iraq reconciles itself to its disadvantageous position at the head of the Gulf, when it perceives itself as no longer "squeezed out". For the long-term stability of the northern Gulf it is perhaps more important for Iraq to lose its negative consciousness surrounding access than for the Baghdad government to have demarcated boundaries at the head of the Gulf. Whether or not access is a genuine problem is less important than the fact that Iraq has always believed it to be so. Notwithstanding the United Nations' final demarcation of the Kuwait/Iraq boundary, the practical problem of Iraqi access to the Gulf may well return as an issue if and when Umm Qasr port is redeveloped. In the medium term, an arrangement that guarantees both the territorial integrity and security of Kuwait and makes access to the sea easier for Iraq may still need to be found. This might involve a relaxation of Kuwait's sovereignty over the network of water channels in the northwestern Gulf (for example, common rights of access over the whole of the Khawr Abdallah), for which the emirate has virtually no practical use, or a land-swap similar to that by which Jordan expanded its coastline on the Gulf of Aqabah. Such concessions are less likely than ever to be made by Kuwait after the Gulf War, however.[246]

Iran's satisfaction at Iraq's apparent readiness to drop its claims to full sovereignty over the Shatt al-Arab and accept once more the *thalweg* delimitation originally prescribed by the 1975 Algiers Accord must be tempered by the knowledge that factors extraneous to the river boundary itself, as was the case back in 1975, were responsible for this turnaround. Saddam Husain's previous abrogation of the Algiers Accord as a prelude to his decision to initiate the 1980–8 Iran–Iraq war went only to prove that a sophisticated boundary agreement will be of lasting value only if the two sides are genuinely reconciled to the document they are signing. Effective co-operation in the management of the Shatt al-Arab river has always eluded Iran and Iraq, though, ironically, the 1975 Algiers Accord and its annexes had provided elaborate guidelines in this direction.[247] Clearly, in the medium term, if one now accepts that the *thalweg* delimitation has to be regarded as the definitive boundary for the Shatt al-Arab, Iran and Iraq will have to co-operate in the conservancy of this shared river. It is to be hoped that if and when Iraq formalizes its reacceptance of the 1975 boundary, joint committees might be appointed to deal with these very issues. The joint economic development of the river may be some decades off, but ultimately it is going to require a radical change in attitude to bring lasting stability to this historically troublesome boundary.

Iraq's negative consciousness concerning access to the Gulf will, almost certainly, continue to inform Iraqi policy towards the Shatt al-Arab question. This dispute must be regarded as dormant rather than permanently settled. As with the Abu Musa and Tunbs dispute in 1992, controversy could be resurrected at short notice. As for Abu Musa, the 1971 Iran–Sharjah Memorandum of Understanding has worked for two decades. It is hard to envisage an arrangement that would improve on its pragmatic accommodation of the claims of both parties to the island.

The only border in Arabia not governed by an agreement of any kind is that between Saudi Arabia and the newly constituted Republic of Yemen, that is, except for its westernmost stretch delimited by the Taif line of 1934. The traditionally large divergence in each state's claims to territory in southern Arabia means that agreement on a boundary line is not going to be easy to reach. Final settlement will come about only when the two sides agree to compromise on their long-standing and frequently overlapping territorial claims in the region. There might be something to be said for instituting a shared political space in the buffer of sand and steppe that currently separates the limits to which effective occupancy has been extended to the southern peninsula by Saudi Arabia and Yemen. All this presumes that the will is there to reach a settlement. Fortunately, with talks in progress between the two sides, this seemed a fair presumption at the end of 1992. Since this is the first time the two states have ever sat down seriously to consider finalizing borders, judgement on the prospects for resolution will have to wait.

Notes

1. This overview is a considerably modified and updated version of the introduction to a recent multi-volume collection of archival materials, "Arabian boundary disputes: a review of the development of borders and territoriality in the Gulf and Arabian peninsula during the twentieth century," in R. N. Schofield (ed.), *Arabian boundary disputes* (Farnham Common, England: Archive Editions, 1992) vol. 1, xvii–lxx.

2. John Duke Anthony "The Gulf Co-operation Council in the postwar period: progress and potential in deterrence and defence", paper delivered to the Annual Conference of the Middle East Studies Association of North America, Washington DC, 23–6 November 1991, 14.

3. There are no explicit provisions in the texts of these rather limited agreements for Western forces to intervene in the face of external threats to guarantee the territorial integrity of the Gulf state concerned, only provisions for low-level military co-operation such as joint exercises, during which time Western forces would enjoy the use of facilities in the territory of the state concerned. Yet there can be little doubt that the Gulf states concerned have seen the conclusion of these agreements as considerably enhancing their security in the face of perceived regional threats from Iran, Iraq and possibly even Saudi Arabia.

4. On 23 November 1992 the United Nations announced that the last of the 106 boundary markers demarcating the line announced in the spring of this year had been laid. The markers were 1.5 m high and spaced at intervals of 2 km. Interestingly, considering that Iraq rejected the United Nations decision on the boundary and consequently pulled out of the commission's activities during early July 1992, a UN spokesman stated that there had been "full co-operation from both sides" in the marker-laying operation. *Middle East Economic Survey* [MEES] **36**, no. 9, 30 November 1992, A10.

5. See "The United Nations and its 'final' settlement of the Kuwait-Iraq boundary, 1991–1993". In R. N. Schofield, *Kuwait and Iraq: historical claims and territorial disputes* 2nd edn (London: Middle East Programme, Royal Institute of International Affairs, 1993), forthcoming.

6. Anthony 1991. *The Gulf Cooperation Council in the postwar period*, 15.

7. In the final statement delivered at the extraordinary summit, Arab League Secretary-General Chedli Klibi expressed the expectation that ongoing UN-sponsored Iran–Iraq peace talks should "guarantee Iraq's rights and sovereignty over its territory, particularly its historic right to sovereignty over the Shatt al-Arab" (Schofield, ed., *Arabian boundary disputes*, vol.3: *Iran–Iraq*, 859).

8. Yet there was no mention of the Hawar/Dibal/Jaradah dispute in the GCC Supreme Council's final communiqué of 25 December 1990. *BBC summary of world broadcasts*: the Middle East: ME/0957/A/9, 29 December 1990.

9. R. N. Schofield, *Kuwait and Iraq: historical claims and territorial disputes* (London: Middle East Programme, Royal Institute of International Affairs, 1991) 46.

10. Jacques Ancel, *Les frontières* (Paris: Delagrave, 1938).

11. Two English-language monographs charting the history of the Shatt al-Arab dispute have been published in recent years. My own *Evolution of the Shatt al-'Arab boundary dispute* (Wisbech: Menas Press, 1986), essentially a survey of published literature, looks at the problem from a geographical perspective. Kaiyin Homa Kaikobad's more recent legal examination, *The Shatt al-'Arab boundary question: a legal reappraisal* (Oxford: Clarendon Press, 1988) relies heavily upon twentieth-century British Government records held at the India Office Library and Records and various United Nations publications. An extensive documentary history of the Iran/Iraq border, comprising nineteenth- and twentieth-century primary materials (including maps) from both the Public Record Office and the India Office Library and Records has also recently been published: R. N. Schofield (ed.), *The Iran–Iraq border* (Farnham Common: Archive Editions, 1989). Gideon Biger has also made the Shatt al-'Arab his case study in the following article: "Physical geography and law: the case of international river bound-

aries", *Geojournal* **17**(3) (1988) 341–7.

12. C. Grundy-Warr & R. N. Schofield, "Man-made lines which divide the world," *Geographical Magazine* (June 1990).

13. See Chapter 6.

14. This chapter has attempted to take full account of the United Nations' recent efforts to settle, once and for all, the historically-problematic Iraq/Kuwait border question. The latter half of 1992 also witnessed a resurrection of Kuwait's historical claim to the entirety of Kuwait, essentially beginning on the second anniversary of the Iraqi invasion of Kuwait. This has been maintained sporadically through 1993. Maurice Mendelson and Susan Hulton provide a rigorous assessment of the Iraqi claim to sovereignty over Kuwait in Chapter 5 of this volume.

15. This tendency is fully explored in the paper (forthcoming in C. H. Schofield & R. N. Schofield, eds, *World boundaries: in the Middle East and North Africa*, London: Routledge, 1993) by R. N. Schofield, "The historical problem of Iraqi access to the Persian Gulf: the interrelationship of territorial disputes with Iran and Kuwait", presented to the International Boundaries Research Unit conference, University of Durham, July 1991.

16. For a comprehensive historical overview of the Kuwait/Iraq border dispute the reader is referred to Schofield, *Kuwait and Iraq*. A useful addition to the literature on the Iraq/Kuwait border has recently been made by D. H. Finnie, *Shifting lines in the sand: Kuwait's elusive frontier with Iraq*, (London: I. B. Tauris, 1992).

17. For example, O.Bengio, "Iraq: al-Jumhuriyya al-'Iraqiyya", offprint from A. Ayalon (ed.), *Middle East Contemporary Survey*, 1990 (Boulder, Colo.: Westview Press, 1991), 2, 18 & 31.

18. Section entitled "The Husain-Rafsanjani correspondence, April–August 1990" in chapter seven of R. N. Schofield, *Kuwait and Iraq* [2nd edn].

19. Schofield, ed., *Arabian boundary disputes*, vol. 3, 373–401.

20. On vacating the Iran/Iraq border in January 1991 UNIIMOG had expressed confidence that its mission had been "fully accomplished".

21. *Iran Focus* (June 1991), 2.

22. *Financial Times*, 9 January 1991.

23. See news section, *Boundary Bulletin* **2**, 55 (International Boundaries Research Unit, University of Durham, 1992).

24. The mandate of the observer force was ultimately expanded with the passage of UN Resolution 806 on 5 February 1993. UNIKOM's terms of reference were extended to actively resist Iraqi violations of the demarcated boundary following serious border incidents in January 1993. See Chapter 7 of Schofield, *Kuwait and Iraq*, 2nd edn (London: Royal Institute of International Affairs, forthcoming).

25. For details of the early operations of UNIKOM and the United Nations Kuwait/Iraq Boundary Demarcation Commission see the articles by R. N. Schofield "Kuwait/Iraq: the problems of refining a poor boundary", and J. Carver "Iraq/Kuwait: the end of the line", in *Boundary Bulletin* **2** (1992), 21–4, 24–5. Also see R. N. "The Iraq/Kuwait boundary: a problem outstanding", *Middle East International*, no. 398 (19 April 1991) 21–2.

26. R. N. Schofield "The question of delimiting the Iraq/Kuwait boundary" *Boundary Bulletin* **1** (1991), 8–13. Also R. N. Schofield, "Flawed history underpins Iraqi claims to Kuwait territory", *The Times*, 5 April 1991.

27. Schofield, *Kuwait and Iraq*, 94–5.

28. R. N. Schofield, *Kuwait and Iraq*, 2nd edn, Ch. 7.

29. See annex to United Nations Document UN S/22558, released 2 May 1991.

30. The map was published in United Nations document UN S/22558 released 2 May 1991.

31. "Kuwait: memo to Arab League outlining consequences of Iraqi occupation", *BBC summary of world broadcasts*, 6 September 1991, A2.

32. G. Butt "A shabby incident", *Middle East International*, 13 September 1991, 8–9.

33. R. N. Schofield, *Kuwait and Iraq*, 2nd edn (forthcoming), Ch. 7.

34. See UN document (press release): IK/101, 16 April 1992.

35. See text of press release issued by UNIKBDC in New York on 24 July 1992, *MEES*, 3 August 1992, A4–A5.

36. Iraq would later object strongly to the encouragement given by the UN Secretary-General for UNIKBDC to go and settle water boundaries between the two states. UNIKBDC was, at this stage, by no means certain that it possessed a sufficient mandate to nominate a boundary delimitation along the Khawr Abdallah. It possessed authority to demarcate only but there was no mention of any water boundaries in the delimitation formula. UNIKBDC's two neutral surveyors had privately doubted whether any boundary could be announced for the water inlet, and the boundary demarcation commission's first chairman, former Indonesian Foreign Minister Mochtar Kusuma-Adjama, publicly expressed such doubts before resigning over the issue in early November 1992: see Schofield, *Kuwait and Iraq*, 2nd edn (forthcoming), Ch. 7. He was replaced as chairman in mid-November by Greek jurist Nicholas Valticos, who evidently harboured fewer reservations. By the end of 1992, UNIKBDC had confirmed that "the principle governing the demarcation of the boundary line in the Khowr Abd Allah should be the median line": see UNIKBDC press release, 16 December 1992. The actual announcement of a median line delimitation for the Khawr Abdallah and the Khawr Shetana, its western arm north of Warbah island, would have to wait until March 1993, following a further session of UNIKBDC in Geneva.

    The nomination of the median line delimitation for the water inlets rested on the assumption that they constituted territorial sea to which no special circumstances applied, an argument also subsequently rejected by Iraq. As a result of UNIKBDC's March 1993 announcement, the principal navigation channel previously maintained by Iraq along the Khawr Abdallah now falls almost entirely within Kuwaiti territorial waters. Conversely, the principal navigation channel previously maintained by Iraq along the Khawr Shetana falls almost entirely within its own territorial waters: see R. N. Schofield, *Kuwait and Iraq*, 2nd edn (forthcoming), Ch. 7.

37. "Further report of the United Nations Iraq/Kuwait Boundary Demarcation Commission", 24 July 1992, IKBDC/Rep. 6, 24.

38. R. N. Schofield, *Kuwait and Iraq*, 2nd edn (forthcoming), Ch. 7.

39. "Iraq: national assembly condemns international demarcation of border with Kuwait", *BBC summary of world broadcasts: the Middle East*: ME/1384/A/1, 19 May 1992. UN Security Council President Paul Noterdaeme, in his reply to Baghdad, dated 17 June 1992, warned Iraq that protesting against the 16 April 1992 UN announcement of the boundary "appears to call into question Iraq's adherence" to the United Nations Gulf war ceasefire resolutions: *MEES*, 22 June 1992, C2.

40. British-based Iraqis have called upon the United Nations Secretary-General to suspend the border question until a truly representative Iraqi Government is in power, adding that the 16 April 1992 announcement will only sow the seeds for future dispute between Iraq and Kuwait. The Shi'ite al-Dawa party has called for the dispute to be referred to the International Court of Justice in the Hague: see *Guardian*, 30 April 1992. The Arabian peninsula's other two major territorial disputes, the Bahrain–Qatar dispute over the Hawar islands and the Dibal and Jarada shoals and the Saudi–Yemen dispute over oil and borders, could well experience international arbitration in the near future.

41. Notably by the renowned international lawyer and acknowledged boundary expert Ian Brownlie of All Souls College, Oxford.

42. Demarcation does, however, usually have the positive effect of obviating future dispute over the precise course of the boundary.

43. Amongst the elaborate, high-tech proposals that have been presented to the Kuwaiti Government for border defences are a fence with rotating laser guns which would automatically "zap any living thing that approached" and another involving a barrier supported by ground radar.

44. It was the approach of a deadline set by the United Nations (15 January 1993) for Iraq to recover weapons and other objects left in UNIKOM's demilitarized zone that seemed to prompt an escalation in violations of Kuwaiti territory, as newly defined by the UN, in early January. On 7 January Kuwait accused Iraqi forces of attacking one of its border posts: see *Reuters* round-up by Inal Ersan, Kuwait, 7 January 1993. Three days later UNIKOM spokesman Abdellatif Kabbaj confirmed that approximately 200 Iraqis had crossed the border in military transport vehicles to seize missiles and munitions: see *Guardian*, 11 January 1993, 1.

45. R. N. Schofield, *Kuwait and Iraq*, 2nd edn (forthcoming), Ch. 7.

46. R. N. Schofield 1992. "The making of a future war?" (in Arabic) *al-Hayat*, 5 April 1992, 8.

47. See United Nations document (press release): IK/101, 16 April 1992.

48. *Kuwait Times*, 15 February 1992.

49. This point, which the author had tried to stress in a letter to the editor published in *The Times* on 3 March 1992, was made forcefully by United Nations Security Council President Paul Noterdaeme in his reply to the Iraqi letter of May 1992 protesting against the 16 April 1992 announcement of the land boundary. He said that the commission was not reallocating territory but "simply carrying out the technical task" of demarcating the boundary. *MEES*, 22 June 1992, C2.

50. There are several variations on this graphic image. Another states that Kuwait is the cork in Iraq's bottle.

51. Schofield, *Kuwait and Iraq*, 25–49.

52. S. Whittemore Boggs, *International boundaries: a study of border functions and problems* (New York: Columbia University Press, 1940). Also, R. Hartshorne, "Suggestions on the terminology of political boundaries", *Association of American Geographers, Annals* **26** (1936), 56–7.

53. It should be noted that this article is not the first to attempt an application of Boggs' and Hartshorne's categories to the Middle East. An exploratory first effort, relating to the Middle East as a whole rather than the Gulf and Arabian peninsula, was made by A. Drysdale and G. Blake, "Interstate land boundaries", in *The Middle East and North Africa: a political geography* (New York: Oxford University Press, 80–3, 1985)

54. Schofield, *Kuwait and Iraq*, 85.

55. Lord Curzon of Kedleston, "Frontiers", *The Romanes lecture*. University of Oxford (London: Oxford University Press, 1908. Colonel T. H. Holdich, *Political frontiers and boundary-making* (London: Macmillan, 1916).

56. Schofield 1991, *Kuwait and Iraq*, 35–46.

57. *Ibid.*, 73.

58. See Foreign Office Research Department memorandum, "Justification of the stand on the Riyadh line from Mughshin to Raiyan", 29 December 1954, FO 371/110102.

59. Schofield, *Kuwait and Iraq*, 57–60. Also, US Department of State, Bureau of Intelligence and Research, *Geographic Notes* **13** (March 1991), 2–4.

60. Foreign Office 1953. *Historical summary of events in the Persian Gulf shaikhdoms and the Sultanate of Muscat and Oman, 1928–1953* [PG 53], 70.

61. Schofield, *Kuwait and Iraq*, 85.

62. Lieutenant-Colonel T. C. Fowle, Political Resident in the Persian Gulf, to Shaikh Abdallah al-Thani, Ruler of Qatar, 11 May 1935, India Office Library and Records [IOLR] *R/15/1/632*.

63. "Notes on Qatar" by A. F. (Hajji Abdallah) Williamson, Anglo–Persian Oil Company, 14 January 1934, and despatch from Lieutenant-Colonel H. R. P. Dickson, Political Agent, Kuwait, to Lieutenant-Colonel T. C. Fowle, Bushire, 18 January 1934, IOLR *R/15/1/627*.

64. The most useful assessment of the two border disputes to be found in the British archives is the Foreign Office memorandum of 30 June 1940, "Ibn Saud's claims in respect of the southeastern frontiers of Saudi Arabia", IOLR *R/15/2/465*. Contemporary accounts of the Jabal Naksh and Khawr al Udaid disputes may be found in the

following publications: J. C. Wilkinson, *Arabia's frontiers: the story of Britain's boundary drawing in the desert* (London: I. B. Tauris, 1991), 218–21; R. Said Zahlan, *The creation of Qatar* (London: Croom Helm, 1979), 84; R. N. Schofield & G. Blake (eds), *Arabian boundaries: primary documents, 1853–1957*, vol. 15: *Saudi Arabia – Trucial Coast I* (Farnham Common, England: Archive Editions, 1988), xvii.

65. Lieutenant-Colonel T. C. Fowle, Political Resident in the Persian Gulf, to the Government of India, 6 April 1934, IOLR *R/15/1/628*.

66. Following the 30 September 1992 Khafus border post incident, a copy of the 1965 treaty (or sections thereof) was published in an early-October edition of the *Saudi Gazette*.

67. See, for example, Zakki Farsi, *National guide and atlas of the Kingdom of Saudi Arabia* (Riyadh: Farsi, 1989).

68. There were other less publicized reports that Saudi Arabia had taken this action on an earlier occasion during 1991.

69. See A. A. El-Hakim, *The Middle Eastern states and the law of the sea* (Manchester: Manchester University Press, 1979), 121; J. B. Kelly, *Arabia, the Gulf and the West* (London: Weidenfeld & Nicolson, 1980), 188; R. Litwak, *Security in the Persian Gulf, vol. 2: Sources of inter-state conflict*, 51; (London: International Institute for Strategic Studies / Aldershot: Gower, 1981, 51; Wilkinson, *Arabia's frontiers*, 338).

Despite Saudi Arabia's apparent acceptance of the limit introduced by the 1965 agreement in the years that have followed, there were some reports of difficulties over the border early in 1992. Specifically, the Saudi authorities closed the major access route from the Khawr al Udaid westwards to Salwah Bay, forcing Qataris to move northwards into Qatar territory and to use the older, slower and much less direct Salwah road. All this happened at a time when Qatar and Iran were considering plans for the exploitation of subsoil gas reserves out beneath the waters of the Gulf. These difficulties were nothing, however, compared with the serious border incident of 30 September 1992 at the Qatari border post of Khafus. An exchange of fire between the respective border patrols apparently resulted in the deaths of two members of the Qatari armed forces and one Saudi. The Saudi authorities have suggested that the whole affair was essentially a tribal dispute, instigated by the action of al-Murrah bedouin. Nevertheless, they have launched a full investigation of the incident.

The Qatari authorities viewed the matter much more seriously. They charged that the Saudi military had quite blatantly attacked the Khafus post, causing not only Qatari fatalities but considerable material damage. An emergency Qatar Cabinet meeting of 1 October 1992 resulted in the following statement being issued: "the incident took place without any justification and is considered a grave precedent in Qatari–Saudi relations. The cabinet has decided to sever the border agreement concluded between the two countries in 1965, and calls for the need to hold bilateral negotiations as soon as possible in order to agree on the final borders between the two countries and to demarcate them" (Qatar broadcasting service in *BBC summary of world broadcasts: the Middle East*, ME/1501/i, 2 October 1992). An undated press release issued by the Qatari Embassy in London at some point during the second week of October 1992 makes it clear that the Qatari Cabinet stopped short of abrogating the 1965 agreement: "It is worth noting here that the Qatari Council of Ministers decided to suspend but not to abrogate the agreement due to the repeated excesses on the part of the Kingdom and its attempts to unilaterally delineate the border". Press release issued by the Embassy of the state of Qatar, London, October 1992.

70. The Egyptian News Agency MENA reported that "There are indications that President Mubarak has succeeded in achieving tangible progress towards containing the differences between the two sisterly states of Qatar and Saudi Arabia". This followed Mubarak's talks of 17 December 1992 with the heads of state and foreign ministers of both Qatar and Saudi Arabia in separate meetings held in Doha and Medina. *BBC summary of world broadcasts: the Middle East*, ME/1568, 19 December 1992, i. Two days later, *Reuters* reported a joint statement by the Qatari, Saudi and Egyptian foreign ministers, made on 20 December 1992. This announced the signature of an agreement to form a joint Qatari–Saudi, committee which would "draw the final borders within

a year". The text of the joint statement was soon published in the BBC *summary of world broadcasts* (29 December 1992). Its most important provisions are as follows:

(a) In implementation of the border agreement concluded between the Kingdom of Saudi Arabia and the State of Qatar on 11th Sha'ban 1385 AH corresponding to 4th December 1965 AD, it was agreed to append a map signed between the two sides showing the final border line to which both sides shall be committed.

(b) The formation of a joint Saudi–Qatari committee in accordance with Article 5 of the agreement to be entrusted with the task of implementing the 1385 AH/1965 AD agreement with all its provisions and articles and the contents of this joint statement.

This committee shall embark upon placing the border demarcations in accordance with the appended map.

71. Details of the 1974 agreement remain scarce. For further information, see Kelly, *Arabia*, 210–11; Litwak, *Security in the Persian Gulf*, 54; Wilkinson, *Arabia's frontiers*, 342–3. Though the line of co-ordinates introduced by the 1974 agreement has, like the text itself, not been made publicly available, the delimitation is shown clearly on contemporary operational navigation charts and tactical pilotage charts produced by the British Ministry of Defence's Directorate of Military Survey. Privately Abu Dhabi officials continued in 1992 to express unhappiness with the 1974 border, which they regarded as having been imposed upon them.

72. See original text of the Anglo–Turkish (Ottoman) Convention of 29 July 1913, IOLR *R/15/5/65.*

73. For a full documentary record of the 1903–5 Anglo–Ottoman boundary delimitation from the British archives, see vol 2 and 3 of Schofield & Blake (eds), *Arabian boundaries: primary documents, 1853–1957* (Farnham Common, England: Archive Editions, 1988), dealing with Ottoman claims in the Arabian peninsula and the evolution of the boundary between the Aden Protectorate and the Imamate of Yemen.

74. For the original text of the 9 March 1914 Anglo–Turkish Convention respecting the boundaries of Aden, etc., which defined the Violet line, the reader is referred to IOLR *L/P&S//10/407.* In the 1914 Anglo–Ottoman Convention no co-ordinates were specified as a starting point for the Violet line at Lakhmat as-Shuwaib in the Wadi Bana. Consequently, the exact alignment of the limit became the subject of dispute during the late 1950s and has remained so ever since. See Foreign Office memorandum "The Riyadh line, and modifications thereof", by K. H. Jones, 22 March 1961, FO *371/156866.*

75. The flawed rationale behind Britain's adoption of the Anglo–Ottoman lines as the legal defence of its territorial claims in southern Arabia during the intermittent and ultimately fruitless Anglo–Saudi frontier negotiations from the mid-1930s to the mid-1950s is fully exposed in John Wilkinson's recent study, *Arabia's frontiers:* His principal arguments are summarized in Chapter 3 of this volume.

76. For English texts of the Anglo–Najdi treaties of 1915 and 1927 see the following IOLR files: *L/P&S/10/387 & L/P&S/10/1166.* Also see appendices in C. Leatherdale, *Britain and Saudi Arabia, 1925–1939: the imperial oasis,* (London: Frank Cass, 1983), 372 & 380–1.

77. See memorandum by W. E. Beckett, Foreign Office Legal Adviser, enclosure to despatch from C. Warner, Foreign Office, to J. G. Laithwaite, India Office, 31 August 1934, IOLR *R/15/1/603.* Also, Foreign Office memorandum, 30 June 1940, IOLR *R/15/2/465.*

78. British Embassy, Jiddah, to the Saudi Arabian Ministry for Foreign Affairs, 4 August 1955, FO *371/114651.*

79. The exchange of ratifications of the 21 March 1990 border treaty was reported to have taken place at the Foreign Ministry in Riyadh on 21 May 1991 (News section, *Boundary Bulletin* **2** (July 1991), 59). It is interesting to note that the Saudi military survey map of 1986 shows a border with Oman running along the modified Riyadh line declared by Britain during the autumn of 1955 (the line that became recognized officially as the Saudi/Oman boundary in the agreement of March 1990): yet the boundary claimed farther west as depicted on the 1986 Saudi military survey map with what were then the Peoples Democratic Republic of Yemen and the Yemeni

Arab Republic (YAR) basically follows the line of Saudi Arabia's 18 October 1955 territorial statement (that is, apart from the section to the east of the old YAR where Saudi Arabia apparently expanded its territorial claims in 1986 – the basis for which is unclear). The Saudi October 1955 claim itself incorporates the earlier Saudi Hamzah line claim of April 1935 for most of its distance. Interestingly there have been reports that Saudi Arabia registered the text of its 1990 border agreement with Oman with the League of Arab States in Cairo and not with the United Nations, as is customary. Following the conclusion of a boundary agreement with Yemen on 1 October 1992, Oman released the text of its 1990 border agreement with Saudi Arabia. This confirmed beyond any doubt that the Saudi/Oman border follows the modified Riyadh line with no exceptions. *MEES*, 2 November 1992, D1–D4.

As for the Oman–Yemen agreement of 1 October 1992, the full Arabic text of the agreement and its annex setting up a regime for the borderland was first published by *al-Hayat* on 20 October 1992 and then subsequently reprinted in the Daily Report (Near East and South Asia) of the *Foreign broadcast information service* [FBIS], FBIS-NES-92–242, 16 December 1992, 21–4.

80. The modified Riyadh line embraced the Sufuq wells southeast of the Qatar peninsula after Saudi evidence of ownership was accepted by Britain and also the Sultan of Muscat's "no claims line", a limit beyond which no territorial claims were harboured. It was never formally presented to Saudi Arabia until 4 August 1955, coincident with the breakdown of the Buraimi arbitration proceedings. See Figure 1.1.

81. Foreign Office Research Department memorandum, 29 December 1954. *FO 371/110102*.

82. See original documents in *FO 371/18907* and *IOLR R15/6/164* and, also, account in Wilkinson, *Arabia's frontiers*, 215.

83. For example, see Sir Bernard Reilly, Colonial Office, to L. A. C. Fry, Foreign Office, 19 March 1954, *FO 371/110102*.

84. L. A. C. Fry, Foreign Office, to Sir Bernard Reilly, Colonial Office, 16 November 1954, *FO 371/110102*.

85. Foreign Office despatch from D. A. Greenhill, 28 March 1953, *FO 371/104858*, and Foreign Office minute by R. C. Blackham, 22 July 1953, *FO 371/104858*.

86. T. Hickinbotham, Aden, to A. Lyttleton, Colonial Office, 23 May 1953, *FO 371/104858*.

87. The Deputy Foreign Minister of Saudi Arabia, Fuad Bey Hamzah, presented the claim to Sir Andrew Ryan, British Minister in Jiddah, on 3 April 1935. See despatch from Sir Andrew Ryan, Jiddah, to Sir John Simon, Foreign Office, 6 April 1935, *FO 406/73*.

88. Fuad Bey Hamzah, Deputy Foreign Minister, Saudi Arabia, to Sir Andrew Ryan, British Legation, Jiddah, 20 June 1934, IOLR *R/15/1/603*.

89. See account in Wilkinson, *Arabia's frontiers*, 194.

90. See statement of 14 October 1949 issued by the Saudi Arabian Government interpreting the boundaries with Qatar and Abu Dhabi in *Arbitration concerning Buraimi and the common frontier between Abu Dhabi and Saudi Arabia: memorial submitted by the British Government*, vol. 2 - Annexes (1955). Also account in Wilkinson, *Arabia's frontiers*, 248–9.

91. See note from the Saudi Arabian Ministry of Foreign Affairs to the British Embassy, Jiddah, 18 October 1955, *FO 371/114651*. Paragraph 4 of this note read as follows:

With regard to the region which lies south of latitude 19°North, His Majesty's Government propose that the frontiers between Saudi Arabia and the territories of the rulers for whom the British government are entitled to act should start at the point 19°North 56°East; the frontier should then be run to the point 17°North 52°East and thence westwards along latitude 17°North until it reaches 48°East; thence it should run through the point at 16°North 46°East to the Yemen border. In the opinion of His Majesty's Government this line depicts a true and moderate estimate of Saudi Arabia's rights in the area in question.

The claim line has been represented cartographically on certain official Saudi Arabian maps since this date (notably that produced by the Ministry of Petroleum and Mineral Resources during 1963) and was shown, accurately as far as can be made out, on a map that appeared in a recent edition of the US State Department's *Geographic Notes* 13 (March 1991), 2.

92. In addition to its interesting maintenance of established Saudi claims to territory north of the Hadhramawt, but its recognition too of previous British claims for western limits to the Sultanate of Oman, the Saudi military survey map of 1986 also claims a greater swathe of the Dahm and Wa'ilah and Abidah tribal territories in the Yemeni *mashriq* than did the Saudi 18 October 1955 claim, depicted faithfully on the maps earlier produced by the Saudi Ministry of Petroleum and Mineral Resources (1963) and Hussein Bindagji (1984).

93. F. Halliday, *Revolution and foreign policy: the case of South Yemen, 1967–87*, 163. (Cambridge: Cambridge University Press, 1990), 163.

94. F. G. Gause III, *Saudi–Yemen relations: domestic structures and foreign influence* (New York: Columbia University Press, 1990), 81, 89. For greater detail on the 1969 al-Wadi'a police post incident, see various issues of the BBC *summary of world broadcasts: Arab world and Israel*, 28 November – 31 December 1969.

95. The al-Jana block was established as a joint exploration area between the Yemen Arab Republic and the People's Democratic Republic of Yemen in June 1988. Following Yemeni unification in May 1990, exploration work was stepped up in this 2,100 km^2 concession area, which stretches north of the Violet line to a point near 16°01'N, 46°12'E. However, exploration work was halted at the beginning of 1991, during the allied offensive during the Gulf war in the northeast of the Arabian peninsula. Drilling in the al-Jana block, originally scheduled to commence during the summer of 1991, began only a couple of months late in early September, though in areas safely to the south of the Violet line. See the announcement "Nabors of Canada spuds first well in Jana block", MEES, A12.

96. MEES, 23 September 1991, A9. As recently as 1 October 1992 Oman and Yemen signed an agreement that provided for the demarcation of the international land boundary and the delimitation of the seabed boundary out into the Arabian sea in accordance with existing principles of maritime law. The Yemeni Cabinet ratified the agreement a week later on 7 October: "The demarcation agreement consists of 10 articles which define the onshore boundary as a straight line running from a point at Ras Dharbat 'Ali on the Gulf of Aden through the Habrut region to latitude 19°N and longitude 52°E." MEES, 12 October 1992, A8.

97. "Yemen: border disputes and relations with Saudi Arabia. A special report by the *Petro Finance* Market Intelligence Service", Washington DC, May 1992, 18.

98. MEES, 27 July 1992, A3.

99. The potential for the institution of common political zones as a means of lessening persistent territorial disputes is investigated in Chapter 9 of this volume by Gerald Blake.

100. Schofield, *Kuwait and Iraq*, 43–6.

101. *Ibid.*, 54 & 57–60.

102. A. Drysdale & G. Blake, *The Middle East and North Africa: a political geography* (New York: Oxford University Press, 1985), 100. The texts of both the 2 July 1975 and the 29 December 1981 treaties can be found in Schofield, *Arabian boundary disputes*, vol. 6: *Saudi Arabia/Iraq*, 785–809.

103. US State Department, Bureau of Intelligence and Research, *Geographic Notes* 13 (March 1991), 2–4.

104. BBC *summary of world broadcasts: the Middle East*, ME/09277/A/2, 23 January 1991.

105. See Chapter 4 of this volume by Julian Walker. Also see Walker's paper (forthcoming in Schofield and Schofield, *World boundaries*) "United Arab Emirates / Oman frontiers", presented to the International Boundaries Research Unit conference, University of Durham, July 1991.

106. Walker recalls the negotiation of these agreements in his unpublished paper "United Arab Emirates / Oman frontiers".

107. *Ibid.*

108. This shared political space is enumerated in Chapter 9 of this volume by Gerald Blake.

109. Walker, "United Arab Emirates / Oman frontiers"

110. Wilkinson, *Arabia's frontiers*, 342–3.

111. Walker, "United Arab Emirates / Oman frontiers".

112. Wilkinson, *Arabia's frontier*, 342–3.

113. Schofield, *Evolution of the Shatt al-Arab boundary dispute*, 2, 13, 50.

114. US Department of State, "Iran/Iraq", *International boundary study* **164**, Washington DC, July 1978.

115. See unpublished PhD thesis by M. Harari, "The Turco/Persian boundary question: a case study in the politics of boundary-making in the Near and Middle East" (New York: Columbia University, 1958).

116. Wilkinson, *Arabia's frontiers*, 19.

117. *Ibid*.

118. J. B. Kelly, *Eastern Arabian frontiers* (London: Faber & Faber), 1964), 17.

119. This was a point well illustrated in the demographic survey undertaken in the *mashriq* (east) of the Yemen Arab Republic by a team from the geography department at the University of Zurich in the mid-1970s. See H. Steffen, U. Geiser, W. Dubach, *Yemen Arab Republic: preliminary report number 4: findings of the demographic surveys carried out in the areas of Marib, Jawf, Barat and Kitaf*, (prepared for Central Planning Office of the Yemen Arab Republic by the Department of Geography, University of Zurich, Switzerland, 1977), 11, 26 & 53.

120. Schofield, *Kuwait and Iraq*, 68–74.

121. Walker, "United Arab Emirates / Oman frontiers".

122. A. Allouche, *The origins and development of the Ottoman–Safavid conflict, 906–962 [1500–1555]*(Berlin: Klaus Schwarz Verlag, 1983, Islamkundliche Untersuchungen 91). This work in its original form was submitted as a doctoral dissertation at the University of Utah in 1980.

123. The translated texts of all of these early Perso–Ottoman treaties may be found in R. N. Schofield (ed.), *The Iran/Iraq border, 1840–1958*, vol. 1: *Negotiations culminating in the 1847 Treaty of Erzeroum, 1840–7* (Farnham Common, England: Archive Editions, 1989).

124. R. M. Burrell & K. S. McLachlan, "The political geography of the Persian Gulf states", in *The Persian Gulf states*, J. Alvin Cottrell (ed.), 122 (Baltimore: Johns Hopkins University Press, 1980); and Majid Khadduri, *The Gulf war: the origins and implications of the Iran–Iraq conflict*, 34 (New York: Oxford University Press, 1988).

125. Drysdale & Blake, *The Middle East and North Africa*, 246.

126. *Ibid.*, 149.

127. Notes on Qatar by A. F. Williamson, 14 January 1934. IOLR *R/15/1/627*. The underdevelopment of central authority in many of the Gulf shaikhdoms at this stage is a subject dealt with by George Joffé in Chapter 2 of this volume: Concepts of sovereignty in the Gulf region.

128. Memorandum on British commitments [during the war] to the Gulf chiefs, Political Intelligence Department, Foreign Office, undated. IOLR *L/P&S/10/606*, 8.

129. Foreign Office memorandum entitled Ibn Saud's claims in respect of the southeastern frontiers of Saudi Arabia, 30 June 1940. IOLR *R/15/2/465*, 7.

130. Zahlan 1979. *The creation of Qatar*, 82.

131. Notes on Qatar by A. F. (Hajji Abdallah) Williamson, Anglo–Persian Oil Company, 14 January 1934. IOLR *R/15/1/627*.

132. *Ibid*.

133. Zahlan 1979. *The creation of Qatar*, 88.

134. Undated report received at the Political Agency, Bahrain, December 1939. IOLR *R/15/2/142*.

135. Wilkinson 1991. *Arabia's frontiers. . .*, 278–9.

136. Drysdale & Blake 1985. *The Middle East and North Africa. . .*, 189.

137. These involved such questions as recognition of Britain's right to represent the Arab rulers of the Gulf, lighting and buoying, a conservancy convention for the Shatt al-Arab, arms traffic and slavery in Gulf waters and the settlement of Persia's wartime debts to Britain.

138. See original Government of India and Foreign Office correspondence in R. N. Schofield (ed.), *Islands and maritime boundaries of the Gulf*, vols 7–9 (Farnham Common, England: Archive Editions, 1991). Also, R. M. Burrell, "Britain, Iran and the Persian Gulf: some aspects of the situation in the 1920s and 1930s", in D. Hopwood (ed.), *The Arabian peninsula: society and politics*, 160–88 (London: Allen & Unwin, 1972).

139. Britain's conventional views of piracy obtaining in the lower Gulf are challenged by the current Ruler of Sharjah in his monograph: Muhammad al-Qasimi, *The myth of Arab piracy in the Gulf* (London: Croom Helm, 1986).

140. R. N. Schofield, "Abu Musa and the Tunbs: the historical background", paper given at a round-table discussion hosted by the Arab Research Centre (London) on 18 November 1992 entitled "The dispute over the Gulf islands" (to be published in Arabic in 1993).

141. India Office memorandum on the status of the islands of Tamb, Little Tamb, Abu Musa and Sirri by J. G. Laithwaite, 24 August 1928. IOLR *L/P&S/18/B397*.

142. Schofield 1992. Abu Musa and the Tunbs: the historical background.

143. For further details see Pirouz Mojtahed-Zadeh, *Political geography of the Strait of Hormuz: the evolution of Iran's role*, a joint Department of Geography / Near and Middle East Centre Occasional Paper, School of Oriental and African Studies, London, 1990.

144. See Laithwaite's memorandum, 24 August 1928. Also, Husain M. al-Baharna, *The Arabian Gulf states: their legal and political status and their internal problems*, 3rd edn, 339–48 (Beirut: Librairie du Liban, 1978); Joseph Churba, *Conflict and tension among the states of the Persian Gulf, Oman and south Arabia*, 41 (Alabama: Air University Documentary Research Study, 1971); Interim report to His Highness the Ruler of Sharjah prepared by Coward Chance and Associates of Swithin House, London (unpublished, 1971).

145. Laithwaite's memorandum, 24 August 1928.

146. Laithwaite's memorandum, 24 August 1928; Also, J. E. Peterson, "The islands of Arabia: their recent history and strategic importance", in *Arabian Studies*, vol. 7 (Cambridge: Cambridge University Press, 1985); R. N. Schofield & G. H. Blake (eds), *Arabian boundaries: primary documents, 1853–1957*, vol. 13: *Issues of Island Sovereignty*, xxi–xxii (Farnham Common, England: Archive Editions, 1988).

147. See the Foreign Office record of this incident in the following Foreign Office files: FO *371/13009–13010*; Also, selections from these files in R. N. Schofield (ed.), *Islands and maritime boundaries of the Gulf*, vol. 7. (Farnham Common, England: Archive Editions, 1990).

148. During July 1932, for example, Monsieur Taimourtache, the Persian Minister of Court, told Hoare, the British Minister in Tehran, that Persia would renounce its claims to Bahrain so long as Britain recognized its sovereignty over Abu Musa and the Tunbs. Despatch from R. H. Hoare, British Legation, Gulahek, to Sir Lancelot Oliphant, Foreign Office, 15 July 1932. FO *371/16070*.

149. The Ruler of Sharjah actually reckoned that his neighbour had taken this action to draw attention to the fact that no rent was received from the British for their use of the Tunb lighthouse, commissioned and constructed by the Government of India during the First World War. (Telegram from the Political Resident in the Persian Gulf, Bushire, to the Government of India, 5 January 1935. FO *371/18901*). The Ruler of Ras al-Khaimah's action, whatever its motivation, led Knatchbull-Hugessen, the British Minister in Tehran, to recommend, albeit reluctantly, that a compromise be struck with Persia over Tunb to move along the general treaty negotiations (telegram from H. Knatchbull-Hugessen to Foreign Office, 9 April 1935. FO *371/18980*), a suggestion which was considered seriously at the Foreign Office before the Ruler of Ras al-Khaimah was persuaded to reassert his sovereignty over the island.

150. For example see despatch from Sir R. H. Hoare, British Minister in Tehran to Sir John Simon, Foreign Office, 7 April 1934. FO 371/17893.

151. In his telegram dated 9 April 1935 to the Foreign Office, H. Knatchbull-Hugessen, British Minister in Tehran, mentioned that "Taimourtache [Iranian Minister of Court] was prepared to abandon the Abu Musa claim in return for Tamb and later even spoke of a long lease Tamb". FO 371/18980. This was not the first time Persia had hinted such a concession was possible. Five years earlier the Persian Minister of Court had indicated that Persia would be willing to drop its claim to Abu Musa if Britain would recognize its claim to the Tunbs. Telegram from Sir R. Clive, British Minister in Tehran to the Foreign Office, 5 October 1920. FO 371/14528.

152. Many secondary sources cover this episode. Amongst those produced in recent years are the following: Gerald Blake, *Maritime aspects of Arabian geopolitics*, Arab Research Centre, Research Paper 11, 1982; R. M. Burrell, *The Persian Gulf*, Washington Papers 1 (Washington DC: Library Press, Georgetown Center for Strategic and International Studies, 1972); R. M. Burrell & K. S. McLachlan, "The political geography of the Persian Gulf states", in Alvin J. Cottrell (ed.), *The Persian Gulf states*, 121–39 (Baltimore: Johns Hopkins University Press, 1979); J. R. Countryman, *Iran in the view of the Persian Gulf Emirates*, US Army War College, Military Studies Program Paper, Pennsylvania, 1976; Alasdair Drysdale & Gerald Blake, *The Middle East and North Africa: a political geography* (New York: Oxford University Press, 1985); Ali A. El-Hakim, *The Middle Eastern states and the law of the sea* (Manchester: Manchester University Press); R. Litwak, *Security in the Persian Gulf*, vol. 2 *Sources of inter-state conflict* (1981, London: International Institute for Strategic Studies / Gower; L. G. Martin. *The unstable Gulf: threats from within* (1986, Lexington, Mass.: Heath Books, 1979); J. E. Peterson, "The Arab response to the Iranian challenge in the Gulf", in *The Middle East in the 1980s: problems and prospects*, Philip H. Stoddard (ed.), (Washington DC: Middle East Institute, 1978); J. E. Peterson, "The islands of Arabia: their recent history and strategic importance", in *Arabian Studies*, vol. 7 (Cambridge: Cambridge University Press, 1985); R. K. Ramazani, *The Persian Gulf and the Strait of Hormuz* (Den Haag: Martinus Nijhoff, 1979); R. N. Schofield & G. Blake (eds), *Arabian boundaries: primary documents, 1853–1957*, vol. 13: *Issues of island sovereignty*, xxi–xxii (Farnham Common, England: Archive Editions, 1988); H. Sirriyeh, "Conflict over the Gulf islands of the Abu Musa and the Tunbs, 1968–71", *Journal of South Asian and Middle Eastern Studies* 7(1984), 73–86; S. Zabih, "Iran's policy toward the Persian Gulf", *International Journal of Middle Eastern Studies* 7(1976), 345–58.

153. al-Baharna 1978. *The Arabian Gulf states. . .*, 339.

154. Private and confidential source.

155. al-Baharna 1978. *The Arabian Gulf States. . .*, 339–41.

156. Text is reproduced in *ibid*, 345.

157. *Ibid.*, 345.

158. Almost a year earlier, during November 1979, the Iraqi Ambassador to Lebanon had called for Iran's evacuation of Abu Musa and the Tunbs. BBC *summary of world broadcasts*: the Middle East, 2 November 1979.

159. In April 1992 the Iranian authorities prevented a group of non-national employees of the Sharjah state (comprising Pakistani, Indian and Philippino labourers and technicians and non-UAE [principally Egyptian] Arab teachers) from entering the island. Iran denied that its authorities on Abu Musa had expelled United Arab Emirates' nationals from the island. Iran's envoy to the United Nations, Kamal Kharrazi, added, however, that "those [nationals of the United Arab Emirates] who have not lived on the island . . . have no right to stay there", implying that only those Sharjah nationals with a proven connection to the island would be allowed to reside there in the future. FBIS-NES-92-076, 20 April 1992. Also, Iranian Foreign Minister Velayati stated at this time (albeit mistakenly) that the 1971 Memorandum of Understanding gave the right only to Sharjah nationals to reside on the island.

The dispute over Abu Musa intensified with reports on 24 August 1992 that Iran had refused entry to a large party of over 100 third-party national (apparently consisting of teachers and their families). In fact, many of these principally Egyptian teachers were the same individuals who had originally been denied entry back in April. Iran had backed down on the first occasion after strong representations from the UAE Federal Foreign Ministry, ostensibly so that pupils in Sharjah could complete their examinations in May/June 1992. It had hinted, however, that the UAE and Iran would need to make strides in addressing the "security problem" on Abu Musa before the beginning of the next academic year in September 1992. With no progress made, the teachers were turned back in late August as they returned to prepare for the commencement of the new school year. *BBC World Service: Persian service news bulletin*, 25 August 1992. Talks aimed at defusing the crisis, held in Abu Dhabi between delegations of the governments of the United Arab Emirates and Iran during late September 1992, broke down when the UAE representatives placed not just Abu Musa but the Tunbs on the agenda for discussion. *BBC summary of world broadcasts: the Middle East*, ME/1498i, 29 September 1992, ME/1501/A/3-A/4, 2 October 1992.

160. Press release, Embassy of the United Arab Emirates, London, October 1992. There are unconfirmed reports that Sharjah and Iran were prepared to reaffirm the provisions of the 1971 Memorandum of Understanding in their entirety before the federal (UAE) government intervened to place the status of the Tunbs back on the agenda. Provisional agreement had apparently been reached at the negotiations in September to abide by the 1971 Memorandum of Understanding before the UAE Foreign Ministry then decided to tie this to a demand that Iran allow the sovereignty of the Tunbs to be adjudicated by international arbitration.

161. This is perhaps best personified in comments made by Abbas Maleki, Deputy Minister of State at the Iranian Foreign Ministry. "The volume of press coverage on Abu Musa is bigger than the island itself", *Iran Focus*, November 1992, 2.

162. See comments by Iranian Foreign Minister Ali Akbar Velayati ascribing the recent dispute over Abu Musa to the misjudgments of "junior Iranian officials" in *Iran Focus*, November 1992, 3. Iran had, during September 1992, sent a senior investigating team from its Foreign Ministry to the island to review the incidents of April and August 1992. As a result of this, Iran's local naval commander was apparently sacked.

163. Especially when one considers that Bahrain has during the last six months occasionally called for Iraq's reintegration into the Arab fold and that Qatar temporarily returned its Ambassador to Baghdad at the height of its border crisis with Saudi Arabia.

164. The fourth part of the GCC's closing statement entitled "Relations with the Islamic Republic of Iran and the Issue of the Islands" contained the following paragraph:
The council also emphasises that the continuation of the Iranian occupation of the three islands (Abu Musa and the Tunbs) and the measures taken by the Islamic Republic of Iran on the island of Abu Musa represent a violation of these principles (good neighbourliness, respect for the sovereignty and territorial integrity of the region's states and non-interference in others' internal affairs) and the declared desire to promote bilateral relations. The Supreme Council calls on the Islamic Republic of Iran to cancel and abolish all measures taken on Abu Musa island and to terminate its occupation of the Greater and Lesser Tunb islands, which belong to the UAE. The Supreme Council affirms its complete solidarity and absolute support for the UAE's position and supports all the peaceful measures and means it (the UAE) deems appropriate to regain its sovereignty over its three islands in accordance with international legitimacy and the principle of collective security. (*BBC summary of world broadcasts*: the Middle East ME/1573/A/7, 29 December 1992).
Iranian President Rafsanjani's reaction to the statement came on 25 December 1992 when he warned the GCC states that "Iran is surely stronger than the likes of you . . . to reach these islands one has to cross a sea of blood" and added that "we (Iran) consider this claim as totally invalid". *MEES*, 11 January 1993, C3.

165. An analysis of recent Iranian policies towards the Arab states of the southern Gulf littoral, specifically where oil and territorial disputes are concerned, is provided in Chapter 11 of this volume by Keith McLachlan: Hydrocarbons and Iranian policies towards the Gulf states: confrontation and co-operation in island and continental shelf affairs.

166. For a thorough account of the early development of Persian claims to the sovereignty of Bahrain see J. B. Kelly's classic and recently reprinted work, *Britain and the Persian Gulf, 1795–1880*, (Oxford: Oxford University Press, 1968); and J. B. Kelly, "The Persian claim to Bahrain", *International Affairs* **33**(1957), 51–70.

For an unabashed articulation of the Iranian claim to the island and its history up until the mid-1950s, see F. Adamiyat, Praeger, *Bahrein islands: a legal and diplomatic study of the British–Iranian controversy*. (New York: 1955).

For a selection of official materials on the history of the dispute from the British archives see vols 11–12 of *Arabian boundaries: primary documents, 1853–1957* (Farnham Common, England: Archive Editions), edited by Richard Schofield & Gerald Blake.

167. See introduction to Schofield & Blake (eds), *Arabian boundaries: primary documents, 1853–1957*, vol. 11: *Iranian claims to Bahrain I*. (Farnham Common, England: Archive Editions, 1988).

168. For a detailed commentary on these comparatively recent events, backed by useful documentary evidence, refer to R. K. Ramazani & J. A. Kechichian, "Coping with Subversion and Terrorism", in *The Gulf Co-operation Council: record and analysis*, 33–59 (Charlottesville: University of Virginia Press, 1988).

169. If, however, the Saudi/Yemen borders dispute ultimately goes to international arbitration, historical claims may be forwarded at the outset which extend farther north than these lines, as it is customary to present maximum territorial claims at the beginning of proceedings, which may then be gradually retracted in the interests of securing a favourable settlement.

170. Viceroy, Government of India to the Secretary of State for India, 12 July 1906. IOLR *L/P&S/18/B166a*.

171. See extracts of report dated 15 May 1866 by Lieutenant-Colonel Lewis Pelly, Political Resident in the Persian Gulf. In J. A. Saldanha (ed.), *Précis of Koweit Affairs*, 3. (Simla: Government of India, 1904).

172. For further details, see Schofield 1991. The creation of a territorially-defined Kuwait. *Kuwait and Iraq. . .*, 25–49: And, B. C. Busch, *Britain and the Persian Gulf, 1894–1914*. (Berkeley: University of California Press, 1967).

173. Schofield 1991. *Kuwait and Iraq. . .*, 46; Wilkinson 1991. *Arabia's frontiers. . .*, 398.

174. See introduction to R. N. Schofield & G. Blake (eds), *Arabian boundaries: primary documents, 1853–1957*, vol. 13: *Issues of island sovereignty*, 165 (Farnham Common, England: Archive Editions, 1988).

175. Schofield 1991. *Kuwait and Iraq. . .*, 54.

176. Foreign Office 1928. *Historical summary of events in territories of the Ottoman Empire, Persia and Arabia affecting the British position in the Persian Gulf, 1907–1928*. [PG 13], 80.

177. Ibn Saud to the Political Agent, Bahrain, 5 September 1920. IOLR *R/15/1/522*.

178. Lieutenant-Colonel H. R. P. Dickson, Political Agent, Kuwait, to Lieutenant-Colonel T. C. Fowle, Political Resident in the Persian Gulf, 18 January 1934. IOLR *R/15/1/627*.

179. H. R. P. Dickson *Kuwait and her neighbours*, 274 (London: Allen and Unwin, 1956).

180. The British authorities in the Persian Gulf had admitted as much two years earlier. For example, see despatch from Major J. C. More, Political Agent, Kuwait, 13 June 1920. IOLR *R/15/1/522*.

181. Drysdale & Blake 1985. *The Middle East and North Africa . . .*, 99.

182. Schofield 1991. *Kuwait and Iraq. . .*, 57–60; United States State Department, Bureau of Intelligence and Research 1991. *Geographic Notes* **13**, 1–4.

183. Drysdale & Blake 1985. *The Middle East and North Africa. . .*, 100; and Chapter 9 by Gerald Blake on "Shared zones as a solution to problems of territorial sovereignty in the Gulf states".

184. Martin I. Glassner & Harm J. De Blij (3rd edn), *Systematic political geography*, 72 (New York: John Wiley, 1980); Drysdale & Blake 1985. *The Middle East and North Africa. . .*, 80–1.

185. As early as 1961, according to recent Foreign Office releases, Saudi Arabia and Jordan had agreed in principle to this landswap. See comment by W. Morris, British Embassy, Amman, to G. F. Hiller, Foreign Office, 5 August 1961. FO 371/157528. "King Hussein told the British Air Adviser that the only success of the meeting was a promise by King Saud that he would rectify the Saudi/Jordanian frontier to give more elbow room for the port of Aqaba".

186. Schofield 1991. *Kuwait and Iraq. . .*, 124–5.

187. Wilkinson's arguments are summarised in Chapter 3. This takes into account recent developments in the territorial affairs of the Arabian peninsula (up until November 1992).

188. Wilkinson 1991. *Arabia's frontiers. . .*, x.

189. For example, *Eastern Arabian frontiers* (London: Faber & Faber, 1974) by New Zealand-born historian John Kelly.

190. See Chapter 4 by Julian Walker.

191. See despatches dated 11 July 1939 from H. Weightman, Political Agent, Bahrain, to the Rulers of Qatar and Bahrain, announcing the award of the Hawar group to Bahrain. IOLR *R/15/2/547*.

192. F. Lawson, *Bahrain*, 133 (Boulder: Westview Press, 1989); John Duke Anthony, *Arab states of the Lower Gulf: people, politics and petroleum*, 91 (Washington DC: Middle East Institute, 1975).

193. R. K. Ramazani & J. A. Kechichian, *The Co-operation Council: record and analysis*, 126 (Charlottesville: University of Virginia Press, 1988).

194. According to Qatar, such a procedure was "concluded in the context of mediation of King Fahd of Saudi Arabia". Unofficial communique no. 91/21 issued by the *International Court of Justice*, 8 July 1991. It is the opinion of some contemporary commentators, however, that Qatar's action of referring the Hawar disputes et al. to the ICJ on 8 July 1991 has since been interpreted by the Saudis as a rejection of their long-standing mediating efforts in this problematic case. This stance has surprised and disappointed the Qatar Government, which maintains instead that reference of the dispute was an agreed procedure, the culmination of two decades of inconclusive Saudi mediation (see quote above).

195. *Foreign broadcasts information service*. FBIS-NES-92-084, 30 April 1992 and *BBC summary of world broadcasts: Gulf states*: ME/1438/A/8-A/9, 21 July 1992.

196. Foreign Office (1953), *Historical summary of events in the Persian Gulf* [PG 53], 71.

197. *Ibid.*, 27.

198. Ramazani & Kechichian 1988. *The Gulf Co-operation Council. . .*, 126 and Lawson 1989. *Bahrain*, 133–4.

199. *The Independent*, 20 September 1991, 10.

200. Text of Decree No.40 issued by the Ruler of Qatar on 16 April 1992 reproduced in *MEES*, 27 April 1992, A3.

201. See original correspondence between the oil companies (BAPCO and Petroleum Concessions Limited) and the British authorities in the Persian Gulf exchanged between April and November 1936 in FO 371/19974 and IOLR L/P&S/12/3895. Earlier in 1936 (April) Charles Dalrymple Belgrave, Adviser to the Ruler of Bahrain, had written to Lieutenant-Colonel Loch, Political Agent in Bahrain, officially recording Shaikh Hamad's claim to the island for the first time. See Foreign Office (1953), *Historical summary of events in the Persian Gulf* [PG 53], 26.

202. Zahlan 1979. *The creation of Qatar. . .*, 89.

203. Reviewing the 1939 award of Hawar to Bahrain during the summer of 1940, Lieutenant-Colonel C. G. Prior, Political Resident in the Persian Gulf, cast doubts upon the legality of acquiring territory in such a way. "It is ridiculous to suppose that territory can be acquired in these waters by the erection of 'national marks'". Telegram from Political Resident, Bushire, to the Government of India, 7 June 1940. IOLR *R/15/2/547*.

204. Memorandum H. Weightman, Political Agent, Bahrain, 29 May 1938. IOLR *R/15/2/547*.

205. C. D. Belgrave, Adviser to the Ruler of Bahrain, to H. Weightman, Political Agent, Bahrain, 22 December 1938. IOLR *R/15/2/547*.

206. Despatches dated 29 May 1938, 24 and 30 March 1939 from the Ruler of Qatar to H. Weightman, Political Agent, Bahrain. IOLR *R/15/2/547*.

207. C. D. Belgrave, *Personal column*, 156 (London: Hutchinson, 1960).

208. Sir Bernard Burrows, Political Resident in the Persian Gulf, Bahrain to Shaikh Salman bin Hamad al-Khalifah, Ruler of Bahrain, 10 August 1957. FO *371/126935*.

209. Foreign Office minute on Halul by C. T. E. Ewart-Biggs, 25 March 1955. FO *371/114647*.

210. Foreign Office minute on Halul by A. R. Walmsley, 8 July 1958. FO *271/132801*.

211. Foreign Office minute on Halul by C. T. E. Ewart-Biggs, 20 August 1958. FO *371/132801*.

212. D. M. H. Riches, Foreign Office, to C. A. Gault, Political Agent, Bahrain, 8 September 1958. FO *371/132801*.

213. D. A. Greenhill, Foreign Office, to the Secretary, Shell Petroleum Company Limited, Ministry of Fuel and Power, 14 October 1952. POWE *33/1976*.

214. On 26 April 1962 the *Daily Telegraph* reported that the British Government, with the approval of Abu Dhabi and Qatar, had chosen Charles Gault, former Political Agent, Bahrain and Professor J. N. Anderson, Professor of Islamic Law at the University of London, to examine and report on the neighbouring shaikhdoms' claims to Halul and other intervening islands. These experts had found that Halul should belong to Qatar but could not decide on the ownership of Sharaiwah and Daiyinah, two much smaller islands lying to the south: for further details see A. A. El-Hakim, *The Middle Eastern states and the law of the sea*, 97, 244. It might also be added that Britain during 1962 considered its decision on Halul as something less than an "outright award". At the time, neither the Ruler of Qatar nor the Ruler of Abu Dhabi was provided with copies of the Gault–Anderson arbitration reports that had determined the verdict.

215. *Ibid.*, 98. Also, for text of 1969 agreement and map showing delimitation introduced, United States State Department, International Boundary Study, Series A: Limits in the seas. *Continental shelf boundary – Abu Dhabi/Qatar* (29 May 1970, Office of the Geographer, Bureau of Intelligence and Research).

216. Foreign Office 1928. *Historical summary of events in territories of the Ottoman Empire, . . .*, [PG 13], 80.

217. For the translated text of this agreement see appendices in Clive Leatherdale, *Britain and Saudi Arabia, 1925–1939: the imperial oasis*, 380–1 (London: Frank Cass, 1983).

218. Zahlan 1979. *The creation of Qatar . . .*, 82.

219. Foreign Office 1953. *Historical summary of events in the Persian Gulf . . .*, [PG 53], 125.

220. For example see *Notes on Qatar* by A. F. (Hajji Abdallah) Williamson, Anglo-Persian Oil Company, 14 January 1934. IOLR *R/15/1/627*.

221. English translation of original Arabic text enclosed in despatch from A. S. Calvert, British Legation, Jiddah, to Foreign Office, 30 July 1934. FO *371/17929*.

222. It was not until the spring of 1934, with the publication of the Saudi Green Book during the brief Saudi–Yemeni war, that Britain was sure about what the August 1920 Najdi–Idrisi treaty had achieved. Sir Andrew Ryan, Jiddah, to Foreign Office, 14 May 1934. FO *371/17928*. Also, enclosure in despatch dated 18 August 1934 from A. S. Calvert, Jiddah, to Foreign Office. FO *371/17930*.

223. For the translated texts of these agreements see FO *371/12235* and the Saudi Green Book concerning the administration of the Idrisi province, published in Mecca-weekly *Umm al Qura*, 23 Jumadi ath Thani, 1349, enclosed in despatch dated 15 November 1930 from Fuad Bey Hamza, Acting Minister for Foreign Affairs, Jiddah in FO *371/14483*.

224. Foreign Office annual report on Saudi Arabia for 1933 in FO *371/17941*.

225. During late December 1937 the Saudi press announced the ratification of an annex to the 1934 Treaty of Taif, recording the agreement of the Sanaa and Riyadh governments to the decisions reached, during late 1935 / early 1936, by the joint commissions on the delimitation and demarcation of the boundary. It would seem that the text of the annex to the Taif agreement never reached the Foreign Office, or at least not until the early 1960s. Nevertheless a translated copy of the annex was finally unearthed at the Ordnance Survey, Southampton. During 1935-6 the Taif line was demarcated by stone cairns at intervals of approximately 1 km. Provisions in the 1937 annex to the Taif treaty to convert them into permanent pillars, long a Saudi objective, have never been acted upon.

226. A brief outline of the history of Yemen during the Muslim period: a note on the Zaidi Imamate of Sanaa. Report by Captain M. Fazluddin, Political Officer, Hudayda. CO 725/17/12.

227. According to an extract from *Al Bilad as Saudiyah* in the despatch dated 1 April 1953 from Mr G. Pelham, British Ambassador at Jiddah, to Mr A. Eden, Foreign Office. FO 371/104532.

228. BBC *summary of world broadcasts: the Middle East*. ME/4249/A/3 20 March 1973. Also, Ali Muhammad al-Ulafi 1978. *Nusus yamaniyya* (Yemeni texts), dar al-huriyya li al-taba'a, Baghdad, 407-9.

229. F. Gregory Gause III, *Saudi–Yemeni relations: domestic structures and foreign influence*, 106 (New York: Columbia University Press, 1990).

230. News section, in *Boundary Bulletin* (July 1991), 59.

231. Quoted in MEES, 10 August 1992, A10.

232. Rodman Bundy provides a legal overview of questions relating to maritime delimitation in the Gulf in Chapter 7.

233. English translation of the Saudi–Bahraini treaty of 22 February 1958 enclosed in despatch from Sir Bernard Burrows, Political Resident in the Persian Gulf, to D. M. H. Riches, Foreign Office, 4 March 1958. FO 371/132794.

234. see introduction to Vol. 10 of R. N. Schofield & G. H. Blake (eds), *Arabian boundaries: primary documents, 1853-1957*, xix. (Farnham Common, England: Archive Editions, 1988).

235. For a detailed record of these negotiations see the correspondence enclosed within the Ministry of Fuel and Power file POWE 33/1952.

236. Gerald Blake, "Maritime boundaries of the Middle East and North Africa", in Gerald Blake & R. N. Schofield. *Boundaries and state territory in the Middle East and North Africa*, 123, 133. (Wisbech, England: Menas Press, 1987). This early example of ways in which rival claims to oil bearing features have been accommodated in the region is one of many enumerated by David Pike in Chapter 8.

237. MEES, 11 January 1993, A2.

238. *Boundary Bulletin* 2(July 1991), 59.

239. Certain rumours have circulated or did at the time of the conclusion of the 1990 Saudi-Omani border agreement, that in return for recognizing Omani territorial claims, Saudi Arabia gained access facilities through Dhufar (western Oman), terminating at Salalah, the principal port in these parts.

240. For an account of current oil exploration and development policies in the Gulf region see Chapter 10 by Paul Stevens.

241. Wilkinson 1991. *Arabia's frontiers . . .*, 344-5.

242. BBC *summary of world broadcasts*: ME/0719i, 23 March 1990.

243. J. Whelan, "Muscat agrees border with Riyadh", in *Boundary Bulletin* 2(July 1991), 26.

244. *Arab Times*, 10 April 1993.

245. Wilkinson 1991. *Arabia's frontiers . . .*, xi.

246. R. N. Schofield, "Borders disputes in the Gulf Region", in *The Middle East and Europe: an integrated communities approach*, 99-110, G. Nonneman (ed.). (London: Federal Trust for Education and Research, 1992).

247. For the text of the 1975 Algiers Accord see Anoushiravan Ehteshami & G. Nonneman, *War and peace in the Gulf: domestic politics and regional relations into the 1990s*,
143–51. (Reading, England: Ithaca Press, 1991). Also, Kaiyan Homa Kaikobad, *The
Shatt-al-Arab boundary question: a legal reappraisal*, 134–42 (Oxford: Oxford University
Press, 1988).

CHAPTER TWO
Concepts of sovereignty in the Gulf region

George Joffé

Introduction

The modern sovereign political structures of the Arab states of the Gulf region are, in virtually every respect, a testimony to British imperial policy, spurred on by a desire for oil and for commercial control. This is particularly true of the small states along the Gulf littoral of the Arabian peninsula, but it is also true, to a greater or lesser extent, of the three major states of the region: Iran, Iraq and Saudi Arabia. Although at least two of them had a sovereign existence before the British-dominated colonial period in the Gulf region began, nonetheless the actual form of sovereignty manifested by all of them today clearly shows the consequences of British interest. This, in turn, derived from concern over access to India and over commerce during the nineteenth century and over control of oil production during the first half of the twentieth century.

The result has been that, in effect, concepts of sovereignty in the region have been dominated by the principles of modern international law, which, in effect, are derived from legal principles and political concepts that were developed in Europe.[1] Crucial to such views has been the principle that sovereignty is linked to territory, since

> Territory is a tangible attribute of statehood and, within that particular geographical area which it occupies, a state enjoys and exercises sovereignty. Territorial sovereignty may be defined as the "right to exercise therein, to the exclusion of any other state, the functions of a state".[2]

Equally crucial has been the associated concept of the state, which, in international law, seems to have a specific meaning. States are entities with populations living in territories effectively controlled by governments, which are also capable of conducting international relations with other states.[3] It should be borne in mind that such a definition does not imply necessarily that the precise borders of the states in question are definitively established or are undisputed, nor that a state ceases to exist if it is occupied by an act of war, provided other states dispute that act of conquest.[4] Indeed, the recent conflict over Iraq's occupation and annexation of Kuwait was implicitly based on just such a principle of international law, even though it may have been explicitly justified by recourse to United Nations Charter. ✓

Although these definitions might seem self-evident within the context of the modern international order, this is not necessarily the case in the Middle East. In fact, there is a corpus of Islamic constitutional law that has traditionally defined an alternative model for political entities within the Islamic world. It might, therefore, have been expected that states within the Gulf region would have sought to justify their independent status by such alternatives. They are, after all, amongst those most directly concerned with Islamic orthodoxy today. Iran, in the aftermath of the Islamic revolution, has claimed to be an embodiment of the Islamic ideal. Saudi Arabia not only contains the two most important religious centres of the Islamic world at Mecca and Medina but is also inspired by the Wahhabi movement. This movement has sought to order social and political life in accordance with strict interpretations of Sunni Islam for the past 250 years.[5]

There is no doubt, too, that Islamic constitutional law offers a very different paradigm from that proposed by modern international law. As far as the state and sovereignty are concerned, "[t]he basis of the Islamic state was ideological, not political, territorial or ethnical and the primary purpose of government was to defend and protect the faith, not the state".[6] Indeed, the concept of the state was unitary, in that ideally the whole of the Islamic world should form a single political unit, the *umma*, under the control of a *khalifa* who was also *imam*. The fact that smaller, discrete political units existed was a practical reality, of course, but these were seen usually as realms of secular authority and power – *sultah* – under the control of a sultan or amir. Sovereignty (*siyada*), in turn, was seen as a divine attribute, not as an inherent attribute of a temporal political construct or of authority within such a construct.[7]

In fact, these principles have not played a dominant rôle in legitimizing the state in the Gulf region, even when, as in the case of Iran and Saudi Arabia, the existence of such an Islamic legal corpus is admitted. Iran, as discussed briefly below, is a state in which ultimately territorial extent and territorial sovereignty are of acute concern to the government. Formally, Saudi Arabia, despite its claim to be an Islamic state controlled by the Wahhabi imams, is a kingdom (*mamlaka*). However, monarchical authority – *mulk* (supreme power, sovereignty or right of possession) - is defined as an attribute of Allah, not of temporal power, precisely because it involves the attribution of sovereignty. The term *malik* is, in consequence, normally used to describe only a non-Islamic or pre-Islamic authority, since an Islamic authority could not lay claim to a divine attribute of this kind.[8]

It has also been argued, in the context of Saudi Arabia at least, that the adoption of the term by Ibn Saud in 1932 was an attempt to associate the divine attributes of *mulk* with those of the Wahhabi *imam*-ate, rather than an overt acceptance of the secular nature of the new Saudi kingdom. This was, no doubt, a factor that was considered. However, it seems difficult to ignore other, perhaps more relevant factors. *Mulk* is an absolute quality and does not depend on conditional authority, as is the case with *sultah* – where the conditional social contract explicit in the *khalifa's* relations with the *umma* is also implicit. In the European context, moreover, monarchy also acquired a quality of divine right, and furthermore it was hereditary – just as became the case in the Middle East and North Africa. Even though primogeniture was not necessarily the preferred mode of succession, there is little doubt that the concept of *mulk* was used to justify the succession process being retained within a small, cohesive family unit – rather as Mawerdi argued should be the case with the caliphate and the Quraish.[9]

It must also be remembered that the term was adopted at a time when relations with Britain as the major regional power were becoming increasingly important to the new kingdom and just in the wake of the appearance of the two British-instituted kingdoms – Jordan and Iraq – in the Middle East region. It is, therefore, difficult to reject the Moss-Helms argument, particularly when the same decision was made in Morocco at the end of the colonial period in 1956 – apparently for similar reasons. Thus the use of the term by Saudi Arabia, Jordan and Morocco implies a recognition of non-Islamic forms of constitutional definition as well – hence, no doubt, the Saudi preoccupation with territorial sovereignty, as described below.

Sovereignty in Iran

Only one state in the region – Iran – occupies a territorial extent that is substantially similar to that which it claimed when the colonial period in the region began, at the start of the nineteenth century. The geographical extent of the modern Iranian state dates from the Safavid conquest between 1501 and 1510,[10] while "Modern Iran inherited from the Safavid period (1501–1722) the pattern of state religions, and tribal (*uymaq*) institutions which would shape its history to the present day."[11] Even there, in the Gulf region at least, the autonomous status of the shaikhdom of Muhammarah up to the reconstitution of Iran by Reza Shah has meant that the nature of sovereignty in the modern Iranian state is very different from that of its predecessor.[12]

Interestingly enough, although the political structures of Iran may have been profoundly changed by the Islamic revolution in 1979, there is little doubt that Ayatollah Khomeini accepted that his *velayat-e faqih* – rule of the Islamic jurisconsult – would, in practical terms at least, be a successor state to its secular precursor under the Shah. In *Hukumat-i Islami*, he argues, "Once you have succeeded in overthrowing the tyrannical regime, you will certainly be capable of administering the state and guiding the masses . . . The entire system of government and administration together with the necessary laws, lies ready for you."[13] The laws referred to comprise the body of *Shar'* and, as Ayatollah Khomeini points out, "Islamic government is a government of law. In this form of government, sovereignty belongs to God alone and law is His decree and command."[14] Nonetheless, the "state" he was concerned with is undoubtedly Iran in terms of its normal geographic definition, as was made clear in his statement proclaiming the formation of the Council of the Islamic Revolution on 12 January 1979.[15]

Sovereignty in Saudi Arabia and Iraq

Both of the other two major states in the region – Saudi Arabia and Iraq are substantially twentieth-century creations, as far as their sovereign status, geographic extent and domestic institutions are concerned.

Saudi Arabia

Furthermore, only Saudi Arabia of all the states in the region (with the possible exception of Yemen and Oman) can claim a degree of legitimacy in terms of traditional Islamic constitutional theory, because of the alliance between Muhammad Ibn Saud, then the Amir of Dariya, and Shaikh Muhammad Ibn Abdul Wahhab, the founder of the Wahhabi movement, in 1744. The Wahhabi movement itself had emerged as a coherent doctrine of religious purification derived from Hanbalism only shortly before the alliance with the al-Sauds.

The al-Saud family itself had come to prominence only two decades earlier as *amirs* of Dariya, one of the many petty principates of central Arabia, based in Wadi Hanifah 20 km to the north of Riyadh. The emirate had been founded by Saud Ibn Muhammad Ibn Muqrin. The al-Saud family had migrated to Wadi Hanifah from Qatif during the fifteenth century, claiming to be part of the Anaizah tribal confederation of northern Arabia.[16] Control of the urban centre of Riyadh was to be its initial and primary concern, as part of its strategy to take over the Najd.

In fact, despite the considerable influence that the al-Sauds were eventually able to exert throughout Arabia as a result of their alliance with the Wahhabi movement, it was only in the twentieth century that they established the essential link with and control over the *badu* (nomadic) population of central and north Arabia that ensured their ultimate territorial expansion. This followed on from a deliberate decision by Abdul Aziz Ibn Saud to encourage the *badu* into a much closer link with Wahhabism and to create the *Ikhwan* movement as the essential component for territorial expansion.[17]

The failure of the combined al-Saud/Wahhabi movement to establish a peninsula-wide territorial base permanently before the twentieth century was also a consequence of its conquest by other powers. Although it rapidly expanded during the second half of the eighteenth century, eventually controlling the Najd, it was subjugated to Ottoman influence, albeit in an indirect form, between 1818 and 1824, when Muhammad Ali conquered the region. The al-Saud family also lost control of the Najd between 1885 and 1901 to the al-Rashid of the Jabal Shammar, with its ruling members (including Ibn Saud) being forced to take refuge in Kuwait.[18]

Through intermarriage, the control of the Wahhabi movement also became integrated into the al-Saud family and its leaders often justified their claim to temporal rights because of their religious status as *imams* – in this respect justifying their constitutional position in purely Islamic terms.[19] However, after the Kingdom of Saudi Arabia was proclaimed in 1932, Ibn Saud was at pains to emphasize his secular rights:

> The Al Saud were therefore forced to validate their rule within Central Arabia by virtue of Wahhabi doctrine and to secure international recognition by emphasizing the historical rights of their family as Arab and secular rulers and not as Wahhabi Imams. It is notable that in all treaties with the Ottomans and the British, Abd al-Aziz insisted that one of the first provisions should be the recognition of his family's historical rights and his own right to choose a successor. Moreover, he was to claim that . . . the territories of Najd and the Badawin world have extended as far north as Aleppo and the river Orontes in north Syria, and included the whole country on the right bank of the Euphrates from there down to Basra on the Persian Gulf . . . and that these territories, having been formerly under Al Saud control, were now his by virtue of his hereditary rights.[20]

In fact, the modern Saudi state was forged by conquest between 1901 and 1925, when the Hijaz was finally occupied[21] and, although today it justifies its sovereign status in both religious and territorial terms, it is the territorial component that has come to be the dominant element.

Iraq

Iraq, on the other hand, is an unambiguously twentieth-century creation. Formed from the former Ottoman *wilayats* of Baghdad, Basrah and Mawsul, it was first a British mandate after April 1920, then a protected monarchy after August 1921 and eventually an independent state after admission to the League of Nations on 3 October 1932. Even then, many Iraqis considered that its sovereignty continued to be infringed by the restrictive terms of the 1930 treaty between Iraq and Britain, which gave the former Mandate power certain specific privileges for a 25-year term.

It was only after the treaty was renegotiated in 1947 and eventually replaced by a special agreement that these restrictions were finally removed. In part, this was made possible because of Britain's decision to join the Baghdad Pact in 1955. The Pact was seen in London as a suitable replacement to ensure those privileges that it wished to reserve.[22] Sovereignty in Iraq, then, has always been couched in terms of territorial sovereignty. This has been particularly demonstrated in its use of the concept of *uti possidetis juris* to justify its claim to Kuwait, despite the effective Ottoman abandonment of that claim in 1913, and the final severance of all Ottoman ties with its former non-Anatolian possessions (excluding Istanbul and Mawsul) with the conclusion of the treaties of Sèvres (1920) and Lausanne (1923).[23]

The origins of the Arab Gulf states

Amongst the Arab states of the Gulf region, perhaps only Oman could claim a substantially continuous sovereign political authority during the past two centuries over much of the territory it controls today. In fact, it was during the latter part of the eighteenth century that the characteristic political division grew up between the secular power of the sultan on the coast and the religious authority of an Ibadi imam in the tribal interior.[24] In short, Oman had, thereby, begun to create a similar political structure to that which existed in Saudi Arabia, except that religious and temporal authority did not coalesce until 1955 when the separate Imamate was suppressed.[25]

Although the future Arab states of the Gulf littoral did exist in embryo by the advent of the nineteenth century, they were in effect only coastal trading and pearling posts, forming part of a mercantile complex stretching from Basrah towards the Indian and East African coasts.[26] Their *mudharabah* (profit-sharing) trading system had been integrated into and dominated by Portuguese maritime trade in the sixteenth century. It was eventually suppressed by Britain after 1839.[27] It is only after this period that a process of expansion of territorial control around these trading centres begins to emerge that, under the pressure of Western demands for oil concession arrangements during the twentieth century, made the issue of territorial sovereignty acute.

The modern Gulf states actually began to develop just as Britain's commercial interest in the Gulf region expanded, in the wake of the assertion of its control over India. In part, of course, this reflected indigenous developments along the Gulf coastline, particularly as a result of tribal attempts to control local trade. However, as the nineteenth century developed, Britain's rôle in protecting these nascent states became ever more important. British influence was exerted by treaty and intermittent supervision from the local British Residency, founded in 1763 in Bushire and transferred to Bahrain in 1946. There were also permanent Political Agents in Muscat,

Bahrain and Kuwait during much of the twentieth-century and a local Residency Agent in Sharjah.[28] By the twentieth century, these few officials had acquired considerable power and were playing a major rôle in delineating sovereign authority amongst the Gulf shaikhdoms, not least because of the shaikhdoms' growing importance as potential sources of crude oil.

Along the northwestern Gulf littoral, the emergence of these small trading entities was closely linked to the new political pre-eminence of the Bani Khalid tribal federation by the eighteenth century. This forced some of the clans of its main rival tribal federation, the Anaizah, particularly the Amarat section, to the coast.[29] Kuwait emerged under the leadership of the al-Sabah branch of the Amarat in 1752 and began to threaten Basrah's commercial pre-eminence at the head of the Gulf after 1792. Bahrain had shortly preceded it as an independent major commercial centre, when the al-Khalifahs, also of the Amarat, moved there in 1783 from their outpost at Zubarah in Qatar. The al-Khalifahs had occupied Zubarah, on Qatar's northwestern coast, in 1766 after migrating there from Kuwait.[30]

Until their arrival, Bahrain had been occupied by the Portuguese (1522–1602) and Persia (1602–1783), with a short period of control by Muscat as well between 1718 and 1720 during the Ibadi expansion northwards up the Gulf after the defeat of the Portuguese at Hormuz.[31] At the same time, the Ibadi movement had seized control of Larak and Qeshm islands. Indeed, Muscat had become the dominant commercial centre at the mouth of the Gulf somewhat earlier as the result of the Ibadi struggle against Portuguese influence towards the end of the seventeenth century.[32] Its interests within the Gulf itself did not persist, as the real focus of its commercial activity turned back towards East Africa and India.

The basic coastal settlements that were to become the United Arab Emirates (UAE) in 1971 began to emerge with the growth of Qasimi power after 1777. During the nineteenth century, however, the Qawasim, based in Sharjah, began to lose control of the region as their sea power declined. They lost control of modern Abu Dhabi to their tribal rivals, the Bani Yas, shortly after the century opened. In fact, the Qawasim – Bani Yas rivalry was really a local reflection of the much wider Hinawi–Ghafiri factionalism which had broken out into open warfare inside Oman during the eighteenth century.

The Bani Yas itself split in 1833, allowing the creation of a separate entity that was to become Dubai. The remaining four modern emirates of Fujairah, Ras al-Khaimah, Ajman and Umm al-Qaiwain were carved out of Sharjah. Ajman and Umm al-Qaiwain were formed towards the end of the nineteenth century and, Fujairah and Ras al-Khaimah developed as distinct political entities in the first three decades of the twentieth century.[33]

The last state to begin its development in modern form was Qatar. There the al-Thani family rose to pre-eminence in the 1860s as the controllers of commerce and pearling in the eastern part of the peninsula, amongst the towns of Dawhah, Wakrah, Dha'ain and Khawr al-Mahadnadah.[34] It was only during the twentieth century that the al-Thani family were able to extend control over the whole of the Qatar peninsula. This was achieved only by astute manipulation of the family's relations with external powers – the Ottoman Empire after the Midhat Pasha expedition to assert Ottoman suzerainty from Mesopotamia in 1871 and, after 1931, Britain.

Social and political organization in the Gulf

The common factor in the development of all these political entities except Oman was the focus of political power around maritime trade and pearling. Each of them also depended on the abilities of the ruling group either to dominate local tribal structures or to come to terms with the tribes concerned, in order to ensure their own political survival. In Kuwait the original Utub settlers who arrived in 1716 – the al-Sabah, al-Khalifah and the al-Jalahimah clans – originally survived only on Bani Khalid sufferance until they were strong enough to establish a separate trading post in 1752.[35] In Qatar, the former al-Khalifah centre of Zubarah continued to be controlled by the rulers of Bahrain until the last quarter of the nineteenth century, while even as late as 1934 an official of the Anglo–Persian Oil Company reported that:

> Ibn Thani, other than the sixty-odd members of his own family, has no tribe which he can claim as his own in Qatar. There are a few scattered semi-nomads of the Naim tribe on the peninsula dating back to the time of Bini Muslim who were the rulers in Qatar before the Thani family. Ibn Thani depends for his fighting force on men drawn from the Bini Hajar and the Bini Murra, two of the three tribes pasturing along the border of Qatar. The third tribe is al-Manasir.
>
> Ibn Thani is definitely dependent on the goodwill of Ibn Saud and his Hassa Governor, Ibn Jalloui: for the safety of his lands from the raids of the Nejd tribes, especially from the Manasir.[36]

The situation in the southern part of the Gulf was similar. Although maritime activities were dominant concerns for the coastal settled populations who formed the majority, the populations of the hinterland, whether *hadar* (settled) or *badu* (nomadic within their own *dar* – nomadic pasture zone – and usually around 10 per cent of the total), also played a crucial rôle. Although local rulers controlled their urban coastal populations through a paternalistic system of absolute authority combined with consultation through a *majlis*, the nomadic tribes had to be cajoled into submission, often with large financial subsidies. Failure to maintain this system of tribal coalition would soon destabilize the political structure, as rivals to the ruler would then seek tribal support in their own right.[37]

This complex system of urban absolutism and rural coalition had little to do with any traditional Islamic constitutional system. It was simply based on the successful exploitation of the segmentary structures of local tribes and the patronage–clientage systems that were their urban variant. In this respect, political power depended on the exploitation of *'asabiya* – the concept of agnatic solidarity, which, according to Ibn Khaldun, provides the driving force for the assertion of political domination of tribal society. Yves Lacoste has argued that this also provides the basis for the creation of patronage–clientage systems as precursors of modern-style class-based societies.[38]

In the future Gulf states, however, ties between the rural hinterland and the coastal focus of political power were far more tenuous. Gulf rulers devoted much attention to avoiding the operation of the process of the circulation of tribal elites that Ibn Khaldun argued formed the underlying theme of political power in the Muslim world.[39] In this respect, the hinterland could have a crucial effect on the ability of a ruler to maintain his position:

> The foremost measure of a coastal ruler's strength and prestige was his ability to command the tribes of the interior; his rise or decline in coastal politics could usually be measured by his ability to enforce his authority over the tribal chieftains in the area he claimed as his territory. Conversely, the extent of a ruler's territory was governed by the extent to which the tribes roaming the area would support him in time of need.[40]

In fact, one of the few recognized assertions of sovereignty was a ruler's ability to collect taxes, known as *zakat*, from tribes whose *dira* ran across the territory he claimed to rule, in addition to the customs dues charged on coastal trade, particularly pearling. Another was the ruler's ability to protect these tribes if they were raided.[41] In effect, therefore, the sovereignty that Gulf rulers sought to assert was territorial sovereignty, even though it was expressed in communal terms (by the collection of *zakat*) because this did not involve any statement about the religious legitimation of the ruler's authority, merely an assertion of his power.

Elsewhere in the Islamic world, the conventional concepts of sovereignty operated by rulers who sought an explicit Islamic form of legitimation were communal in nature. Territorial control was not the crucial factor in the definition of sovereignty, popular consent and obedience were instead. Sovereign control in terms of Islamic constitutional law was related to the obedience accorded to a ruler by a population that recognized his religious orthodoxy. The obedience was granted on condition that the ruler preserved Islamic society in an appropriate state for the correct practice of Islam – in accordance with *sharia* law.[42]

The Gulf rulers' assumptions about the basis of their assertion of territorial sovereignty did not operate in a vacuum, however. All the small Gulf states also had continually to contest their territorial sovereignty against encroachment from the tribal confederations of larger states around them. Chief amongst these states were Iran and Saudi Arabia. Bahrain, for example, always had to be prepared to counter Persian claims to sovereignty over it, claims that were formally abandoned only in 1969–70. In the 1930s, Iran was still arguing over the control of Abu Musa and the Tunb islands with Sharjah and Ras al-Khaimah, to the irritation of the British Political Resident[43] – and eventually Iran annexed them in 1971, having forced a hastily arranged accommodation on Sharjah concerning Abu Musa only a day or so earlier. While Abu Musa continues to be jointly administered, the Tunbs remain firmly in Iranian hands.[44]

Kuwait had to confront Ottoman claims, which forced it on the one hand into an intermittent suzerainty arrangement after 1829 with the authorities in Basrah and on the other into temporary alliances with the Egyptian occupiers of the peninsula sent by Muhammad Ali. It also had to accept more formal – even if formalistic – Ottoman control between 1871 and 1899.[45] It also faced Saudi pressure in the mid-nineteenth century and again at the turn of the 1920s until finally a border was formally established with Ibn Saud's young Najdi state in December 1922 through the signature of the Uqair Protocol.[46] Thereafter, of course, there were continual tensions with Iraq to the north, which began to be addressed only by United Nations Security Council Resolution 687 in April 1991.[47]

Qatar and the emirates of the lower Gulf – on the so-called Trucial Coast – continually had to deal with growing Saudi and Wahhabi pressure on their hinterland tribes to pay *zakat* and thereby recognize Saudi sovereignty. Shaikh Abdullah al-Thani in Qatar actually paid an annual subsidy to the al-Sauds of 100,000 rupees up to 1935.[48] In the case of Abu Dhabi, this sort of pressure continued intermittently throughout the nineteenth century and was most notable in the period following the Second World War, particularly in the Buraimi oasis complex. In fact, in the oasis complex, Abu Dhabi had to contest control with both Saudi Arabia and supporters of the Ibadi Imam in Oman.[49]

The British rôle in the Gulf

In this complex picture of fluctuating territorial control and pragmatic assertion of sovereign rights, Britain's rôle was, first, to act as guarantor of the small Trucial shaikhdoms and states such as Kuwait, Bahrain and Qatar against external pressure. Later on, this rôle became more codified, as Britain began to involve itself directly with Gulf affairs, particularly over border definition, and eventually provided the military guarantees required to defend the delineated territorial sovereignty claimed by the states concerned. It was this latter process that was stimulated by British anxiety to capture control of Gulf oil.

The creation of protectorate status

British interest in the Gulf began in 1763 with the establishment of the Bushire Residency as a new commercial outpost of the East India Company.[50] It is notable that it was the British presence in India that first stimulated interest in the region. Indeed, as well as their interest in commercial possibilities there, the British authorities in India were also concerned over the threat to their communications with Britain from piracy in the Gulf. Interestingly enough, apart from a period in which responsibilities were in effect divided between the India Office and the Colonial Office between 1921 and 1933, it was British India that retained control of Gulf affairs until the end of the Raj in 1947, when responsibility passed to the Foreign and Commonwealth Office.

As a result of British anxiety over their seaborne communications, from 1798 onwards[51] a series of treaties were signed with the coastal rulers of the Gulf by which they agreed to abstain from piracy. In 1820, after a punitive expedition from Bombay, the Trucial shaikhdoms signed a General Treaty of Peace with the British authorities in India which protected British shipping from attack. In 1853, this was codified into the Perpetual Maritime Truce, whereby – as a result of British pressure – local rulers agreed to stop all maritime hostilities. It was a move that, indirectly, did much to cause the decline of the sea-based Qawasim strongholds of Sharjah, Ras al-Khaimah and Lingeh and the corresponding growth in the power of Abu Dhabi and Dubai.[52]

As the nineteenth century wore on, British interest in the shaikhdoms, and in Muscat, where Britain intervened in support of the Al Bu Said family in 1871,[53] became more acute. By the end of the century, there were considerable fears that the shaikhdoms might fall under Wahhabi as well as Ottoman influence. The result was the 1892 treaties, which bound the shaikhdoms to let Britain handle their foreign policies. Bahrain, having also signed an anti-piracy agreement in 1820, followed the Trucial shaikhdoms into protected status in 1892.

Qatar fell into line with the protected states to its south after 1868, when it first signed an anti-piracy agreement and agreed to allow Britain to intervene in any future dispute with Bahrain over control of the problematic locality of Zubarah.[54] Britain nonetheless accepted Ottoman suzerainty over Qatar until its formal offer of territorial guarantees in 1916. A British agent, however, was not appointed there until 1949.[55]

In the northern Gulf, as a result of British anxiety over German links with the Ottoman Empire and the possibility of the Berlin–Baghdad railway extending down to Kuwait, a similar treaty was signed with the Ruler of Kuwait, Shaikh Mubarak. There had been intermittent temporary agreements between Britain and Kuwait before, dating from the late 1820s, over British commercial interests there and over piracy. However, until 1899, Britain had conceded Ottoman sovereignty over the emirate. With the 1899 agreement, Kuwait had also in effect become a British protectorate and, by 1913, even the Ottoman Empire had virtually abandoned claims to suzerainty over it.[56] Technically, however, Kuwait had been defined in the Anglo–Ottoman settlement of Gulf questions as an independent *qadha* of the Ottoman Empire.

Oil concessions and sovereignty

Despite the formal treaty system, which, by the end of the First World War, had turned the Gulf into a region of exclusive British influence, the British authorities there took little interest in direct intervention in regional affairs as far as the Trucial shaikhdoms were concerned. This was not the case in the upper Gulf, however. There was acute concern over delimiting territorial control between Kuwait, the new state of Iraq and Saudi Arabia – in theory resolved by the Uqair Protocol in 1922 and by an Iraqi–Kuwaiti exchange of letters in the spring of 1923. Bahrain, too, was a focus of attention because of its island status and the strong British presence there. The British agent had to ensure that Bahrain renounced its residual claims on Zubarah on the Qatari mainland in a dispute that simmered on from 1937 until 1957. He also had to resist periodic Iranian pressure over its residual sovereign claims to Bahrain.

The Trucial shaikhdoms, however, were largely left to their own devices. In this respect of course, they were not true protectorates, even though British officials often had to adjudicate in squabbles between rulers or inter-tribal strife that threatened local stability. In foreign affairs, however, Britain maintained very close control, particularly in its protégés' dealings with the neighbouring states of Saudi Arabia, Iran and Iraq.

Even the question of direct airlinks between Britain and India did not involve any real change in the policy of *status quo* over domestic affairs. This development in communications within the Empire involved the creation of staging posts in the Gulf at Dubai and Sharjah, along with military posts at Abu Dhabi and Kalba (an urban settlement recognized by Britain as an independent settlement in 1937 but that was absorbed into Sharjah two decades later). As the Political Resident remarked when the air agreements were concluded: "There is only one test of a policy and that is its success or failure. Judged by this test our policy on the Trucial Coast . . . however hand-to-mouth and peculiar it may appear . . . emerges with flying colours."[57]

The crucial factor that altered this *status quo* approach was the issue of oil. The British Government had been aware of the potential problems that could be created by the search for oil even before the First World War. It began to apply pressure on all the Gulf states to sign new agreements with it to grant oil exploration concessions only to persons nominated by itself. In 1913, Kuwait signed such an agreement, followed by Bahrain in 1914 and by the Trucial shaikhdoms in 1922.[58] Qatar had made a similar commitment within the 1916 Anglo–Qatari agreement.[59]

Britain was not, however, very anxious to prosecute a rapid search for oil – partly, no doubt, because of British oil interests in Iran through the Anglo–Persian Oil Company (APOC) and, after the war, in the new mandate territory of Iraq through the Turkish (later Iraq) Petroleum Company (TPC). Furthermore, Foreign Office officials believed British interests to be guaranteed by the Red Line agreement (more correctly known as the Foreign Office agreement), an agreement drawn up in 1914 originally, whereby foreign oil companies agreed not to institute separate oil concessions within the Ottoman Empire except through the TPC, which was to act as a holding company for individual oil companies. In February 1928, the Red Line agreement was revived to include US companies interested in Middle East exploration.[60] As far as the Gulf states were concerned, Britain believed that the Red Line agreement applied to Kuwait and Bahrain. Indeed, oil prospecting by the US company, the Standard Oil Company of California (SOCAL), in Bahrain – where the first major Gulf oil strike was made in May 1932 – was permitted only once the Iraq Petroleum Company (IPC, the successor to TPC) had expressed its lack of disinterest.[61]

The consequent transformation of the Bahraini economy and the evidence of US interest in oil concessions in Saudi Arabia after 1933 spurred interest amongst other Gulf rulers as well. Shaikh Shakhbut of Abu Dhabi was the first, asking APOC to start prospecting in 1934. The following year Ras al-Khaimah followed suit and APOC – which changed its name to the Anglo–Iranian Oil Company (AIOC) – took up an option during 1935. In Abu Dhabi and Dubai, however, the British authorities ensured that the IPC took over concessions because they considered that the two states fell within the area covered by the Red Line agreement. Soon IPC was reconstituted for exploration along the Trucial Coast as Petroleum Concessions Ltd – a company that had no Iraqi directors, unlike IPC – and pressure for oil exploration really began.

There were two problems, however. First, US companies continued to try to persuade the Trucial States' rulers to accept their concession proposals, with their typically more generous terms – a move scotched by the Political Resident in 1937 when he warned the recalcitrant rulers that Britain would not approve concessions to any but British companies. Secondly, it rapidly became clear that the hinterlands of the Trucial shaikhdoms themselves were now of vital importance, as was political control over them. Inland tribes simply obstructed geological surveys, despite the grant of concessions, because of the weakness of central power. In addition, the actual territorial extent of the various states along the Trucial Coast and Qatar became of paramount importance. In February 1936, the India Office and the Foreign Office held an interdepartmental meeting over the issue. The Foreign Office, with the experience of territorial disputes between Oman (Muscat), Abu Dhabi and Saudi Arabia over the previous two years uppermost in their minds, argued that outstanding inter-emirate issues should be quickly resolved. The India Office resisted this approach, arguing that it would cause problems with the Trucial shaikhs.[62]

The delay proved to be a fatal mistake, for, although a review of territorial claims was made in 1937, the disputes between the various shaikhdoms were never resolved because the Second World War intervened. Only Shaikh Shakhbut of Abu Dhabi actually sought to delimit his territory with Dubai and only Dubai claimed at the end of the Second World War to have precise territorial limits. The result has been the confused and confusing fragmentation of the small emirates in the UAE today. Even in Qatar, the 1935 oil concession agreement provoked a dispute with Saudi Arabia over the future border that persisted for 30 years until the agreement of 1965, though it is fair to say that it was actually Britain and Saudi Arabia that disputed Qatar's southern boundaries. Qatar and Saudi Arabia had long maintained a tacit understanding on where their boundaries lay. Saudi Arabia refused to accept British arguments of the 1920s and early 1930s that Qatar's western boundaries had been in effect delimited with the conclusion of the Anglo–Ottoman Blue and Violet lines of 1913–14. Qatar and Saudi Arabia contested ownership of Jabal Naksh up until the Second World War, after which time the issue died down.

The one major dispute that has been settled is the Buraimi oasis dispute, which lasted for a good quarter-century until it was apparently resolved in 1974. However, by that time there had been regular disputes over the control of villages in the complex, culminating in a British military intervention in 1955. Soon afterwards, Britain imposed boundaries between the states involved. Britain continued to argue for the line it unilaterally imposed until the agreement between Saudi Arabia and Abu Dhabi in 1974.[63]

Conclusion

In general, the states of the western Gulf littoral entered into independence in 1971 (1961 for Kuwait) with territorial disputes still in being but with a sense of territorial sovereignty well developed. It is very unlikely that any of the rulers in the Gulf would subscribe today to the views of the Residency Agent after his review of boundary status in the summer of 1937:

> In his report, the Agent said that the rulers had admitted that they had no fixed frontiers with their neighbours, but that they had given him instead details of what they considered their *ihram* (sacred possession, and therefore inviolable). The only ruler who was absolutely sure of the extent of his territory was Sa'id of Dubai. Sultan of Sharjah, by contrast, was the only one who refused to state what territory he claimed.[64]

Territorial sovereignty has, instead, become the essential source of legitimacy for statehood in the Gulf. Perhaps, along with that, *'asabiya* has finally been solidified into a modern society that will, in time, demand the other attributes of modern states as well.

Notes

1. M. Akehurst, *A modern introduction to international law*, 6th edn, 203 (London: Unwin Hyman, 1987), 203
2. R. M. M. Wallace, *International law* (London: Sweet & Maxwell, 1986), 81.
3. Akehurst, *A modern introduction to international law*, 53.
4. *Ibid.*
5. A. Al-Azmeh, "Wahhabite polity", in *Arabia and the Gulf: from traditional society to the modern state*, I. R. Netton (ed.), 75–90 (London: Croom Helm, 1986).
6. A. K. S. Lambton, *State and government in medieval Islam: an introduction to the study of Islamic political theory: the jurists*, 13 (Oxford: Oxford University Press, 1981).
7. E. G. H. Joffé, "International law, conflict and stability in the Gulf and the Mediterranean", in *The state and instability in the south*, C. Thomas & P. Saravanamuttu (eds), 231 (London: Macmillan, 1989).
8. C. Moss-Helms, *The cohesion of Saudi Arabia*, 109–10 (London: Croom Helm, 1981).
9. A-H. A. Mawerdi 1982. *Les statuts gouvernementaux* (translated by E. Fagnan), 8 (Paris: Le Sycomore, 1982).
10. I. M. Lapidus, *A history of Islamic societies*, 287 (Cambridge: Cambridge University Press, 1988).
11. *Ibid*, 571.
12. Joffé, 154.
13. Imam R. Khomeini, *Islam and revolution: writings and declarations* (translated by H. Algar), 137 (London: Kegan Paul International, 1985).
14. *Ibid*, 56.
15. *Ibid*, 246–8.
16. Moss Helms, 76–77.
17. *Ibid*, 128.
18. *Ibid*, 77.
19. Joffé, 231–3.
20. Moss Helms, 110.
21. F. Al-Farsy, *Saudi Arabia: a case study in development*, 42 (???PLACE: KPI, 1986).
22. E. Penrose & E. F. Penrose, *Iraq, international relations and national Development*, 42–56, 123 (London: Benn, 1978).
23. R. N. Schofield, *Kuwait and Iraq: historical claims and territorial disputes* (London: Royal Institute for International Affairs, 1991).
24. K. H. Al-Naqeeb, *Society and state in the Gulf and the Arab peninsula*, 44 (London: Routledge, 1990).
25. B. Pridham, "Oman, change or continuity?", in *Arabia and the Gulf: from traditional society to a modern state*, I. R. Netton (ed.), 136 (London: Croom Helm, 1986).
26. Al-Naqeeb, 8.
27. *Ibid*, 28.
28. R. Said Zahlan, *The origins of the United Arab Emirates: a political and social history of the Trucial States*, 22–3 (London: Macmillan, 1978).
29. Lapidus, *A history of Islamic societies*, 677.

30. R. N. Schofield & G. Blake (eds). *Arabian boundaries, 1853–1957: volume 10, Bahrain Qatar* (Farnham Common, England: Archive Editions, 1988).

31. H. M. Al-Baharna, *The Arabian Gulf states: their legal and political status and their international problems*, 3rd edn, 167 (Beirut: Libraries du Liban, 1978).

32. Al-Naqeeb, 42–3.

33. Said Zahlan 1978, 8–16, 65–71.

34. A. F. Williamson, *Notes on Qatar*, 14 January 1934. *IOLR R/15/1/1627*.

35. Schofield 1991, 2.

36. A. F. Williamson, *Notes on Qatar*, 14 January 1934, IOLR *R/15/1/627*.

37. Said Zahlan 1978, 4–7.

38. Y. Lacoste, *Ibn Khaldoun: naissance de l'historie du tiers monde*, 156 (Paris: Maspero, 1966).

39. Lacoste, 129–31.

40. Said Zahlan 1978, 6.

41. *Ibid*.

42. Joffé, 232–4.

43. Said Zahlan 1978, 126.

44. For a resumé of the Iranian/Qasimi dispute over Abu Musa and the Tunbs, see Chapter 1.

45. Schofield 1991, 11–17.

46. *Ibid*, 60.

47. See Chapters 1, 5 and 6 for greater detail.

48. R. Said Zahlan, *The creation of Qatar*, 82 (London: Macmillan, 1979).

49. Said Zahlan 1978, 133.

50. *Ibid*, 23.

51. I. M. Lapidus, *A history of Islamic societies*, 678.

52. Said Zahlan 1978, xiii.

53. D. Hiro, *Inside the Middle East*, 10 (London: Routledge & Kegan Paul, 1982).

54. Said Zahlan 1979, 47.

55. *Ibid*, 60.

56. Schofield 1991, 17–22.

57. Said Zahlan 1978, 106.

58. *Ibid*, 26–27.

59. R. N. Schofield (ed.), *Arabian boundary disputes*, vol. 16, 9–16 (Farnham Common, England: Archive Editions, 1992).

60. Penrose & Penrose, 67–8.

61. Said Zahlan 1978, 109.

62. *Ibid*, 112–3.

63. A. Drysdale & G. Blake, *The Middle East and North Africa: a political geography*, 90 (Oxford: Oxford University Press, 1985).

64. Said Zahlan 1978, 148.

CHAPTER THREE

Britain's rôle in boundary drawing in Arabia: a synopsis[1]

JOHN C. WILKINSON

Introduction

Not one of the states of the Arabian peninsula recognized by the international community – Kuwait, Saudi Arabia, Bahrain, Qatar, the United Arab Emirates, Oman and Yemen – would be able to put up a watertight case at the International Court of Justice at The Hague to retain the territory it actually occupies. Even where boundary agreements have been made between neighbours, such agreement could be challenged by a third party. So, for example, although progress has been made in southeast Arabia (even since this chapter appeared in its original form as a conference paper in May 1991), as the result of Saudi Arabia and Oman ratifying their boundary agreement of March 1990 and of Oman and Yemen signing an agreement on their common boundary in October 1992,[2] this does not mean the tripartite frontier point with Saudi Arabia has been fixed. It would seem that Saudi Arabia maintains *vis-à-vis* former South Yemen a frontier line that it declared on 18 October 1955[3] in repudiation of the British unilateral declaration of August 1955, with the result that there is a major discrepancy in the alignment of the Saudi boundary on either side of the Yemen/Omani boundary (see Figs 1.1, 1.3). For Yemen to defend its *de facto* boundary in law, it would have to make recourse to the old British legal arguments and these, in turn, would query the validity of the Oman–Saudi agreement.

Indeed, the only proper and fully ratified international boundary agreement that has ever been demarcated on the ground of Arabia is the short section extending from the Red Sea to the Wadi Bana. An Anglo–Ottoman Convention of 1914 gave recognition to a boundary delimitation of 1903–5 between the Ottoman *wilayat* of Yemen and the "nine cantons" of British Aden. Within months of this boundary fulfilling the conditions for becoming inviolable, permanent and final it was breached, and when the First World War ended the Imam of the newly independent Yemen absolutely refused to recognize its legality: military action had to be taken to drive his government to behind a modified pre-war line. British force had also to be used to impose on Saudi Arabia a boundary with the Aden Protectorate (subsequently South Yemen), with the Sultanate of (Muscat and) Oman, where the putative independent Imamate government was also forcibly removed, and with Abu Dhabi (now part of the United Arab Emirates). A few years earlier the British had likewise used force to refute Saudi claims to islands that Britain considered belonged to Bahrain and Kuwait. Treaties following war laid down the boundaries between independent Saudi Arabia and (North) Yemen and also that between (South) Yemen and Oman.

So, disregarding the additional internal disputes between the seven constituent states of the United Arab Emirates, as too the on and offshore boundaries of the Arabian peninsula states with their regional neighbours (Iran, Iraq, Jordan, Israel and Egypt), we are today still left with 12 boundaries that, within living memory, have been the scene of acrimonious dispute or violence. Assuming the union of the two Yemens survives, that figure has now been reduced to 10 international boundaries within the peninsula itself. Some of these seem now to be of little concern; but that apparently quiescent situations can suddenly flare up is evidenced by the serious boundary incident of 30 September 1992, which led the Qataris to suspend the 1965 boundary agreement with Saudi Arabia. That agreement had seemed to settle their old dispute and the boundary legacy there appeared to be one of the least problematic in the region.[4]

The colonial legacy

There are two clear reasons for this general state of affairs. First, the region's boundaries have not fully met the precepts of international law; secondly, local concepts of territorial organization have been largely ignored in imposing or otherwise deciding boundaries. In many other areas of the world where external powers have imposed state boundaries, local concepts have been conclusively overridden by arrangements between the protecting powers; it is these boundaries that are generally recognized when the ex-protected states or colonies are accepted as fully-fledged, independent members of the "family of nations". In Arabia such "colonial" boundaries devolved only on Britain's former protégés with respect to each other (and even then independence saw some unresolved disputes, notably Qatar–Bahrain). With respect to Saudi Arabia, Yemen, Iran and Iraq, such arrangements are *res inter alios acta*, and do not affect their own claims unless they become a party to the agreement. For most of the history of defining territories in Arabia, Britain has been the sole arbiter of boundaries. The only other external international powers to challenge its rôle were the

Ottoman Empire and, marginally and ineffectually until the 1950s, Iran. After the First World War there was no counterbalancing "colonial" power in the peninsula and only one indigenous independent state – Yemen – was prepared to stand up to Britain. It was not until 1949 that Saudi Arabia obtained proper advice on its sovereignty rights from lawyers hired by the Arabian American Oil Company (ARAMCO) and formulated onshore and offshore territorial claims that exhibited the political will to challenge Britain's claims. Later, in the contemporary context of the Cold War and of increasingly strident Arab nationalism, Yemen, Saudi Arabia and the Imamate of Oman learnt to reformulate local concepts of sovereignty in terms of "effective occupancy". These new territorial claims were certainly exacerbated, but by no means created, by the potential oil fortunes that lay under the ground of the disputed land.

It was because the rulings applicable by an international body arbitrating the boundaries with Britain's protégés would generally have been unfavourable to its claimed sphere of territorial control that Britain decided in 1955 to resolve the situation by unilaterally declaring a frontier that it was claimed defined territory that incontestably belonged to its protégés. Britain then drove the Saudis back across the new lines, notably from Buraimi; it also supported the Sultan's suppression of the Imamate of Oman and repelled incursions by the Yemenis into Aden. Thus, when Britain withdrew from its formal protecting rôle in the region during the 10-year period from 1961 to 1971, it left a heritage of *de facto* boundaries. To some extent the countries concerned have tried to resolve this frontier heritage in recent years, but even when they appear to have reached understanding they are reluctant to finalize their agreements according to those international rules which that entitle them to consider that their arrangements constituted an inviolable and permanent feature of the political map.

Traditional concepts of territory

There is a third underlying reason for this unsatisfactory situation, namely the fact that the corpus of international law relevant to deciding sovereignty over sparsely populated territory was singularly ill suited to the needs of the region. All territorial boundaries are in some measure artificial, but the imposition onto Arabia of sovereignty concepts that basically started with feudal rule over areas of sedentary subsistence agriculture and ended up with European rules designed to partition Africa, inevitably cut across the very flows of migration, trade and political loyalty that permitted the local population to exist in its traditional way of life. Before oil revenues began to make a serious impact on the region after the Second World War (the first oil was not discovered in commercial quantities anywhere in the peninsula until 1932), land-based resources were generally so limited that survival depended on integrating the human and largely seasonal physical resources of mountain, desert, oasis and sea. Each zone had its own specialized way of life, but none provided self-sufficiency. So complex patterns of complementary migrations as well as exchanges of goods developed between them. Such local "circulation" was extended immeasurably since the peninsula as a whole was not economically self-supporting and was closely integrated into the seasonal monsoon circulation of the Indian Ocean system.

Mobility was the key to survival. So, even though individual groups and places might compete to concentrate those flows towards individual nodes or to extract local "protection costs", the fact that no centre was indispensable to the traditional "circulation" militated against centralized power and perpetuated the tribal ethos of the *hijra*, the tradition of upping stakes and forming a new community (whether religious, commercial or tribal) when government began to become "oppressive". True, certain regions played particularly important rôles in the system, but there was no irreplaceable site that predetermined where the local controlling centre would be located, as any detailed study of the history of the entrepôt and carrying trade, naval power and piracy in the area will show. Long established custom determined the "moral economy", the acceptable contribution made to rulers and tribes as payment for protection, passage and other services, but when local dynasts became too exacting they were either removed or avoided.

All this is not to say that indigenous territorial structure in Arabia did not exist, or that boundaries were unknown. On the contrary! Tribes had a strong sense of territorial rights. But their notion of exclusive territorial space (*dars/diras*) stemmed from their need to control access to the scarce grazing and water resources essential for nomadic pastoralism, and was primarily designed to prevent over-exploitation of natural and unimproved resources. Ownership notions in Arabian tribal societies were confined to mobile property and to nodes of intensive land use where inputs of labour and capital had created agricultural land, permanent wells, towns, etc. Such nodes of intensive settlement gave rise to usufructuary rights in the surrounding areas, both on the coast and in the desert. In these peripheries it was the use of resources that mattered and the interests of groups could overlap and indeed complement each other. The essential right that had to be preserved in territorial organization was mobility in space. Boundary drawing lay in the social system, that is, in who was recognized as a member of the group, while reciprocal relationships were defined in terms of family, clientship, neighbourliness and military alliance. The whole was rationalized in personal terms of descent, and the accompanying code of behaviours translated into terms of "honour and shame", stemming from *asl* (origin). Family and clan networks, perceived or real, therefore determined the relationships of trade, society and political power, not exclusive territorial units.

Political power could also certainly translate itself into terms of regional sovereignty. Resource-rich areas in the traditional geographic cores of Greater Bahrain, Greater Yemen and Greater Oman offered opportunities for a degree of social stratification and the development of a quasi-permanent central government system. The fact that in such areas "circulation" patterns were relatively highly internalized also helped reinforce a sense of regional identity. But the tribal ideology that prevailed in all areas of Arabia was geared to minimizing such centralization of power and wealth. So, even when rulers developed a hold over commercial or tribal empires, they were never able to transform their society into the hierarchically organized social, urban and administrative structure that characterizes full, permanent statehood. Arabia remained at the two-tiered "chiefdom" level in state and class formation.

Only the universal claim to act as an Islamic ruler could override the political units of the shaikh and amir (shaikhdoms, emirates). The Wahhabi-al-Saud state was the most aggressive manifestation of the Islamic tribal state and recognized no compromise with others, Muslim or otherwise. In practice the al-Saud rulers might be forced into accepting some limits to their expansion, but the fact that this could only be at the cost of deviation from the state's constitution meant that tension developed automatically between foreign and domestic policy. When Ibn Saud was obliged to accept his frontier in the north with the Hashimite rulers of Iraq and Jordan he had no alternative but to suppress those very Ikhwan tribesmen who had originally conquered the Hashimite homeland in the Hijaz. One result of this was that, even after Ibn Saud accepted the legal constraints of the "family of nations", he had no inherent notion of what the limits of his state should be. It ought to be that of his forebears and he certainly believed that it should at least incorporate the nomadic tribes inhabiting the hinterlands of the British protégés on the coast. In the Ibadi form of Islam, which had been established in Oman since the eighth century, the Imam could recognize no other and simply signed himself as *Imam al-Muslimin* (Imam of the Muslims, that is, the true believers) and the Zaidi Imam of Yemen had similar pretensions to universality. The first goal of the Ibadi Imamate was to throw off the corrupt regime of the Sultan of Muscat in the core of the country and then to bring the local shaikhs of the peripheries of Greater Oman under proper rule. The Zaidi Imam of Yemen similarly sought to reunite Greater Yemen under his sway, and an immediate goal was the southern province, that is to say the Aden Protectorate. By definition, therefore, the system of government in the territories that Britain upheld was considered as illegitimate in all three indigenous forms of Arabian Islam: not just because the rulers had compromised with "Christians", but because their governments were either increasingly oppressive of their own people or could lay no claim to legitimacy above the level of the tribal order (as in the case of the shaikhdoms of the western Gulf littoral). The Islamic state order was there-

98

fore fundamentally in conflict with British rule in Arabia, and, although in Oman and Yemen, unlike the case of the Wahhabi state, the Imamates could constitutionally recognize some constraints on their sovereignty, those concessions never extended to permanently limiting their territories. So, the 1920 Treaty of Sib that came to regulate relations between the Imam and Sultan in Oman was no more than an accommodation and laid down no boundaries, while the Imam of Yemen absolutely refused to recognize any *de jure* boundary between his state and Aden and simply accepted a *status quo* under the provisional Anglo–Yemeni Treaty of San'a (1934). Meanwhile Ibn Saud never fully abandoned his ancestral claims. The only boundaries with his peninsular neighbours he reluctantly agreed were those that separated his territory on the mainland from Kuwait as defined by the Uqair Protocol (1922) and, implicitly (through his recognition of the territorial independence of Bahrain), some sort of boundary between the Hasa coast and the island state.

Legitimacy of government and historic tradition lay at the core of frontier problems in Arabia. At first sight these may seem to be about oil. Oil was never of any import in western Arabia and scarcely, if at all, entered the frontier dispute with the Imam of Yemen. Interest in eastern Arabia was really aroused only by the discovery of oil in Bahrain in 1932 and it was only then that Britain adopted the Iraq Petroleum Company (IPC) as the sole candidate for concessions in the territories of its protégés. Until after the Second World War the interest of this international conglomerate in Arabia remained essentially pre-emptive. IPC was determined that Standard Oil of California (SOCAL), which held Bahrain and had recently obtained a concession from Ibn Saud, should not get any more. Qatar became the first focal point of competitive interest and to this extent it is true to say that the frontier problem with Ibn Saud really surfaced only when the British Government decided that IPC should get the concession there. In reality that simply brought to the boil a potential dispute that had been quietly heating up over a number of years, namely the limit of Ibn Saud's and the British sphere of influence. In the time of the Ottoman Empire that problem had been more or less solved just before the First World War with the conclusion of two conventions that laid down the limit of Ottoman spheres of influence in Yemen and along the coast of eastern Arabia. These two areas were joined by two lines drawn straight across the map to meet in the Empty Quarter (Rub al-Khali), the Blue and Violet lines. After the Ottoman Empire disappeared and the Imam of Yemen and Ibn Saud emerged as independent local authorities capable of effecting some control over the tribes of Arabia's interior, the problem for the British became how to stop them from expanding into their own sphere, which lay to the east and south of the Anglo–Ottoman lines. The answer was not to draw boundaries around the territory of the protégés, for they were coastal rulers and generally controlled little hinterland, but to delimit the territory of these "new" states. So it was decreed that Yemen and Saudi Arabia were successor states to the Ottoman Empire in this part of the world and that the boundaries of the pre-war conventions devolved on them. Thus came into existence the British legal case, which was adhered to right to the bitter end.

The British legal argument

Its starting point is the Blue line, which was laid down in Article 11 of the Anglo–Ottoman Convention of 29 July 1913 to run from the island of Zakhnuniyah due south to the Rub al-Khali. This line defined the southern boundary of the Ottoman *sanjaq* of Najd, separating it from the peninsula of Qatar. Qatar, the article further stipulated, was to remain under the rule of the al-Thani shaikh and Britain was to ensure that the Shaikh of Bahrain did not interfere in the affairs of that autonomous country. This 1913 convention was unratified, but the Blue line was referred to in the ratified 1914 Anglo–Ottoman Convention which, after confirming the agreements reached in 1905 and earlier concerning the boundary between the Ottoman *wilayat* of Yemen and the "nine cantons" of the Aden Protectorate, then went on to say in Article 3 that from the last surveyed point in the Wadi Bana the boundary of Ottoman territories would follow a straight line (marked in violet on the accompanying map), northeastwards until it intersected the Blue line in the Rub al-Khali at 20°N (Fig. 1.1). According to the British legal argument this article "had a larger scope than Article 11 of the 1913 Convention, since it dealt with the limits of Turkish territory across the whole breadth of the peninsula, from the frontier of the Aden Protectorate to the shores of the Persian Gulf".[5]

With the disappearance of the Ottoman Empire after the First World War, the British view that the boundary line laid down in the ratified 1914 Anglo–Ottoman Convention devolved on the now independent Imam Yahya was soon made abundantly clear to him. He absolutely refused to accept it, but the line was more or less imposed on him as part of the *status quo* to which he agreed under the terms of the provisional 1934 Anglo–Yemeni Treaty of San'a. The Blue line argument, however, was sprung on Ibn Saud only in 1934. This was in spite of: the (Darin) treaty he signed with Britain in 1915 in which it was laid down that the common boundaries with Britain's protégés would be settled later; the fact that the 1913 Anglo–Ottoman Convention was not raised with respect to either Kuwait or Qatar when signing the Uqair Protocols in 1922; and that in 1927 the British produced neither the 1913 nor the 1914 conventions when Ibn Saud asked for all treaties relevant to his undertaking to maintain friendly relations with the protégés under the new definitive Treaty of Jiddah he was just about to sign with Britain.[6] His total rejection of the Blue line brought the frontier issue into the open so that after some initial negotiations his government produced a frontier line that represented the maximum concession he was prepared to make in order to settle the dispute. This was rejected by Britain, which now itself offered a major concession from the Blue and Violet lines. The two 1935 territorial claims (sometimes referred to respectively as the Saudi 1935 or Hamzah line, and the Ryan or Riyadh line) covered the whole frontier from the tripartite junction with Yemen (Raiyan area) round to Qatar. Subsequent negotiations in effect reached deadlock by 1937, with both sides resting on their respective lines.

Saudi transgressions of the British Riyadh line in 1949 led to the so-called Stobart incident and the reopening of negotiations. It now became clear that Saudi Arabia was extending its territorial claims and, when pressed for clarification of its position, the kingdom responded on 14 October 1949 with a "statement of frontier" that opened an entirely new phase in the history of the dispute. It specified a boundary line for Abu Dhabi that made an enormous advance on the 1935 claim and argued that in the hinterland of this coastal borderland, that is, in Buraimi and Oman, the shaikhdoms and the lands of the Imam Muhammad bin Abdallah al-Khalili (Imam of Oman, 1920–54) were independent and therefore of no concern to the British or their protégé states: Saudi Arabia would settle the frontier directly with them. A specific statement about the southern frontier would follow in due course.

In the resulting exchange of views Britain maintained that the Buraimi oasis belonged in part to Abu Dhabi and in part to the Sultan of Muscat and Oman, who also held sovereignty over the adjoining Dhahirah region beyond. Furthermore, Britain did not recognize the independence of the Imam and claimed he was a subject of the Sultan under the terms of the 1920 Treaty of Sib. Negotiations were reopened but were suspended *sine die* after a conference held at Dammam early in 1952 showed the two sides to be as wide apart as ever. At this, Britain put forward a new statement of Abu Dhabi's frontier, but little else was discussed. A few weeks later, the Saudis occupied that part of the Buraimi oasis claimed by the Muscati Sultan and started "subverting" the tribes of the region, notably in the Dhahirah where the Imam of Oman also had little influence.

This started the so-called Buraimi crisis and it was not until July 1954 that agreement was reached to refer to arbitration the issue of the common frontier between Saudi Arabia and Abu Dhabi, plus the sovereignty of a small circle of territory enclosing the Buraimi oasis. Existing legal standpoints were refined with the exchange of Memorials in the summer of 1955. Britain stuck to its case concerning the legality of the boundaries introduced by the Anglo–Ottoman conventions (in the same way as it did in the co-existing and acrimonious frontier dispute with Yemen). The onus, it claimed, was therefore on Saudi Arabia to show how it had established rights since signing its 1915 treaty with Britain, at which date Ibn Saud exercised no sovereignty beyond the Blue line. Any prior "ancestral" rights were completely rejected: "Even under the international law of the 19th century, the forcible seizure and annexation of territory did not generate rights of sovereignty . . . Moreover, a sovereignty acquired by force was equally liable to be lost by force". This is what happened in 1869 when the Saudis were first evicted from Buraimi.[7] Furthermore, since the dispute could officially be held to have crystallized in 1935 (the critical date), no evidence aimed at improving the legal position of either Party was admissible after that year, *a fortiori* following the Saudi "violation" of the territory in 1952. For its part, Britain held that the evidence presented in its Memorial demonstrated that the Ruler of Abu Dhabi and the Sultan of Muscat and Oman had "maintained a continuous and peaceful display of sovereignty" since 1915 in the areas referred to arbitration, so "any attempts by the Sa'udi Rulers to assume, or to lay claim to, the sovereignty of the disputed areas were necessarily illegal and invalid".

The Saudi legal argument

The Saudi Arabian counter-argument basically built on Ibn Saud's legal position, which from the start had always been the simpler of the two: "no frontier lines have ever been agreed upon by the parties." Like the Imam of Yemen, he denied any authority of the Ottomans (and implicitly the British) to make agreements binding on the peoples of the area; the Anglo–Ottoman conventions had absolutely no relevance to him and history had moved on with the First World War. His was not a successor state to the Ottoman *sanjaq* of Najd and this was perfectly clear from both the spirit and the actual terms of the 1915 treaty, which recognized that his state existed in continuation with that of his forebears and stipulated that the respective frontiers of both his state and Britain's protégés were to be subsequently laid down. It was not until 1934 that anyone had said anything to him about the Blue and Violet lines and it was not on this basis that he and Sir Percy Cox had reached agreement about Kuwait in 1922 at Uqair. All he wanted was to be recognized as sovereign over the areas over which he exercised actual jurisdiction, and that was the tribal areas of the *badu* (nomads). His 1935 claim was an absolute minimum statement of his territory and he could have gone much further, by claiming not only all the *badu*, but also his ancestral rights which the British had recognized with the 1915 treaty. He had refrained from doing so in the interests of reaching settlement, but his 1935 statement was non-negotiable. The Imam of Yemen showed no such spirit of compromise. He had to be pushed back by force to recognize a *status quo*.

Ibn Saud never moved an inch from this line between 1935 and 1949. But by the end of the Second World War circumstances had again changed.

Now his arguments that the loyalty of the tribesmen inhabiting the disputed areas was to him and that it was his government that exercised traditional jurisdiction were reinforced by the fact that many tribesmen were conspicuously being drawn increasingly into the Saudi orbit, thanks to the inducements oil wealth offered. As the Saudi Memorial[8] explained:

The Stobart incident made it clear that the wartime lull was over with respect to boundary matters. Nearly a dozen years had elapsed since they had last received the serious attention of the two Governments, and new negotiations were clearly called for . . . The considered position of Saudi Arabia was presented . . . on 14 October 1949 . . . In formulating these lines, Saudi Arabia took up its position once again on what it considered to be its full legal rights . . . In the negotiations of 1934–1938 it had agreed to lay these rights aside temporarily, and had gone far in discussing a compromise solution on which agreement might be possible. Its overtures went not merely unheeded; they were rejected by the other side, which argued its own version of a suitable line. There can be no doubt that the breakdown of the discussions in which it was offered, and with the passing of the special circumstances in which it was set, the Saudi proposal of 1935 became defunct.

The 1949 Saudi statement of frontier had the effect of putting the British on the defensive, rather than the Saudis, as had been the case before the war. What Britain now had to put forward on behalf of its protégé states to justify claims to an effective occupation of the disputed areas, the Saudis dismissed with some reason. The fact was that only the Imam exercised any central government authority in the interior of Oman and, since the British would not even produce the 1920 Treaty of Sib, which purportedly showed that he was a subject of the Sultan, how could the Saudis be expected to take that claim seriously? In so far as central government authority was exercised over the shaikhs of the border zone from near Ibri to the immediate hinterland of the coastal settlements of the Trucial shaikhdoms, this originated from the Saudi state, they claimed. Furthermore it was argued that, since the British had now raised the issue of Ibn Saud's ancestral rights, it could be shown that these had only temporarily lapsed since 1873 (cf. the British terminal date of 1869). The Saudi Memorial then tried to show how this relationship was renewed, pointing to various acts purporting to illustrate the desires of the people to reunite with Ibn Saud as soon as he was restored to power, and how authority was indeed exercised in the area by Ibn Jiluwi, his Governor in the Eastern Province of Saudi Arabia. To the fore in such evidence was the active collection of *zakat* tax from the local *badu* in the 1920s through to the early 1930s. Abu Dhabi's rights in the Buraimi oasis were dismissed, partly on the grounds that the shaikh of the Al Bu Falah ruling family had merely usurped Saudi rights during this temporary lapse of sovereignty in the area, and partly because the Al Bu

Falah were no more than a dynasty of petty squabbling shaikhs, continually assassinating each other and incapable of effective rule. Only British intransigence had prevented Saudi Arabia from fully exercising its rights. Thus, when negotiations broke down in 1952, Saudi Arabia saw no reason why it should not respond to the wishes of the people and establish an actual Saudi Government presence in Buraimi.

In the end, arbitration proceedings were aborted by the resignation of the British member on the tribunal on the grounds that proceedings were being improperly influenced by Saudi Arabia. The British Government declared that the arbitration had lapsed (Saudi Arabia considered it suspended) and military action was taken to remove the Saudis from Buraimi. A coup soon afterwards also temporarily removed the new Imam, Ghalib bin Ali al-Hina'i, from interior Oman. British forces ultimately had to be used to evict him finally and establish the rule of the Sultan over his "rebellious subjects", in both Oman and Dhufar. Whilst arbitration proceedings were still under way, Britain had already declared (4 August 1955) a boundary line enclosing land that was stated to be "indisputedly within the territories of the Sultan of Muscat and Oman or of the Aden Protectorate". It was the 1937 modified Riyadh line, embracing the Muscati Sultan's "no-claims" line.[9] So there remained only the need to decree the effective frontier for the area referred to arbitration and the modified Riyadh line was declared "without prejudice" to Abu Dhabi's 1952 claim. In the case of Yemen, the *de facto* frontier remained what had been laid down by the *status quo* agreement of the 1934 Anglo–Yemeni Treaty of San'a. This basically forced the Imam to accept virtually all of what Britain considered to be the *de jure* frontier (that is, that laid down in the ratified Anglo–Ottoman Convention of 1914 with its minor concession in the Baihan salient). These were the frontiers inherited by the ex-protégé states on achieving independence.

Most of this never need have happened if Britain had taken a realistic attitude at the start of negotiations with Ibn Saud in the mid-1930s. It speaks for itself that when Britain was considering what frontier to declare for Abu Dhabi at the time of the collapse of arbitration proceedings, the Foreign Office suggested it should be the very line Ibn Saud had put forward, 20 years earlier in 1935!

Fundamental issues

At the heart of this whole issue was law versus politics. The problem was essentially legal: how to negotiate sovereignty rights and draw boundaries in the desert according to the "norms" of contemporary international law. What was at issue, however, was the conflict between the "ancestral rights" of Britain (or rather, for much of the time, the India Office which administered the Gulf up until Indian independence in 1947) and those of the al-Saud. In the first half of the nineteenth century a balance between the authority of the Wahhabi–al-Saud state and Britain's maritime interests in the region was established and the cyclical fortunes of the Saudi–Wahhabi state were absorbed in flexible expressions of sovereignty. The collapse of the al-Saud in dynastic squabbling and the arrival of the Ottoman Empire claiming sovereignty along the Gulf littoral after 1871 complicated the issue. Just before the First World War, however, an understanding had been reached on respective spheres of influence in Arabia. In 1915, Ibn Saud's putative state emerged under the British aegis, but it was not until the Treaty of Jiddah in 1927 that he was sponsored as ruler of an independent sovereign state, a member of the "family of nations" and the theoretical equal of Britain in international law. No longer were the old arrangements sufficient. What Britain had in fact agreed with the Ottoman Empire had been boundaries defining their spheres of influence. But a "sphere of influence" had no status in international law and the area was either under sovereignty or it was *res nullius*, thereby open to whichever party first established "effective occupancy". So the old criteria governing the concepts of personal rule took on new significance when translated into the terminology of the internationally recognized sovereign state. How far could the fickle loyalties of tribes be equated with the desires of the people? To what extent were the collection of *zakat* and obedience to the call to *jihad* to be regarded as continuous displays of peaceful acts of sovereignty? Whatever the answer, it was a great deal more than the protégé states could offer as evidence to support their claims to sovereignty. The translation of tribal territory and loyalty into the feudal concepts underlying European notions of sovereignty also posed major problems. The territorial rights of nomadic tribes were rooted in the variable use of natural resources, so their flexible and often overlapping *dars/diras* were not a good basis for determining fixed and permanent boundaries for states incorporating land with oil potential. No feudalization without sedentarization![10]

But what other alternatives were there? As we have seen, the easy way out was for Britain to maintain that Saudi Arabia (and Yemen) inherited the boundaries of the Ottoman Empire in this part of the world. That argument in fact began to be dreamed up only when Britain decided not to establish formal Protectorates over the Gulf states (1927–8) and became adopted as policy only from about 1932; in 1922, at Muhammarah and Uqair, the British had taken every care when negotiating the Kuwaiti/Saudi/Iraqi frontiers to ensure that there was no question of any of these states employing successor state arguments. The Blue line thesis was largely based on slovenly research without proper legal advice, but by the time its limitations were realized Britain had committed itself and it had no alternative but to try and bluff Ibn Saud. So the British Government, largely at India Office instigation, resorted to a fiction that it knew perfectly well would not stand before an international tribunal. It simply asserted its legal position over its protégés, and used its power and prestige with Ibn Saud to try to impose an invalid interpretation of international law on the new Saudi state, in much the same way as it had done earlier with the Ottomans. The only real justification was that Ibn Saud's state was probably ephemeral and that any territorial concession would be permanent and detrimental to Britain's continuing position. Right through to the 1950s the British pinned their hope on the fact that when Ibn Saud died the problem would disappear, more or less with Saudi Arabia itself. Another such legal fiction was the one it had earlier created in Oman through deliberately introducing an ambiguity into the wording of the 1920 Sib agreement. When all this bluff was at last called by Ibn Saud's new American international lawyers, the British had no alternative but to resort to force to save their interests.

First and foremost in realizing that "effective occupation" was the law's key requirement for defining sovereignty were the concessionary oil companies. Until surprisingly late in the day, the Saudis were woefully ignorant about the places to which their king laid claim and or how to substantiate his case legally. At the same time, the British-protected coastal rulers had not even visited the hinterlands purportedly under their rule. On the British side, the Foreign Office huffed and puffed about Saudi expansionism, but it signally failed to prod the Shaikh of Abu Dhabi or the Sultan of Muscat into action to substantiate their territorial claims; rather it was the local officials of the IPC group who eventually gave some effect to the Sultan's claims to rule the Dhahirah. The driving force behind the post-war frontier situation was oil interests, but the issue remained, as ever, *amour propre*. Thus it was that a brash ARAMCO, born out of the Second World War, doped the Saudi chargers with a vision of reviving past glories to ride against the dying British imperial order, harnessed to the failing IPC hack, born out of the First World War. Neither side had a better morality. Few of the protégé shaikhs were of a calibre to rule or command the respect and loyalty of their tribesmen, whilst such influence as Saudi Arabia had in the disputed areas was a product of fear of the old Wahhabi regime and hope of reward from the corrupt new oil order. Yet international law abhors a vacuum. Tribesmen could not be independent and these areas had to belong to one side or another. So the race was run in blinkers, and the self-interest disguised in ever brighter colours of self-righteousness and self-delusion. The outcome was inevitably collision. Britain considered it had won the race by Saudi default and imposed a frontier; Saudi Arabia rejected this unilateral declaration and maintained that the frontier issue was merely postponed.

So it is impossible either not to be biased when writing a study on such politically sensitive issues, or not to be cynical with the benefit of hindsight. There is no right balance if the issues concerned are seen in the perspective of the time. In retrospect, it is difficult not to consider Britain's final effort to cling on in Arabia by force when it had honourably withdrawn from India as immoral as it was futile, but how does one weigh this against King Saud's corrupt attempts to buy a Saudi hegemony of Arabia, or the kind of regime that came to power in Aden once Britain adopted a realistic policy and vacated its position in 1967? Earlier, Britain had failed to treat Ibn Saud's honest offer for settlement with the consideration it had deserved and temporarily won its way by bullying; but then it should also be remembered that Ibn Saud's state was expected to be ephemeral while Britain had a permanent rôle to play in the region. If it surrendered territory to Ibn Saud, it was surrendering it not to a person but to a state.

To the end, the frontier problem remained about spheres of influence: but spheres of influence have no status in international law. International law, if not exactly an ass, was certainly not designed to solve the problem of drawing boundaries in the desert, and it also had a built-in bias that favoured Ibn Saud's interests, once he learned, with the help of the American lawyers, how to manipulate it. There is thus no absolute right and wrong that should decide frontiers in Arabia, merely a series of legal and moral problems. But it is a great pity Britain did not start from a realistic point of view when dealing with Ibn Saud back in 1934. Had it started honourably, as Sir Andrew Ryan advocated, and recognized in 1934 what it had acknowledged in solemn treaty in 1915 – that no boundaries had ever been drawn between Ibn Saud's state and its protégés – then maybe it would have taken Ibn Saud's 1935 line with the seriousness it deserved. Indeed, if it had obtained the opinion of its own lawyers before, rather than after, making its declaration to Saudi Arabia concerning the Anglo–Ottoman lines, it would probably have never used the Blue line. Even when it discovered that Ibn Saud was perfectly entitled to establish an effective occupation beyond this line, it clung to the bitter end to the fiction it had invented and so had no alternative but to impose by force the unilateral declaration of frontier it made in 1955. The result is that Arabia has *de facto*, not *de jure* boundaries (see Figs 1.1–1.3).

Notes

1. This paper is largely based on the introduction to J. C. Wilkinson, *Arabia's frontiers: the story of Britain's boundary drawing in the desert* (London: I. B. Tauris, 1991). Detailed references and elaborations of the themes discussed will be found in that work, and no attempt has been made to quote sources in this chapter.

2. The text of this agreement, which was announced from San'a in June 1992, was published in *Middle East Economic Survey*, 2 November 1992. From this it appears that the agreement was not actually signed until 1 October 1992. The text of the Oman–Saudi agreement is also given in the same publication. It is dated 21 March 1990 and was ratified in May 1991. The boundary agreed appears identical with the line unilaterally declared by the British Government in 1955.

3. Details of this line are given in R. N. Schofield's review of *Arabia's frontiers* in *Boundary Bulletin* **3** (January 1992), 75–7. The claim was articulated in a note of 18 October 1955 from the Saudi Foreign Ministry to the British Embassy in Jiddah, which appears in the file, *PRO FO 371/114651* at the Public Record Office, London. It appears on various official maps, which Schofield describes in his comments. The text of the most relevant paragraph of the Saudi statement of 18 October 1955 is quoted in the footnotes to Chapter 1 of this book. Furthermore, the claim would seem to be inconsistent with the (North) Yemen–Saudi agreement of 1934, for it appears to consider the Dahm as a Saudi tribe. It is also worth noting that the whole of this Saudi/Yemen boundary situation is further complicated by the fact that the 1934 Treaty of Taif, which regulated relations between the two countries, has to be renewed every 20 lunar years. It is possible that the actions taken by the Saudis to expel Yemenis during the Gulf crisis may be construed as contrary to the terms of that agreement and provide the opportunity for Yemen to repudiate the boundary which was more or less laid down by the victorious Ibn Saud when he took the Asir province (see M. N. Katz, "Yemeni unity and Saudi security", *Middle East Policy* **1** (1992), 117–35).

4. That bilateral agreement is further complicated by the fact that it disregarded Abu Dhabi's putative rights in the area. And it is worth noting that the boundary of Abu Dhabi (UAE) with Saudi Arabia still has an element of dispute in it centring on the location of the line towards the Qatar peninsula.

5. British Memorial of 1955, *Arbitration concerning Buraimi and the common frontier between Abu Dhabi and Saudi Arabia*, Part 10, section 38. This work is hereafter abbreviated BM, whilst its Saudi Arabian counterpart is abbreviated SM.

6. This treaty was a "treaty of friendship and good understanding" between what were now two equal parties in the eyes of international law.

7. BM, Part 9, section 18.

8. SM, Vol. 5, sections 55–7.

9. The modification was the line beyond which the Sultan agreed he had no territorial claims in 1937 when the British Government was looking for potential concessions in southeast Arabia. This concession, along with those also wrested from the Aden Government at that time, had never been offered to the Saudis.

   The Saudi counter to this unilateral declaration was issued on 18 October 1955 (see note 3). It followed the breakdown of the Buraimi arbitration, but preceded the eviction of the Saudis from Buraimi (26 October 1955). This declaration makes a statement about the southern frontier, which it will be remembered was still under investigation according to the 1949 statement, and also Oman. This line explains the boundary that has appeared on various official Saudi publications and also in H. H. Bindagji, *Jughrafiyyat al-Mamlika al-'Arabiya al-Sa'udiyya* (Riyadh: University of Riyadh, 1977), (and also apparently taken up in his *Atlas of Saudi Arabia* (Oxford: Oxford University Press, 1978).

10. Cf. E. Gellner in the introduction to the English translation of A. M. Khazanov, *Nomads and the outside world* (Cambridge: Cambridge University Press, 1983).

CHAPTER FOUR
Practical problems of boundary delimitation in Arabia: the case of the United Arab Emirates

JULIAN WALKER[1]

Introduction

I have mildly the same sort of feeling that I had when I faced the prospect of frontier settlement for the first time, with many of my questions about how to start and make progress unanswered. In the present circumstances I have decided to play safe and not to deal with the problems of straight-line frontiers, stretching between a series of co-ordinates, of the sort that straddle the Arabian peninsula, and which have produced many of their own difficulties, even if the task of delineating them may, at first sight, have been comparatively simple. Instead I intend to deal with the frontiers that I know best, the squiggly tribal frontiers that separate the shaikhdoms of what was the Trucial Coast and that has now become the United Arab Emirates, and the similar lines that divide the UAE from the Sultanate of Oman. These frontiers were settled, if you can call them settled, by a process of arbitration between the Emirates and of mediation between the Emirates and the Sultanate. The first line, that running southeast from the coast at Ras Hasian between Abu Dhabi and Dubai, was laid down by the British Political Agent in the Trucial States, John Wilton, soon after the end of the war between Abu Dhabi and Dubai in the late 1940s. But it caused Shaikh Shakhbut of Abu Dhabi so much indignation that he refused to have anything more to do with frontier arbitrations by the British.

However, the other rulers of the Trucial Coast, anxious to reduce friction among themselves and to encourage exploration by oil companies in the hopes that this would foreshadow the end of poverty, which had afflicted the area ever since the collapse of the pearl trade at the beginning of the 1930s, agreed with John Wilton's successor, Christopher Pirie-Gordon, to accept his arbitration on the boundaries between them, and undertook not to dispute his decisions. Christopher decided to work on the easiest frontier, that between Ras al-Khaimah and Umm al-Qaiwain, about which there was said to be no dispute. So one day early in 1955, accompanied by the Arab adviser to the Agency, he met the two rulers, each in their separate transport and accompanied by their bedouin retainers, at a point on the coast between their two capitals. The Ras al-Khaimah representatives asserted that the frontier started further to the west. But the Umm al-Qaiwain team appeared more authoritative and led the cavalcade to a prominent sand dune a little further east then started southwards. Christopher followed them in his Land Rover, bouncing from one indistinguishable sand dune to the next, followed by the Ras al-Khaimah contingent which gave every indication of being in unknown territory but who complained plaintively that they were plunging deep into the Ras al-Khaimah heartlands. Tempers rose between the two parties, and Christopher had to resort to his diplomatic skills to calm them. At the end of the day he returned to the Agency weary, gritty and hard tried, to the solace of several pink gins. The frontier over which there had apparently been no dispute had been revealed as a bone of contention by no means easy to settle. He had had enough. There was more important work to do in the office. Frontier settlement had best be left to his assistant, who happened to be myself.

Concepts

It was some time before I began to understand the basic difficulties behind frontier settlement in the Arabian peninsula. When I did, I realized that we were trying to impose the alien Western concepts of nation states, and of territorial sovereignty, in a region where these were not understood. Instead there were important families settled in coastal towns who had influence over the tribes wandering in the hinterland. What really mattered was the number of men a leader could call to his assistance in times of trouble. The barren desert sea had little value, except in that it might provide grazing for the ships of the desert, the camels, and the men that crossed it, and it was the latter who were important. The influence of each family in the coastal towns, and of each tribal group, would fluctuate with the reputation and competence of the man who led it and his ability to attract men to his support. This was especially significant when the ruling family, such as the Qawasim of Sharjah and Ras al Khaimah, were not shaikhs of the tribes they attempted to control, and had no blood links with them. At times the Ruler of Sharjah was unable to visit his oasis of Dhaid in the interior in the face of opposition from his Bani Qitab "subjects". Furthermore there were anomalies on the coast where the British, for political or other reasons, had failed to recognize a virtually independent family as the ruler of a state. Fujairah had to wait 50 years from the time of the Battle of Bithnah in 1902, when it won its independence from the Qawasim, until 1952 for British recognition. The Rulers of Jazirat al-Hamrah and Rams (Dhayah), whose forebears signed the original Truce of 1820, and the shaikhs of Hamriyah, never made it. The imposition of frontiers meant the rigidification of the traditional ebb and flow of influence between the families of the coast at a chance point in history. If one realized that, how much did one aim off against the current, and demand that the claims of the expanding power must be proven, while those of the contracting one should be taken as read?

Practical difficulties

But it was immediate practical problems that faced me when I started. There were no maps of the coast other than the nearly blank sheets produced by the surveyors of the Petroleum Development Trucial Coast Limited (PD[TC]L) oil company, naval charts, and a few compass traverses recorded by Wilfred Thesiger. I had to make my own maps, and started by climbing mountains, where these existed, to sketch the countryside around me. A useful book called *Hints for travellers,* published by the Royal Geographical Society, gave me clues about surveying, and I borrowed alidades, plane tables, range finders, clinometers and other instruments from the Directorate of Overseas Survey. In the end the need for speed overcame hopeless attempts towards perfection, and I relied on compass traverse and the milometer in the Land-Rover. Half way through, air photography came to my rescue. But the maps had to be drawn, and in primitive Dubai only the PD[TC]L accountant had paper large enough to sketch maps on. I cadged some sheets, pinned them on a beaverboard and set to work armed with a fountain pen. Later problems included the insertion of grids and the reconciliation of the PD[TC]L one with the Universal Transverse Mercator [UTM] grid. The final product was neither artistic or particularly accurate, but certainly better than working without any maps at all. There was a tendency for the maps near the coast to be dotted with innumerable names, which gave one the impression that one was looking at suburbia, while those of the Rub al-Khali were largely blank, and sometimes a feature held two names given by different tribes who seldom met. The most pressing difficulty was not the maps, but a requirement for speed and progress in a society that was largely oblivious to the passage of time, which was measured only by the hours of prayer. Even the day of the month might differ between neighbouring shaikhdoms after Ramadhan, and Arab hospitality lasting hours, if not days, was traditional. Of course there were no telephones.

There were other difficulties. In a world of raiding parties every stranger was suspect. Shots would often greet one's approach to a village. Only if one was patently no threat, walking ahead of one's Land Rover and obviously unarmed, or came in the company of friendly tribesmen, would the traditions of hospitality and curiosity prevail over fear. Often I was warned off. In some cases I came with the wrong companions and was detained and threatened. Once, when I sent my Awamir guides to fetch water at a Duru well, the Duru on the well, at feud with the Awamir, promised to come and cut all our throats. The need for speed dictated that our party was usually small, but a small party was easy prey to raiders. We went armed, since everyone was armed, but a rifle is an awkward companion in bed. So we avoided wells as camping spots and lit no bright fires at night. Further south, in the Buraimi oasis and beyond, there were land-mines on the beaten tracks, largely because of Saudi claims to the oasis, and their support for the rebellious Imam Ghalib and his brother Talib in the interior of Oman. We cadged armour plate from the oil company to protect our legs, but then the Trucial Oman Scouts, whose Land Rovers were not so well protected, wanted us to lead the way over tracks that out of discretion (or was it cowardice?), we would have preferred to avoid. Normally we travelled alone, but that meant that a breakdown could be serious, so we were loaded with spares and supplies. Other supplies, such as petrol, had to be dumped in the desert.

I have talked of Land Rovers as though they were the only form of trans-port. They were certainly the preferred one, for both comfort and speed. Even then one's bedouin guide might easily become car sick or be disori-ented by the speed of travel. And there were many places, especially in the mountains, where Land Rovers could not go. Then one could choose a camel. But have you tried making notes perched, without reins and stirrups, on a camel, where conversation with one's guide was normally conducted in a series of shouts? A donkey was far less prestigious, but a good deal more comfortable. In places where donkeys could not go, walking, or climb-ing, was the only alternative. Otherwise, if one was lucky enough to be by the sea, a launch would provide a place where one could be comparatively clean, comfortable and have a base for one's supplies. However much we tried to hurry in the cooler months, the heat of the summer overtook us, making all travelling more difficult. When subsequently I went out to the Gulf from the Foreign Office for winter periods of frontier settlement there would be impatient signals emanating from London telling officials on the coast to ask, if they saw me, when I planned to return to my proper (seri-ous) work.

Bureaucratic and other obstacles

One problem faced over frontier settlement was that posed by the British official who believed that if a frontier was causing no problem it should be left well alone, at least while he had responsibility for the area. The last thing to be done was to create work and friction, and sleeping dogs should be left to lie. Of course, if there was trouble then one had to do one's best to damp it down, or even settle the frontier. The difficulty was that, with trouble, tempers flared and settlement became all the more difficult. Very often the British at home failed to understand the problems involved. In the end I found it best to provide settlements, if I could, that looked good on a map. A 15-mile frontier in barren desert looked far more impressive than 2 miles in valuable rugged mountain territory, which was less likely to contain an oilfield, and the labour taken to achieve its settlement might be a fraction of that needed in the mountain area, however much more important the latter might be to the locals. On the Arab side there was a similar desire not to stir up difficulties, expressed normally by statements that the frontier was known to all, and not disputed since both neighbours were so friendly to each other that they treated each other's capitals and houses as their own. The tendency for neighbours to be at odds with one another and to seek support from families two steps away was blandly disregarded. When one did get down to brass tacks, they were most uncomfortable. Then one discovered that the "known undisputed frontier" lay miles inside territory that the neighbour had no doubt was his own. To approach a settlement the arbitrator, or mediator, had to spend hours trying to prove that "just claims" were wildly exaggerated and unreasonable. Once again he became the unwanted visitor, this time attempting to convince the rulers that they had no title to land that they had long considered indisputably theirs, and apparently using dubious arguments to deprive them of their just rights.

Methods

Evidence

To be able to argue with any hope of convincing reluctant rulers, one had to have evidence of all types. There was the history of the disputed area, to be gleaned from the files held by the Political Agency in Dubai and the Political Residency in Bahrain, together with the invaluable Lorimer's *Gazetteer*,[2] which listed the names of villages and settlements that had been largely forgotten since the time it had been printed. There were local historians on the coast who had details to contribute, and there were elderly *badu* whose memories of incidents might be as clear as if they had happened yesterday. That was one of their troubles, as their impressions of the passage of time could be wildly misleading. Everything in the past, whether 50 years before or a few weeks earlier, was often stated to have happened *ams* – yesterday. One then had to dig into their memory for other contemporary events, or personalities who had been involved or alive at the same time, which might help one to date the evidence. Every bit of evidence of acts implying suzerainty or sovereignty could be helpful. Who had sent out a party to pursue the killers of an itinerant tailor who had been murdered at a certain spot, or to recover camels that had been stolen from a disputed area? In contemporary times, who organized *sakham*, the cutting of wood in certain areas for the production of charcoal for sale? Who collected *zakat* – officially a 10% tithe for Islamic charity levied on crops and livestock, but in local practice one of the rulers' traditional sources of income? Although *zakat* on livestock could be taken from your tribesmen on territory to which you had no claim, that on palms and other crops was a significant indication of the control of territory. In desert areas it was useful to know who had cemented desert wells, and, in agricultural areas, who maintained the water channels and taxed the farmers for the provision of irrigation water.

There was some uncertainty about when property was purely private and about when its proprietor had begun to practice some of the attributes of sovereignty. The Ruler of Ajman had gradually converted the ownership of the estates at Manamah, which his grandfather had inherited, into overlordship of the small surrounding area. In the mountains, where there was valuable wood and water, evidence of control over territory was easier to come by than in the desert. On rare occasions villagers in the mountains could even point to a well or a pile of stones that marked the dividing line between them, and might have marked the front line in past skirmishes. Naturally the allegiance of the tribesmen was important, since it affected the ability of a ruler to enter the territories to which he laid claim. But in some cases the tribesmen would fight for one ruler and pay taxes to another. In such cases, as occurred between the Rulers of Ras al-Khaimah and Fujairah in the mountains between them, one could only divide rights; and where the Ruler of Ajman and the Shaikh of the Bani Kaab both had strong titles – as in the Wadi Hadf – it was necessary to create a neutral zone. But the allegiance of the tribes was not necessarily straightforward. There were split tribes. For instance, some sections of the Sharjah Bani Qitab had given their allegiance to Abu Dhabi during the Abu Dhabi – Dubai war. And several tribes did not acknowledge the overlord that the British considered to be their suzerain. The Bani Kaab, Al Bu Shamis and the Duru all considered themselves to be independent of the Sultan of Muscat and Oman. If they were independent, they could claim payments from the foreigners, especially oil men, who wanted access to their territories.

Tactics

Luckily many of the problems connected with the delineation of frontiers could be minimized. Above all, as one was bound to stir up trouble and acquisitiveness, it was important to keep the temperature down. The arrival of an oil company prospecting team excited outrageous claims and aroused hopes of instant wealth. So it was far better if work could be completed

114

before the appearance of such a team. It was wise to avoid taking the disputants to see the area they claimed, as this excited possessive instincts. In any case, it was often easier to explain the situation to them through the use of maps. To have two claimants meeting on disputed territory risked argument and passion and was certainly not wise. In fact it was better that rivals should not meet to discuss the frontier between them at all. A go-between could dampen down friction and transmit compliments and understandings rather than suspicion and take the blame himself for any differences of opinion. It was vital to get evidence from witnesses, but these would be fearful that anything they said would anger the ruler it disadvantaged and result in his wrath being wreaked upon them. The coast was still a world where, as in medieval times, the villager was largely at the mercy of the barons. Therefore one had to gain the trust of the witnesses and assure them that sources would remain confidential to save them from suffering as a result of their honesty and frankness. Even though the evidence was disguised, one had to persuade the rulers that one was being fair and impartial. It would be disastrous to attempt to outsmart them in a field where they might expect trickery, at which they were far more adept than the westerner. At the same time, when the rulers attempted trickery, bribery or unfair pressure, it was necessary to warn them off but not so openly as to involve their face and honour. The whole process involved hours of listening to claims, requests, allegations and complaints, searching for answers to questions put by the rulers and revising decisions in the light of all the evidence and indications. In the end persuasion might achieve reluctant assent, or exhaustion intervened, with the result that a disputant might accept, grudgingly, the decision painfully arrived at. If two disputing parties were equally dissatisfied there was a chance that the division was just. In some ways mediation was easier than arbitration, since an imposed, arbitrated decision might nurture resentment whether or not a ruler had undertaken, before the work had started, not to dispute the findings of the Political Agent. In mediation, the party to the dispute could easily refuse his consent if he was not really satisfied or prepared, at least for the time being, to honour the agreement he was being asked to subscribe to.

However, even when an agreement was achieved by mediation, it was wise not to impose Western standards and concepts too heavily. The Arab of the coast did not regard a written and signed scrap of paper with the same reverence as does the European, let alone the European lawyer. A written contract was understood to indicate the attitudes of the parties to it at the moment it was concluded, rather than as an undertaking fixed forever in time. The rigidity of the West could not easily encompass the flexibility of the East, where Allah, not man, disposes. On the other hand, a Western arbitrator or mediator must be wary of changing any decision that he has finally arrived at. Any modification to a frontier settlement opens up a "Pandora's box" of demands for further changes, and for the righting of wrongs newly perceived by each party to the dispute. Once the first decision has been overthrown, each subsequent decision has lesser force and is more easily exposed to assault and correction. And the decisiveness and resolution of the judges are also seen to be progressively weaker. Once again one is back to the incompatibility of the Western concept of territorial sovereignty bounded by fixed frontiers in an area where individual influence, and its fluctuations, are still of underlying importance.

In delimiting frontiers in that area of Arabia,[3] I believed that it was important that the drawing of those strange lines should itself alter the local way of life, and the position on the ground, as little as possible. The new frontier arrived at should try to be a recognition of an existing situation. The erection of state barriers in the face of long custom and bedouin migration could only disrupt, upset, and create further friction. Even the erection of markers on the ground introduces a new element. It also arouses avidity and disputes over the last few hundred feet of territory, where sufficient evidence for a fair decision is almost certainly lacking. Therefore, I avoided demarcation, if only because there was not enough time or energy to deal with the consequences. It seemed best to rely on maps and descriptions of the frontier, however uncertain these might be, and to use natural markers – stones, wells, tracks, mountains, dunes, trees, palm groves and wadis. But, although mountains are fixed, most of the other features are mutable; trees die and disappear, wells can silt up, and tracks and wadis and even dunes can shift. Memories of names and places fade, especially where, with an oil boom, open desert is gradually converted into the suburbia of expanding towns, so that the London solicitors argue over features that, in the past, not even the townsmen of the Trucial Coast would have considered as having any importance for their comparatively penurious and simple lives.

Notes

1. Julian Walker continues to grapple with outstanding territorial issues at the Foreign Office Research Department at the time this book goes to print. This chapter is a personal reflection on the question of delimitation in and between the shaikhdoms that today constitute the United Arab Emirates by the person who was responsible above anyone else for the contemporary territorial framework in these parts. For this reason and the more technical one that many of these events being discussed are still covered by strict confidentiality rules, no references or notes are included in this chapter.

2. J. G. Lorimer, *Gazetteer of the Persian Gulf, Oman and central Arabia*, vols 1 & 2 (Calcutta: Superintendent Government Printing, 1908, 1915).

3. Julian Walker's arrangement for territorial division in these parts with its subsequent modifications is shown in Figure 9.3. Also, the reader is referred to a paper entitled *"United Arab Emirates / Oman frontiers"* presented by the author of this chapter at the 1991 International Boundaries Research Unit conference (forthcoming in C. H. Schofield and R. N. Schofield (eds) *World boundaries: the Middle East and North Africa* (London: Routledge, 1993).

CHAPTER FIVE
Iraq's claim to sovereignty over Kuwait[1]

MAURICE MENDELSON & SUSAN HULTON

Introduction

Historical claims are often merely excuses for action taken to promote present objectives. So it may have been with President Saddam Husain's invasion of Kuwait in August 1990. However, it no doubt increases popular support if the leaders can say that they are fighting to regain part of the homeland. Moreover, the reactions – sometimes decisive – of third parties may very well be influenced by their perception of the legal merits of the dispute.

When Iraq purported to annex Kuwait six days after the invasion, part of the justification it proffered was that the emirate had encroached upon its territory during Iraq's war with Iran and that, in any case, the whole of Kuwait rightfully belonged to it. It was suggested in some quarters that the adjudication of these disputes might form part of a negotiated settlement. The launching of hostilities by the coalition forces in January 1991, under the authority of UN Security Council Resolution 678 of 29 November 1990, and the enforced withdrawal of Iraq removed the prospects of an adjudication of the latter's claims to sovereignty over the whole country, though it was obvious that at some stage the boundary would have to be demarcated, if not by agreement, then by arbitration or adjudication. In the end the United Nations was given the authority to demarcate the existing Iraq/Kuwait boundary as referred to in the 1963 "Agreed Minutes" between the two states, a task completed as far as the land boundary was concerned by the end of November 1992.

An examination of the background to and genesis of the Iraqi claims may nevertheless be of interest, even though, as we shall argue, Iraq's invasion of Kuwait would have been illegal even if its claims had been justified.

Though the official and other documentation we have seen is not entirely clear, there seem to have been five main legal issues between Iraq and Kuwait immediately prior to the invasion. They related to: Kuwait's right

117

to a separate existence; Iraq's claims to Warbah and Bubiyan islands; the exact course of the frontier; a dispute about oil extracted from the Kuwaiti side of the Rumailah oilfield, which straddles the boundary; and a dispute about Kuwait's oil-pricing policies.

This chapter, however, is confined to the disputes concerned with sovereignty. That is to say, we shall concentrate on the claims to dominion over the whole of Kuwait, or to sovereignty over Warbah and Bubiyan. These questions alone give rise to a multiplicity of issues of fact and of law. As we shall also show, prior to the 1990–1 Kuwait crisis, the boundary between the two states had been agreed with binding effect in general terms, though it had not been demarcated on the ground and certain points of detail remained unsettled. These detailed questions of demarcation raise rather different legal issues from those that we shall be considering with regard to sovereignty over the whole country or over the two islands, and for reasons of space we shall not go into the former at comparable length here.[2] Rather, we shall confine ourselves to a brief account of the history of the boundary, and an identification of what seemed during the spring of 1991 to be the main issues with regard to its delimitation.

We begin, then, with an account of the historical facts relating to the question of sovereignty over Kuwait, including the islands of Warbah and Bubiyan, touching only tangentially on the boundary. This historical account is necessarily compressed. Moreover, it is admittedly based on incomplete evidence. Not all of the official documents have been published; many languish still in the comparative obscurity of the British Public Record Office and India Office archives, amongst other places – and, indeed, some are still not open to public inspection. It is also possible that there are relevant documents in these archives that we have not seen – though we believe that we have been able to consult the key files. Nor have we had recourse to the archives of other states, such as Turkey, or to materials in Arabic, or to private collections. It is not claimed, therefore, that this is a definitive account of the facts, though we think it unlikely that further research will throw a very different light on matters.[3]

This historical account is followed by a legal analysis of Iraq's claims, as set out in various official government documents and statements made before international bodies. We then give a summary account of the boundary between the two countries and of the issues arising in connection with its demarcation. Thereafter, we consider briefly the question whether, if Iraq did have valid territorial claims against Kuwait, this would have justified the use of force to vindicate them.[4] A final section summarizes the developments with respect to the boundary question from the spring of 1991 to the end of 1992.

The history of sovereignty over Kuwait

It seems that at the end of the seventeenth century three families of the Utub tribe, driven by a great drought in central Arabia, settled in Zubarah on the west coast of the Qatar peninsula. These three families were the al-Sabah, the al-Khalifah and the al-Jalahimah. Some 50 years later, after disputes with the Qatari tribes, they moved to Kuwait, in about 1716.[5] The dominant tribe there were the Bani Khalid, but within 50 years the three families, together with some other local tribes, managed to supplant them; and in about 1756 they designated Sabah ibn Jabir, of the al-Sabah, as chief. Ten years later the al-Khalifah emigrated back to Zubarah, to be followed by part of the al-Jalahimah. In due course they moved over to Bahrain, but that is another story. Meanwhile, the al-Sabah were left as the dominant family in Kuwait – a position that they continue to this day.

However, in the latter part of the nineteenth century the Ottoman Turks decided to strengthen and expand their control over Arabia – partly to compensate for their loss of the Balkans.[6] In 1871 Midhat Pasha, the Turkish governor of Baghdad, launched an expedition into the Hasa, in the interior of the Arabian peninsula, and the Shaikh of Kuwait, Shaikh Abdallah, gave him extensive assistance. For this he was rewarded with considerable date gardens in the region of the Shatt al-Arab, and was appointed as Ottoman *qaimmaqam* (sub-governor) of Kuwait, attached to the *wilayat* or province of Basrah.[7]

Though it seems that Ottoman control was fairly nominal, this is where the problems stem from. Before proceeding, it may be useful, therefore, to take a closer look at the nature of that control at the turn of the century (without, however, evaluating its legal significance at this stage). The most outwardly visible signs of Ottoman influence were three. In the first place, there was the acceptance by the shaikh of the title of *qaimmaqam*. According to one viewpoint, however – that of Stavrides, Legal Adviser to the British Embassy in Constantinople – this was little more than an honorary title and was accepted only because the shaikh held property in non-Kuwaiti Ottoman territory.[8] Secondly, the Ottoman flag was flown.[9] In so far as this was on Kuwaiti ships, this was nothing new, having been adopted as a flag of convenience at an earlier stage.[10] Thirdly, an Ottoman customs house was established at Kuwait; however, it was apparently not maintained for long.[11] It appears that, in 1900 and 1901, the population of Kuwait was included in Basrah province by the Ottoman authorities for census purposes.[12] On the other hand, it would appear that Kuwait was not treated as part of Basrah for currency purposes. The basis of the currency in Ottoman Iraq was the Turkish pound or *lirah*, which circulated in the form of Turkish gold coins; there was a prohibition against the use of foreign coins under which Indian coins were sometimes seized.[13] In Kuwait, however, Indian rupees and other coins were current tender,

119

although the basis of the currency was the Maria Theresa thaler or *riyal*.[14]

Returning to our narrative, in 1896 Mubarak al-Sabah murdered his reputedly pro-Ottoman brothers and took over the leadership. Since the Ottoman Empire would not at first recognize his independence and he was surrounded by enemies, he requested the protection of Britain, then the principal power in the Gulf. After much hesitation the latter finally agreed, and in January 1899 a secret agreement (known typically as the Anglo-Kuwaiti Secret Bond) was entered into, whereby Britain offered him its "good offices" – though not formally a protectorate – plus 15,000 rupees, in return for which he undertook to cede no territory and not to receive any foreign representative without British consent.[15] This did not, however, prevent the shaikh from making his submission in Basrah when the Ottoman authorities found out what he had done.[16] (The al-Sabah long suffered from the difficulty that they had valuable property in territory under Ottoman sovereignty.)

However, in 1901, Shaikh Mubarak was defeated in an attack upon Ibn Rashid, the Amir of Najd – an ally of the Ottomans. The latter threatened him and the British came to his aid with a show of force. This action prompted the Ottoman Government to enquire whether the British Government intended to establish a protectorate in Kuwait. The latter gave an assurance that it would not occupy Kuwait or establish a protectorate there, so long as the Ottoman Empire respected the *status quo*.[17] The British were less concerned about the safety of Mubarak than about the danger of a Russian or, still worse, German railway to Basrah and the Gulf. For much of the time it was thought that this would emerge at Kuwait.

Apart from the Shatt al-Arab, the only outlet to the Gulf was through the Khawr Zubair / Khawr Abdallah, the entrance to which was controlled by the islands of Warbah and Bubiyan (see Fig. 5.1).[18] In 1902, the establishment by the Ottoman Empire of military posts at Umm Qasr (on the western shores of the Khawr Zubair, at the head of the Khawr Abdallah) and on Bubiyan island evoked a protest from the Shaikh of Kuwait, who claimed sovereignty over both places. The British viewed the Ottoman action with concern, bringing as it did the shores of the mainland and of Bubiyan within the hands of a single power. In the event, however, they took no action to assert the shaikh's claims beyond informing the Ottoman Government that its action was regarded as constituting a disturbance of the *status quo*, and that the occupation could not be regarded as in any way prejudicing the shaikh's rights and authority over these territories.[19] The importance of securing the withdrawal of the Ottoman post from Bubiyan and of asserting the shaikh's claim to the island, and, if possible, also to Warbah, was stressed by an Interdepartmental Committee on the Baghdad railway terminus in October 1907.[20] Before executing this policy, the British authorities investigated the question of Kuwait's title to the islands in 1907-9.[21] They concluded that, although the investigations had gone far to-

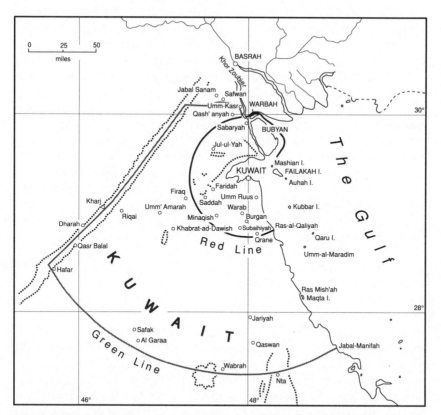

Figure 5.1 Red and Green lines introduced to define Kuwaiti territory after the Anglo–Ottoman Convention, 29 July 1913.

wards establishing its title to Bubiyan, no satisfactory evidence had been produced in support of its claims to Warbah, and so it was decided that it was inadvisable to raise the question of the shaikh's rights to either island.[22]

Late during the first decade of the twentieth century Shaikh Mubarak asserted himself against the Turks, refusing to register as an Ottoman subject, despite the fact that this precluded him from registering in his own name valuable private property in territory under Ottoman control.[23]

Between 1911 and 1913 the British and Ottoman Governments were engaged in protracted negotiations concerning the Baghdad railway question, during the course of which they decided also to define formally their respective spheres of influence in the Gulf area. The result was the Anglo–Turkish Convention of 29 July 1913[24] which dealt with, amongst other things, the status of Kuwait. The Ottoman Empire recognized the validity of the 1899 agreement and promised to refrain from interfering in the affairs of Kuwait and from any administrative act as well as any occupation or military act. The territory of Kuwait was defined and divided into two zones, in which the Shaikh of Kuwait was recognized as having varying degrees of authority. Within a semi-circle having a radius of approximately 40 miles from Kuwait town, marked as the red line on Figure 5.1, the "complete administrative autonomy" of the al-Sabah was acknowledged. The islands of Warbah and Bubiyan (as well as of Mashjan, Failakah, Awhah, Kubr, Qaru, Maqtah, and Umm al Maradim) were shown as being, and expressly stated to be, included within this zone. Within an outer zone, bounded by a green line, which was occupied by tribes recognized as being dependants of the Shaikh of Kuwait, he was to continue to collect their tithes, as in the past, and to exercise the administrative rights belonging to him in his capacity of *qaimmaqam* of the Ottoman Empire. The Ottoman Empire would not perform any administrative act there independently of the shaikh, and would not establish garrisons or undertake any military activity without prior understanding with Britain. The British, for their part, acknowledged that Kuwait was an autonomous *qadha* (or administrative subdistrict) of the Ottoman Empire, and undertook not to establish a formal protectorate so long as the *status quo* continued. They also accepted that the Ottoman Empire could appoint an agent in Kuwait.[25] The shaikh was to continue to hoist the Ottoman flag, as in the past, though he could add the word "Kuwait" to it. (We will return to consider the delimitation of the northern boundary of Kuwait as envisaged in this treaty.)

The outbreak of the First World War prevented the Anglo–Ottoman Convention from being ratified and the entry of the Ottoman Empire into the war in November 1914 against the Allied Powers produced a new situation. The Ruler of Kuwait revolted against the Ottoman Empire, throwing in his lot with the British who, in return for his attacking Umm Qasr, Safwan and Bubiyan, promised recognition as an independent principality under their protection[26] (though not technically establishing a protectorate since Britain did not at this stage take over Kuwait's international relations, but merely undertook to protect the shaikhdom from external attack).[27] Although this was formulated as a personal promise to Shaikh Mubarak, it was renewed to his two successors during the course of the war[28] (in the event, the territories concerned were taken by British forces very shortly after the commitment was made[29]). From the commencement of operations in the Shatt al-Arab region, the Shaikh of Kuwait ceased to fly the Ottoman flag, replacing it with one consisting of the word "Kuwait" in white lettering on a red background.[30]

Following the defeat of the Ottoman Empire and the signing of a formal armistice in October 1918, Mesopotamia (the Ottoman provinces of Baghdad, Mawsul and Basrah) held the status of enemy-occupied territory, having been occupied by the British. The latter thereupon gave consideration to defining the nature and boundaries of a new non-Ottoman

Mesopotamian state, and in December asked the Civil Commissioner in Baghdad to formulate a draft definition of the frontiers of Mesopotamia. In his reply, he observed that the boundary between the new state and Kuwait would have to be delimited with the consent of the Shaikh of Kuwait[31] (the British had, in the meantime, in internal discussions, confirmed that, as far as they were concerned, the status of Kuwait remained as set out in the declaration of 1914: that is, it continued to be recognized as an independent principality under British protection – a proposal to declare it a British protectorate having been rejected).[32]

It was decided by the Allied Supreme Council at the San Remo Conference of 25 April 1920 that Mesopotamia should be provisionally recognized as an independent state, subject to a League of Nations mandate administered by Great Britain until such time as it was ready to stand alone. The boundaries of Mesopotamia were to be determined by the Principal Allied Powers.[33] The terms of the peace agreed between the Allied Powers and Ottoman Turkey in the Treaty of Sèvres of 10 August 1920 incorporated this arrangement, clarifying that the frontiers of Mesopotamia – other than with Anatolian Turkey – were to be determined by the Principal Allied Powers.[34]

Owing to resistance by Turkish nationalists, this treaty was never ratified. The strength of nationalist sentiment also had ramifications for the mandate: in August 1921 a constitutional monarchy under the Hashimite dynasty was installed in the new state territory of Iraq, and the terms of the mandate were embodied in an Anglo–Iraqi Treaty of Alliance of 10 October 1922, but which was not ratified until 19 December 1924.[35] This arrangement was formally approved by the League of Nations Council on 27 September 1924.[36] By the 1923 Treaty of Lausanne, which eventually re-established the peace between Turkey and the Allied Powers, Turkey renounced "all rights and title whatsoever over or respecting the territories situated outside" its present borders, the future of such territories being settled or to be settled "by the parties concerned".[37] No provision was made in this treaty for the determination of the boundaries of Iraq, apart from its frontier with Turkey.[38]

The frontier between Kuwait and Najd was settled by the Uqair Protocol of 2 December 1922.[39] Shortly thereafter Britain decided that the boundaries between Iraq and Kuwait should also be settled. This was effected by an exchange of letters in April 1923 involving the British Political Agent in Kuwait, the British High Commissioner for Iraq and the Ruler of Kuwait. In a memorandum dated 19 April 1923 to the Political Agent, the High Commissioner for Iraq (Sir Percy Cox) stated that the Shaikh of Kuwait could be informed that his claim to the frontier and islands as therein set out was recognized "in so far as His Majesty's Government are concerned".[40] We will return to this agreement in connection with the frontier[41] but, for present purposes, it is relevant to note that Warbah and Bubiyan were among the islands included on the Kuwaiti side and also that the agreement constituted an implicit recognition of Kuwait's separate existence.[42]

The mandate for Iraq was terminated on 3 October 1932, Iraq having on the same date become an independent sovereign state and been admitted to membership of the League of Nations.[43] Meanwhile, at the instigation and through the intermediary of Britain, an agreement had been reached between Iraq and Kuwait to "reaffirm the existing frontier" between the two countries, by means of an exchange of letters in July and August 1932 between the Iraqi Prime Minister, Nuri al-Said, and the Ruler of Kuwait. By a letter dated 21 July 1932, the former suggested to the High Commissioner for Iraq that the time had come when it was "desirable to reaffirm the existing frontier", and asked him to take the necessary action to obtain the agreement of the "competent authority or authorities in Kuwait" to the description of the frontier as therein set out. This was done, with the Ruler of Kuwait agreeing, in his reply of 10 August 1932 to the Political Agent, to "reaffirm the existing frontier between Iraq and Koweit as described in the Iraq Prime Minister's letter".[44] Iraq subsequently challenged the validity of the 1923 and 1932 agreements on grounds to which we will return later.[45]

In 1938 Iraq formally claimed, for what appears to have been the first time, that, as a former part of the Ottoman *wilayat* of Basrah to which Iraq had succeeded, Kuwait ought to be incorporated within Iraq.[46] The British Foreign Office, to which this proposition was put by the Iraqi Foreign Minister at a meeting in October, firmly rejected it, refuting as inaccurate the premise on which it was based.[47] It appears not to have been persisted in; and indeed it had originally been put forward as an alternative negotiating position, Iraq's other expressed aim and perhaps its real goal having been to secure a slight modification of the boundary for the purpose of developing a port on the Khawr Abdallah and securing the approaches thereto. Thereafter, the Iraqis pressed for Warbah and Bubiyan to be ceded to them, but without success, Kuwait maintaining that demarcation of the land boundary should take precedence.[48] We will return to this below.

On 19 June 1961 the British agreements with Kuwait were brought to an end,[49] and the latter applied to join the United Nations as a fully independent state. Six days later the Iraqi leader, General Qasim, claimed sovereignty over the whole of Kuwait, contending that Ottoman sovereignty had not been lost before Iraq had succeeded to its rights over the province of Basrah.[50] Following reports that Iraqi troops were moving southwards towards the shaikhdom, British and Saudi troops went to Kuwait's defence, to be replaced shortly afterwards by an Arab League defence force. In the debates that took place in the United Nations Security Council in July of that year, the United Kingdom and Kuwait (admitted by invitation of the Security Council) disputed the Iraqi contention, asserting that Kuwait had, *de facto*, been an independent sovereign state for some time, and that the 1961 exchange of notes between the two countries simply constituted formal recognition of that fact.[51] Kuwait pointed to the fact that it had, by this time, been recognized by "most of the nations of the world", and had been admitted as a member of several international organizations.[52] Iraq itself had supported Kuwait's application for membership in the International Labour Organization in 1961, and had entered into discussions with Kuwait concerning the exchange of consular representatives. On 5 July 1961, the Arab League recognized Kuwait as an independent state and accepted it as a member.[53] Kuwait's application for membership in the United Nations was defeated later that year (the Soviet Union having cast a negative vote), but was approved two years later in 1963.[54]

Following the overthrow of General Qasim in February 1963 and his replacement by President Arif, relations between Iraq and Kuwait improved; and on 4 October an agreement was entered into by which Iraq "recognized the independence and complete sovereignty of the state of Kuwait with its boundaries as specified in the letter of the Prime Minister of Iraq dated 21.7.1932 and which was accepted by the Ruler of Kuwait in his letter dated 10.8.1932".[55] However, it became apparent that this recognition did not extend to acceptance of precise delimitation of the boundary, and disagreement and discussions between the two countries dragged on for years. With the development of the Iraqi port of Umm Qasr in the Khawr Zubair as an egress to the Gulf alternative to the Shatt al-Arab, the controlling position of Warbah and Bubiyan became more important to Iraq; and at the same time, the precise location of the boundary became a matter of great importance. Following the outbreak of the Iraq–Iran war, in which Kuwait leaned towards the former, relations improved; but, with the ending of that war in 1988, the problem came to the fore again. Iraq stepped up its complaints and claims, adding to them the complaints that Kuwait, by overproduction of oil, had deliberately undermined the Iraqi economy, that it had stolen vast amounts of oil from the southern section of the Rumailah oilfield, and also that it had, during the war, encroached upon Iraqi territory.

On 2 August 1990, Iraq invaded and overran Kuwait. Initially President Saddam Husain claimed that he had been invited in by internal Kuwaiti revolutionaries, and a "Provisional Free Kuwaiti Government" (PFKG) was proclaimed, though it was generally regarded as a sham. On 8 August, the day after the PFKG proclaimed Kuwait a republic, Iraq formally annexed the whole country, albeit allegedly at the request of the new government.[56] All foreign embassies in Kuwait were ordered to move to Baghdad, but many refused to comply.

Legal validity of Iraq's claim to sovereignty over Kuwait[57]

Apart from the dubious assertion that it had been invited into Kuwait, Iraq sought to justify the invasion and annexation of 1990 by reasserting its claim to sovereignty over the whole country, contending – as it had in 1961 – that

Kuwait had always formed an "integral part of Iraq" and had wrongfully been separated from it.[58] This claim was based on the argument that Kuwait had been part of the province of Basrah in the Ottoman Empire, to which Iraq had succeeded on its establishment in 1921, an argument that was elaborated upon by the Iraqi Foreign Minister, Mr Tariq Aziz, in a letter of 4 September 1990 to the foreign ministers of all countries.[59]

Before considering whether that was indeed the case, a word should perhaps be said about the standards to be applied. Although Iraq initially sought to characterize the events taking place in Kuwait as a purely internal matter,[60] this was roundly rejected by the United Nations Security Council, that has treated it from the outset as an inter-state dispute. The status of an entity which purports to be independent can be determined not solely, or even mainly, by the municipal law of the state claiming sovereignty over it, but only by public international law. And, in the ultimate analysis, the legal arguments relied on by Iraq itself are arguments about the application of international law. What, then, does this body of law, when applied to the facts, reveal?[61]

Succession

It was not entirely clear prior to 1914 whether or not the Ottoman Empire claimed sovereignty or suzerainty in respect of Kuwait and what the British understood by this. There are documents using both terms, as well as analogous ones.[62] One must bear in mind that the authors of these documents (as, for example, India Office officials) may not necessarily have had in mind the legal meaning of the terms they employed. But, in any case, based upon the facts, the relationship appears to have been more in the nature of suzerainty than sovereignty, certainly by 1913. According to Oppenheim–Lauterpacht, the former concept, as used on the international plane, lacks legal precision, but its general attributes are defined in the following terms:

> Suzerainty is by no means sovereignty. It is a kind of international guardianship, since the vassal state is either absolutely or mainly represented internationally by the suzerain state. . .[T]he vassal remains nevertheless a half-sovereign state on account of its internal independence.[63]

Certainly suzerainty appears to be a more suitable description of the relationship described in the Anglo–Turkish Convention of 1913.[64] That agreement – which Iraq relies upon as evidencing Ottoman sovereignty over Kuwait[65] – in fact reveals, when taken as a whole, the purely nominal nature of Ottoman control over the country at that time. The actual wording, it must be said, is a masterpiece of compromise. Kuwait was recognized as an "autonomous *qadha* of the Ottoman Empire". The history of negotiations up until this point reveals that this term was adopted specifically so as to avoid use of either the term "sovereignty", which was preferred by the British, or "suzerainty", favoured by the Ottoman Government.[66] Moreover, as we have seen, by the other provisions of the treaty, the Ottoman Empire effectively denied itself any rôle in the shaikh-dom: it recognized that, within the designated inner circle of Kuwaiti territory, the shaikh had "complete administrative autonomy"; and, in the outer circle, it undertook not to interfere either administratively or militarily without the consent of, respectively, the shaikh and the British. At the same time, the Ottoman Empire acknowledged the validity of the 1899 agreement by which Kuwait had acquired the status of a British quasi-protectorate. The argument might perhaps be made that the 1913 Convention did not describe an existing state of affairs, but was part of a bargain that did not come into effect since the Convention was never ratified. Such an argument could be to some extent, at least, countered by referring to a Secret Additional Protocol,[67] in which the Ottoman Government declared that orders had been given to the relevant authorities "at the time of signing" to ensure the withdrawal from Kuwait of civil, police and military personnel stationed there within the shortest possible time. In any case, the Convention certainly described the way in which things were developing and, if the First World War had not broken out, this kind of shadowy suzerainty would probably have been the most that the Ottoman Government could have hoped for.

As it happens, however, the link with the Ottoman Empire – whatever its nature – was severed in 1914 as the result of acts carried out by the Kuwaitis: the revolt by the al-Sabah against the Ottomans during that year, their attack on the latter, the British promise to make Kuwait a protectorate and the adoption by Kuwait of its own flag. These would all seem to constitute fairly clear evidence that it had established its independence from the Ottoman Empire. Moreover, at no time subsequent to this rebellion did Turkey claim sovereignty or suzerainty over Kuwait. On the contrary, Turkey renounced claims to both in the (unratified) Treaty of Sèvres and the Treaty of Lausanne.[68] If that is the case, then the question of Iraq's succession to sovereignty over Kuwait does not arise.

Furthermore, if for any reason that is wrong and the link between the Ottoman Empire and Kuwait did remain, there could have been a suc-cession only if what the Ottoman Empire had retained was territorial sovereignty over Kuwait. If the only bond with the Sublime Porte was – as seems to have been the case – one of suzerainty, that is not something that would have been inherited by Iraq.

It was the Republic of Turkey that was the continuation of the Ottoman Empire,[69] not Iraq. Iraq was a new state carved out of former Ottoman territory.[70] Turkey therefore retained all the rights and obligations of the Empire except in so far as they related directly to ceded territory or were, by treaty, transferred to that territory.[71] Conversely, Iraq would have inherited only such international rights and duties of the Empire as were, in Oppenheim–Lauterpacht's phrase, "locally connected" with the ceded territory, that is with its land, rivers, roads, railways and the like (e.g. a boundary treaty); and not rights and duties of a political nature (such as, for example, a treaty of alliance), which are regarded as being personal to the contracting states.[72]

The relationship of suzerainty between the Ottoman Empire and Kuwait would seem to fall into the latter category, the personal aspect of the relationship being paramount. In feudal law, from whence the term derived, it was used to describe the relation between the feudal lord and his vassal. On the international plane, as we have seen, it was employed to denote a relationship short of sovereignty, described variously as a kind of "international guardianship" or a relationship of dependency, since the vassal state was either wholly or mainly represented by the suzerain state.[73]

That being the case, Iraq could have succeeded (and did, in our submission, succeed) only to the borders of the *wilayat* of Basrah and the territory within those borders, but not to any relationship of suzerainty that the Ottoman Empire had over Kuwait, even if that relationship had been exercised administratively through the province of Basrah. The relationship – had it survived[74] – would have been taken over by the Turkish Republic.[75]

To sum up so far, a strong case can be made that, by the time Iraq was created as a territory under mandate, the link between the province of Basrah and its former dependency, Kuwait, had been broken, in which case the question of succession simply does not arise. Even if the tie – at most one of suzerainty – still subsisted at that stage, it seems that that relationship would have devolved not upon Iraq, but upon the Republic of Turkey.

If this is so, then Iraq's claim to sovereignty over the whole of Kuwait falls to the ground. So, too, does its claim to Warbah and Bubiyan, over which Kuwait either already possessed sovereignty before the outbreak of the 1914–18 war, or acquired it during that war.

The effect of recognition by Iraq

Even if the foregoing analysis were for some reason wrong, recognition by the competing claimant would cure any defects in title.[76] As we shall show,[77] there has also been recognition of Kuwait by third states, but, even if that were not so, recognition on the part of Iraq would be opposable to it and would defeat its claims. As we have seen, there was recognition of Kuwait's separate existence and of its title over the islands of Warbah and Bubiyan in the agreements of 1923, 1932 and 1963. Baghdad has objected, however, that, for various reasons, none of these agreements is binding on it. In the interests of completeness, these objections[78] – together with others that might be raised on Iraq's behalf – are considered *seriatim* below, even though, in our view, the 1963 agreement would in any case have cured any possible defects in the earlier agreements. The objections relate, put briefly, to breach of mandate, dependent status, and failure to comply with constitutional procedures.

Breach of mandate. Iraq has challenged the validity of the 1923 agreement on the ground, *inter alia*, that it was a breach of mandate. It argues that, in entering into that agreement on its behalf, the British High Commissioner for Iraq acted *ultra vires* by disposing of part of Iraqi territory to Kuwait "in a manner contravening the terms of the Mandate approved by the League of Nations in 1923 [*sic*], which prohibited the surrendering by the Mandatory Power of any territory belonging to the mandated state".[79] Consideration of the merits of this argument requires a closer look, in the first instance, at the terms of the mandate over Iraq.

The mandate over Iraq, which had initially been allocated to Britain by the Allied Supreme Council in April 1920, was no ordinary one. Because of the strength of nationalist sentiment, a mandate agreement in the usual form, between the League and the mandatory, was not drawn up. Instead, Britain concluded a Treaty of Alliance in 1922 with the King of Iraq, who had been installed as a constitutional monarch after the Cairo Conference during the previous year. Under this agreement, the British were to provide King Faisal with "advice and assistance" in the administration of the country, and had the right to give binding "advice" to him on "all important matters affecting the international and financial obligations and interests of His Britannic Majesty".[80] Article 8 specified that "No territory in Irak shall be ceded or leased or in any way placed under the control of any foreign Power". Although the term "mandate" does not appear in the Treaty, it was certainly treated as such and, on 27 September 1924, the Council of the League of Nations approved the treaty and supplementary British pledges as defining the mandatory's obligations[81] (in fact Wright suggests[82] that the form of these documents seems to comply more accurately with the requirements imposed by Article 22(4) of the Covenant of the League of Nations[83] than was the case with any other class A mandate).

There are several difficulties with the Iraqi argument that the 1923 exchange of letters violated the mandate. In the first place, it presupposes that Kuwait formed part of the mandated territory and, as we have seen,[84] this appears not to have been the case. That the Principal Allied Powers did not themselves seem to have had Kuwait in mind is demonstrated to some extent by the fact that they conferred the mandate in respect of "Mesopotamia". Geographically, this denoted the land between the Euphrates and the Tigris, comprising the Turkish provinces of Baghdad and Basrah as well as the more northern province of Mosul, and, as such, would have excluded Kuwait, which lies some distance below the confluence of the two rivers.[85] There is also the fact that the British Foreign Office – whose views are particularly relevant inasmuch as Britain was the mandatory power – expressed the view in July 1921, in addressing the question of the post-war status of Kuwait, that:

from the legal standpoint and *on the understanding that there was no intention of including Kuwait within the boundaries of Mesopotamia*, the status of this territory [Kuwait] would appear to be governed by Article 132 of the [unratified] Treaty of Sèvres [by which Turkey renounced its claims to territory outside its present-day borders].[86]

On this view, the question of compliance or otherwise with the mandate does not even arise.

A second difficulty with the Iraqi argument is one of timing. There was an express prohibition on the cession of territory in the Anglo–Iraq Treaty of 1922, which constituted the mandate; but that treaty was not ratified until 19 December 1924, i.e. *after* the 1923 exchange of letters by which the British High Commissioner recognized Kuwait's separate existence and territorial extent. Nor was the mandate over Iraq formally approved by decision of the League of Nations Council until 27 September 1924.

There appears to have been no other prohibition on alienating prospective mandate territory apart from that in the Anglo–Iraq agreement itself. According to Wright,[87] prior to confirmation of the mandates, all the mandatories that were actually governing the territories – as was Britain in the case of Iraq, the mandate having been conferred by the Allied Supreme Council in 1920 – had assured the League Council of their intention to observe the spirit of Article 22 of the League of Nations Covenant and, in some cases, had published reports that were examined by the Mandates Commission and the Council.[88] Article 22 of the Covenant does not assist, however, as it does not contain any prohibition on the alienation of territory. In short, there was no agreement in force in 1923 forbidding the cession of Iraqi territory.

Thirdly, it is doubtful whether the fixing of the boundaries of a mandated territory could in any case be said to involve an "alienation" or "cession" of territory. Such a proposition begs the question that the territory in question appertained to the country concerned in the first place. Moreover, it was for the Principal Powers to determine the territories' boundaries. According to an influential report by M. Hymans, the Belgian rapporteur who examined the legal foundations of the mandates system, the League of Nations itself had no original authority to define the mandated areas. This, like the appointment of the mandatories, was to be done by the Principal Powers.[89] The resolution adopted by the League Council in August 1920 to give effect to Hymans' report accordingly requested the Principal Powers to name the mandatory powers, to define the terms of the mandates, and "to inform it as to the frontiers of the territories to come under these mandates".[90] From the point of view of logic, therefore, until Britain had made this determination in respect of Iraq, it could not be argued that any particular territory either belonged to the latter or had been ceded from it. That the states concerned in fact proceeded on this basis is evidenced by an agreement entered into on 23 December 1920 between Britain and France, readjusting the boundaries of the mandated areas of Palestine, Mesopotamia, and Syria.[91] The consent of the League Council was apparently not sought to the readjustment, it having been effected *before* the mandates in question were confirmed.[92]

There does not seem to be any force, therefore, in the Iraqi argument that the 1923 agreement constituted a breach of mandate. Still less could it be argued that the 1932 agreement, which was entered into during the currency of the formal mandate, but merely confirmed a pre-existing boundary, constituted a "cession" of territory contrary to the mandate.[93]

Agreements entered into prior to independence. We have not seen this argument put forward by Baghdad, but it has been suggested that it further objects that in 1923 and 1932 Iraq was not independent, and so recognition by the British High Commissioner in 1923, and by the Iraqi Prime Minister, Nuri al-Said, in 1932, does not count.[94] This does not seem to be a good point for a number of reasons, the most compelling of which is that the independence of Kuwait and the boundary between the two countries were affirmed in 1963, at a time when Iraq plainly was independent. This would, strictly speaking, seem to rule out the necessity of considering the validity of the 1923 and 1932 agreements at all. But, for the sake of completeness, we will do so.

As regards the 1932 agreement, it is true that Iraq was not formally independent in July and August 1932 when the exchange of letters took place. However, it was evidently in *statu nascendi*, as evidenced by, *inter alia*, the Treaty of Alliance of 1930 between Britain and Iraq.[95] As such, Iraq was endowed with sufficient legal personality to enter into such an agreement on its own behalf and, provided that it was freely entered into,[96] the agreement would have continued to bind it after independence.[97] Indeed, the League of Nations Council expressly required, as a condition of terminating the mandate, that Iraq give an undertaking to comply with all the international agreements entered into by it or on its behalf during the period of the mandate, and Iraq did so in May 1932.[98] The 1923 agreement is the only agreement made when Iraq was plainly still in a state of dependence. Assuming that the agreement was made on behalf of Iraq,[99] it would appear to be binding on it on the basis of the principles enunciated in the case of *US Nationals in Morocco*.[100] There, the International Court of Justice (ICJ) held that Morocco, as a protectorate, had retained its personality as a state under international law, and that agreements made by the protecting power within the scope of its authority, touching the affairs of and intending to bind the protected state, bound, and inured to the benefit of, that state. According to some writers,[101] mandated territories – of the

A type at any rate, of which Iraq was one – also had a certain degree of international personality and, having been represented in international affairs by the mandatory power, were bound by the treaties concluded on their behalf. Iraq may be seen to present an even clearer case for such continuity, since Britain recognized its independence in the Anglo–Iraq Treaty of 1922, the League having previously recognized its "provisional" independence.[102] If, therefore, the 1923 agreement was concluded on Iraq's behalf, and within the scope of Britain's authority as mandatory, it seems reasonable that Iraq should continue to be bound by it.[103]

Moreover, even if one were to reject the proposition that *all* treaties concluded on its behalf are binding on the former mandated territory, there is strong authority for the proposition that *boundary* treaties are. State practice, arbitral awards, and decisions of the International Court of Justice establish that internal administrative boundaries of a single colonial power, boundaries agreed between colonial powers, and boundaries between colonial powers and independent states are to be respected after independence.[104] In the *Frontier Dispute (Burkina Faso/Mali)* case,[105] a Chamber of the ICJ stated that the principle of respect for existing boundaries – *uti possidetis*, as it is known – was a firmly established principle of international law and one that was applicable in several different contexts. At p. 566 (paras 23 and 24), the Court said:

> Such territorial boundaries might be no more than delimitations between different administrative divisions or colonies all subject to the same sovereign. In that case, the application of the principle of *uti possidetis* resulted in administrative boundaries being transformed into international frontiers in the full sense of the term.
>
> The territorial boundaries which have to be respected may also derive from international frontiers which previously divided a colony of one State from a colony of another, or indeed a colonial territory from the territory of an independent State, or one which was under protectorate, but had retained its international personality.

It is true that the preamble to the special agreement whereby the case was brought before the Court expressly recognized this principle, but the Chamber evidently treated it as one of general application.[106] The 1923 agreement seems to fall broadly within these categories, which, in any event, should not, in our view, be regarded as exhaustive. The fact that Iraq was not fully independent at the time does not, therefore, seem as such to affect the issue.

Alleged non-compliance with constitutional requirements. Iraq also claims that the 1932 and 1963 agreements were invalid because the approval of the proper Iraqi authorities – the House of Representatives (or National Council) and the National Revolutionary Council, respectively – was not obtained.[107] Accepting, *arguendo*, that such approval was not secured (a matter on which we have no independent evidence), is it the case that this would have rendered the agreements invalid? This is a question that falls to be considered under both national[108] and international law. As the facts and the applicable law differ as between the two agreements, it will be convenient to consider them in turn.

Turning first, then, to the 1932 agreement, it will be recalled that this took the form of an exchange of letters between the Prime Minister of Iraq and the Ruler of Kuwait.[109] The Iraq Constitution (or "Organic Law") of 21 March 1925, as amended on 29 July 1925,[110] which was in force when these letters were signed, provides in Article 26(4) that:

> The King concludes treaties. He may not ratify them, however, until they have been approved by Parliament.

Article 28 goes on to provide, in relevant part:

> Legislative authority is vested in Parliament and the King. Parliament is composed of the Senate and the Chamber of Deputies.

The issue arises, therefore, whether or not the exchange of notes was a "treaty" for purposes of Iraqi constitutional law. The term "treaty" is not defined in the Constitution, but the way in which Article 26 is drafted seems to contemplate a treaty subject to ratification in the international sense, i.e. the procedure whereby the executive power of a state signifies its formal consent to be bound.[111]

It does not appear that such a treaty was involved here. The 1932 exchange of letters contained no provision as to whether or not it required ratification before entering into force. British treaty practice at the time was that treaties in general did not require ratification unless this was expressly stipulated.[112] In any case, it seems to have been widespread practice, at the time and subsequently, that exchanges of notes or letters, which constituted a particularly informal means of concluding a treaty, were not normally subject to ratification, although they could be made so.[113] It appears to follow from this that the 1932 agreement was probably not one requiring ratification under international law, and hence did not, as a matter of Iraqi constitutional law, require the approval of Parliament.[114]

If, however, Iraqi constitutional law did require parliamentary approval,[115] and this was not given, would this have affected the binding force of the agreement? It is questionable whether, as a matter of the law of treaties, non-compliance with such a requirement could be relied upon to invalidate the agreement (we return below to consider this matter – as well as the possibility of characterizing the exchange of notes as an act of recognition rather than as a treaty – in connection with the 1963 agreement).

Turning to the 1963 agreement, this took the form of "Agreed Minutes" of a meeting held between a high-level Kuwaiti and Iraqi delegation in October 1963, aimed at rectifying "all that blemished the Iraqi–Kuwaiti relations as a result of the attitude of the past Qasim regime towards Kuwait before the dawn of the blessed revolution of the 14th of Ramadhan". The

Minutes were signed at Baghdad on 4 October 1963 by the Heads of the two delegations: respectively, Shaikh Sabah al-Salim al-Sabah, Heir Apparent and Prime Minister of Kuwait, and Major-General Ahmad Hasan al-Bakr, Prime Minister of Iraq. They were registered with the United Nations by Kuwait on 10 January 1964.[116] They said nothing about the manner in which the agreement was to enter into force. However, a footnote in the UN Treaty Series states that the agreement "came into force on 4 October 1963 by signature".

We do not know whether, as a matter of domestic law, the alleged failure to obtain the approval of the Iraqi National Revolutionary Council of this agreement was a constitutional flaw.[117] Even if it was, however, there are serious problems in international law in relying on such a defect to invalidate the 1963 agreement or that of 1932. Article 46 of the Vienna Convention on the Law of Treaties, 1969 (which is not binding in the present case, not least because it is not retrospective, but which in this respect is regarded by at any rate some authorities as declaratory of the position in customary law),[118] provides as follows:

(1) A state may not invoke the fact that its consent to be bound by a treaty has been expressed in violation of its internal law regarding competence to conclude treaties as invalidating its consent unless that violation was manifest and concerned a rule of internal law of fundamental importance.

(2) A violation is manifest if it would be objectively evident to any state conducting itself in the matter in accordance with normal practice and good faith.

There are thus three requirements to be met: there must be a defect; it must be of fundamental importance; and it must be manifest.

Whether the proviso has been satisfied in this case is a question of fact; but the burden of proof is on the state alleging invalidity – in this case Iraq – and it is not an easy burden to discharge, as the arbitral award of 31 July 1989 in the case of *Guinea–Bissau/Senegal*[119] shows. Even if the Iraqi Constitution did require the consent of the Revolutionary Council, that might not be enough if it was usually dispensed with in practice. In the *Guinea–Bissau/Senegal* case, the former sought to invalidate a boundary agreement entered into by an exchange of notes between Portugal (Guinea–Bissau's former colonial ruler) and France (on behalf of Senegal), on the ground, *inter alia*, that it had not been concluded in conformity with Portuguese constitutional law. The Tribunal held that, in assessing whether a treaty had been concluded in accordance with a state's internal law, it was necessary to take account of the law in force in the country – as actually interpreted and applied (para. 56). It found that the Portuguese Government (then led by President Salazar) had regularly dispensed with obtaining the National Assembly's approval of international conventions. This, amongst other considerations, led the Tribunal to hold that the French Government had had reason to believe, in good faith, that the treaty signed was valid (para. 59).

We do not know the facts here, but it may be the case that the constitutional provision (if any) was either not fundamental or not complied with in practice.[120] There is, moreover, the further hurdle that the alleged constitutional defect must have been "manifest", i.e., to paraphrase Article 46(2) of the Vienna Convention, objectively evident to a negotiating party acting in good faith and in accordance with usual practice.[121] On the question of the normal practice followed by those negotiating exchanges of letters, the arbitral tribunal in the *Guinea–Bissau/Senegal* case had this to say:

Lorsque deux pays concluent un accord par échange de lettres, accord qui, pour des raisons constitutionelles, exige l'approbation du Parlement de l'un d'eux, il est d'usage de faire mention de cette circonstance dans le texte ou au cours de la négociation (para. 58).

There is no indication that that was done in the present case.

Even if these formidable difficulties could be overcome, the question arises whether Iraq has not, by its conduct, effectively renounced any right it might have had to invoke invalidity.[122] The agreement had not been formally denounced on this or any other ground at the time of Iraq's invasion of Kuwait. Nor does the argument of invalidity appear to have been raised by Iraq until September 1990 – 27 years after the agreement was signed. Moreover, there has been at least partial performance of the agreement, with the establishment of diplomatic relations between the two countries and the exchange of ambassadors, as envisaged therein.[123]

There is another way altogether, though, of looking at the 1932 and 1963 exchanges of letters. They could be treated not as treaties, but as the exchange of unilateral acts of recognition of the boundary, etc. by Iraq and Kuwait. Acts of recognition are, as a matter of constitutional law, usually (or perhaps always) the province of the executive alone, and, as a matter of international law, the question of failure to comply with internal constitutional arrangements seems not to arise, when one is dealing with recognition, not treaties.[124]

Other acts of recognition by Iraq

This brings us to a further point concerning recognition. Quite apart from the specific acts of recognition embodied in the 1923, 1932 and 1963 agreements, Iraq has performed various other acts amounting to implied recognition of Kuwait as a separate entity (if not recognition of the precise boundary between the two countries). Since 1963, Iraq has exchanged diplomatic representatives at the ambassadorial level with Kuwait.[125] Since 1958, at least, Iraq has entered into diplomatic correspondence on a state-to-state basis with Kuwait, in which, *inter alia*, it has expressed the desire to enter into consular relations. It has stated that it would recognize judicial documents produced by the Department of Justice in Kuwait.[126] It supported Kuwait's application for membership in the International Labour Organization in 1961. Moreover, the fact that Iraq entered into lengthy negotiations with Kuwait for the lease or cession of Warbah and Bubiyan would seem to constitute implied recognition of Kuwait's sovereignty over the islands. It would be tedious to multiply further examples.

Recognition by other states

Recognition by the claimant state is not, of course, the only factor in determining statehood; nor is it even a necessary one. If one takes a declaratory view of international legal personality, then, certainly by 1990, Kuwait was an independent state by all the usual indicia: that is to say, it had a permanent population, a defined territory, and a government, and it was independent in the sense of not taking instructions from any other state. If, on the other hand, one thinks recognition is important because one either takes the constitutive view or considers recognition to be significant evidence of statehood, then the overwhelming recognition of Kuwait by other states by 1990[127] is strong evidence of its independent statehood and separate existence from Iraq.

The boundary[128]

Turning to the question of the actual boundary between Iraq and Kuwait, there was agreement as to the main route it should follow, but this was expressed in rather imprecise terms.

The first formal definition of Kuwait's northern boundary was contained in the (unratified) Anglo–Turkish Convention of 1913. Article 7 had defined the outer limits of the territory in which the Ruler of Kuwait was recognized as having administrative authority, in relevant part, as follows:

La ligne de démarcation part de la côte à l'embouchure du Khawr-Zoubair vers le nord-ouest et passe immédiatement au sud d'Oumm-Kasr, de Safouan et de Djebel-Sanam, de façon à laisser ces endroits et leur puits au vilayet de Basrah; arrivée au Batine, elle le suit vers le sud-ouest jusqu'à Hafr-el-Batine qu'elle laisse du côté de Koueit.[129]

It was stated in the Convention that this line was marked in green on the map attached as Annex V thereto (see Fig. 5.1); but there was some controversy in later years as to whether the Green line (outer limit) did in fact accurately depict the boundary as described.

When the question of delimiting the Iraq/Kuwait boundary came to the fore late in 1922 (the other boundaries of the two countries having been settled), Sir Percy Cox, the British High Commissioner for Iraq, proposed to the Colonial Office that the Green line be confirmed as the Kuwait/Iraq boundary. In the ensuing exchange of letters between the Ruler of Kuwait, the British Political Agent in Kuwait and the High Commissioner for Iraq, the latter stated in his memorandum of reply dated 19 April 1923 that:

[T]he Shaikh of Kuwait is understood [by his letter of 4 April 1923 to the Political Agent] to claim the frontier of Kuwait with Iraq to be as follows:

From the intersection of the Wadi-el-Audja with the Batin and thence Northwards along the Batin to a point just south of the Latitude of Safwan; thence Eastwards passing south of Safwan wells, Jabal Sanam and Um Qasr, leaving them to Iraq and so on to the junction of the Khawr Zobeir with the Khawr Abdallah.

Shaikh Ahmed at the same time claims as appertaining to Kuwait the Islands of Warbah, Bubiyan, Maskan (or Mashjan), Failakah, Auha, Kubha, Qaru and Um-el-Maradim.

The Shaikh can be informed that his claim to the frontier and islands above indicated is recognised in so far as His Majesty's Government are concerned.[130]

Cox asserted that this definition was identical to the frontier indicated by the Green line of the Anglo–Turkish Convention of 1913, but saw no need for the Political Agent to make special allusion to that document in his reply to the shaikh. (In fact, it will be noted that the definitions in these two instruments were not quite identical. Apart from the fact that the line was now described as running from west to east, there were several changes in wording.)

The 1923 definition was reaffirmed word for word by the Prime Minister of Iraq, Nuri al-Said, and the Ruler of Kuwait in their exchange of letters of July/August 1932. On that occasion, the former requested, in a letter to the High Commissioner for Iraq dated 21 July 1932, that the necessary action be taken to obtain the agreement of the Kuwaiti authorities to "the following description of the existing frontier between the two countries", the description that followed was a verbatim repetition of the 1923 definition of the boundary. In his reply of 10 August 1932 to the Political Agent, the Ruler of Kuwait noted "that the frontier proposed by the Iraqi Prime Minister is approved by His Majesty's Government", and agreed to "reaffirm the existing frontier between Iraq and Koweit as described in the Iraq Prime Minister's letter".[131]

The following would appear to be the main issues left unresolved by the 1923/1932 definition, issues that had not subsequently been agreed between the parties before the 1990–1 crisis, although they had been the subject of internal and inter-state discussions.[132]

Proceeding from west to east, there is, first, the problem of what exactly is meant by the phrase "along the Batin". The Batin is a long and fairly wide *wadi* or valley, which is dry except when it rains and is used for grazing and recreation. The questions that arise in this regard are whether the boundary here should run in a straight line or whether, in view of the later discovery that the course of the Batin is rather sinuous, the line should follow that course; and, if so, whether it should run along one of the banks, the *medium filum aquae* (median line) or the *thalweg* (deepest navigable channel or line of continuous deepest soundings).

Secondly, what is meant by "just south" of the latitude of Safwan and what marks the point at which the frontier should leave the Batin and turn eastwards? Similarly, what is meant by "south of Safwan wells", which is the point through which the line passes on its course to the east? This, of course, raises a question of fact as to what the parties had in mind. There is some suggestion that the frontier here was originally marked by a large notice board located 1 mile south of Safwan, which had been erected by the Ruler of Kuwait and the British Political Agent in Kuwait in 1923. This was apparently removed, however, by the Iraqis in 1932, restored by them, but once again removed in 1939 by persons unknown. In June 1940, the Political Agent had it replaced again in the presence of an Iraqi frontier official, giving rise to a protest by the Iraqis that the new board had been erected at a point far from the site of the old one – at a distance of 250 metres within Iraqi territory. They removed it and it was not subsequently replaced, leading to suggestions that it should be reinstated or that some other point, selected by reference to co-ordinates or to a fixed landmark, should be used. At one stage, the most southerly palm in Safwan was considered for the landmark, but matters were complicated by the Iraqis placing new plantations south of Safwan during or after the Second World War.[133]

A third issue concerns the course to be followed by the boundary in the segment from Safwan to the Gulf. Does it run in a straight line from the point south of Safwan to the junction of the Khawr Zubair and Khawr Abdallah, or in a direct line to a point immediately south of Umm Qasr, then turning southeast to the junction of the two Khawrs? (see Fig. 5.2)[134] The difference concerns a small wedge of territory, but potentially an important one as regards oil and the development of the port of Umm Qasr during the past two decades at least.

A fourth issue, which is not dealt with by the definition at all, is how the boundary runs from the junction of the Khawr Zubair with the Khawr Abdallah to the open sea.

Commencing in 1940, Britain, acting on behalf of Kuwait, put forward a number of proposals concerning these points. The Iraqis did not reject any of them out of hand; the proposals met with either silence or the response that demarcation of the boundary should wait until the question of the lease or cession of Warbah and Bubiyan had been resolved. We do not have access to archival materials postdating 1961; but it seems that no agreement had subsequently been reached on these issues, and the boundary had not been formally demarcated.[135]

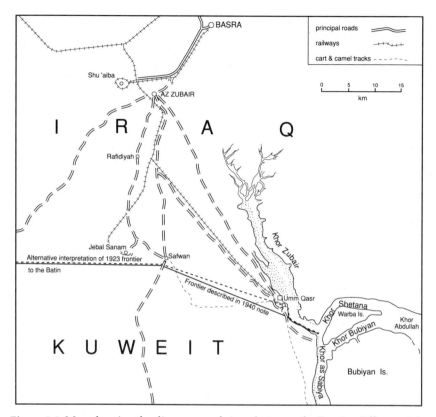

Figure 5.2 Map showing the divergence of views between the Foreign Office and the Government of India evident during 1941–2 on where the land boundary should terminate on the Khawr Zubair.

Legality of the use of force to vindicate territorial claims

Supposing, however, and purely for the sake of argument, that (contrary to the conclusions reached above) Iraq's claim to sovereignty over Kuwait and/or the islands of Warbah and Bubiyan was valid, would this have justified the use of force to vindicate them?

The answer must be a categorical "no". By Article 2(4) of the UN Charter, all members (which includes Iraq) undertake to refrain from the use of force against "the territorial integrity or political independence of any state". Even though the admission of Kuwait by the General Assembly, on the recommendation of the Security Council, in 1963 does not formally amount to collective recognition, we would argue that it does not lie in the mouth of a member of the United Nations to dispute that a fellow-member is a state for the purposes of, at any rate, Article 2(4). In any case, however, that provision goes further, also imposing an obligation on members to "refrain . . . from the use of force . . . in any . . . manner inconsistent with the Purposes of the United Nations". And the very first purpose of the organization is "to bring about by peaceful means . . . settlement of international disputes" (Article 1(1)). The whole object of the Charter régime is to prohibit the unilateral use of force in the resolution of international disputes.[136]

In the context of territorial disputes, a state must use peaceful means to achieve possession, however good its claim to title. The one exception is the right of self-defence; but the right of self-defence cannot be invoked to justify an attempt to recapture territory that has long been peacefully occupied by another state. That this is so is demonstrated by the international reaction to Argentina's invasion of the Falkland islands in April 1982 in pursuit of its claims to sovereignty over them. That invasion was condemned by virtually the entire international community, notwithstanding that quite a few states, especially in Latin America, supported Argentina's claim to territorial sovereignty.[137] A fortiori, the use of force is impermissible as a means of vindicating a merely economic claim, such as that arising out of alleged overproduction of oil or the siphoning off of oil allegedly belonging to Iraq.

This analysis was endorsed by the Security Council in this particular case, especially in Resolution 662, declaring the annexation null and void, and calling on all states and institutions to refrain from recognizing the annexation or doing anything that might be interpreted as indirect recognition.

Often in an international legal dispute, there are some good, or at least plausible, legal arguments on both sides, matters are rarely black and white. The present case is an exception. For the reasons we have given, it seems that Iraq's claims to sovereignty over Kuwait and the islands of Warbah and Bubiyan were completely unfounded in law, and the means by which it sought to vindicate them completely inadmissible.[138]

Postscript

Since the core of this chapter was written, the Security Council adopted Resolution 687 on 3 April 1991, which (*inter alia*) affirmed the inviolability of the international boundary between Iraq and Kuwait and the allocation of islands, as recognised in the agreement of 4 October 1963; demanded that the two countries respect that boundary; and called upon the Secretary-General to lend his assistance to the parties in demarcating it. The Secretary-General was asked to draw upon all appropriate materials for this purpose (including a topographic map of Kuwait produced by the UK Director General of Military Survey and transmitted to the Security Council on 28 March 1991) and to report back within one month. This resolution was accepted by Iraq and Kuwait and, by his report of 3 May 1991 to the Security Council, the Secretary-General proposed the establishment of an Iraq/Kuwait Boundary Demarcation Commission (comprising one representative each of Iraq and Kuwait and three independent experts appointed by himself) to demarcate the boundary, as set out in the 1963 agreement. The Security Council approved his report and the members of the commission were duly appointed. The commission can decide by a majority and its decisions are final.

The main factual and legal issues before the boundary commission were identified and examined by us at length in our article "The Iraq/Kuwait boundary: legal aspects" , *Revue Belge de Droit International* **23** (1990–2), 293. Decisions on the various sections of the land boundary have now been taken and that part of the boundary has been physically demarcated. These decisions were broadly along the lines envisaged in our article. In brief, following the frontier from west to east, the commission identified the key boundary points as follows:

(1) the boundary monument on the Iraq / Saudi Arabian border, Pillar No. 1, shall be the starting point for the boundary along the thalweg of Wadi Al Batin, and therefore, the tri-point of Iraq, Kuwait and Saudi Arabia;

(2) the boundary south of Safwan shall be located at the distance of 1,430 metres from the south-west extremity of the compound wall of the old customs post along the old road from Safwan to Kuwait;

(3) the boundary at the northern end of the Wadi Al Batin shall be the intersection of the thalweg of the Wadi and the latitude of the point south of Safwan;

(4) the boundary south of Umm Qasr shall coincide with the location at which the boundary line on map sheet 5549-I of series K7611, edition 2 (1990), produced by the military survey of the United Kingdom, crosses the western shore of Khowr Zhobeir; and

(5) the junction of Khowr Zhobeir and Khowr Abd Allah shall be the one best identified for the Epoch 1932 and transposed onto modern ortho-photo maps produced by the Commission.[139]

The commission further decided on the boundary lines connecting these points. They were described as follows:

(A) The boundary line in the Wadi Al Batin shall be a series of straight line segments of about two kilometres length best approximating to the lowest point line in the Wadi;

(B) The boundary line from the point at the northern end of the Wadi Al Batin to the point south of Safwan shall be a line running along the common latitude of the points;

(C) The boundary line from the point south of Safwan to the point south of Umm Qasr shall be the shortest line between the points;

(D) The boundary line from the point south of Umm Qasr on the shore shall follow the low water line up to the location of [sic] directly opposite the junction of Khowr Zhobeir and Khowr Abd Allah.

A report on the land boundary was submitted to the Security Council in August 1992. It was circulated as a restricted document and not made generally available.

The Security Council welcomed the report in Resolution 773, adopted on 26 August 1992, and urged the commission to demarcate, as soon as possible, the eastern section of the boundary, including the offshore boundary. In the same resolution – in the wake of renewed claims by Iraq to Kuwait, particularly on 2 August 1992 (the second anniversary of the Iraqi invasion) – the Security Council "underlined" its guarantee of the inviolability of the boundary.[140]

Notes

1. An earlier version of this chapter was originally published in French in 1991 under the title "La revendication par l'Iraq de la souveraineté sur le Koweït", *Annuaire français de droit international* **36**, 195. We are grateful for permission to reproduce it here in English.

2. We examine the boundary question in more detail in our article, "The Iraq/Kuwait boundary: legal aspects", *Revue Belge de Droit International* **23** (1990–2), 293.

3. A particularly helpful recent source is R. N. Schofield, *Kuwait–Iraq: historical claims and territorial disputes* (London: Royal Institute of International Affairs, 1991). Other useful sources include the following:
   B. C. Busch, *Britain and the Persian Gulf: 1894–1914* (Berkeley: University of California Press, 1967); J. G. Lorimer, *Gazetteer of the Persian Gulf, Oman and central Arabia*, vol. 1 & vol. 2 (Calcutta: Superintendent Government Printing, 1915 & 1908); "Historical summary of events in territories of the Ottoman Empire, Persia and Arabia affecting the British position in the Persian Gulf, 1907–28" (printed for the Committee of Imperial Defence) [PG 13], in *The Persian Gulf historical summaries 1907–53*, vol. 1 (Farnham Common, England: Archive Editions, 1987); "Historical summary of events in the Persian Gulf shaikhdoms and the Sultanate of Muscat and Oman, 1928–53" (printed by the British Foreign Office) [PG 53], in *ibid.*, vol. 2; R. N. Schofield & G. Blake (eds), *Arabian boundaries: primary documents 1853–1957* [AB], vols 1, 7, 8 (Farnham Common, England: Archive Editions, 1988); E. Lauterpacht, C. J. Greenwood, M. Weller, D. Bethlehem (eds), *The Kuwait crisis: basic documents*. (Cambridge: Research Centre for International Law, Grotius Publications, 1991).

4. For reasons of space, some points of detail have been omitted.

5. See, e.g., S. al-J. Al-Sabah, *Les Émirates du Golfe: histoire d'un peuple* (Paris: Fayard, 1980), 43–4.

6. Prior to that, it would appear that the Ottomans had pretensions to, but little control over, the Arabian peninsula. For this earlier period, see Schofield, *Kuwait–Iraq*, Part I. According to the reports of two British Political Residents in the Persian Gulf, writing in 1863 and 1866, neither the Ruler nor the inhabitants of Kuwait paid tribute or taxes to the Turkish treasury (respectively, L. Pelly, Political Resident, 1862–72, "Report on the tribes, etc. around the shores of the Persian Gulf, 13 April 1863",

Foreign Office Confidential Print (London: Public Record Office [PRO]), *FO 881/8843*, 23; and extract from letter dated 18 April 1866 from C. A. Kemball, Political Resident, 1852–5, in J. A. Saldanha, *Précis of Koweit affairs* (1904) (reprinted in *Persian Gulf précis 1903–1908*, vol. 5 [Farnham Common, England: Archive Editions, 1986]).

7.   R. V. Harcourt, "Memorandum respecting Koweit", Foreign Office, 30 October 1901, India Office Library and Records [IOLR] *L/P&S/18/B133*, reprinted in AB, vol. 7, 3 [Harcourt memorandum]; see also Lorimer, *Gazetteer*, vol. 1, 1014. Without going into detail on the system of administration employed by the Turkish Empire, it may be noted that, as applied by the Porte in Iraq, the largest territorial unit was the *wilayat*, ruled by a *wali*; each *wilayat* consisted of divisions, known as *sanjaqs*; and each *sanjaq* was again divided into *qadhas* (*qazas*) or districts, administered by a *qaimmaqam* (Lorimer, *Gazetteer*, vol. 2, 834–42).

8.   Despatch of 6 July 1899 from Stavrides to M. Herbert (British chargé d'affaires), as reported in Harcourt memorandum, at 8. Cf. Lorimer, *Gazetteer*, vol. 2, 842–3, observing that there was little correlation between appearance and reality as regards the Turkish administration in Iraq, *qaimmaqams* being sometimes "merely illiterate tribal Arabs whom it is desired to placate".

9.   Harcourt memorandum.

10. Pelly, "Report on the tribes, etc.", *FO 881/8843*, 25. Cf. the case of the *Muscat Dhows 1905*, *Reports of international arbitral awards* [RIAA], **11** (1905), 83.

11. Harcourt memorandum.

12. Lorimer, *Gazetteer*, vol. 2, 767–8.

13. *Ibid.*, 810–11. Lorimer's information was based on investigations carried out between 1904 and 1907.

14. *Ibid.*, 1055.

15. Copies of the Agreement of 23 January 1899 between Shaikh Mubarak, Shaikh of Kuwait, and Lieutenant-Colonel M. J. Meade, the British Political Resident, and of the accompanying letter of the same date from Meade to Shaikh Mubarak, are reproduced in Lorimer, *Gazetteer*, vol. 1, 1048–50; in J. C. Hurewitz (ed.), *The Middle East and North Africa in world politics: a documentary record*, vol. 1 (New Haven, Conn.: Yale University Press, 1975), 475–7; and in Lauterpacht et al., *The Kuwait crisis*, 9–10.

16. In October 1900, a decoration was conferred upon him as *qaimmaqam* of Kuwait (Harcourt memorandum, at 11). The following month, after the Wali of Basrah settled a dispute between Kuwait and the neighbouring territory of Najd, Mubarak accompanied the Wali to Basrah where he made solemn professions of allegiance to the Sultan, and promised to cease "coquetting with foreign Powers": *ibid.*, AB, vol. 7, 10 at 12.

17. Exchange of notes dated 9 and 11 September 1901 between, respectively, the Ottoman Ambassador in London (Anthopoulo Pasha) and the British Foreign Secretary (the Marquess of Lansdowne), in G. P. Gooch & H. Temperley (eds), *British documents on the origins of the War, 1898–1914*, vol. 10 (London: HMSO, 1938), 49; reprinted in Lauterpacht et al., *The Kuwait Crisis*, 10.

18. A version of those parts of the map forming Annex 5 to the Anglo–Turkish Convention of 29 July 1913 pertaining to Kuwait was produced by the Research Department of the Foreign Office in 1954: *PRO FO 371/114644*. A modern copy of the map has been reproduced here as Fig. 5.1.

19. Foreign Office, "Memorandum respecting British interests in the Persian Gulf", 12 February 1908, *L/P&S/18/B166*, reproduced in AB, vol. 1, 167 at 224 and 230–31.

20. *Ibid.*, 231.

21. See, generally, IOLR *R/15/5/68*, reprinted in AB, vol. 7, 35.

22. PG 13, 74. While these investigations were proceeding, the British Government entered into a secret agreement with the Shaikh of Kuwait on 15 October 1907 (reprinted in PG 53, 236, and in Lauterpacht et al., *The Kuwait crisis*, 25–7), whereby, *inter alia*, it acquired, for a yearly rent, a perpetual lease of a portion of the foreshore at Bandar Shuwaikh (2.5 miles southwest of Kuwait port), which was considered to possess greater capacities as a railway terminus than any other place on the Gulf. By

this agreement, the British also secured a right of pre-emption over the island of Warbah and its foreshore. A few years later, when the limits of Kuwait territory came to be discussed with the Turkish Government, the British Political Agent in Kuwait and the Government of India took the view that this right of pre-emption amounted to, or would be regarded by Shaikh Mubarak as amounting to, recognition of his title to the island. (The view of the Political Agent, Shakespear, is set out in his "Note on the boundaries of the Kuwait principality", 9 August 1912, R/15/5/65, reprinted in AB, vol. 7, 123 at 126; that of the Government of India in an undated Foreign Office minute, *ibid.*, 109.)

23. Schofield, *Kuwait–Iraq*, Ch. 1.

24. Anglo–Turkish Convention: collection of documents signed on 29 July 1913, original French version, IOLR R/15/5/65, reproduced in AB, vol. 7, 185–99 at 191, with map at 199; relevant extracts concerning Kuwait in English, reprinted in AB, vol. 1, 389; in Hurewitz, *The Middle East and North Africa*, vol. 1, 567–9; and in Lauterpacht et al., *The Kuwait crisis*, 33–4.

25. Shaikh Mubarak, whose approval was sought to a draft of this Agreement, strongly objected to the idea of a Turkish agent being appointed in Kuwait. The British Political Resident, Cox, managed to assuage his concerns, however, by pointing out that the appointment was in fact a useful indication and necessary consequence of his administrative autonomy (see letter of 6 July 1913 from Cox to Shaikh Mubarak, IOLR R/15/5/65, reproduced in AB, vol. 7, 179; and letter of 10 July 1913 from Cox to the Government of India, *ibid.*, 175 at 177).

26. "Letter of 3 November 1914 from the Political Resident to Shaikh Mubarak", in C. U. Aitchison, *Collection of treaties, engagements and sanads relating to India and neighbouring countries* (Delhi: Government of India Printing Press, 1933), vol. 11, 265–6; and in Lauterpacht et al., *The Kuwait crisis*, 37–8.

27. On the distinction between a state "under protection" and a "protectorate" or "protected" state, see L. Oppenheim, *International law*, 8th edn, ed. H. Lauterpacht, vol.1 (London: Longman, Green, 1955), 191–6; M. Whiteman, *Digest of international law*, vol. 1 (Washington DC: Department of State, US Government Printing Office, 1963), 431–40.

28. Shaikh Mubarak's eldest son, Shaikh Jabir, who succeeded him on his death in November 1915, was informed in March 1916 by the Viceroy of India that "so long as you act up to existing arrangements with the British Government you may expect the same support as was enjoyed by your father". Shaikh Jabir himself died within the year and was succeeded by his brother, Shaikh Salim, to whom a similar assurance was conveyed by the Viceroy in March 1917: PG 13, 75–6.

29. Schofield, *Kuwait–Iraq*, Ch. 3.

30. L. Lockhart, "Outline of the history of Kuwait", *Journal of the Royal Central Asian Society* 34 (1947), 262, 271. That this was the case is corroborated by the Iraqis: see the press release issued by the Press Office of the Embassy of the Republic of Iraq, London, 12 September 1990, "The political background to the current events", 7.

31. Schofield, *Kuwait–Iraq*, Ch. 3.

32. PG 13, para. 22.

33. The text of the Council's decision is contained in *Documents on British foreign policy*, Series 1, vol. 8, 172, 176; and in Lauterpacht et al., *The Kuwait crisis*, 38.

34. *British and Foreign State Papers* 113 (1920), 652, Article 94. By Article 132 of the Treaty of Sèvres, Turkey renounced in favour of the Principal Allied Powers "all rights and title which she could claim on any ground over or concerning any territories outside Europe" not otherwise disposed of by the Treaty.

35. Cmnd 2370 (1925); reproduced in Q. Wright, *Mandates under the League of Nations* (Chicago: University of Chicago Press, 1930), Appendix 2 (b), 595.

36. "Decision of the Council of the League of Nations relating to the Application of the Principles of Article 22 of the Covenant to Iraq", reprinted in Wright, *Mandates*, Appendix 2 (a), 593–4.

37. The Treaty of Lausanne, League of Nations Treaty Series [LNTS], vol. 28, 12, Article 16. The Treaty was signed on 24 July 1923 and entered into force on 6 August 1924.

38. *Ibid.*, Article 3.

39. *British and Foreign State Papers* **133** (1930), 726; Aitchison, *Collection*, vol. 11, 213–14; also in Lauterpacht et al., *The Kuwait crisis*, 48.

40. For the relevant text, see below, p. 137. The complete exchange of letters is in IOLR *R/15/1/523*, folios 14–17. This comprises a letter of 4 April 1923 from the Shaikh of Kuwait to the British Political Agent in Kuwait, setting out his claim as regards the frontier between Kuwait and Iraq; a letter of the same date from the Political Agent in Kuwait to the British High Commissioner for Iraq, forwarding the Shaikh's claim; and a memorandum from the High Commissioner for Iraq (Sir Percy Cox) to the Political Agent in Kuwait, 23 April 1923, confirming that the Shaikh's "claim to the frontier and islands [as] indicated is recognised in so far as His Majesty's Government is concerned". The text of the High Commissioner's memorandum is reprinted in Aitchison, *Collection*, vol. 11, 266; and in Lauterpacht et al., *The Kuwait crisis*, 49.

41. See "The boundary", p. 136.

42. The language used in Cox's memorandum – that the Shaikh's claim was recognized "in so far as His Majesty's Government are concerned" – raises the question whether this recognition was on behalf of Iraq or only of Great Britain. The Anglo–Iraq Treaty of 1922 (Article 1) envisaged that there would be a British High Commissioner in Iraq who would represent British interests there. On the other hand, before the entry into force of the treaty, Cox was the representative of the mandatory and in that capacity conducted Iraq's foreign relations. Consequently, he had the power to make this commitment on behalf of Iraq, although whether that is what he intended to do is less clear in the light of the language he used. The Iraqis themselves have treated the agreement as one that was made on their behalf, challenging it on the basis not that it did not purport to bind them, but that it constituted a breach of the mandate: see "Breach of mandate", p. 129.

43. As a condition precedent of the termination of the mandate and membership in the League, Iraq gave the following undertaking, amongst others, to the League Council:
    Iraq considers itself bound by all the international agreements and conventions, both general and special, to which it has become a party, whether by its own action or by that of the mandatory Power acting on its behalf. Subject to any right of denunciation provided for therein, such agreements and conventions shall be respected by Iraq throughout the period for which they were concluded. (Declaration by the Kingdom of Iraq, 30 May 1932, Article 13, in M. O. Hudson, ed., *International legislation* (Washington, DC: Carnegie Endowment for International Peace, 1932–4, vol. 6, 39). The ratification of this declaration by Iraq was deposited with the Secretariat of the League of Nations on 29 June 1932: *ibid.* The declaration had been required by resolution of the Council of the League adopted on 28 January 1932: *League of Nations Official Journal* (1932), 471, 474.

44. IOLR *R/15/5/184*; reprinted in AB vol. 7, 372 and 376. The frontier was described in exactly the same terms as in the 1923 agreement. See, further, "The boundary", p. 136.

45. See below, pp. 128–35.

46. In April 1938, the then Iraqi Foreign Minister, Tawfiq al-Suwaidi, expressed this view in discussion with the British Ambassador to Baghdad, Sir Maurice Peterson (letter dated 26 August 1938 from L. Baggallay, Foreign Office, to R. T. Peel, India Office, IOLR *R/15/5/208*). The same view was expressed in an aide-mémoire on Kuwait enclosed in a letter dated 28 September 1938 from the Iraqi Foreign Minister to the UK delegate to the League of Nations, PRO FO *371/21858*.

47. See record of conversation with the Iraqi Minister for Foreign Affairs held at the Foreign Office on 4 October 1938, IOLR *R/15/5/208*; and undated Foreign Office minutes in PRO FO *371/21858*. See also Note Verbale dated 6 October 1938 from the British Embassy, Baghdad, to the Iraqi Ministry of Foreign Affairs, IOLR *R/15/5/159*.

48. See, generally, *IOLR R/15/5/208–10*; *PRO FO 371/114644–5*; and *PRO FO 371/126960–1*: all reprinted in AB, vol. 8.

49. "Exchange of Notes between the United Kingdom and Kuwait regarding relations between the United Kingdom and the state of Kuwait", 19 June 1961, United Nations Treaty Series [UNTS], vol. 399, 239; also in Lauterpacht et al., *The Kuwait crisis*, 50.

50. *Keesing's Contemporary Archives* (1961), *18187A*; elaborated upon in a statement issued by the Iraqi Foreign Ministry on 26 June 1961, Appendix 2 to *The truth about Kuwait*, (The Republic of Iraq, Ministry of Foreign Affairs, July 1961, 24). See also Whiteman, *Digest*, vol. 1, 442–6.

51. *Security Council Official Records*, 16th yr, 957–8th meetings, 2 and 5 July 1961; relevant extracts in Lauterpacht et al., *The Kuwait crisis*, 51–4. Kuwait's right to territorial integrity and political independence was affirmed in the debate by Chile, China (Nationalist), Ecuador, France, Liberia, Turkey, the United Arab Emirates and the United States. A British draft resolution calling upon all states to respect the independence and territorial integrity of Kuwait obtained seven votes, but failed to be adopted owing to the negative vote of the Soviet Union: *ibid.*, 54–5.

52. Namely, the International Telecommunications Union in 1959; the International Civil Aviation Organization, the Universal Postal Union, the World Health Organization, Inter-governmental Maritime Consultative Organization, and UNESCO in 1960; and the International Labour Organization in 1961. See M. H. Mendelson, "Acquisition of membership in selected international organizations". Doctoral thesis, Oxford University, 1971, 105; cf. the views of the British and Kuwaiti representatives in the Security Council debates in July 1961 (see note 51); and *The truth about the crisis between Kuwait and Iraq* (Government of Kuwait Printing and Publishing Department, 26 June 1961), 20.

53. Resolution 1777, 35th Ordinary Session, 8th meeting, 20 July 1960 [*sic*], in Lauterpacht et al., *The Kuwait crisis*, 55.

54. *Resolutions and decisions of the Security Council* (1963), 12.

55. "Agreed Minutes between the state of Kuwait and the Republic of Iraq regarding the restoration of friendly relations, recognition and related matter", 4 October 1963, UNTS, vol. 485, 321. According to the UN Treaty Office, Iraq had not revoked this instrument as of 2 August 1990.

56. *Keesing's record of world events* (1990), 37631, 37632 and 37634. See also 37635, concerning Iraq's announcement on 28 August 1990 that Kuwait had become the 19th province of Iraq.

57. Legal discussion of Iraq's claims is to be found in R. V. Pillai & M. Kumar, "The political and legal status of Kuwait", *International and Comparative Law Quarterly* 11 (1962), 108; and H. Al-Baharna, *The Arabian Gulf States*, 2nd edn (Beirut: Librairie du Liban, 1975), 250–8. However, there are many respects in which our analysis diverges from, or goes beyond theirs, although we share their general conclusions.

58. *Keesing's record of world events* (1990), 37635; and the views expressed by the representatives of Iraq in the Security Council and General Assembly debates that followed the invasion (respectively, statement by Mr Al-Anbari, S/PV2934, 9 August 1990, para. 42, quoting a resolution adopted by the Revolutionary Command Council in Iraq, the country's supreme authority; and statement by Mr Kadrat, A/45/PV23, 17 October 1990, paras 54–62), reprinted in Lauterpacht et al., *The Kuwait crisis*, 109 & 191.

59. "Letter on The Kuwait question from Mr Tariq Aziz, Deputy Prime Minister and Foreign Minister of Iraq to the Foreign Ministers of all Countries", Baghdad, 4 September 1990, 7–11. See also the press release "The political background to the current events", 12 September 1990.

60. Cf. statement by the Iraqi representative, Mr Kadrat, to the Security Council, S/PV2932, 2 August 1990, para. 11.

61. For reasons of space, some detailed arguments have had to be omitted from the present exposition, but we do not think that this affects either the analysis or the conclusions reached.

62. In 1863, Pelly, the then Political Resident, described Kuwait as "nominally recognising the *suzerainty* of the Turkish Government but practically independent" (Foreign Office, "Memorandum respecting British interests in the Persian Gulf", 225–6); and three years later, his successor, Kemball, asserted that the Shaikh of Kuwait "acknowledges *fealty* to the Sultan", the feudal obligation lying not in the payment of taxes or tribute, but in protecting the shores of the Shatt al-Arab from foreign attack by sea (Saldanha, *Précis of Koweit Affairs*, 3–4). In statements made to the Sublime Porte between 1880 and 1893, Great Britain, through its Ambassador in Constantinople, recognized or impliedly recognized, variously, Turkish territorial sovereignty or jurisdiction on the coast from Basrah to Udaid or Qatif – both considerably south of Kuwait (Harcourt memorandum, at 4). Yet in 1897 the British Ambassador to Constantinople was informed by the Foreign Office that "His Majesty's Government have never admitted that Kuwait is under the protection of the Turkish Government. But since it is practically under Turkish *influence*, it is doubtful whether we could deny the latter" (Foreign Office, "Memorandum respecting British interests in the Persian Gulf", 167, 226). And, in 1908, the Foreign Office contended that Pelly's above-mentioned description of the status of Kuwait expressed in a nutshell the attitude HMG had consistently adopted on the question (*ibid.*, 226). During the 1911–13 negotiations, the Ottoman Empire claimed *sovereignty* over Kuwait, whereas Britain maintained that it was prepared to recognize Turkish *suzerainty* (see IOLR R/15/5/65, reprinted in AB, vol. 7, 69).

63. Oppenheim, *International law*, vol. 1, 189–90.

64. See pp. 121–2.

65. "Letter on The Kuwait question from Tariq Aziz", 11, 16.

66. See, generally, the correspondence in IOLR R/15/5/65, reprinted in AB, vol. 7, 69. Asked by the Shaikh of Kuwait what might be involved in accepting Turkish suzerainty, the Political Agent invoked the analogy of Egypt "where the Khedive, though nominally a Turkish viceroy and a subject of the Sultan, enjoyed British protection and was for all practical purposes, quite independent of the Porte, who had no word in his internal administration, the collection of revenue and the like" (letter of 28 May 1913 to the Political Resident, *ibid.*, 161). See also "Report on the negotiations with Hakki Pasha on the Baghdad railway and the Persian Gulf", 3 May 1913, in Lauterpacht et al., *The Kuwait crisis*, 32.

67. Secret Additional Protocol to the Anglo–Turkish Convention, signed 29 July 1913. French original in Gooch and Temperley (eds), *British documents*, vol. 10, 196; English translation in Lauterpacht et al., *The Kuwait crisis*, 35.

68. By contrast, Turkey did persist in its claim to Mosul, which had been occupied during the war by British and Iraqi troops, on the ground that it had had sovereignty and never renounced it (Q. Wright, "The Mosul dispute", *American Journal of International Law*, 20 (1926), 453, 454–5). The frontier between Turkey and Iraq remained unsettled by the Treaty of Lausanne, but under the terms of that treaty the question was submitted to the League of Nations Council, which awarded most of Mosul to Iraq on 16 December 1925 (*ibid.*, 453).

69. C. Rousseau, *Droit international public*, vol. 3 (Paris: Sirey, 1977), 341; J. Crawford, *The creation of states in international law* (Oxford, Clarendon Press, 1979), 404; Arbitrator Borel, *Ottoman debt arbitration*, RIAA 1 (1925), 529 at 573; and *Annual Digest of Public International Law Cases*, vol. 3, Case No. 57 (1925), 78; *Roselius & Co. v. Karsten & Turkish Republic*, ibid., Case No. 26 (1926), 35.

70. *Ottoman debt arbitration*, 573, 608–9; *Annual Digest*, vol. 3, Case No. 29 (1925), 42.

71. D. P. O'Connell, *State succession in municipal and international law*, vol. 2 (Cambridge: Cambridge University Press, 1967), 39; and the cases cited in n69.

72. Oppenheim, *International law*, vol. 1, 165–6.

73. *Ibid.*, 188–90; M. J. De Louter, "La question du Transvaal", *Revue de droit international et de législation comparée* 28, 1st series (1896), 117, 122. Cf. *contra*, however, W. E. Hall's view that "a state under suzerainty of another, being confessedly part of another state, has those rights only which have been expressly granted to it" (*A treatise on international law*, 8th edn [Oxford: Clarendon Press, 1924], 32); criticized by

W. H. H. Kelke as unwarranted and erroneous in the light of state practice, in "Feudal suzerains and modern suzerainty", *Law Quarterly Review* **12** (1896), 215, 223.

74. Any such claims were in fact, as we have seen, foresworn by Turkey in the Treaty of Lausanne, Article 16: p. 123.

75. Unless, of course, provision had been made otherwise by treaty (as it was in the case of sharing the debt of the Ottoman Empire). But that was not the case here. There was no provision in the relevant instruments stipulating that the "dependencies" of the provinces forming Mesopotamia were to be included in the new state – a provision that could easily have been inserted had that been the intention.

76. I. Brownlie, *Principles of public international law*, 4th edn (Oxford: Oxford University Press, 1990), 159–62.

77. See pp. 136.

78. Iraq's objections are not contained in a single document, and have varied over time, different ones being invoked in 1961 from those in 1990: see, respectively, *The truth about Kuwait*; "Letter on The Kuwait question from Tariq Aziz"; and the press release "The political background to the current events".

79. *The truth about Kuwait*, 15, 18.

80. Cmnd 2370 (1925), Articles 1 and 4; also in Wright, *Mandates*, Appendix 2 (b), 595; extracts in Lauterpacht et al., *The Kuwait crisis*, 39.

81. "Decision of the Council of the League of Nations relating to the Application of the Principles of Article 22 of the Covenant to Iraq", reprinted in Wright, *Mandates*, Appendix 2 (a), 593–4; see also *ibid.*, 59–60, 503.

82. Wright, *Mandates*, 60.

83. The Covenant of the League of Nations is contained in Part I of the Peace Treaty of Versailles of 28 June 1919; relevant extracts reproduced in Lauterpacht et al., *The Kuwait crisis*, 38. Article 22(4) thereof provides that: "Certain communities formerly belonging to the Turkish Empire have reached a stage of development where their existence as independent nations can be provisionally recognized subject to the rendering of administrative advice and assistance by a Mandatory until such time as they are able to stand alone. The wishes of these communities must be a principal consideration in the selection of the Mandatory."

84. See pp. 122–3.

85. See Lorimer, *Gazetteer*, Vol. 2, 760–1, who notes that, in British official terminology, this area was known as "Turkish Arabia". He considered this to be an unfortunate expression, however, for "it obviously suggests the Red Sea provinces of Yemen and Hejaz rather than *Mesopotamia which is no part, either physically or politically, of the Arabian peninsula*" (emphasis added).

86. PG 13, para. 22, emphasis added. Cf. the analogous provision, Article 16, in the Treaty of Lausanne.

87. Wright, *Mandates*, 119.

88. Britain fell into the latter category in respect of Iraq, having submitted Reports on Iraq administration, 1920-2 and 1922-3 – both of which pre-dated confirmation of the mandate.

89. Wright, *Mandates*, 441.

90. *Ibid.*, 112.

91. Cmnd 1195 (1921); Wright, *Mandates*, 51. According to Wright, the readjustment was effected so as to allow Great Britain to construct a railway and pipeline entirely in its mandated area connecting the Hedjaz railway with the Mosul oil region and to permit France also to tap this oil region within its mandated territory.

92. Wright, *Mandates*, 119.

93. The League Council was confronted with a similar situation in the case of the agreement pending in March 1926 between France and Turkey defining the boundary of Syria. The Council initially intimated that it should be given the opportunity to confirm the agreement, on the ground that the mandatory did not have the power "to cede or lease on its sole authority, any part, however small of the territory". The

French representative maintained, however, that this was unnecessary as the treaty in question was "merely for the delimitation on the spot of the Angora agreement of 1921 and did not involve any cession of territory" (Wright, *Mandates*, 122, citing League of Nations Council, March 1926, XXXIX, *Official Journal*, vol. 7, 522). This contention was endorsed by the Permanent Mandates Commission at its 8th session (*ibid.*, citing Minutes of the Permanent Mandates Commission, vol. 8, 204; vol. 10, 192).

94. Schofield states in AB, vol. 7, viii, that such an argument has been advanced by Iraq in respect of the 1932 agreement, but we have not seen it. Similarly, although a memo by the Association for Free Kuwait has dealt with the point (see Lauterpacht et al., *The Kuwait crisis*, 82), it is unclear whether this is in response to an argument already put forward by Iraq.

95. League of Nations Treaty Series [LNTS], vol. 132, 363 (No. 3048), the preamble of which affirmed Great Britain's intention to support the candidature of Iraq for admission to the League of Nations in 1932 (thus terminating the mandate).

96. Tariq Aziz suggests that the Iraqi Prime Minister was actually forced to enter into this exchange of letters ("Letter on The Kuwait question", 10). We do not know what evidence there is of this, and without further information are unable to pursue the point. Cf. on the question of coercion of a state's representative, A. D. McNair, *The law of treaties* (Oxford: Clarendon Press, 1961), 206–11; Vienna Convention on the Law of Treaties 1969, Article 51.

97. See, for example, *Deutsche Continental Gas-Gesellschelt v. Polish State*, German–Polish Mixed Arbitral Tribunal 1929, *Annual Digest*, vol. 5, 11; *Poznanski v. Lentz and Hirschfeld*, German–Polish Mixed Arbitral Tribunal 1924, *Annual Digest*, vol. 2, 288; and Brownlie, *Principles*, 79–80.

98. See n43.

99. There may be seen to be some doubt in this regard, the British High Commissioner's memorandum of April 1923 having stated that the boundary set out therein was recognized "in so far as His Majesty's Government are concerned"; but the context suggests that it was signed by him on behalf of Iraq: see n42.

100. International Court of Justice Reports [ICJ Rep.] (1952), 172, 185, 193–94.

101. O'Connell, *State succession*, vol. 2, 141, 150–9; A. P. Sereni, "La représentation en droit international", *Recueil des cours de l'académie de droit international* 73 (1948–II), 69 at 109; and R. W. G. De Muralt, "The problem of state succession with regard to treaties" (1954), 119, in Whiteman (ed.), *Digest of international law*, vol. 2, 965.

102. Cf. the League of Nations Covenant, Article 22(4).

103. It is true that, in the Vienna Convention on the Succession of States in respect of Treaties (1978), the *tabula rasa* principle for newly independent states would, by virtue of the definition of Article 2(1)(b) and (f), appear to apply also where a mandated territory becomes fully independent and takes over responsibility for governing that territory. However, this Convention is not in force. Moreover, it is not retrospective, and it is questionable whether these principles represent the law as it stood in 1932, whatever may be the position today: see the authorities cited at note 101 above.

104. Brownlie, *Principles*, 669–70.

105. ICJ Rep. (1986), 554.

106. See to the same effect the Award of the Arbitral Tribunal in the *Guinea/Guinea–Bissau Maritime Delimitation Case 1985*: ILR **77**, 635 at 657 (para. 40). See also Article 62(2)(a), Vienna Convention on the law of treaties (1969), stipulating that the principle of a fundamental change of circumstances may not be invoked in respect of a "treaty which establishes a boundary", and Article 11, Vienna Convention on succession of states in respect of treaties (1978), which also contains a saving for boundaries. Although neither treaty is retrospective, and only the earlier one is in force, in the present respect they may well codify existing customary law.

107. "Letter on The Kuwait question from Tariq Aziz", 10, 18; press release "The political background to the current events", 14–15.

108. We are not, we should stress, experts in Iraqi law.

109. See p. 125.

110. English translation, as approved by the Iraqi Ministry of Justice, transmitted by the British Government to the Secretary General of the League of Nations, 28 November 1928, and communicated by the latter to the Council on 20 February 1929, C.49. 1929.VI. There were apparently no amendments to this prior to 1943. A. J. Peaslee (ed.), *Constitutions of nations*, 1st edn (Concord, N. H.: Rumford Press, 1950), vol. 2, 218, note 1.

111. See, for example, Sir Gerald Fitzmaurice, "Do treaties need ratification?" *British yearbook of international law* **15** (1934), 113 at 113–14.

112. See McNair, *Law of treaties*, 85-7.

113. See H. Blix, "The requirement of ratification", *British yearbook of international law* **30** (1953), 352; International Law Commission [ILC] commentary to draft Article 11 (now Article 14) Vienna Convention on the Law of Treaties, Report of the ILC on the 2nd part of its 17th session and on its 18th session (1966), General Assembly Official Records 21st session, Supp. No. 9, 30; E. Satow, *Guide to diplomatic practice*, 5th edn (New York: Longman, 1979), 247.

114. Cf., by way of contrast, two other agreements entered into contemporaneously by Great Britain and Iraq that specifically provided for ratification: the Anglo–Iraq Treaty of Alliance of 1922, Article 18, Cmnd 2370 (1925), in Wright, *Mandates*, 595; and the Anglo-Iraq Treaty of Alliance of 30 June 1930, Article 11, 132 LNTS 364. It might also be – though we do not know – that there was a doctrine of Iraqi constitutional law, like that in the United States, differentiating between treaties, which required parliamentary approval, and "executive agreements", which did not (see, *United States v. Belmont* (1937), 301 U.S. 324; *American Journal of International Law* **31** (1937), 537). If such a distinction did exist in Iraqi law, the fact that this was an agreement merely recognizing something that had already been done might well suggest that the present case fell into the executive agreement category.

115. Some suggestion that this may have been case is implicit in the assertion by Tariq Aziz that the Iraqi National Assembly "refused" to ratify the 1932 agreement (see "Letter on The Kuwait question", 10); but we have not seen anything to substantiate this contention.

116. UNTS, vol. 485, 326.

117. The agreement was entered into by the Baath régime that had seized power in February 1963, but was itself overthrown by a military coup on 18 November 1963. According to Tariq Aziz, the present Iraqi Foreign Minister, it was the "interim constitution of 1963" that required the National Revolutionary Council to ratify the agreement ("Letter on The Kuwait question", 18). We have not seen this constitution; nor is it mentioned by Peaslee or Blaustein in their outlines of Iraqi constitutional developments, though other interim and provisional constitutions are (A. J. Peaslee, ed., *Constitutions of nations*, 3rd edn [The Netherlands: Martin Nijhoff, 1966], vol. 2, 472; *ibid.*, 4th rev. edn, vol. 2, 1985, 375; A. P. Blaustein & G. H. Flanz, eds, *Constitutions of the countries of the world* [New York: Oceana publications, 1990], "Iraq", 1, 11). The press release issued by the Iraqi Embassy in London on 12 September 1990 asserted that the requirement to obtain the Council's approval was imposed by "Provision II of the National Revolutionary Council Act No. 75 of 1963", 15. We have not seen this either.

118. See Sir Ian Sinclair, *The Vienna Convention on the law of treaties*, 2nd rev. edn (Manchester: Manchester University Press, 1984), 19; P. Reuter, *Introduction to the law of treaties* (London: Pinter, 1989), 14-15, 35; McNair, *The law of treaties*, 60-77; and *Determination of the Maritime Boundary Guinea–Bissau/Senegal*, Arbitral Award of 31 July 1989 (not yet published), para. 55.

119. *Ibid.*, paras 53–60.

120. It may be noted in this regard that Tariq Aziz described the situation prevailing in Iraq at the time the agreement was signed as one of "political confusion and instability" ("Letter on The Kuwait question", 18).

121. Cf., to similar effect, McNair, *The law of treaties*, 63, 77, who asserts that the irregularity must be "notorious", citing, as an example, the well known requirement of the constitution of the United States that the President has the power to make treaties "by and with the Advice and Consent of the Senate".

122. For the position at customary international law, see McNair, *ibid.*, 76. Cf. the Vienna Convention on the Law of Treaties, Article 45.

123. See the memorandum produced by the Kuwait Embassy in London, "Refuting the falacies [*sic*] of Saddam and his gang: Kuwait is a historic, political and legal entity", circa September 1990, 11, 16–17, asserting that the provisions of the 1963 agreement were implemented immediately after the signing of the agreement. See also memorandum by the Association for Free Kuwait on behalf of the Embassy, circa November 1990, in Lauterpacht et al., *The Kuwait crisis*, 82.

124. Provided always, of course, that the person according recognition is competent to do so by virtue of his or her office or has been granted the appropriate powers by a person holding such office.

125. See n123 and related text. See also Brownlie, *Principles*, 95–6, citing Lauterpacht to the effect that such an exchange constitutes implied recognition.

126. *The truth about the crisis between Kuwait and Iraq*, 18–19, 29–38.

127. See pp. 124–5.

128. We expand on these points in our article "The Iraq/Kuwait boundary", 293. For an historical account of the boundary question, see Schofield, *Kuwait–Iraq*, Parts 4–5.

129. Text reproduced in AB, vol. 7, 192.

130. "Memorandum from the High Commissioner for Iraq to the Political Agent, Kuwait", 19 April 1923, in Aitchison, *Collection*, vol. 11, 266; Lauterpacht et al., *The Kuwait crisis*, 49. Actually, the language Cox used in the quotation is not quite the same as the language used by the Shaikh.

131. *IOLR R/15/5/184*, in AB, vol. 7, 372–76.

132. For the internal British consideration of these issues, see letter from H. R. P. Dickson, Political Agent, Kuwait, to the Political Resident, 27 August 1935, IOLR *L/P&S/12/3737*, in AB, vol. 7, 251; letter from Sir Archibald Clark Kerr, British Ambassador to Baghdad, to the Foreign Office, 30 October 1935, *IOLR R/15/5/184*, in AB, vol. 7, 463; Foreign Office reply to Clark Kerr of 22 January 1936, *ibid.*, 481.

133. PG 53, para. 46.

134. A map showing this segment of the Iraq/Kuwait frontier, with lines depicting these two possibilities, was produced by the Research Department of the Foreign Office in 1948, and reproduced in AB, vol. 24, as map 26. We reproduce it here as Figure 5.2.

135. See, further, the postscript. It is unclear whether Iraq's claim (see press release "The political background to the current events", 4) that Kuwait was stealing oil from the south Rumailah oilfield was a claim that Kuwait was drilling diagonally across the border; that Kuwait was drilling vertically, but in a location that was on Iraq's side of what should be the border (an argument incidentally inconsistent with the position it adopted that there was no entity of Kuwait entitled to a border); or thirdly that, even though Kuwait was drilling vertically, on its side of the border, it was tapping into a field that straddled the border and that the manner of extraction was unlawful.

136. See also Article 2(3) of the UN Charter and General Assembly Resolution 2625 (XXV), "Declaration on principles of international law concerning friendly relations and co-operation among states in accordance with the Charter of the United Nations", para. 1. Cf. the reasoning of the ICJ in the *Corfu Channel Case* (UK v. Albania) (Merits) , ICJ Rep., 1949, 4, 33–5, and, on the position at customary international law, *Case concerning military and paramilitary activities in and against Nicaragua* (Nicaragua v. USA) (Merits), ICJ Rep., 1986, 14, 98–103.

137. See the debates of the Security Council on Resolution 502 (1982), 3 April 1982: UN documents S/PV2345, 2346, 2349, 2350, 2360, 2362–64, 2366, 2368, 1–3 April 1961.

138. By contrast, the question of the precise course of the frontier has raised many difficulties and questions. We allude briefly to these matters in the short section "The boundary" above. They are explored more fully in our article "The Iraq/Kuwait boundary", 293. Since the latter was written, there have been further developments, which are dealt with in the postscript, as well as in Richard Schofield's chapter in this volume.

139. UN Document IK/101, 16 April 1992.

140. We hope to publish a detailed analysis of the commission's decisions.

CHAPTER SIX

The Kuwaiti islands of Warbah and Bubiyan, and Iraqi access to the Gulf

RICHARD SCHOFIELD

Introduction

This chapter examines the origins of Kuwait's ownership of the islands of Warbah and Bubiyan in the northwestern reaches of the Gulf and the constantly voiced Iraqi demand in the years since the late 1930s that the islands should be ceded or, at the very minimum, leased by Kuwait, so as to improve Iraq's access to the high sea. It takes us up to but not beyond the 1990–1 Kuwait crisis and Gulf war. Readers are referred to Chapter 1 for information on the recent deliberations of the United Nations. The chief characteristic of the territorial relationship between the two states during the past half-century has been Iraq's total inability to reconcile itself to the boundary delimitation it agreed with Kuwait in an exchanges of notes of 1932, which clearly specified Kuwaiti ownership of the islands. This is despite the conclusion, during October 1963, of an agreement in which the Baghdad Government recognized an independent Kuwait with its boundaries (according to the 1932 correspondence) for the first time since Iraq's admission to the League of Nations as an independent state in October 1932. Both before and after the false dawn of 1963 the Iraq–Kuwait islands and border questions have generally remained entrenched in the following intractable pattern of dispute: Iraq would agree to the final demarcation of the land boundary as defined by the 1932 exchange of notes, or, more accurately, Britain's 1951 interpretation of the alignment introduced by this correspondence,[1] only if Kuwait first agreed to the cession or lease of Warbah and Bubiyan; conversely Kuwait, which has tenaciously resisted all suggestions that it might cede or trade portions of its northern land and islands territories, has traditionally refused to consider leasing Warbah unless Iraq first agreed to the demarcation of the existing land boundary.

Why has Kuwaiti ownership of Warbah and Bubiyan proved so contentious historically? After all, these islands are low-lying alluvial flats largely incapable of inhabitation or effective development, while Warbah island is partially submerged at high tide. The answer lies in their strategic location and Iraq's deep-rooted belief that Kuwait's ownership of the features squeeze it out from the Gulf. Kuwait's ownership of the islands has meant that Iraq has been in no position to control the principal navigation channel linking the Khawr Zubair, an important, navigable water inlet on which Iraq's second dry cargo port of Umm Qasr is situated, with the waters of the Gulf. Instead of utilizing this route – the Khawr Abdallah with its westward extension along the Khawr Bubiyan lying between the islands of Warbah and Bubiyan – Iraqi shipping has been forced instead since the opening of Umm Qasr port in 1961 to navigate the Khawr Shetana channel, also a westward extension of the Khawr Abdallah lying north of Warbah island. This narrow access channel, theoretically shared with Kuwait according to Britain's 1951 interpretation of the boundary delimitation, needs constant dredging to remain navigable, unlike the Khawr Bubiyan, which is naturally navigable and reasonably deep (Fig. 6.2). It is hardly surprising that the Iraqis have sought to develop the Khawr Zubair. The economic and strategic potential of the water inlet had been recognized as early as 1866 by Political Resident Lewis Pelly, who had noted promising, natural anchorage facilities at what is today the site of a modern port, which he suggested might be suitable for a railway terminus. As will be seen, it was the perceived threat of this very development in the first years of the twentieth century that encouraged the Government of India to support the Shaikh of Kuwait's claim to Bubiyan and, indeed, to encourage him to claim the tiny island of Warbah to its immediate north. For the British authorities in the Gulf almost certainly calculated that the Khawr Zubair could not be successfully developed if another power (in this instance Kuwait under Britain's protection) held sovereignty over these islands.

The insecure status of the Shatt al-Arab, Iraq's principal arterial link with the waters of the Gulf and the southernmost constituent of the international boundary with Iran, has encouraged Iraq to look to develop an alternative access channel to the sea and one over which complete control is exercised. Hence the consistent demands over the past half-century for the cession or lease of Warbah and Bubiyan. In the 1960s and 1970s it was apparent that the capacity of Basrah, Iraq's principal dry cargo port laying 72 miles upstream from Faw at the mouth of the Shatt al-Arab, was approaching saturation point. Before the outbreak of the Iran–Iraq war in 1980, it was noticeable that all plans to expand port capacity were directed towards Umm Qasr and not Basrah. For the duration of the Iran–Iraq war and the two-year period between the 1988 ceasefire and the Iraqi invasion of Kuwait in August 1990 (and thereafter), the Shatt al-Arab remained blocked and Iraq needed to utilize the Khawr Zubair – Khawr Abdallah link if it was not to become in effect landlocked.

There are, of course, other considerations lying behind the demands of successive Baghdad regimes for Iraqi control of the islands in the northwestern Gulf. If Iraq were ever to gain sovereignty over the islands of Warbah and Bubiyan, then its narrow salient of developable coastline on the Gulf (less than 15 miles) would be at least doubled. This would also considerably enlarge the area of Gulf seabed to which Iraq would be entitled for the exploitation of hydrocarbons deposits. Iraqi leasehold rights over the islands, which were, rather than sovereign rights, generally the subject of negotiations over the 35-year period culminating in Iraq's invasion of August 1990, would, however, provide no alteration to Iraq's meagre seabed entitlement.

Iraq's frustration at not being able to secure some sort of control over the islands has probably encouraged the prosecution of the historical claim to the entirety of Kuwait. This claim, which is not difficult to rebut for historical and legal reasons,[2] has been pursued much less consistently but much more aggressively than demands that Warbah and Bubiyan should be leased or ceded. It is not proposed to delve deeply into the history of this claim in the present discussion, but a few comments might be made in summary by way of background.[3] The Iraqi claim to the whole of Kuwait has been pursued with varying degrees of purpose and intensity. In 1938, the Iraqi Foreign Minister, Tawfiq al-Suwaidi, made rather half-hearted calls for Kuwait to be administered as an integral part of Iraqi territory as significant instability prevailed within Kuwait during the period of the *majlis* movement.[4] Early in 1958, with the institution of the Hashimite Union of Iraq and Jordan, Nuri al-Said requested that Britain actively support moves for the incorporation of Kuwait within the Hashimite domain. In 1961, after displaying little interest in the emirate for nearly three years, General Qasim dramatically resurrected the Iraqi historical claim to Kuwait. In 1990 Iraqi President Saddam Husain utilized such arguments to justify the Iraqi occupation of Kuwait. These historical arguments were once again voiced loudly in Baghdad on the second anniversary of the Iraqi invasion in August 1992. They have remained a feature ever since. The case actually rests on Kuwait's incorporation within the former Ottoman province of Basrah at the turn of the century. Because of its generally latent characteristics, it has been almost impossible to predict when the argument will be employed. With the exchange of ambassadors following Iraq's recognition of Kuwait in the October 1963 agreement, it seemed as though no more would be heard of the historical claim. The events of 2 August 1990 squashed this assumption and suggest that it will be impossible to say for certain at any point in future that the claim has disappeared for good. To return to the islands question and the issue of Iraqi access to the Gulf. Practical considerations aside, Iraq has pointed to its narrow coastline as limiting any Gulf rôle that it might otherwise play. During April 1973 the Iraqi Foreign Minister was reported to have stated that Iraq could not possibly be a Gulf state without Warbah and Bubiyan.[5] Only a few months earlier, after hearing renewed Iraqi demands

155

for the lease of facilities on the islands and further complaints of its disadvantageous geographical position on the Gulf, a prominent Kuwaiti minister
neatly likened Iraq to "a big garage with a very small door"[6]. (Fig. 6.1).

The origins of Kuwaiti sovereignty over Warbah and Bubiyan, 1902–13

Up until the first two months of 1902, when Ottoman garrisons were positioned at Umm Qasr, Safwan and then Ras al-Qaid on the southeastern tip
of Bubiyan island, there had been no reason to consider what, even approximately, were the territorial limits of Kuwaiti Ruler Shaikh Mubarak's authority. In the years since 1896, largely by playing off Britain and the Ottoman
Empire against one another, Mubarak had done much to guarantee the
future of an independent Kuwait, protected as it now was against direct
Ottoman aggression by the "good offices" clause of the 1899 Secret Bond
negotiated with Britain and the *status quo* understanding reached between
London and Constantinople in the autumn of 1901.[7] The latter agreement
had done nothing to clarify the blurred international status of Kuwait,
which remained technically a part of the Ottoman Empire, despite its new
treaty relations with Britain. The basic importance of the *status quo* agreement lay in its specification that Britain would not establish a formal protectorate over Kuwait unless the Porte intervened militarily in the shaikhdom.
This understanding would continue to be the basis of Anglo–Ottoman relations over Kuwaiti for the next decade or so. When in November 1901, only
one month after the conclusion of the Anglo–Ottoman *status quo* understanding, the British authorities in the Gulf gave force to the arrangement by
preventing the Ottoman *naqib* of Basrah from landing at Kuwait, the Porte
probably realized that it would never directly control or maintain a presence
in Kuwait in the future.[8] The new policy of territorial encroachment at the
head of the Gulf embarked upon by the Porte during the first two months
of 1902 reflected such thinking. It was almost certainly calculated that by
moving southwards until stopped by the British, it would discover the
territorial limits that Britain was prepared to defend for Shaikh Mubarak.

After no protests had been received from Britain over the placing of Ottoman troop detachments at Safwan and Umm Qasr, the Porte deployed a
small garrison on Bubiyan island during February 1902. Although the Foreign Office initially doubted whether such an advance could be construed
as a breach of the recently agreed *status quo* understanding, considering at
this stage that Britain should defend no greater extent of territory than
Kuwait Bay for Mubarak, the Government of India viewed matters quite
differently. Its resolve to uphold Kuwaiti claims to Bubiyan, based upon the

periodic use of the feature by fishermen from the Awazim tribe, who generally paid allegiance to Mubarak, largely resulted from the findings of Commander Kemp's survey of the Khawr Abdallah and Khawr Zubair during late February 1902.[9] He noted, like Pelly some 40 years earlier, that an anchorage lying a couple of miles southeast of Umm Qasr might make a suitable railway terminus. One of the chief reasons that had prompted Britain to conclude the 1899 secret bond with the Ruler of Kuwait had been the successive plans of the Russian and German governments to run a railway to the Gulf. It was presumed that the terminus of the railway would lie on Kuwait Bay. By guaranteeing to protect this area, Britain calculated that it would have the final say in the form and location of the railway terminus or an effective veto should any plans be judged detrimental to its interests. Kemp had also discovered an anchorage on the Khawr Bubiyan to the southwest of Warbah island, which he considered, with adequate dredging, might make a better harbour for ocean-going vessels than Kuwait Bay itself. So the thought suddenly occurred to the British Government that, if no action were taken, the Porte might develop a railway head that Britain could do little to prevent or influence. In early March 1902, the Ottoman Foreign Minister confirmed to Sir Nicholas O'Conor, British Ambassador in Constantinople, that garrisons had been stationed at Safwan, Umm Qasr and Bubiyan because of the Porte's anxiety to keep an outlet for the railway under its own protection.[10]

So, later that month, O'Conor made a representation to the Grand Vizier that the British Government could not admit that the occupation of Bubiyan was anything but an infringement of the *status quo*. It was added that the Ottoman occupation could in no way be held to prejudice the rights of the Ruler of Kuwait to the island.[11] No action was taken, however, to pressurize the Porte into removing its post at Ras al-Qaid, which remained until the Ottoman Empire and the Porte commenced Great War hostilities in November 1914. In the spring of 1903, despite initial Foreign Office support, Britain shelved plans, for the immediate future at least, to participate in the German Baghdad railway scheme.[12] This only encouraged the Government of India to make good the Shaikh of Kuwait's claims to Bubiyan so as to deny any opportunity for the development of a railway terminus in the Umm Qasr / Khawr Zubair area. After a visit to the northwestern Gulf during November 1903 Indian Viceroy Lord Curzon had concluded that the anchorages in the Umm Qasr / Warbah island area would afford "an impregnable harbour",[13] which would be far easier to defend than a site on Kuwait Bay. Curzon, who had always been firmly opposed to the idea of a foreign railway venture reaching the Gulf coastline, recommended that the Shaikh of Kuwait should be assisted in establishing a post on the northern shores of Bubiyan island to counterbalance the Ottoman garrison at Ras al-Qaid. The Foreign Office stopped short of adopting this action, not wishing to antagonize the Porte unduly at a time when its co-operation was valued in other spheres of

157

foreign policy, and issued instructions for O'Conor to remind the Porte of its previous remonstrances and to press for the removal of the post. If, after an interval of time, the Ottoman post remained on Bubiyan, O'Conor would be instructed to make a further representation to the Porte announcing that Mubarak would be assisted in placing his own post on the island.[14]

One year later, in March 1905, the Government of India asked whether it was not now time to exert further pressure on the Porte to remove its garrison from and to support the Shaikh of Kuwait in establishing a post on the northern shores of Bubiyan island.[15] Before any instructions were passed on to O'Conor, the newly installed Political President in the Persian Gulf, Major Percy Cox, was instructed to ascertain Shaikh Mubarak's views on the establishment of a Kuwaiti post on Bubiyan island. He wanted not one but three posts: one alongside the Ottoman post at Ras al-Qaid; one on the northeast tip of Bubiyan island and, one on a tiny mud flat known locally as wool island lying east of Umm Qasr in the Khawr Zubair. No direct indication was given to Cox that Warbah island was also claimed.[16] British Foreign Secretary Lord Lansdowne eventually suggested that no action on the matter should be taken until the Committee of Imperial Defence had examined the question in relation to the connected issue of the terminus for the Baghdad railway.[17] This did not happen until late in 1907, despite further representations from the Government of India in the autumn of 1906.

By the time the Committee of Imperial Defence met, Britain had again decided to press for full participation in the Baghdad railway scheme. The Government of India's anxieties that a totally German railway might terminate at Basrah, after Captain Mahon's survey of possible terminal sites in 1905, had been primarily responsible for this turnaround.[18] Mahon concluded that, although Warbah island seemed the most suitable choice from an engineer's point of view, a line linking up with the Shatt al-Arab at Basrah had much greater economic potential. Viceroy Minto and Lord Kitchener considered that a German line to Basrah, which Britain could do little to prevent, would inevitably lead to the "Germanisation of the Baghdad or Basrah *wilayets*, the diminution of British prestige and commerce in these provinces, and the disturbance of our relations with the Arab Chiefs on the southern and western shores of the Persian Gulf". In the same despatch, the Government of India admitted, significantly, that the recent attempts made to consolidate British influence at Kuwait and to support Mubarak's claims to Bubiyan had been made only "in anticipation of the day when the port of a trans-continental railway system should be located in the neighbourhood".[19] There was the clear implication, therefore, that were it not for the threat of imperial competitors reaching the Gulf via the Baghdad railway, then Kuwait would not have received so generaous a definition for its northern limits. Britain's staunch defence of Kuwaiti claims to the islands was designed to "squeeze out" the Ottoman Empire from the Gulf so as to deny a rôle there for its European rivals.

By mid-1907 Britain again tended to the view that Kuwait Bay would make the most suitable terminus for the Baghdad railway. Importantly, during the previous year, Vice-Admiral Poe had highlighted the deficiencies of Umm Qasr and Warbah as possible termini, the former lying a good 30 miles or so from the waters of the Gulf proper, the latter practically submerged at high tide.[20] It was now decided during interdepartmental consultations in London that Britain should secure pre-emption rights over the most likely terminal sites for the Baghdad railway. So, by a secret agreement of 15 October 1907, Mubarak sold pre-emption rights over Bandar Shuwaikh, now considered the most likely terminal site, Kadhamah (Kazima) Bay (the previous favourite) and Warbah island, along with any other territory.over which the Ruler of Kuwait might exercise jurisdiction.[21] Britain had gained pre-emption rights over Warbah island yet there was no record of Mubarak ever having put forward a convincing claim to the island. On 2 October 1907, a fortnight before the Bandar Shuwaikh lease was signed, the Committee of Imperial Defence eventually met to consider what policy should be adopted towards the continuing presence of the Ottoman post at Ras al-Qaid. They came up with the following conclusions:

We therefore recommend, if diplomatic considerations permit, that the Shaikh of Kuwait should be invited to specify the nature of his claims to Warbah Island . . . and that the continued occupation of Bubiyan Island by a Turkish post . . . should be neutralised by the establishment forthwith of a Koweiti post, with the countenance of His Majesty's Government, on Warbah Island, or, if that should prove undesirable, on the northern shore of Bubiyan Island. If practicable, we would even recommend the establishment of posts on both islands.[22]

Before enacting such a policy it was agreed that the exact nature of the Shaikh of Kuwait's claims to Warbah island should first be ascertained by Major Knox, who since 1904 had been established as Britain's first Political Agent in Kuwait. No rights of pre-emption were to be exercised before such corroborative information had been gathered.

In the geographical and statistical sections of J. G. Lorimer's sprawling *Gazetteer of the Persian Gulf, Oman and central Arabia*, published in 1908 and 1915 for internal use by Government of India employees, the opinion was expressed that Kuwaiti rights to Warbah naturally followed from Kuwaiti ownership of the Ottoman-occupied island of Bubiyan.[23] This judgement had been made before Knox had been given a chance to investigate the exact nature of Kuwaiti claims to Warbah. In the summer of 1908, Mubarak informed Knox that the claim to Warbah was justified on the grounds by which Kuwaiti jurisdiction had been recognized over the neighbouring island of Bubiyan, namely the Awazim tribe had maintained fishing nets on the island for around 200 years.[24] Knox then interviewed a number of Awazim fishermen, who flatly contradicted Mubarak's claims. No ownership had ever been exercised over this mud flat, which was regarded as

159

useless for fishing purposes. While strong evidence was provided by the Awazim for long-established contacts with Bubiyan, Knox considered that Mubarak's claims to Warbah would have to be based on other arguments. Like Lorimer before him, he wondered whether, on geographical grounds, it might not be argued that Warbah was an offshoot of Bubiyan or, alternatively, whether the island had a stronger connection with the mainland to the west. If the latter were the case, Knox that argued a claim for Kuwaiti sovereignty could still be made as, "from Umm Qasr down the coast, I can myself testify without hesitation to the fact that the land is regarded as the grazing ground of Koweit Arabs and that Shaikh Mubarak's will throughout the region is law".[25] The India Office remained unconvinced by these arguments and instructed Knox to search for further evidence to support a Kuwaiti claim to the island. There is no record to show that these investigations were ever undertaken. However, Knox asked Mubarak in March 1909 whether he had any further evidence to substantiate his claim over Warbah. The al-Sabah ruler replied that "Warbah Island was almost entirely submerged at some high tides and that no-one could live there".[26] Though the weakness of a Kuwaiti claim to Warbah based on geographical contiguity had been readily acknowledged, the claim continued to be employed by the Government of India. In December 1910, a memorandum argued that since "it [Warbah] is separated only by a narrow channel from Bubiyan, it might fairly be argued on geographical grounds that the ownership of Warbah followed from that of Bubiyan".[27]

There was to be no more active consideration of the strength of Kuwaiti claims to the islands of Warbah and Bubiyan. In the protracted Anglo–Ottoman negotiations that resulted in the 29 July Convention (a settlement of a fairly broad package of outstanding Gulf questions), Britain insisted that the Porte must recognize Kuwaiti ownership of the two islands. The Constantinople Government ultimately had little option but to comply, though this admission was not given lightly. Recognition of Kuwaiti rights to Warbah and Bubiyan remained the last concession to be extracted from the Porte before the Convention could be signed.[28]

Confirmation of Kuwaiti sovereignty over Warbah and Bubiyan in international agreements, 1913–32

In the unratified Anglo–Ottoman Gulf settlement of July 1913, Kuwait was recognized as an autonomous *qadha* of the Ottoman Empire. It was further specified that the Ottoman flag was to be flown by the al-Sabah shaikh, who had the right to insert a distinctive emblem in its corner. He was to continue to be the Ottoman *qaimmaqam* (sub-governor), while his successors were bound to be appointed to a similar position by the Ottoman Porte. Importantly, however, the full autonomy of the shaikh was to be recognized within the territories of Kuwait proper, the limits of which were defined by a red semi-circle, some 40 miles in radius, on a map annexed to the July 1913 settlement (Figs 5.1 & 9.2). Within this inner zone of absolute authority were also included the islands of Warbah and Bubiyan (also circumscribed by the red line on the map), Mashjan, Failakah, Awhah and Kubr. In a more extensive outer zone of diminished Kuwaiti authority, prescribed by a green line also marked on the map annexed to the 1913 settlement, the al-Sabah shaikh was to continue to levy tribute and perform the administrative duties of Ottoman *qaimmaqam*. In both the inner and outer zones of Kuwaiti authority, the Ottoman Empire undertook to abstain entirely from any interference.[29]

In return for 'coming in on Britain's side at the onset of hostilities with the Ottoman Empire in November 1914, Kuwait was promised independence under British protection. The Ottoman garrison at Ras al-Qaid was finally removed a few days later as British forces landed on the shores of the northwestern Gulf.[30] The July 1913 Anglo–Ottoman settlement of Gulf questions was now therefore officially redundant. Kuwaiti claims to Warbah island having never been substantiated, the British Deputy Civil Commissioner of the Basrah *wilayat* enquired in March 1918 whether the feature was still claimed by the Shaikh of Kuwait. To this, Captain McCallum, Political Agent in Kuwait, replied that Kuwaiti rights to Warbah were recognized by Britain and that, if asked, Shaikh Salim would certainly claim the island. During the autumn of 1920, as Britain tried to effect a settlement of the deteriorating dispute between Salim and Ibn Saud, the al-Sabah shaikh did just this. Having apparently been told by McCallum during 1919 that Britain recognized the 1913 Green line as delimiting his shaikhdom, Salim claimed this delimitation for his northern boundary on 17 September 1920.[31] Despite the redundancy of the 1913 Anglo–Ottoman Convention, its zonal territorial provisions were employed to define the territorial extent of the Kuwaiti state in 1922 and 1923. The Uqair Protocol of December 1922 placed a boundary between the al-Sabah shaikhdom and Ibn Saud's Najdi state to the south along the inner zone or Red line of the 1913 settlement. Conversely, an exchange of correspondence between Kuwaiti Political Agent Major J. C. More and the British High Commissioner in Baghdad, Sir Percy Cox, during the following spring (April 1923), defined the boundary between the shaikhdom of Kuwait and the British-mandated territory of Iraq, administered by the Colonial Office since the Cairo Conference of 1921, as running along the outer zone or Green line of the 1913 settlement and confirmed Kuwaiti sovereignty over Warbah and Bubiyan. The boundaries claimed by Kuwaiti Ruler Shaikh Ahmad, as recognized in the British exchange of letters of 1923, were identical to those earlier claimed by his predecessor Salim during September 1920.[32]

The decision to reaffirm the Kuwait/Iraq boundary (with the specification that Warbah and Bubiyan belonged to Kuwait) as originally delimited by the Green line of the unratified Anglo–Ottoman Convention of July 1913 and confirmed by the 1923 exchange of notes was taken at a British interdepartmental meeting of April 1932. The Colonial Office, which considered that it was important when applying for membership of the League of Nations that the Iraqi Government should be in a position to show that it possessed well defined frontiers with all bordering states, thought that there would be no difficulties in getting the Iraqi Prime Minister, Nuri al-Said, to confirm this delimitation. So it proved. By letters dated 21 July 1932 and 10 August 1932 Nuri al-Said and Shaikh Ahmad of Kuwait respectively agreed to confirm the existing boundary delimitation between the two states. Kuwaiti sovereignty over Warbah and Bubiyan was also confirmed.[33] Yet there were some reports of dissent at an Iraqi Cabinet meeting of late July 1932. Defence Minister Jaafar al-Askari reportedly expressed strong reservations about admitting Kuwaiti sovereignty over the islands, which, it was suggested, might be claimed by the Iraqis on the basis that these features were formed by Mesopotamian mud.[34]

Iraqi demands for the cession of Warbah and Bubiyan, 1938–54

In March 1938, the Iraqi Foreign Ministry intimated that it would like to possess an alternative outlet to the Gulf to the Shatt al-Arab, preferably an Iraqi-controlled port on Kuwait Bay.[35] The idea was seriously considered in interdepartmental meetings held in London during the summer of 1938, with opinion generally divided as to the advisability of offering Iraq certain facilities in Kuwaiti territory. A new development occurred in August 1938 with the visit to the Foreign Office of Colonel Sir John Ward, Head of the Basrah Port Directorate and Director-General of the Iraqi railways. He contended none too convincingly that the capacity of the Shatt al-Arab was reaching breaking point, but that alternative port facilities should be sought on the Khawr Zubair rather than Kuwait Bay itself. Lacy Baggallay of the Foreign Office quickly pointed out that Kuwaiti sovereignty over Warbah island meant that Iraq owned only the northern bank of the Khawr Abdallah, the strategically important waterway linking the Khawr Zubair with the waters of the Gulf. He suggested that Iraq might secure Warbah by making other territorial concessions to Kuwait.[36]

In his bizarre aide-mémoire dated 28 September 1938, which included, for the first time since Iraq's admission to the League of Nations as an independent state in October 1932, an articulation of Iraq's historical rights to the entirety of Kuwait, Iraqi Foreign Minister Tawfiq al-Suwaidi listed three reasons why new port facilities were sought on the Gulf coastline adding that these could be situated on Kuwait Bay or along the Khawr Zubair. First, the reliability of the Shatt al-Arab was vulnerable to the long-standing dispute with Iran over its alignment and international status; secondly, the Shatt al-Arab was becoming increasingly congested, owing principally to the activities of the Anglo-Iranian Oil Company at Abadan; thirdly, Iraq wished to extend its railway beyond Basrah to the Gulf coast.[37] In a meeting held at the Foreign Office during early October 1938, C. W. Baxter advised Tawfiq to concentrate upon the Khawr Zubair as the site for any new Iraqi port facilities outside the Shatt al-Arab. When Tawfiq replied that certain territorial concessions would need to be made by Kuwait before the water inlet could be effectively developed, Baxter authorized him to enter into discussions with Shaikh Ahmad on the subject. Baxter argued that, if Iraq wanted Kuwait to cede sovereignty over Warbah and the southern waters of the Khawr Abdallah, it would probably have to offer compensation to the Shaikh of Kuwait that considerably exceeded the actual value of this territory.[38] Another change in the line-up of the Baghdad Government during 1939 meant that the projected bilateral discussions never took place.

During the summer of 1939 Colonel Ward secretly undertook a survey of the Khawr Zubair and communicated his findings to the British Government. He established that the most suitable site for the development of the proposed port was at a point 2½ miles southeast of Umm Qasr, at the natural anchorage Pelly had first discovered in 1866. Even if Iraq chose not to develop this site, he suggested that Britain should be aware of its potential strategic benefits during wartime.[39] At an interdepartmental meeting of August 1939 it was decided that Ward's findings should be communicated to the Iraqi Government. What the Iraqis were not informed of was the utter confusion prevailing in British governmental circles about whether Ward's proposed site lay within Iraqi or Kuwait territory. That is another story.[40] In November 1939 the new Iraqi Foreign Minister, Jawdat Ali, admitted to being impressed by Ward's report and announced that wharves and moorings for two ships would be erected at the site south of Umm Qasr. For the effective protection of the port and its approaches, Iraq would require Kuwait to cede the islands of Warbah and Bubiyan. Jawdat argued that, as these islands were merely barren, occasionally sandy mud flats, they could be of no possible use to Shaikh Ahmad, who therefore need receive no compensation for their cession. The British Chargé d'Affaires in Baghdad, Houston-Boswell, insisted that there must be a *quid pro quo* and if this could not be territorial then it should be financial.[41]

The questions of whether Iraq should be allowed to secure control over the Khawr Abdallah and, if it should, what inducements might be offered to Kuwait, were then broached by the various departments of the British Government. Baggallay had commented in August 1939 that complete Iraqi control of the water channel would be most convenient for practical administration. During December 1939, evidently backed by the Foreign Secretary, he added that there would also be some justice in this arrangement:

[I]t is understandable that the State which controls the Mesopotamian plain should desire to have undivided control of at least one good means of access to the sea, and Lord Halifax thinks that on a long view it is likely that, if Iraq were given this access, it would make for steadier conditions in that part of the world in years to come.[42]

The Foreign Office added that Kuwait need not necessarily give up sovereignty over Bubiyan for Iraq to control the whole of the Khawr Abdallah. It was implied here that Kuwaiti rights could stop at the low-water mark of Bubiyan island. It might be added, though, that 100 years of dispute between the Ottoman Empire and Persia and their successors over a similarly arranged Shatt al-Arab boundary hardly augured well for such a scheme's workability. Importantly, however, the Foreign Office stressed that, whatever Iraq's desiderata, the Shaikh of Kuwait was under no obligation to cede to Iraq any part of his territory, except in return for what he considered to be adequate compensation.[43]

Yet another ministerial reshuffle in Baghdad of early 1940 saw Nuri al-Said regain control of Iraq's foreign affairs. Nuri requested during February 1940 that Britain support Iraqi efforts to obtain territorial concessions from Shaikh Ahmad to safeguard the approaches to Umm Qasr. While giving no details, he hinted that economic satisfaction would be given to the shaikh if he complied.[44] Meanwhile Baggallay and the Foreign Office continued to argue that Iraqi control over the Khawr Abdallah was desirable. Yet the Government of India now argued quite the reverse. The Political Resident doubted whether Iraq really needed a port on the Khawr Zubair and maintained that, if there had to be one, it should be administered jointly by Britain, Iraq and Kuwait. A purely Iraqi port, it was argued, would threaten the further economic wellbeing of Kuwait, which might itself be justified in wanting to develop port facilities on the Khawr Zubair inlet. The Indian authorities also suggested that to allow Iraqi control over both shores of the Khawr Abdallah would be inimical to British interests:

As a point of principle in British interests, as distinct from those of Kuwait, we are entirely opposed to any territorial cession. The last twenty years have demonstrated Iraqi fickleness and we should not abet the transfer of an important point from a sheikhdom to a State whose future attitude to the Empire is hard to predict.[45]

Any chances that Shaikh Ahmad might have agreed to Iraqi inducements to him to cede sovereignty over Warbah and Bubiyan disappeared in late March 1940. In an interview with Political Resident Lieutenant-Colonel Charles Prior, the Kuwaiti ruler stated that he would give Iraq "nothing at all" and that "all he wanted . . . was that they should keep out of Kuwait".[46] The evident tenacity with which Shaikh Ahmad defended every inch of his territory persuaded the Home government that there was no realistic prospect of Kuwait ceding Warbah and Bubiyan. In any case, no more was heard of the Iraqi proposal to construct a port on the Khawr Zubair after Sir Basil Newton, the British Ambassador in Baghdad, informed Jawdat Ali in May 1940 that Britain could not promise any assistance to finance the scheme until further enquiries had been made concerning the precise location of the proposed port, namely whether it lay within Iraqi or Kuwaiti territory.[47] With Kuwait unwilling to make any concessions on the islands issue, the Foreign Office now considered that any proposals offered to the Baghdad Government as a basis for the final demarcation of the land boundary would have to be a legitimate interpretation of the express terms of the vaguely worded 1932 correspondence which had described the boundary and confirmed Kuwaiti sovereignty over Warbah and Bubiyan. Thus Britain offered its basis for the demarcation of the land boundary to the Iraqi Ministry of Foreign Affairs during October 1940.[48] Sir Basil Newton was soon privately informed by C. J. Edmonds, a British Adviser to the Iraqi Ministry of the Interior, that the Iraqi Ministry of Defence strongly deprecated any demarcation of the land boundary before the islands of Warbah and Bubiyan had first been ceded by Kuwait. This answer was communicated formally to the British Ambassador during March 1941.[49] So the border and islands question had been set in the pattern of deadlock that persisted right up to the Iraqi invasion of Kuwait on 2 August 1990.

During the Second World War, the Allied Powers erected landing facilities on the Khawr Zubair at the precise spot where the Iraqis had wished to develop their own port only a few years earlier. As the Foreign Office and the Government of India had been unable to agree on the terminal point of the Iraq/Kuwait land boundary on the Khawr Zubair, the sovereignty of the site in question was temporarily set to one side while the port was erected in the disputed strip of territory and administered on a purely military basis. It was completely dismantled at the end of the Second World War, in part because of its sensitive location.[50] The shipping that actually made use of the short-lived allied military facilities at Umm Qasr used the Khawr Abdallah and its westward extension along the Khawr Bubiyan to reach the Khawr Zubair from the Gulf. This was, of course, the navigable channel over which Iraq sought control through its demands that Kuwait cede Warbah and Bubiyan. Instead, Iraq has had to content itself with sharing the much less satisfactory westward arm of the Khawr Abdallah, the Khawr Shetana, running north of Warbah island.

During the summer of 1949 the Iraqi Government again announced plans for the development of Umm Qasr port and repeated its hopes that Kuwait would cede the islands of Warbah and Bubiyan so that sole control might be gained over navigation in the channels leading to the Gulf. Soon afterwards, in his last days as Ruler of Kuwait before his death in January

1950, Shaikh Ahmad requested that Britain should finally fix Kuwait's northern boundaries with Iraq as soon as possible.[51] Eventually, by December 1951, Britain had decided what boundary the vague 1932 correspondence had meant to introduce. This interpretation was offered to the Iraqi Government as a basis for the demarcation of the boundary, having earlier been agreed with the Ruler of Kuwait.[52] By the summer of 1952 the Iraqis had replied, with their agreement to Britain's demarcation proposals contingent upon Kuwait ceding the island of Warbah, so that Iraq might secure the approaches of the port it intended to develop at Umm Qasr. The Iraqi Foreign Ministry reminded the Foreign Office that it was they who had suggested that Iraq should try to obtain the island of Warbah by offering Shaikh Ahmad financial inducements or territorial concessions elsewhere only a decade earlier.[53]

Iraqi demands for the cession or lease of Warbah and Bubiyan, 1955–8

In May 1955 the Iraqi Government announced their desire "to advance its frontier to a depth of some four kilometres, covering a desert strip, the uninhabited island of Warbah and the waters of the Khawr Abdallah which surround it" (Fig. 6.1).[54] The Iraqi Government sought such changes, it was maintained, only to provide solid foundations for the future expansion of the town and port of Umm Qasr, and so that its approach channels might be dredged and marked in reasonable security. All oil rights in these places Iraq would renounce in favour of Kuwait. If Shaikh Abdallah of Kuwait could be persuaded to accede to such demands, Iraq would agree to the demarcation of the rest of the boundary on the basis of the British note of December 1951. Sir Michael Wright, the British Ambassador in Baghdad, immediately hit upon the idea of linking this proposal with the projected scheme, under consideration since 1952, to pipe fresh water from the Shatt al-Arab across the Faw peninsula to Kuwait. As it was Britain's experience that the al-Sabah rulers would not relinquish sovereignty over territory that had previously been recognized as belonging to them, Wright also suggested that both the Umm Qasr scheme and the Shatt al-Arab water carrier scheme (as it concerned Iraqi territory through which the Kuwaiti water pipeline would run) should be arranged on corresponding long-lease (99 years) terms.[55] So, the idea of leasing the islands from Kuwait, rather than demanding their outright cession, had been born.

Wright's proposals to link the leasehold schemes were presented to Shaikh Abdallah in June 1955 and, encouragingly, the al-Sabah ruler gave his provisional approval.[56] For its part, the Iraqi Foreign Ministry was not interested in the proposed linkage of the Umm Qasr scheme with the Shatt al-Arab water carrier proposal, but had no objections to the simultaneous signing of two separate agreements. It was also apparent that Iraq would insist on policing and administering its leased area in Kuwait. The British authorities in the Gulf and the British Embassy in Baghdad both considered that this would be acceptable so long as adequate safeguards for the protection of Kuwaiti interests were built in to the draft 10-article Umm Qasr lease agreement. In the end the Iraqis demurred at only one of these conditions – an undertaking that property privately owned by Kuwaitis in the area would not be disturbed.[57]

No sooner had the Foreign Office begun to make final preparations for the conclusion of the Umm Qasr and Shatt al-Arab water carrier agreements than the prospects for their settlement suddenly receded. In October 1955, Nuri al-Said, now back in place as Iraqi Prime Minister, introduced a new element into the bargaining – the Iraq Petroleum Company wished to run an oil pipeline from its Zubair field to Mina al-Ahmadi on the Gulf coast of southern Kuwait. By way of enticement Nuri offered Kuwait a 50 per cent share in the development of the proposed port at Umm Qasr.[58] These proposals produced little reaction from Kuwait. In December 1955, however, Shaikh Fahad, the brother of the Kuwaiti ruler, commented that it was extremely dangerous for Kuwait to give up any land to Iraq in the long term, even if this was by lease. Gawain Bell, Political Agent in Kuwait, also reported that the al-Sabah were visibly weary of the pressure Britain was exerting to secure Kuwait's agreement with Iraq on Umm Qasr port and the water carrier scheme.[59] Meanwhile, further information was coming to light concerning Iraq's plans to develop the area surrounding Umm Qasr, should it be acquired on lease. There were plans to develop the natural anchorage south of Warbah island, which Lord Curzon had described as "impregnable" in 1903. There were also reports that Iraq intended to go ahead with the development of Umm Qasr, with or without the blessing of Kuwait.[60]

It was no surprise when Kuwait decided against concluding the Shatt al-Arab water carrier scheme in January 1956. Opposition had long been mounting against an arrangement that would have left Kuwait totally dependent on its northern neighbour for the supply of a vital natural resource. The Kuwaiti ruler opted instead for extensive investment in distillation plants.[61] This decision led the Iraqi Government to reiterate that the time was not right for a demarcation of the Kuwait/Iraq boundary.[62] So, after all their early promise, the efforts to promote a territorial settlement within a larger framework of improved bilateral relations had not succeeded. The failure of this more imaginative approach threw the border and islands question straight back into its previous deadlock.

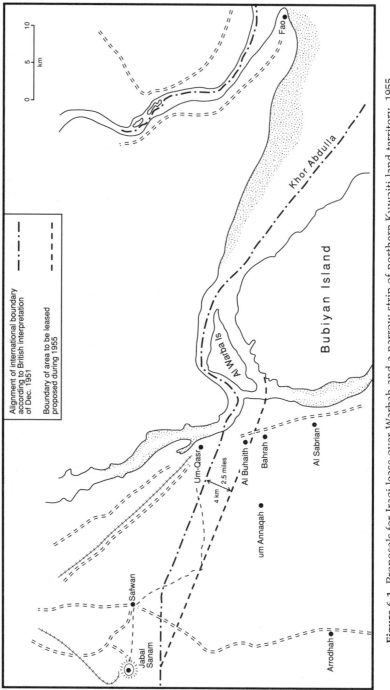

Figure 6.1 Proposals for Iraqi lease over Warbah and a narrow strip of northern Kuwaiti land territory, 1955.

Britain tried to revive proposals to demarcate the boundary and also the Shatt al-Arab water carrier scheme during the next two years, but met with little success. Iraq held to its position that it could not reaffirm and demarcate the boundary until Kuwait had agreed first to cede or lease the 4 km strip of territory south of Umm Qasr and the island of Warbah.[63] At around the same time, Shaikh Fahad intimated that the cession of Warbah might be contemplated, but only after the Kuwait/Iraq land boundary, as defined by the British interpretation of December 1951, had been fully demarcated.[64]

"More of the same", 1958-90

Apart from the dramatic interlude provided by Qasim's reassertion of the historical claim for the amalgamation of Kuwait within Iraq on the announcement of the emirate's independence in June 1961,[65] the history of the Kuwait–Iraqi border question up until 1990 could be described as being "more of the same". Following the 1988 ceasefire in the Iran–Iraq war, Iraq still sought the lease or cession of the islands of Warbah and Bubiyan before Kuwait's requests for the demarcation of the boundary would be considered. Certainly, throughout this period the two sides never came anywhere near as close to finding a solution to the borders and islands question as they had been in 1955.

This lack of progress was in spite of the conclusion during October 1963 of an agreement in which Iraq recognized an independent Kuwait for the first time and the borders between the two states as defined by the 1932 exchange of notes.[66] The failure of the two sides in 1963 to take the same opportunity to fix provisions for the final demarcation of the boundary suggested either that the border question had not been seriously considered between the two states in the run-up to the signature of the treaty or that Iraq still hankered after the lease of the islands. The latter scenario soon proved well founded as, within only a few years, Iraq returned to the offensive on the islands issue.

Very few new proposals for a resolution of the border and islands question were made during this period. Established ones were unavailingly resurrected, such as schemes to lease the islands on terms varying from 20 to 99 years and renewed attempts to make a territorial solution part and parcel of a much wider package of bilateral agreements between the two neighbours. Proposals were reportedly made as recently as early 1989 to exchange Kuwaiti sovereignty over Warbah and Bubiyan for relatively well watered inland strips of Iraqi territory.[67] During 1977, proposals were made that the two sides should agree to differ on territorial questions but promote bilateral relations to such a healthy state that the failure to settle the border and islands question would be largely irrelevant.[68] These have all been recurring yet ultimately fruitless suggestions for the resolution of the boundary dispute. They have foundered on Iraq's basic determination to improve its access to the sea and Kuwait's resolve not to cede any part of its national territory.

Even before the Iraqi invasion of Kuwait on 2 August 1990, it seemed that Kuwait had bolstered its sovereignty over Warbah and Bubiyan, but especially the latter, to the extent that it would be almost impossible to cede or lease these features to Iraq. This was a process that began, essentially, with the Iraqi attack during March 1973 on the Kuwaiti border post of al-Samtah, a few miles to the southwest of Umm Qasr, which resulted in the death of two Kuwaitis. The incident's chief long-term significance was its effect on the territorial consciousness of the Kuwaiti Government and public alike. From this point onwards Kuwait became visibly defensive about Warbah, Bubiyan and its northern territories. Ships and businesses began to be named after the islands of Warbah and Bubiyan and northern border posts such as al-Samtah and Abdaly.[69] During the Iran–Iraq war, Kuwait took physical steps to assert its sovereignty over the islands of Warbah and Bubiyan. After warnings from the Speaker of the Iranian *majlis*, Ali Akbar Hashemi Rafsanjani, against granting Iraq naval facilities on the islands in

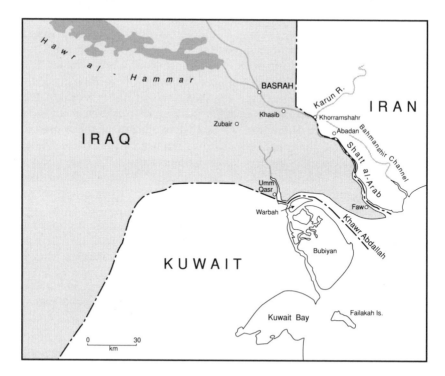

Figure 6.2 Iraq's limited access to the Gulf.

November 1984, Kuwait installed its own forces with rockets and anti-aircraft batteries on Warbah and Bubiyan during the following month.[70]

Steps taken to reinforce the physical evidence for Kuwaiti sovereignty over Warbah and Bubiyan were not restricted to the military sphere. In early 1983 an economically useless bridge was hastily constructed to link Bubiyan island with the Kuwaiti mainland at Sabiyah, at the northern entrance to Kuwait Bay. The purely symbolic value of the bridge was clear for all to see since the feature initially possessed no connecting roads. Hence it was jokingly referred to by Kuwaitis as "linking nowhere to nowhere".[71] During 1984 the Kuwaiti Ministry of Information announced that a further bridge was to be constructed to link Bubiyan with Warbah further north, though there were no indications that this had been completed by the end of the 1980s. The Ministry also revealed further proposals to develop research centres, along with fish-canning plants on Bubiyan.[72] These strategically motivated developments were overtaken by the Iraqi invasion of 2 August 1990.

Concluding remarks

The border and islands question had remained in deadlock long before Iraq's calamitous action of invading Kuwait. Iraq's acceptance during the spring of 1991 of United Nations terms for a Gulf ceasefire (United Nations Resolution 687 passed in New York during the late afternoon of 3 April 1991) committed it to respect the inviolability of the boundary as referred to in the Iraq–Kuwait "Agreed Minutes" of 4 October 1963. As this agreement itself bound Iraq to respect the boundary delimitation introduced by the 1932 exchange of correspondence, Kuwaiti sovereignty over the islands of Warbah and Bubiyan was, once more, formally recognized. The United Nations Iraq/Kuwait Boundary Demarcation Commission (UNIKBDC) announced its decision on the land boundary on 16 April 1992. Its decision on the water boundaries between the two states was announced in the spring of 1993 to follow the median line along both the Khawr Abdallah and its western arm north of Warbah island, the Khowr Shetana. Since June 1992 Iraq took no part in UNIKBDC's deliberations. It all but rejected the findings of the United Nations with respect to the boundary. Yet both UNIKBDC and the United Nations Iraq–Kuwait Observation Mission (UNIKOM) – the peacekeeping force that monitors the demilitarized zone along the border, and since February 1993 has been empowered to actively resist serious Iraqi violations of the newly-demarcated land boundary – reported that Iraq and Kuwait had co-operated as the UN laid permanent pillars to demarcate the land boundary during the late autumn of 1992 (see Ch. 1). This having been said, Iraqi incursions into UNIKOM's demilitarized border zone were partially responsible for the West's action of resuming limited bombing against Iraq early in January 1993.

171

Notwithstanding the current "successes" of the United Nations in settling the border issue, there are no reasons to believe that the constantly asserted positional demand that Kuwait cede or lease the islands of Warbah and Bubiyan so that Iraq might improve its access to the waters of the Gulf would simply disappear with the current Baghdad regime, if and when this occurs. Most prominent Iraqi opposition groupings for instance have denounced or rejected the recent United Nations' decisions on the border. Presuming the eventual resumption of normal relations between Kuwait and Baghdad, the same problems of finding a long-term solution to the border and islands question, so apparently unbridgeable during the past half-century, may well have to be addressed once more. Ultimately a formula might have to be found that satisfies Kuwait's legitimate security concerns but also addresses the long-established Iraqi desire for secure access to the Gulf outside the Shatt al-Arab waterway. It is of the utmost importance for the future stability of Kuwaiti–Iraqi relations, and also Iranian–Iraqi relations for that matter, that Iraq no longer perceives itself as "squeezed out" of the Gulf. Given its narrow coastline and the fact that Iraq exercises complete sovereignty over neither the Shatt al-Arab nor the Khawr Abdallah (its two means of access to Gulf waters), this will probably prove a very difficult perception to assuage.

This chapter has perhaps highlighted some historical antecedents for Iraq's negative consciousness concerning access to the Gulf. After all, the original support given to Kuwaiti claims to Bubiyan and the encouragement given to Shaikh Mubarak to claim Warbah in the first decade of this century were prompted, above all, by the Government of India's desire to squeeze the Ottoman Empire out of the northwestern Gulf and thereby to deny a footing there for its chief imperial rivals. Unless a satisfactory long-term solution to the problem, genuine or illusory, of Iraqi access to the Gulf can by found, then successive Baghdad Governments may well continue to argue that Kuwait should compensate Iraq for its geographic and strategic misfortune.

Notes

1. Up until the United Nations settlement of the Iraq/Kuwait land boundary in the aftermath of the 1990–1 Kuwait crisis and Gulf war, Britain's demarcation proposal of December 1951 remained the most detailed existing interpretation of the vague 1932 definition of the boundary, clearly informing those maps depicting this limit produced before the UN announced its decision on the land boundary in April 1992. The decision of the United Nations on the land boundary, released on 16 April 1992, has itself been described by a leading protagonist as a "refinement of Britain's 1951 interpretation". For post-1990 developments, see Chapter 1.

2. See Chapter 5.

NOTES

3. For an analysis of the emerging international status of Kuwait up to the dissolution of the Ottoman Empire, see R. N. Schofield, *Kuwait and Iraq: historical claims and international disputes*, Middle East Programme Report (London: Royal Institute of International Affairs, 1991), 1–49. Also see B. C. Busch, *Britain and the Persian Gulf, 1894–1914* (Berkeley: University of California Press, 1967); and B. C. Busch, "Britain and the status of Kuwayt, 1896–1899", *The Middle East Journal* **21** (1967), 187–98. Also, D. H. Finnie, *Shifting lines in the sand: Kuwait's elusive frontier with Iraq* (London: I. B. Tauris, 1992).

4. See J. Crystal, *Oil and politics in the Gulf: rulers and merchants in Kuwait and Qatar* (Cambridge: Cambridge University Press, 1990), 47-61; J. E. Peterson, *The Arab Gulf states: steps toward political participation* (New York: Praeger, 1988) 30-1; Alan Rush, *Al-Sabah: history and genealogy of Kuwait's ruling family, 1752–1987* (London: Ithaca Press, 1987), 57.

5. The *Kuwait Times*, 5 April 1973.

6. Schofield, *Kuwait and Iraq*, 110.

7. *Ibid.*, 13–22.

8. *Ibid.*, 21-2.

9. Commander T. W. Kemp to Captain F. S. Pelham, Senior Naval Officer in the Persian Gulf, 20 February 1902, Public Record Office PRO FO 78/5251.

10. See Busch, *Britain and the Persian Gulf*, 217.

11. Telegram from Sir N. O'Conor to the Marquess of Lansdowne, Secretary of State for Foreign Affairs, 11 March 1902, PRO FO 78/5251.

12. Schofield, *Kuwait and Iraq*, 28-9.

13. L. W. Dane, Government of India, to the Secretary of State for India, 20 November 1903, PRO FO 78/5285.

14. Telegram from the Foreign Office to Sir N. O'Conor, 10 May 1904, PRO FO 78/5385.

15. Viceroy to the Secretary of State for India, 16 March 1905, PRO FO 78/5468.

16. Major P. Z. Cox to the Government of India, 11 June 1905, India Office Library and Records IOLR R/15/5/68.

17. Foreign Office to India Office, 9 August 1908, IOLR R/15/5/68.

18. E. W. S. Mahon, "Report on the country adjacent to the Khawr Abdallah, and places suitable as a termini of proposed Baghdad railway", 1905, IOLR L/P&S/18/B165, 5.

19. Viceroy, Government of India, to the Secretary of State for India, IOLR L/P&S/18/B166a.

20. Vice-Admiral Poe to the Admiralty, 26 April 1906, IOLR L/P&S/18/B166a.

21. See texts of lease agreement dated 15 October 1907, IOLR L/P&S/10606.

22. See Foreign Office, "Memorandum respecting British interests in the Persian Gulf", 1908, PRO FO 881/9161.

23. J. G. Lorimer, *Gazetteer of the Persian Gulf, Oman and central Arabia*, vol. 2: *Geographical and statistical* (Calcutta: Superintendent Government Printing Press, 1908), 1059-61.

24. See translation of confidential correspondence of June 1908 passing between Mubarak and Knox, IOLR R/15/5/68.

25. Major S. G. Knox to Major P. Z. Cox, Bushire, 9 June 1908, IOLR R/15/5/68.

26. Political Agent, Kuwait, to the Political Resident in the Persian Gulf, 17 March 1909, IOLR R/15/5/18.

27. See Government of India, "Memorandum on British relations with Turkey on the Persian Gulf", 1910, IOLR L/P&S/18/B181.

28. Schofield, *Kuwait and Iraq*, 42-4.

29. *Ibid.*, 41-6.

30. *Ibid.*, 47-8.

31. Major J. C. More to the Political Resident in the Persian Gulf, 17 September 1920, IOLR R/15/1/522.

32. Schofield, *Kuwait and Iraq*, 60-1.

33. *Ibid.*, 60-1; Finnie, *Shifting lines*, 70-84.

34. Press release of the Iraqi Embassy, London, 12 September 1990, "The political background to the current events", 13–14.
35. Sir Maurice Peterson, Baghdad, to Foreign Office, 30 March 1938, *IOLR R/15/1/541*.
36. Lacy Baggallay to R. T. Peel, India Office, 26 August 1938, *IOLR R/15/5/208*.
37. See aide-mémoire dated 28 September 1938 by Tawfiq al-Suwaidi, *PRO FO 371/21858*.
38. Schofield, *Kuwait and Iraq*, 75.
39. See summary of report by J. C. Ward in despatch dated 8 August 1939 from Lacy Baggallay, Foreign Office, to C. G. Jarrett, Admiralty, *PRO FO 371/23200*.
40. Schofield, *Kuwait and Iraq*, 76–86.
41. Houston-Boswell, Baghdad, to Lord Halifax, Foreign Office, 14 November 1939, *PRO CO 732/86/17*.
42. Lacy Baggallay, Foreign Office, to India Office, 16 December 1939, *PRO CO 732/86/17*.
43. *Ibid*.
44. Telegram from Sir Basil Newton to Foreign Office, 27 February 1940, *PRO CO 732/86/17*.
45. Telegram from the Government of India to the Secretary of State for India, 18 March 1940, *PRO CO 732/86/17*.
46. Telegram from the Political Resident in the Persian Gulf to the Secretary of State for India, 22 March 1940, *PRO FO 371/24559*.
47. Foreign Office minute dated 7 June 1943 on the discussions held during 1938–42 regarding the construction of a port on the Khawr Zubair, with reference to the question of the Kuwait/Iraq frontier, *PRO FO 371/34999*.
48. Schofield, *Kuwait and Iraq*, 81–2.
49. Sir Basil Newton to Lord Halifax, 29 November 1940, *PRO FO 371/61455*; Foreign Office, *Historical summary of events in the Persian Gulf, 1928–53* [PG 53](1953), 70.
50. Schofield, *Kuwait and Iraq*, 82–6.
51. *Ibid.*, 87–8.
52. See appendices in PG 53, 247–9.
53. British Embassy, Baghdad, to Foreign Office, 21 August 1952, *PRO FO 1016/364*.
54. British Ambassador, Baghdad, to Foreign Office, 24 May 1955, *PRO FO 371/114644*.
55. Sir M. Wright to Foreign Office, 24 May 1955, *PRO FO 371/114644*.
56. Telegram from Gawain Bell, Political Agency, Kuwait, to Foreign Office, 28 June 1955, *PRO FO 371/114644*.
57. Sir M. Wright to Foreign Office, 4 July 1955, *PRO FO 371/114644*.
58. Telegram from British Embassy, Baghdad, to Foreign Office, 4 October 1955, *PRO FO 371/114644*.
59. Bell to Foreign Office, 10 December 1955, *PRO FO 371/114644*.
60. Bell to Burrows, 19 December 1955, *PRO FO 371/114644*.
61. Bell to Burrows, 23 January 1956, *PRO FO 371/120598*.
62. A. R. H. Kellas, British Embassy, Baghdad, to D. A. Logan, Foreign Office, 12 March 1956, *PRO FO 371/120598*.
63. Telegram from Bahrain to Foreign Office, 28 May 1958, *PRO FO 371/126961*.
64. Telegram from Bahrain to Foreign Office, 20 May 1957, *PRO FO 371/126961*.
65. Mustafa M. Alani, *Operation Vantage: British military intervention in Kuwait, 1961* (Surbiton: LAAM, 1990); Schofield, *Kuwait and Iraq*, 94–104.
66. Schofield, *Kuwait and Iraq*, 104–6.
67. *Ibid.*, 117–18.
68. *Ibid.*, 113. It might also be noted that the Japanese Government proposed the internationalization of water channels in the northwestern Gulf as a means of defusing tensions in the countdown to the Kuwait crisis during July 1990.
69. Schofield, *Kuwait and Iraq*, 111.
70. *Ibid.*, 115–6.

71. G. Nonneman, *Iraq, the Gulf states and the war: a changing relationship, 1980–1986 and beyond* (London: Ithaca Press, 1986), 58.
72. Government of Kuwait, Ministry of Information, *Facts and figures* (1984), 88–90.

CHAPTER SEVEN
Maritime delimitation in the Gulf

Rodman R. Bundy

Introduction

Under the United Nations Convention on the Law of the Sea, maritime states have a right to a 200 nautical mile exclusive economic zone and at least a 200 nautical mile continental shelf. Although the convention has not yet entered into force, owing to the lack of requisite ratifications, it is undisputed that these entitlements reflect well established principles of customary international law.

In the Gulf, not only are the mainland coasts of Iran and the Arab littoral states separated by much less than 400 nautical miles, but the presence of islands further complicates the picture and prevents any state from enjoying its full complement of continental shelf or exclusive economic zone. Every state abutting the Gulf, in fact, faces a dual delimitation situation: first with its adjacent neighbours and, second, with states lying opposite. This factor has potentially important implications since the law of maritime delimitation, as developed by the International Court of Justice (ICJ), has tended to arrive at different results depending on whether the boundary is being drawn between opposite or adjacent states.

State practice in its legal context

With the discovery and development of offshore hydrocarbons in the 1960s, the need for fixed boundaries became more pressing. Oil companies in particular were reluctant to spend considerable amounts on the exploration and development of areas whose title was in dispute. Not surprisingly, during this period a whole series of bilateral delimitation agreements were entered into amongst the states of the Gulf.

Strictly speaking, this body of state practice has a limited legal relevance under international law in as much as it does not point to the existence of any particular method of delimitation that is legally obligatory or that has a privileged status over other methods. In practice, it is not always possible to determine the exact principles that were applied in determining the course of a boundary line from a reading of the agreements. Accordingly, it can be dangerous to attempt to extract general rules from the practice in question. As the ICJ observed in its very first decision concerning a continental shelf delimitation in 1969:

> [T]here is no legal limit to the considerations which States may take account of for the purpose of making sure that they apply equitable procedures, and more often than not it is the balancing-up of all such considerations that will produce this result rather than reliance on one to the exclusion of all others.[1]

In order for state practice to reflect a general principle of customary international law, two criteria must be met. First the practice must amount to a "settled practice", in the sense of being "extensive" and "virtually uniform" with regard to the method of delimitation employed. Second, evidence must exist that the states concerned considered that their choice of a particular method of delimitation was rendered obligatory by the existence of a rule of law requiring it – in other words, that they were conforming to a legal obligation when they agreed to a particular boundary.[2]

Neither of these requirements is met with respect to delimitation agreements in the Gulf. As will be seen, a variety of delimitation methods have been employed, and it cannot thereby be concluded that the states concerned felt that they were under a legal obligation to use any particular method. Nonetheless, this does not mean that these agreements are devoid of all legal significance. Indeed, a close scrutiny of subsequent ICJ and arbitration decisions reveals that the practice in the Gulf has often been drawn upon as precedential support for particular methods of delimitation.

Individual delimitation agreements

The first delimitation agreement to be signed in the Gulf was between Saudi Arabia and Bahrain on 22 February 1958.[3] The agreement itself stated that the boundary had been drawn "on the basis of the median line". The delimitation appears to be based generally on equidistance, with some deviations possibly due to the existence of a number of shoals, low-tide elevations and islets in the area (Fig. 9.4).

Of particular interest, as Figure 7.1 also shows, is the hexagonal area in the northern sector of the delimitation labelled "joint development zone". The agreement provides that the actual delimitation line in this area runs along the eastern boundary of the zone. Saudi Arabia's rights of sovereignty

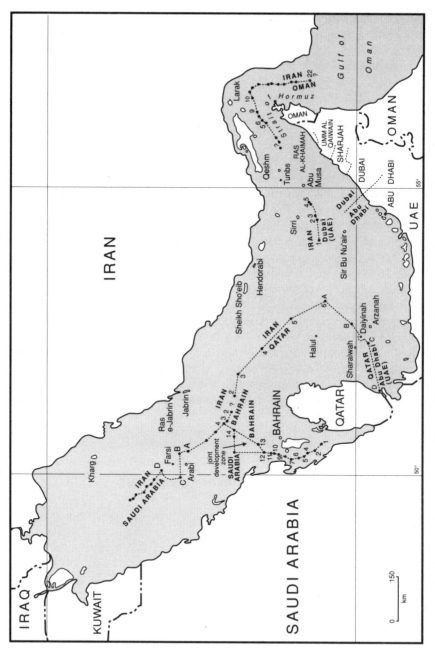

Figure 7.1 Maritime delimitation in the Gulf.

and administration over the zone are thus not impaired and Saudi Arabia may develop the area in any manner it chooses. However, the agreement further provides that, if development is carried out, Saudi Arabia will give Bahrain half of the net income derived from such development (Article 2).

As such, the Saudi Arabia/Bahrain delimitation provides an interesting example of one way states can deal with mineral resources which straddle international boundaries. Subsequent to the Saudi Arabia–Bahrain agreement, a number of other maritime boundaries have been established incorporating joint development zones. Such zones exist between Japan and Korea, France and Spain (in the Bay of Biscay), and Iceland and Norway, to name just a few.

The next delimitation agreement entered into was between Abu Dhabi and Dubai on 18 February 1968. The agreement is very short – just over one page – and says little about the principles of delimitation adopted. It refers instead to a pre-existing agreement starting at the coastal point of Ras Hasian and proceeding "seawards in a straight line in a northwesterly direction passing to the west of the Fateh wells belonging to the Amirate of Dubai".

The new agreement signed in 1968 transposed the boundary, which still followed the same seaward projection, 10 miles in a westerly direction measured along the coast in Dubai's favour. Although the agreement does not indicate how far seaward the boundary extends, the intention clearly must have been for it to intersect with an eventual Iran / Abu Dhabi delimitation (discussed below) since when that agreement was subsequently drafted, it incorporated as its terminus on the east the point of intersection with the Abu Dhabi/Dubai lateral boundary.

As far as the principles upon which the Abu Dhabi–Dubai agreement was based are concerned, the boundary appears to follow a course roughly perpendicular to the general direction of the coast. This is a fairly common method (corresponding roughly to a simplified equidistance line) used by states with adjacent coasts where there are no unusual coastal features or islands. Other examples of state practice where such a method has been employed include the delimitations between Uruguay and Brazil and between Panama and Costa Rica. Moreover, the International Court of Justice has also resorted to a line running perpendicular to the general direction of the coast in its judgments: notably for the first sector of the continental shelf boundary decided between Libya and Tunisia in the court's 1982 judgment.

Eight months after the Abu Dhabi–Dubai agreement was signed, Iran and Saudi Arabia finalized their maritime delimitation.[4] This is one of the most significant agreements in the Gulf owing to the way in which offshore islands were treated, and it has often been cited as a precedent in international jurisprudence.

The first notable characteristic of the agreement is that it settled the question of sovereignty over the islands of Farsi and Arabi. Under Article

1, the parties recognized Iran's sovereignty over Farsi and Saudi Arabia's over Arabi. In the light of current disputes involving other islands in the Gulf, particularly Abu Musa and the Greater and Lesser Tunbs, this agreement provides an interesting example of how it is possible to compromise questions of sovereignty in a highly practical manner.

The second significant feature of the agreement is that Farsi and Arabi have been partially enclaved in the delimitation. Between the two islands, an equidistance line has been drawn (see the section of the line between points B and C in Fig. 7.1). To each side of this line (points C–D and A–B), 12-mile arcs have been constructed, corresponding to a 12-mile territorial sea for each island. Obviously, the resulting line would have been much different if, instead of being restricted to a 12-mile enclave, each island had been used as a basepoint in constructing an equidistance boundary.

The balance of the delimitation north of the islands appears to be based on modified equidistance. According to the Geographer of the US State Department, the Iranian island of Kharg, which has important oil installations and loading facilities, was given a one-half effect in the delimitation.[5] This was most probably accomplished by constructing two equidistance lines – one using the mainland Iranian coast as the baseline and the other using the low-water mark on Kharg – and splitting the difference.

Under international law, the Iran – Saudi Arabia agreement is *res inter alios acta,* meaning that it is legally binding only between those two states but not opposable to others. Nonetheless, international courts and tribunals have had little hesitation in referring to this agreement as precedent for according islands a partial or "half-effect" in other situations.

In the 1978 arbitration between the United Kingdom and France regarding their maritime boundary in the English Channel, for example, the arbitral tribunal granted only a half-effect to the Scilly islands in constructing a median line between the two countries in the Atlantic portion of the boundary. The tribunal justified this treatment in the following way:

> A number of examples are to be found in State practice of delimitations in which only partial effect has been given to offshore islands situated outside the territorial sea of the mainland . . . in one instance, at least, the method employed was to give half, instead of full, effect to the offshore island in delimiting the equidistance line.[6]

Almost certainly the example referred to by the arbital tribunal was the Iran – Saudi Arabia agreement. Undoubtedly, the International Court also had this agreement in mind when it decided the Libya–Tunisia continental shelf case in 1982. In that case, the Kerkennah islands lying off the Tunisian coast were also given a half-effect in the delimitation. In words that echoed those of the Anglo–French arbitration, the court stated:

> The Court would recall . . . that a number of examples are to be found in State practice of delimitations in which only partial effect has been given to islands situated close to the coast.[7]

South of Farsi and Arabi islands, the delimitation appears to revert to a strict equidistance line. Kharg island no longer has an effect on the line because it is too far away, and the last point on the line forms a tripoint with the starting point of the Iran/Bahrain and Bahrain/Saudi Arabia boundaries.

Moving down the Gulf, the next agreement signed was between Abu Dhabi and Qatar on 20 March 1969.[8] Like the Abu Dhabi – Dubai agreement, it too involved a delimitation between adjacent states.[9] Unlike the former, however, it was not based on a line drawn perpendicular, or "normal", to the general direction of the coast.

First of all, the agreement confirmed that the island of Daiyinah formed part of the territory of Abu Dhabi, while the islands of al-Ashat and Shuraiwah belonged to Qatar (Fig. 9.5). Thereafter, the delimitation line was defined by a series of geographic co-ordinates passing through four turning points.

Point A coincides with point 6, the easternmost point on the Iran/Qatar boundary, and point 1 on the Iran / Abu Dhabi boundary. It thus represents another tripoint roughly equidistant from all three states.

Point B is specified as coinciding with the location of well no. 1 in the Bunduq oilfield. Articles 6 and 7 of the agreement stipulate that the field is to be equally shared by the parties even though the Abu Dhabi Marine Areas Company retains full authority to develop the resources in accordance with a pre-existing concession with the Ruler of Abu Dhabi.

While the agreement thereafter provides that the boundary will be a straight line between points B and C, such a line would pass almost directly over Daiyinah island. Since at the time both Qatar and Abu Dhabi claimed 3-mile territorial seas, a 3-mile arc has been drawn around the island. It is not known whether this line has changed in the light of both the 1982 United Nations Convention on the Law of the Sea, which allows states to claim a 12-mile territorial sea and the passage of new maritime legislation by the United Arab Emirates in 1993.

The final point, point D, lies at the mouth of the Khawr al-Udaid outlet. Because of the presence of small islands on both sides of the line, it is difficult to identify the principles upon which the line was agreed. This highlights one of the shortcomings of trying to draw broad-reaching legal conclusions from state practice. In the final analysis, such agreements are the product of negotiation and it is not always possible to identify the considerations that underlay a particular boundary.

Nonetheless, the Abu Dhabi – Qatar agreement, like the agreement between Bahrain and Saudi Arabia, is significant to the extent that it illustrates another way in which states deal with boundaries that pass through areas rich in natural resources.

Not surprisingly, the Abu Dhabi – Qatar agreement was followed shortly afterwards by the conclusion of an agreement between Iran and Qatar.[10]

The westernmost point of the boundary, point 1, was left undefined pending conclusion of a delimitation agreement between Bahrain and Qatar. The other points appear to be approximately equidistant from the mainland coasts of each party, including point 6, which forms the tripoint between Iran, Qatar and Abu Dhabi. While it is clear that the small Qatari island of Halul does not affect the course of the delimitation line, it is less apparent whether the Iranian islands of Lavan, Hendorabi or Qais have been given a reduced (perhaps one-half) effect. The agreement itself simply refers to establishing a "just, equitable and precise" boundary. It also provides that, in the absence of agreement, neither party will place the producing section of any well closer than 125 m to the boundary. In the event that development of the oil resources takes place, the parties undertake to endeavour to reach agreement on how operations can be co-ordinated.

Iran extended its maritime boundaries in the central Gulf in 1971 with the signature of an agreement with Bahrain.[11] The agreement again seems to be based on equidistance, with the westernmost point forming a tripoint between Iran, Saudi Arabia and Bahrain and the easternmost point left undefined pending resolution of the Qatar/Bahrain boundary dispute. In other respects, the language of the Iran–Bahrain agreement is virtually identical to that appearing in the Iran–Qatar agreement, including the prohibition against drilling within 125 metres of the boundary.

Although the State Department's boundary series, *Limits in the Sea*, does not appear to have recorded the existence of a delimitation agreement between Iran and Abu Dhabi, the evidence suggests that such an agreement, or at least a working arrangement, does exist in this part of the Gulf. During the course of legal proceedings before the Iran – United States Claims Tribunal in The Hague concerning the alleged expropriation of contractual rights that four American oil companies held on the Iranian side of the median line prior to the Iranian revolution, a copy of a delimitation agreement between Iran and Abu Dhabi was produced. One of the issues in the case involved a dispute over the amount of oil that hypothetically could have been produced from the Sassan oilfield – a field that straddled the boundary. In view of this situation, it was important to determine whether the agreement had any bearing on the disposition of resources from the joint field.

Once again, the agreement is cast in the same terms as the Iran–Qatar and Iran–Bahrain agreements. Point 1 of the boundary line in the west coincides with the end-points of the Iran/Qatar and Qatar / Abu Dhabi boundaries, and point 6 in the east is defined as coinciding with the intersection of the lateral boundary between Abu Dhabi and Dubai. Otherwise, the line is basically a median line, and was referred to as such during the proceedings before The Hague Tribunal.

With respect to the joint management of the mineral resources from the Sassan field, the agreement did not set any production limits or quotas on either party. Nonetheless, before the Iranian revolution there were periodic meetings between the parties to exchange technical information relating to the field. These discussions broke down when Iran was forced to interrupt its production from the field owing to the Iran–Iraq war and particularly following the bombardment of certain oil installations by the US Navy in April 1988.

Extending eastwards from the Iran / Abu Dhabi boundary is the last boundary of the central Gulf – the delimitation between Iran and Dubai signed on 31 August 1974.[12] Its starting point also depends on the point of intersection with the Abu Dhabi / Dubai lateral boundary.

The language of this agreement is similar to the others involving Iran, except for the treatment of the Iranian island of Sirri, which was accorded a 12-mile arc of territorial sea between points 3 and 4 in much the same way as the islands of Farsi and Arabi were treated in Iran's agreement with Saudi Arabia.

The boundary stops at point 5 in the east owing to the presence of Abu Musa. Because sovereignty over Abu Musa and the Greater and Lesser Tunbs is disputed, it has not been possible to complete the delimitation in this area. Moreover, Sharjah has entered into lateral delimitation arrangements with Dubai (as a result of a 1981 arbitration award) and Umm al-Qaiwain, but these apparently extend only up to a 12-mile band of territorial water around Abu Musa. Iran has no delimitation agreement with any of the smaller shaikhdoms of the United Arab Emirates, including Sharjah, Umm al-Qaiwain, Ajman or Ras al-Khaimah. Nor do the emirates as yet have an offshore boundary with Oman in the eastern reaches of the Gulf.

The last boundary in the Gulf is between Iran and Oman in the Strait of Hormuz.[13] Both end-points depend on delimitations that have yet to be agreed between Oman and Ras al-Khaimah and Sharjah, respectively.

Because of the presence of numerous islands on both sides of the boundary, it is difficult to deduce the precise method of delimitation used. Nonetheless, the line appears to be broadly equidistant from the territory of each state. What is known is that the agreement specifies that, between points 9 and 10, Larak island has been allocated a 12-mile arc of territorial sea, in a manner that is consistent with the practice elsewhere in the Gulf.

Outstanding disputes

Having completed this *tour d'horizon* of the Gulf, it can be seen that three principal areas remain to be delimited. These lie in the northwest between Iran, Iraq, Kuwait and Saudi Arabia, in the central section between Qatar and Bahrain, and in the east around Abu Musa and the Tunb islands.

If there is one common thread to each of these areas, it is that fundamental questions of sovereignty remain to be resolved before the issue of delimitation can be finalized. Hence, it is not simply the failure of the states concerned to agree on principles of delimitation that has prevented boundaries from being fixed – indeed, the Gulf states have shown themselves to be both practical and imaginative when it comes to agreeing methods of delimitation. Rather, the fact that sovereignty over territory that could affect the delimitation is disputed represents a serious stumbling block to final agreement.

Although it is beyond the scope of this chapter to examine the political aspects of each dispute, it is quite clear that delimitation in the north will probably have to await resolution of at least three thorny problems: the dispute between Iran and Iraq over the Shatt al-Arab waterway (see Ch. 1); the recent resolution of the Iraq/Kuwait boundary in the light of the United Nations' ultimate demarcation efforts (see Ch. 1); and the resolution of the offshore boundary between Saudi Arabia and Kuwait, including the disposition of certain small islands.

Further south, delimitation between Qatar and Bahrain depends in part upon which country has sovereignty over the Hawar islands and the nearby shoals. This dispute has recently been submitted to the International Court of Justice by Qatar after mediation efforts by Saudi Arabia failed to bridge the differences. Bahrain has contested the court's jurisdiction to hear the case and the court will hear oral arguments on this issue early in 1994. Even if the Court accepts jurisdiction, final resolution of the dispute would appear to be several years away. Lastly, there is the question of Abu Musa and the Tunbs. Without recanvassing the history of this particular dispute, it can be safely said that, in the past, islands have posed one of the trickiest problems for maritime delimitation. It can be assumed, therefore, that, no matter how the issue of sovereignty is resolved in the future, agreement on delimitation in this area, which affects several states (Iran, Dubai, Sharjah and possibly Oman), will still pose a difficult issue. In such circumstances, recourse to the World Court or arbitration may provide the most practical solution.

If guidance on how to resolve these matters is sought from the principles and rules of international law governing maritime delimitation, the basic tenets are straightforward. According to the International Court of Justice: "Delimitation is to be effected in accordance with equitable principles and taking account of all relevant circumstances, so as to arrive at an equitable result."[14] In applying such broad-brush principles, it is evident that the identification, assessment and weighing of the relevant circumstances are of vital importance. Here, the courts are influenced by a number of factors, some of which are geographic (such as the lengths and configurations of the coasts involved and the element of proportionality) and some of which are historical or political (such as the conduct of the parties and the question of whether the contesting states can demonstrate any historic or prescriptive rights). States that find themselves in judicial proceedings of this sort will have to marshall these kinds of facts to support their positions.

It is not excluded, however, that some of the answers to the disputes mentioned above may be found in the practice of the Gulf states generally. For example, in at least two of the agreements (Iran – Saudi Arabia and Abu Dhabi – Qatar) the parties resolved questions of sovereignty over disputed islands in the same agreement that fixed the delimitation. There is precedent, therefore, for negotiating a comprehensive solution dealing with sovereignty and delimitation at the same time, which might have application in the Abu Musa and Tunbs situation.[15]

As for the principles of delimitation that might be applied, although the practice in the Gulf is no more legally binding than any other delimitation agreement, it is striking that most of the delimitations in the Gulf between opposite states (principally involving Iran) have involved the use of a median line adjusted to take into account the presence of islands. Under Article 121(2) of the United Nations Convention on the Law of the Sea, islands in principle generate the same maritime zones as mainland coasts (e.g. a territorial sea, exclusive economic zone and continental shelf). In practice, however, smaller islands lying close to the mainland of the state to which they appertain, such as Kharg island, have been given a half-effect. Still other islands lying in the middle of the Gulf, such as Farsi, Arabi and Sirri, have been left with 12-mile belts of territorial sea and no economic zone or continental shelf. Whether these same principles could be constructively applied to the undelimited parts of the Gulf remains to be seen.

With respect to the question of how to delimit the rest of the boundaries between adjacent states in the Gulf (Iraq–Kuwait, Kuwait – Saudi Arabia, Oman–UAE), the practice is less clear. Up to this point, equidistance seems to have been abandoned as a strict rule in favour of lines running roughly perpendicular to the general direction of the coast or representing a projection of the land boundary. The appropriateness of these kinds of solutions, taking into account any relevant historical factors, will undoubtedly need to be considered for the remaining delimitations.

Finally, there is the question of mineral resources that straddle international boundaries. It is perhaps ironic that this factor, which arguably provided the principal impetus for states to agree their boundaries in the Gulf, can also act as an impediment to agreement when proven resources are at stake.[16] In such cases, it may be useful to bear in mind the precedents created by the Saudi Arabia – Bahrain and Qatar – Abu Dhabi agreements, the former creating a joint development zone and the latter calling for a sharing of the resources from the oilfield involved.

In summary, the Gulf provides a rich source of state practice for maritime delimitation. With the exception of the North Sea and parts of the Caribbean, the Gulf is more fully delimited than any other comparable area of the globe. While complex questions of sovereignty and delimitation still remain to be resolved, useful guidance may be obtained from the precedents that already exist.

Notes

1. North Sea continental shelf cases, ICJ Reports 1969, 50, para. 93.
2. Ibid, 44, para. 77. In the 1985 Libya–Malta continental shelf case, the Court confirmed that State practice falls short of proving the existence of a rule of law prescribing any method, whether it be equidistance or otherwise, as legally obligatory. ICJ Reports 1985, 38, para. 44.
3. Reproduced in the US State Department's publication, Limits in the sea 12, 10 March 1970. See Figure 9.4 in Chapter 9 for map showing the line introduced by the 1958 agreement.
4. United Nations Treaty Series (UNTS), vol. 696, 189.
5. US Department of State, International Boundaries series 24.
6. HMSO, Cmnd 7438, 117, para. 251.
7. ICJ Reports 1982, 89, para. 129.
8. US Department of State, Limits in the sea 18, 29 May 1970.
9. The adjacent state – opposite state distinction can be important. While the ICJ has consistently held that there is no one method of delimitation that is legally obligatory in all cases, it has also suggested that there is far less difficulty involved in applying equidistance or a median line, at least as a first step in delimiting maritime areas between states with opposite coasts. This "provisional" boundary can be modified if other relevant circumstances so dictate. Consequently, there are strong grounds for arguing that equidistance does enjoy a quasi-privileged status, at least as a preliminary step, in opposite state delimitations.
10. UNTS, vol. 787, 165, 20 September 1969.
11. UNTS, vol. 826, 227 17 June 1971.
12. US Department of State, Limits in the sea 63, 30 September 1975.
13. Agreement entered into force on 28 May 1975. UNTS, vol. 972, 265.
14. Case concerning the continental shelf (Libyan Arab Jamahiriya / Malta), Judgment, ICJ Reports 1985, 57, para. 79(A)(1). This principle closely mirrors the provisions of the United Nations Convention on the Law of the Sea, Article 83 of which states that: "The delimitation of the continental shelf between States with opposite or adjacent coasts shall be effected by agreement on the basis of international law, as referred to in Article 38 of the Statute of the International Court of Justice, in order to achieve an equitable solution."
15. This is precisely what Qatar has sought by submitting its dispute with Bahrain over the Hawar islands, the shoals and the maritime delimitation generally to the International Court.
16. In both the Libya–Tunisia and Libya–Malta continental shelf disputes, for example, the parties were unable to negotiate the boundary largely because of the existence of potentially important oil reserves in the disputed areas. In the end, both cases were submitted to the World Court by the agreement of the parties involved.

CHAPTER EIGHT
Cross-border hydrocarbon reserves

DAVID PIKE

Introduction

The problem of cross-border hydrocarbon reserves is a global one, not confined to the Gulf states. Oil and gas fields do not respect international boundaries and their exploration and development can provoke at best disagreement and at worst military conflict.

Such disputes can be hard to resolve, with few clear legal guidelines in place. The United Nations Law of the Sea Convention includes rules for the establishment of maritime borders but has still to be fully ratified 20 years after talks on the agreement got under way. There is no such accord for land borders. Instead, delineation or sharing of cross-border fields relies on hard bilateral negotiations, backed up by a political will to reach agreement.[1]

Examples of global disputes include disagreement between China and Vietnam over exploration in the Tonkin Gulf and Spratly islands, between Argentina and the UK about seismic work off the Falkland islands, and between Norway and Russia about prospecting rights in the Barents Sea. Even the Timor Gap controlled by Australia and Indonesia, where a complex agreement on joint offshore development was signed in 1989, has been the scene of dispute. Portugal has challenged the agreement in the International Court of Justice, on the grounds that it was colonial ruler of East Timor until Indonesia's invasion in 1975 but was not included in the accord.[2]

However, in the Gulf such disputes are more numerous and more intense (see Fig. 8.1). The region's enormous hydrocarbon resources and the profusion of small state territories mean cross-border reserves are far more likely to occur. Coupled with this are vague or disputed boundaries, often the legacy of British colonial rule. No clear border between Saudi Arabia and former South Yemen was ever drawn up, while other frontiers are controversial, often ignoring local tribal claims.

More recently, several states of the Gulf – Arabian peninsula region have stepped up exploration and development in border regions previously igno-

Figure 8.1 Transboundary resource reserves and disputes in the Gulf region and Arabian peninsula.

red, either to support economic development or to compensate for maturation of older oilfields. Initial successes in such border work, particularly by Saudi Arabia, suggest the issue is set to assume more importance than in the past.

Despite the region's volatility, cross-border reserves in the Gulf do not always result in dispute. Backed by cordial political ties, Saudi Arabia has peacefully shared oil reserves in border regions with Kuwait and Bahrain. Yet other frontiers witnessed conflict – varying from a war of words between Saudi Arabia and Yemen to the military invasion of Kuwait by Iraq – with real or potential oil reserves a contributing factor. Other cross-border fields, such as that between Qatar and Iran or those straddling the Saudi Arabia / UAE boundary, have not yet provoked problems, but differences could emerge as development leads to production.

Sharing reserves

The few examples of successful long-term co-operation in developing cross-border reserves are not based on complicated agreements defining precise exploration and production rights. Rather, they involve a straightforward split of ownership or revenues, relying heavily on the persistence of sound bilateral relations.

The most significant joint development programme is in the Divided (formerly Neutral) Zone between Saudi Arabia and Kuwait, which contains recoverable reserves currently estimated at 5 billion barrels.[3]

Development of the area started in 1948 when a US consortium, the American Independent Oil Company (AMINOIL), was awarded the first concession in Kuwait's onshore share of the zone. AMINOIL discovered the Wafrah field in 1953 and the Umm Gudair field (both onshore) in 1966, but was nationalized by Kuwait in 1977. The Kuwait Oil Company (KOC) took over responsibility.

Co-operation between Kuwait and Saudi Arabia in the Divided Zone dates from 1958 when the (Japanese) Arabian Oil Company (AOC) was granted what has proved to be the zone's most productive concession, including the offshore Khafji and Hout fields with capacity now in the order of 300,000–400,000 barrels a day (b/d). The Kuwaiti and Saudi governments each hold a 10 per cent shareholding in AOC with the rest owned by Japanese interests. A smaller concession in the zone, covering the onshore Wafrah oilfield, is held by the Getty Oil Company, a subsidiary of Texaco, which produces 65,000– 90,000 b/d.

Reserves and output in the zone are split equally between Kuwait and Saudi Arabia. Development projects in the concessions are also co-ordinated with the two governments, although these were set back by damage incurred during the Gulf crisis.[4] AOC has plans to spend $400 million on a gas-gathering project at Khafji to produce 140 million cubic feet/day of gas, with output to be split between Kuwait and Saudi Arabia. Getty Oil has drawn up plans for a $2 billion enhanced oil recovery scheme involving steam flooding at the Wafrah field, but this may not go ahead because of doubts that costs will be recovered before expiry of the concession agreement in 2009. The project could increase Getty's production to 250,000 b/d and boost recoverable reserves from 700 million barrels to 3–4 billion barrels.[5]

Saudi Arabia also shares oil development with Bahrain. Revenues from the 140,000 b/d Bu Saafah field, lying offshore between the two countries and operated by state oil company Saudi ARAMCO, were until very recently split equally between the two countries. The 1958 Saudi–Bahraini seabed boundary agreement, the first to be negotiated in the Gulf, had recognized Saudi sovereignty over Bu Saafah, previously a disputed shoal lying to the northwest of Bahrain, but had specified that all future revenue accruing from the associated oil-bearing structure be shared equally (see Chs 1 and 9). The economic importance of revenue from Bu Saafah for Bahrain is considerable, often matching or exceeding Bahrain's revenues from its own onshore production. Only in late December 1992, Saudi Arabia agreed to Bahrain increasing its share of revenue from the Bu Saafah hexagon from 50 per cent (70,000 b/d) to over 70 per cent (100,000 b/d). This development is regarded by many as in effect a form of economic aid by Saudi Arabia to its poorer offshore neighbour.[6]

Saudi Arabia's third main agreement for allocation of hydrocarbons shared with a neighbouring state covers its southeastern boundary with the UAE. The two countries' border agreement signed in 1974 includes a clause referring to cross-border reserves, and specifically a field with around 7 billion barrels of high-quality light crude discovered in the early 1970s, called Shaibah on the Saudi side of the border and Zararah on the UAE side. The treaty states that sovereignty over Shaibah and any other fields along the border will be granted to the country with the majority of the field. Shaibah, with 80 per cent of its reserves in Saudi territory, thus belongs solely to Saudi Arabia, including the part on the UAE's side of the frontier. According to contemporary press reports, negotiations on the 1974 agreement included possible joint development of Shaibah, but this was apparently not written into the treaty.[7]

This unusual and arbitrary definition of ownership was academic until 1992, as the field's remoteness on the edge of the Rub al-Khali (Empty Quarter) meant exploitation was very expensive compared with other more accessible oilfields and it was left untouched for two decades.[8]

However, Saudi Arabia decided in November 1992 to proceed with development of Shaibah, despite its estimated total cost of $8 billion. Initial plans aimed for production of 350,000–600,000 b/d by 1997 through the drilling of 175–225 wells and construction of three gas–oil separation plants (GOSPs), each with a capacity of 175,000–225,000 b/d.[9]

The decision fell under Saudi ARAMCO's capacity expansion programme, which aims to reach a sustainable 10 million b/d in 1995 and will continue beyond that with Shaibah and other developments. Exploitation of Shaibah has become necessary as older fields mature, making it hard to extract further output from the main producing area in Eastern province (Hasa). Shaibah's light crude reserves will also complement the Kingdom's traditional heavier export grades.

The Shaibah decision also comes in the context of increased Saudi attention towards its borders, both to gain a clearer idea of the country's total reserves and to stake a claim to any finds in frontier areas.

Until the late 1980s, Saudi exploration and development were limited to the Eastern province. But in 1986, Saudi ARAMCO's prospecting mandate was expanded to cover the whole country. Initially, it explored a central area south of Riyadh where a series of promising discoveries of very high quality oil was made. Since 1989, it has moved on to a northern area near the Jordanian border, the western Red Sea coast, the southern border area near Yemen and the southeastern areas near the Qatar and UAE frontiers.

By mid-1992, most work was confined to seismic studies, and actual drilling in border regions had taken place only in the northern Jawf region, in the Nafud desert. Gas was struck here in November 1991 but no other discoveries were reported. Late in 1992, drilling also started at Midyan on the northern Red Sea coast and Jizan, lying on the Asir coast 70 km from Yemen. A seismic crew was deployed to work on the Qatar and UAE borders in mid-1992, with a second one starting work at Shaibah in 1993. Drilling along the UAE border is also scheduled to start in 1994. Saudi officials have made few public comments on the border activity. One rare statement in July 1992 on exploration near Yemen said only that the drilling was in an undisputed area.[10]

Three wells drilled at Midyan in late 1992 and early 1993 found oil and gas, but the likelihood of their development was not immediately clear. No official announcement was issued about work near Jizan but small discoveries are believed to have been made, confirming the area has some hydrocarbon reserves. Drilling in mid 1993 moved onto the Jiddah and al-Wajh regions.[11]

Oil on troubled borders

Cross-border hydrocarbon reserves are not the exclusive cause of any regional border dispute. In some, they do play a central rôle but are accompanied by political differences or other sources of grievance. In other cases, oil is used simply as a weapon in political disputes.

Rumailah, the most controversial cross-border oilfield in the Gulf during recent times straddles the Iraq/Kuwait frontier. Before the events of 1990–91 it was not established beyond doubt that this was the case (see below). Iraq pumped up to 2 million b/d from its northern and southern sections of its Rumailah field before the Gulf War. Kuwait calls its southern, smaller part of the field Ratgah, claiming it produced only 10,000 b/d before the Iraqi invasion. In rhetoric before and after the 2 August 1990 invasion, Baghdad employed a combination of territorial and historical claims on its southern neighbour and also deprecated Kuwait's exploitation of the cross-border field and its pursuit of moderate price levels within OPEC. Kuwait may well have been pumping more than its declared 10,000 b/d at Ratgah and its OPEC pricing policy did affect the oil revenues of other producers. But such differences would not on their own have provoked Iraq's military aggression. The issue of oil, particularly cross-border reserves, was one of Iraq's excuses not its reason for invading.

Before the United Nations settlement of the Iraq/Kuwait boundary question, no reliable geological maps of the Rumailah–Ratgah area were known to exist. There remained two views within oil company circles over the relationship between the massive Iraqi Rumailah field and the much smaller Ratgah oilfield to its immediate south. The first and more widely held view, which has since been confirmed, is that Ratgah is the southern continuation of the Rumailah field, lying on the lower slope of the main dome structure, which rises in Iraq. The other, now discredited view, held by a respected Palestinian geologist (Z. R. Beydoun), was that the Rumailah field did not straddle the international boundary. He estimated that the large, anticlinal structure of the "super-giant" oilfield consisted of two principal sections, north Rumailah and Rumailah, which lay totally within Iraq. He described the exact location of the Ratgah field as uncertain and provisionally characterized its geology as a crescentic trend near and along the Iraqi border.[12]

The liberation of Kuwait has not put an end to the issue, as exploration of Rumailah–Ratgah continues to bear the seeds of dispute. The United Nations Iraq/Kuwait Boundary Demarcation Commission (UNIKBDC), charged after the war with finally settling the historically problematic border issue, made several controversial decisions in its award for the land boundary in April 1992. It ruled that a strip of land overlying the southern tip of the Rumailah oilfield containing six wells should be handed over to Kuwait, as should parts of Iraq's Umm Qasr port. In its interim report of July 1992, UNIKBDC defended its decision by highlighting that it had not been the first to suggest areas operated by Iraq actually belonged to Kuwait. "The oil wells in the fields between Safwan and the Batin exploited in the past by Iraq fell already in Kuwait according to the boundary shown on the British map referred to in [UN] Security Council resolution 687 (1991)."[13] In other words, maps existing before UNIKBDC commenced its operations showed the strip containing the wells operated by Iraq as Kuwaiti territory. The reader is referred to Chapter 1 for greater detail on the confusing matters of maps, boundaries and oil.

Iraqi Foreign Affairs Minister Ahmad Husain al-Samarai warned in June 1992 that "imposing the border by force would leave the region in a state of boiling tension".[14] In November 1992, Oil Minister Osama al-Hiti said the six wells belonged to Iraq "and will remain Iraqi". He said Baghdad was keeping a close eye on its border oilfields and, if a neighbouring country – Kuwait – tried to increase production from one, "We will insist on having our full share."[15] The author of this chapter established that Iraq was actually required to hand over 11 wells to Kuwait following the United Nations' demarcation (November 1992) of the land boundary it first announced in April 1992. Of the 11, 8 were below the old Arab League line established by the British and Arab League forces placed in Kuwait to protect it from an earlier Iraqi threat during 1961. The remaining three apparently lay between the 1961 Arab League line and the boundary line awarded by the United Nations during 1992.[16]

Another border dispute, between Saudi Arabia and Yemen, flared up in 1992, this time revolving more clearly around oil exploration along their indeterminate border. However, other factors were also at play, notably pretensions to tribal loyalties in frontier regions, Saudi opposition to the unification of Yemen and its plans for elections, Riyadh's distrust of San'a since it supported Iraq in the Gulf crisis, and political posturing in advance of negotiations on the renewal of a border accord.

Saudi drilling in the area suggests the border region could contain important reserves. Yemen in turn has awarded several exploration concessions along the frontier, including areas where sovereignty is disputed by Saudi Arabia. If the area is confirmed as containing significant reserves and production starts by either country, the other government is bound to be concerned about possible depletion of a common reservoir. A resurgence of the border dispute through territorial claims to areas in which discoveries are made cannot be ruled out.

The border between Saudi Arabia and former North Yemen, or at least its western stretch from the Red Sea coast near Midi to Jabal al-Thar southeast of the Najran oasis, was defined by the 1934 Taif agreement, which was due for renewal in September 1992, that is if one discounts Yemen's reported statements that this stretch of the border was "permanent and final", made during 1973 in rather obscure circumstances in Riyadh. But this agreement does not provide for delineation of maritime borders. Moreover, the frontier between Saudi Arabia and former South Yemen has never been defined and is not covered by any formal bilateral agreement, a direct legacy of British control of Aden.

After unification in May 1990, the Yemeni Government accelerated its search for oil to support development efforts, breaking up the Shabwah concession previously held by Soviet interests, then awarding this and a series of other exploration blocks to foreign firms. By the start of 1992, 24 blocks had been awarded, with only 15 still vacant. The country's oil production of 170,000–200,000 b/d was limited to the Marib/Jawf concession operated by the American firms, Hunt Oil and Exxon. It was augmented in September 1992 by a limited output of around 10,000 b/d by the Saudi-owned Nimr Petroleum Company at Shabwah block 4.

Some of the most important exploration blocks let to foreign companies lay along the border with Saudi Arabia, including the ill defined offshore and former South Yemeni parts. With renegotiation of the 1934 agreement approaching – or at least still an issue – Saudi Arabia provoked a sharp deterioration in relations by warning foreign companies in Yemen against exploration along the border. In March 1992, Riyadh sent letters to four companies accusing them of trespassing upon disputed territory.[17] The firms were British Petroleum (BP), which held offshore block 23 (Antufash);

Elf Petroland, a subsidiary of France's Elf Aquitaine, with block 11 (Sirr Hazar); Ireland's Tullow Oil, a partner in block 12 (North Sanaw) operated by Arco of the USA; and Petro-Canada, with block 30 (Habarut). All four blocks were adjacent to border areas not covered by a formal agreement between Saudi Arabia and Yemen. The offshore area of BP's block was not mentioned in the Taif Treaty; Yemen defined the northern limit of the concession by drawing a straight line extending the mainland Taif border line out to sea equidistant from the two countries, but Saudi Arabia claims some islands that would thus fall under Yemeni administration. In other words, these islands (which lie south of the Farasan archipelago) lie south of the line of latitude declared by the Republic of Yemen to constitute the northern limit of the concession area. Indeed Saudi Arabia and Yemen dispute the exact point at which the 1934 Taif line terminates on the Red Sea coast. Blocks 11, 12 and 30 lie along the former South Yemeni border, with concession limits based on frontiers unilaterally declared by Britain but never formally agreed with Saudi Arabia.[18]

The Washington-based *Foreign Reports* wrote in October 1992: "Although there have been a number of lines proposed or claimed over time in regard to this section of the border, these past proposals have no particular legal weight and, since much of the area in question has not been inhabited or exploited by either side, most of the legal arguments rest in vague assertions of who has had constructive control over the area."[19]

Following the letters of March 1992, Riyadh sent similar letters to two American companies, Hunt Oil – operator of the only producing concession at that time, block 18 (Marib/Jawf) – and Phillips Petroleum, block 20 (the first relinquished area). These lie along the former North Yemeni part of the border but a section not covered by the Taif accord. Instead, the concessions' northern limits were based on what is known unofficially as the straightened-out Philby line (denoted as Zurich line in Fig. 1.3), which is disputed by Saudi Arabia. Nor is the Philby line (in whatever variant) – a suggestion for a Yemeni/Saudi boundary made in the late 1930s by the eccentric and sometimes unreliable British traveller, H. St John B. Philby, – recognized by the Republic of Yemen in 1993. The only two blocks on the Saudi/Yemen border that lie along the Taif line, and are thus less controversial, are blocks 21 (central highlands) and 22 (Zaidiah). Both of these were vacant when the dispute flared up.

However, Yemeni officials claimed that the government had tried specifically not to provoke Saudi Arabia when drawing up the concessions. In an August 1992 interview, Foreign Affairs Minister Abdul Karim al-Iryani said: "We were careful as we did not wish to initiate any indirect disputes with the Saudis when dividing the area into blocks, because we didn't want to reveal our eventual territorial claim before we negotiate, in order not to exacerbate the existing situation. They chose to do the reverse and go directly to the oil companies. Definitely, the existing contracts are in no way a declaration of adherence to that line, and they cannot construe it in such a way that it is our frontier." He added that Yemen tried "to normalise, to negotiate, to sit down and solve our problem" but Saudi Arabia "chose to communicate with a third party".[20]

The response to the Saudi letters was mixed. Petro-Canada, Arco, Hunt and Phillips continued their exploration and production activities, although in some cases the pace of work slowed down. In June 1992, Tullow sold its 10 per cent stake in block 12 to Arco, the operator, saying the decision was partly influenced by the border controversy. BP halted all development at its offshore Antufash block in May because of the dispute, declaring *force majeure* on relevant contracts. Elf adopted a low profile, suspending further drilling plans and concentrating on evaluation of a well drilled in December 1991. The company had already experienced problems with Saudi Arabia in its concession, when an exploration team had to stop work in 1989 because of interference by a Saudi border patrol.

The opening of talks between Riyadh and San'a on the border issue removed much of the pressure from the oil companies. After an initial round of negotiations in July 1992 and a later round in September/October, BP resumed its work at Antufash, drilling its first well on 8 November. The well, 10 km from the northern limit of the concession, was described by BP as the "closest ever Yemeni oil well to be drilled near the Saudi border".[21] In late July, San'a had also awarded a new border block to a US company, Mayfair Petroleum. The onshore concession is adjacent to BP's Antufash block and opposite the site of drilling by Saudi Arabia on its side of the frontier. But in early 1993 both BP and Petro-Canada relinquished their disputed blocks after failing to find oil.

The dispute arose again in August 1993 when Riyadh sent new warning letters to firms still working in border blocks – Hunt, Arco, Phillips and Elf. The three US companies continued operations, now regarding the letters largely as a Saudi negotiating tactic in the ongoing border talks. Elf continued to suspend its work with government approval until resolution of the border issues.

Yemen's relations with its eastern neighbour Oman, and the question of possible border reserves, have been established more clearly. The two countries signed a full border agreement early in October 1992 (see Ch. 1), which catered for the eventuality of hydrocarbon discoveries, albeit in only a vague manner. Article 6 of the treaty states: "In the event of the discovery of joint natural resources, an agreement shall be reached on ways and means of exploiting and sharing these resources in accordance with established international conventions and regulations and in an equitable and just manner."[22]

Soon after the treaty was signed, San'a awarded an Omani company, Saad al-Qawi, an offshore exploration concession in southeast Yemen. Concessions bordering on the Oman land boundary had already been let to

Nimr Petroleum and Petro-Canada, the latter being the same block (Habarut) involved in the Saudi dispute.

Problems similar to those being experienced by Saudi Arabia and Yemen concerning ill defined borders are present on the western coast of the Red Sea. In 1992 Egypt and Sudan became embroiled in the classic case of establishing oil rights where a frontier is disputed. The coastal section of the border between the two countries has two formal frontiers drawn up by Britain at the end of the nineteenth century – a political boundary and an administrative one. The area between the two lines, called the Halaib triangle, covers 16,000 km^2. Since the 1950s it has been administered by Sudan but under the sovereignty of Egypt.

In December 1991, Sudan granted an onshore and offshore exploration block covering 10,300 km^2 in the triangle to Canada's International Petroleum Corporation (IPC).[23] Cairo voiced strong objections to the award. A telex from the state owned Egyptian General Petroleum Corporation (EGPC) to foreign oil companies stated: "The Canadian company's concession regarding its acquisition of Halaib from the Sudanese government is illegal since it was granted from an authority which does not own the property."[24] EGPC responded in early 1992 by issuing a tender for four Red Sea exploration blocks, one of which, block D, included Halaib and overlapped with the IPC concession. EGPC maintained it was serious about awarding block D right up to the 30 September 1992 deadline, although a lack of foreign company interest obliged it to postpone the tender at the last minute, allowing time for talks to defuse the row. IPC had in the meantime suspended its work programme at Halaib until resolution of the dispute.[25]

Proven and unproven oil reserves figure in other of the region's border disputes, but do not have the same central importance. Qatar and Bahrain have a long-standing dispute over maritime boundaries, with Qatar rejecting territorial awards made by Britain and claiming sovereignty over the Hawar islands and two coral reefs controlled by Bahrain. This is primarily a territorial dispute, but it has inhibited offshore exploration by the two countries in the area between them, at a time when both are stepping up prospecting activity. According to one report, the definition of an offshore concession awarded by Bahrain to the American Harken Energy Corporation has been left vague because of the dispute. This follows an old-established pattern. An oil concession given by the Ruler of Bahrain to BAPCO (Bahrain Petroleum Company) in 1940 was similarly non-committal concerning its eastern limits, eventually utilizing "present and future dominions". Harken has concentrated on drilling in regions away from the area at stake.[26] Two Qatari offshore exploration blocks, 3 and 4, near the disputed waters off the west coast are vacant and the Qatar General Petroleum Corporation (QGPC) announced in late 1992 that there were no immediate plans to award them.

Similarly, the re-emergence in 1992 of a dispute between Iran and the UAE (Sharjah) about Abu Musa island was determined largely by strategic

196

considerations, but it did contain important implications for the oil sector. Iran's actions on Abu Musa, effectively shared between Iran and Sharjah under a 1971 agreement (see Ch. 1), threatened operations at the Mubarak oil and gas field lying to the southeast of the island. Abu Musa's proximity to oil tanker shipping lanes also means the dispute has the potential to threaten the safety of oil exports from the Gulf. This remains highly theoretical, but unsubstantiated reports of an Iranian military build-up on its northern half of the island on occasions during the past year (e.g. November 1992) have periodically raised tensions, especially if the local media is to be believed.[27]

The 1971 Abu Musa agreement stated that all government revenues from exploitation of hydrocarbon resources in the island's waters should be split evenly between Sharjah and Iran. Sharjah then passes on smaller shares of its revenues to Ajman and Umm al-Qaiwain. The Mubarak field was developed soon after the agreement by Sharjah's Crescent Petroleum Company. It produced 60,000 b/d of oil/condensate when the field first came on stream in 1974, but technical problems have limited output since the mid-1980s to 5,000–8,000 b/d. Crescent stated in October 1992 that both production and the revenue-sharing arrangement had been unaffected by the Abu Musa dispute, and that it was proceeding as planned with both a $100 million enhanced recovery project to raise oil/condensate production to 15,000–20,000 b/d and also with plans to sell 100 million cubic feet/day of gas to Dubai. The field has estimated remaining reserves of 50 million barrels of oil and 1.5 trillion cubic feet of gas.[28]

Still to come?

Currently one of the biggest current hydrocarbon developments in the Gulf involves the huge offshore gas reserves shared by Qatar and Iran. Qatar is already developing its share of reserves in the deep Khuff-4 structure, which it calls the North Field and which has estimated recoverable reserves of 250 trillion cubic feet. Iran in late 1992 started to develop its part of the field, which has estimated reserves of 100 trillion cubic feet and which it refers to as South Pars.

A 1969 agreement signed by Iran and Qatar clearly defines their maritime border, but does not say how any cross-border reserves should be shared. There have been no differences over the issue to date and the two governments consulted each other on their respective development plans. However, any deterioration in political relations between the two could have the potential to affect the field's development.

The legality of Saudi Arabia's plans to develop the cross-border Shaibah field on the UAE frontier was reportedly established in the 1974 border agreement. Despite having been in existence for three years or so, the UAE federal government did not actually sign the 1974 agreement with Saudi Arabia; this was left to Abu Dhabi, its dominant shaikhdom. However, the clause giving full ownership to Saudi Arabia has only recently assumed relevance and, as development progresses, could cause resentment in the UAE. Current Saudi plans involve only its side of the border and Saudi officials said in 1992 there had been no objections from the UAE. But Western diplomats in Saudi Arabia said Abu Dhabi officials visited Riyadh in early 1992 to discuss possible co-operation in development of Shaibah, including a proposed export pipeline across UAE territory, the shortest and cheapest route.[29] The officials are reported to have received a lukewarm response, as Saudi Arabia apparently guards its rights to the field. Abu Dhabi officials continue to express dissatisfaction with the 1974 border agreement. To date, unlike Saudi Arabia's border agreements with Qatar (1965) and Oman (1990), the text of the 1974 agreement has not been made available to the public. Saudi ARAMCO's plans for export of Shaibah crude involve a far more expensive option of building a $1 billion, 600 km pipeline across the desert to existing Saudi processing facilities at Abqaiq in Eastern province, from where existing pipelines run to the Ras Tanurah export terminal.

Notes

1. "Exploration drive deepens territorial disputes", *Petroleum Argus*, 12 October 1992, 3.
2. "First Timor Gap oil drilling to start in December", *Reuter*, 5 November 1992.
3. The manner in which the former Saudi–Kuwaiti Neutral Zone was created (during 1922) and then divided (by agreements of 1965 and 1969) is reviewed in Chapters 1 and 9.
4. Post-Gulf war reconstruction efforts in the Divided Zone shared by Saudi Arabia and Kuwait have now pushed capacity above 400,000 b/d. Further onshore expansion plans mean it should top 500,000 b/d by the end of 1995. *Petroleum Argus*, 1 February 1993, 4.
5. AOC's concessions were awarded by Saudi Arabia and Kuwait for offshore areas and are valid up to 1999. Getty has a Saudi concession valid up to 2009 for Saudi Arabia's half of onshore rights in the Divided Zone. It operates in the Kuwaiti part of the zone in close co-operation with the Kuwait Oil Company. Getty's steam flooding programme involves an Eocene reservoir, which necessarily makes it very expensive. The programme would go ahead only if Getty's concession was renewed in 2009. The company's exploration and water injection projects are viable irrespective of whether the concession is renewed. "A survey of the Saudi Arabian oil industry", Embassy of the USA, Riyadh, Saudi Arabia, July 1991, 21–2.
6. "1991 Oil survey", Embassy of the USA, Riyadh, Saudi Arabia, July 1991. Also, *Middle East Economic Survey* [MEES], 11 January 1993, A2.
7. "Development plans advance for cross-border field", *Petroleum Argus*, 5 October 1992, 5.

8. A field straddling the maritime border between Iran and Oman has similarly been left undeveloped since discovery, largely because of its cross-border nature. The Henjam field was discovered by Elf Aquitaine in 1976. The first well was on the Iranian side of the border but a later well and seismic studies showed it to cross the border. Elf relinquished the concession in 1984 without developing the field. A warming of relations between Iran and Oman led to an agreement in 1991 to undertake a joint study on development of Henjam, but no further progress has been reported. *MEES*, 21 May 1990, A7.

9. "Saudi Arabia to revive border field", *Petroleum Argus*, 13 July 1992, 6.

10. *Petroleum Argus*, 5 October 1992, 6; "New drilling marks out territorial claims", *Petroleum Argus*, 27 July 1992, 3; "ARAMCO explores depths and breadth of Saudi territory. *Petroleum Intelligence Weekly*", [PIW], 3 August 1992; "ARAMCO drilling in disputed area", *Reuter*, 21 July 1992.

11. *Petroleum Argus*, 30 August 1993, p. 6.

12. R. N. Schofield, *Kuwait and Iraq: historical claims and territorial disputes* Middle East Programme Report (London: Royal Institute of International Affairs, 1991), 126-7.

13. *MEES*, 3 August 1992, A4–5; and, for further details, see Chapters 1 and 5.

14. *MEES*, 8 June 1992, A11–12. An earlier editorial comment in *MEES* says it is "conceivable (but unlikely) that the Iraqis might go along with such a demarcation as far as Rumaila is concerned", but "there would appear to be no chance whatsoever" for acceptance of the recommendation for handover of part of Umm Qasr port. *MEES*, 24 February 1992, C2.

15. "Iraq tells OPEC to curb output", *Reuter*, 18 November 1992.

16. See Chapter 1 for a further discussion of these issues.

17. The text of the letter reads: "The kingdom of Saudi Arabia has information that some of the international oil companies granted concessions by the government of the Yemen Republic for oil exploration and drilling had exceeded in this exploration into areas on the borders between the two countries that have not been agreed upon and the government of the kingdom of Saudi Arabia considers these areas a part of its territory. Needless to say, the government of the kingdom of Saudi Arabia will not recognise any legal implications for these excesses and will not allow any aggression against the sanctity of its borders and rights, and will take all necessary actions to protect its rights against any unlawful activity. At the same time, these companies will bear full responsibility for any actions that would be considered against the rights of the kingdom of Saudi Arabia." *Middle East Economic Digest* [MEED], 29 May 1992, 35.

18. *Yemen: border disputes and relations with Saudi Arabia* (Washington DC: MAY 1992); Petro Finance Market Intelligence Service, "Border stakes rise", *Petroleum Economist*, July 1992, 24.

19. "Borders, borders, everywhere", *Foreign Reports Bulletin*, 2 October 1992, 2.

20. *Energy Compass Weekly Review*, 14 August 1992, 13–15.

21. *MEES*, 30 November 1992, A11.

22. *MEES*, 2 November 1992, D1–2.

23. *MEES*, 10 February 1992, A12–13.

24. *Ibid*.

25. *Petroleum Argus*, 5 October 1992, 7; 17 August 1992, 6.

26. *Energy Compass Weekly Review*, 24 July 1992, 4.

27. *Ibid*, 30 October 1992, 13.

28. *Petroleum Argus*, 19 October 1992, 6; "Crescent to raise output from Mubarak oil field", *Reuter*, 4 November 1992.

29. *Petroleum Argus*, 5 October 1992, 5; also, "Saudis look east to tap alternative light crude field", *PIW*, 6 July 1992, 1. This report claims that officials from Abu Dhabi proposed to Saudi Arabia that Abu Dhabi National Oil Company (ADNOC) develop the reservoir on its side of the frontier.

CHAPTER NINE

Shared zones as a solution to problems of territorial sovereignty in the Gulf states

GERALD BLAKE

Introduction

Seen in a global context, the political map of the Gulf region has a number of remarkable geopolitical features. It includes some of the world's smallest states both by area and by population even allowing for high rates of population increase (Table 9.1).

Table 9.1 Micro-states of the Gulf.

	Area (km)	World rank/140	Estimated population 2000	World rank/140
Bahrain	598	137	693,000	130
Kuwait	9,375	125	3,007,000	109
Qatar	10,360	128	569,000	132
UAE	93,970	99	1,939,000	115

Source: World resources 1987. New York: Basic Books.

The Gulf itself is the world's smallest semi-enclosed sea (230,000 km²), and with eight coastal states it is clearly one of the most congested. Bahrain is one of the world's few non-archipelagic island states. Iraq, with only 19 km of coastline, is generally regarded as a "geographically disadvantaged" state. The territorial divisions of the seven component shaikhdoms of the United Arab Emirates are the most complex of any federal state in the world. The strategically important Musandam peninsula at the entrance to the Gulf is a political outlier of Oman. Another unusual geopolitical feature of the territorial framework of the Gulf states is the number of areas where state sovereignty is modified in some way. Such modifications may be regarded as temporary attempts to resolve problems of territorial competition on land,

Table 9.2 Examples of non-state and restricted state sovereignty in the Middle East.

	Parties/sponsors	Dates
(a) Land territories		
Turkish Straits zone	International Straits Commission	1923–36
Suez Canal zone	Britain–Egypt	1882–1954
Cyprus Buffer zone	United Nations	1974–present
Lebanon Protected zone	United Nations	1978–present
Neutral zone*	Iraq–Saudi Arabia	1922–81
Neutral zone*	Saudi Arabia–Kuwait	1922–66
Neutral zone*	Abu Dhabi–Dubai	1961–present
Shared zone*	Sharjah–Oman	1964–65?
Shared zone*	Fujairah–Sharjah	1956–58?
Shared zone*	Ajman–Oman	1964–65?
Joint administration* (Abu Musa)	Iran–Sharjah	1971–present
Partitioned zone*	Saudi Arabia–Kuwait	1966–present
Kurdish safe haven	United Nations	1991–present
Demilitarized zone*	Kuwait–Iraq–UN	1991–present
(b) Seabed		
Partitioned zone*	Saudi Arabia–Kuwait	1966–present
Shared revenues*	Saudi Arabia–Bahrain	1958–present
Shared revenues*	Abu Dhabi–Qatar	1969–present
Shared revenues*	Iran-Sharjah (Abu Musa)	1971–present
Restricted exploitation*	Iran–Saudi Arabia	1968–present

* Gulf region example

or resource competition at sea. The aim of this chapter is to suggest that such alternatives to absolute state sovereignty generally appear to have worked well in the Gulf region. A wide range of types of non-state sovereignty has been established in the Gulf at various times, most of which remain in operation today. Six examples are briefly examined below. The Middle East as a whole exemplifies an even greater range of examples than the Gulf region (see Table 9.2). More thought needs to be given to the definition of terms and to the development of a proper classification of non-state or restricted state sovereignty. For the purpose of this chapter, terms in common use to describe various zones are adopted; they do not necessarily give reliable indications of differences in status. Whether the Kurdish "safe havens" established in northern Iraq in the early months of 1991 will ultimately develop into another type of non-state territory remains to be seen. United Nations policy is not to create any territorial enclaves in Iraq, but it is a fair guess that the safe haven will remain a feature of the political map for some time to come (see Fig. 9.1).

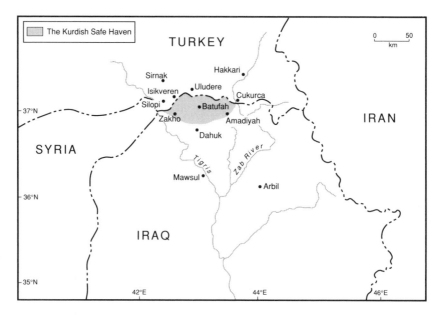

Figure 9.1 The Kurdish safe haven in northern Iraq, May 1991.

The Anglo–Ottoman Agreement of July 1913

The Anglo–Ottoman Agreement of July 1913 concerning Kuwait provides an interesting curtain-raiser to the concept of restricted state sovereignty in the Gulf region, although it was never ratified or put to the test because of the outbreak of the First World War. Kuwait was recognized as an autonomous *qadha* within the Ottoman Empire, and within an inner zone contained by a Red line (see Fig. 9.2) autonomy was absolute. Here, the Ottomans had no right of intervention, not least because of a number of earlier agreements giving Britain considerable influence, including control of foreign policy. Within a zone bounded by a Green line (see Fig. 9.2), tribes were acknowledged to be dependent on the Shaikh of Kuwait; though Article Six of the agreement appeared to allow the possibility of Ottoman intervention, this was only with the agreement of the Shaikh of Kuwait (or, in the case of military activity, after notifying Britain).[1] The status of the area bounded by the Green line was sufficiently ambiguous to satisfy Britain, Kuwait and the Ottomans in 1913, but it proved to be no deterrent to the territorial claims of Ibn Saud of Najd. In 1920 and 1921 his forces had invaded almost all of the territory contained within the Green line, and raided Jahrah within the Red zone. The Treaty of Muhammarah (May 1922) was a first attempt to define approximate territorial limits in northern Arabia between Iraq, Najd and Kuwait. The subsequent protocols signed at the Uqair conference (December 1922) defined Najd's northern boundaries with Iraq and Kuwait and introduced the Neutral Zone to the territorial landscape of Arabia.

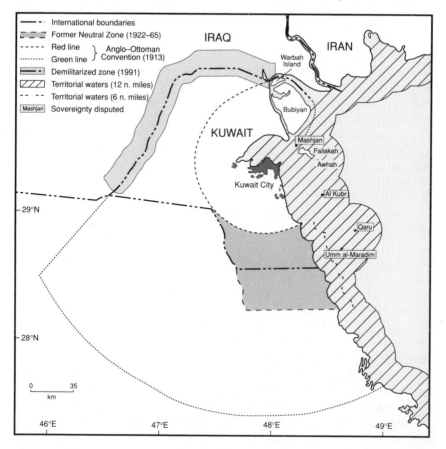

Figure 9.2 Kuwait, showing the 1913 Red and Green lines, the former Kuwaiti–Saudi (Najd) Neutral Zone (1922–69) and the United Nations demilitarized zone (1991 to the present).

The Kuwait–Saudi Arabia Neutral Zone

The Kuwait–Saudi Arabia (Najd) Neutral Zone was established by the Uqair Protocol of 1922. Under the treaty, the Shaikh of Kuwait lost about two-thirds of the territory within the outer zone bound by the 1913 Green line, and the provision of a large Neutral Zone may have been an attempt to mollify him. Far more important were reports of oil in the vicinity of Khawr

Maqtah, which Britain wished to ensure was not lost entirely to Kuwait. In the Neutral Zone, "the government of Najd and Kuwait will share equal rights until through the good offices of the government of Great Britain a further agreement is made between Najd and Kuwait concerning it."[2] Although the Saudi Arabia–Kuwait Neutral Zone was equivalent to 36 per cent of the area of Kuwait, and although it was thought to contain oil, no guidelines were laid down for the joint administration of the area. There was no reference to offshore arrangements, no provision for government, and no guidance about what to do in cases of dispute. In later years a number of agreements were reached that helped define the rôles of the two states. One such agreement recognized the jurisdiction of each state over its own nationals in the Neutral Zone. From 1953, however, oil production in the Neutral Zone created strains and stresses between the parties as the number of workers rose to over 4,000. There were accusations by Kuwait, for example, that the Saudis were treating the entire workforce as though it were under Saudi law.[3] Saudi Arabia proposed the creation of a proper joint administration for the Neutral Zone headed by a council of four, but Kuwait rejected the idea as too complex. In 1963, after much discussion going back a number of years, the principle of equal partition was agreed.

The partition agreement of July 1965 provided for the division of the Neutral Zone into two equal parts, which would be annexed as integral parts of the territories of the parties.[4] Equal rights to exploit hydrocarbon resources were to continue, and the citizens of Saudi Arabia and Kuwait had the right to work in either part of the partitioned zone. The width of the territorial sea of the annexed territories was fixed at 6 nautical miles. Beyond the 6-mile limit, the parties have equal rights to resources by means of joint exploitation unless they agree otherwise. The offshore arrangement is greatly complicated by the existence of a dispute over the sovereignty of Qaru and Umm al Maradim islands which are claimed in full by Kuwait. Saudi Arabia apparently argues that the islands should be subject to co-sovereignty to reflect their position off the former Neutral Zone, although this position has not been clearly stated.[5]

The Iraq–Saudi Arabia Neutral Zone

The 7,044 km^2 Saudi Arabia–Iraq Neutral Zone was also established by a protocol signed at the Uqair conference of December 1922 (Fig. 1.2). The parties agreed to an equal division of the zone in December 1981, perhaps because it had largely fulfilled its original purpose of allowing nomadic tribes free and unhindered access to traditional wells and pastures. The 1922 Treaty of Muhammarah and the 1925 Bahrah Agreement had previously sought to settle the difficult question of tribal loyalties in the border zone between Najd and Iraq. Both sides had made "ridiculous" claims to vast territories based on tribal allegiance,[6] but it was finally agreed that the Muntafiq, Dhafir and Amarat tribes would be assigned to Iraq, and the Shammar Najd to the Najd. On this basis, ownership of wells and pastures was to be established and a boundary drawn, but in the area of the Neutral Zone it proved too problematic and a territorial compromise was adopted. Since the right of access to wells was a concern in other sectors of the boundary, it is perhaps surprising that the Neutral Zone concept was not used more widely. The Treaty of Muhammarah promised certain Najd tribes access to wells close to the border within Iraq, but there was clearly no way in which this could be guaranteed once an international boundary was in place.

The Abu Dhabi–Dubai Neutral Zone

The Abu Dhabi–Dubai Neutral Zone (see Fig. 9.3) appears to have had similar origins to the former Iraq–Saudi Arabia Neutral Zone, but it is of lesser significance and far smaller. The area measures only some 30 km by 5 km, but it contains several important wells disputed by each party since the 1950s. The territorial claims of Abu Dhabi and Dubai were once very much greater and their 1969 Neutral Zone is, in a sense, a symbol of earlier struggles. It has very little practical importance today. Three other small territories in the United Arab Emirates are also shared, two of them with neighbouring Oman (see Table 9.2). In these areas tribal allegiances were complex and ambiguous and territorial compromise had to be reached.

The Bahrain/Saudi Arabia maritime boundary

There are already at least 13 joint arrangements worldwide for the exploitation of resources near maritime boundaries, three of which are in the Gulf.[7] The 1958 Bahrain–Saudi Arabia continental shelf agreement was not only the first offshore boundary to be agreed in the Gulf (Fig. 9.4), but it was also the first in the world to incorporate the sharing of revenues from seabed resources. Several features of this boundary are interesting, such as the decision to ignore certain small islands when determining the median-line boundary between the mainland and Bahrain island. The most important feature from the point of view of this chapter, however, is the Fasht Bu Saafah hexagon (see Fig. 9.4), whose oil revenues are divided equally between Saudi Arabia and Bahrain. In many years these revenues

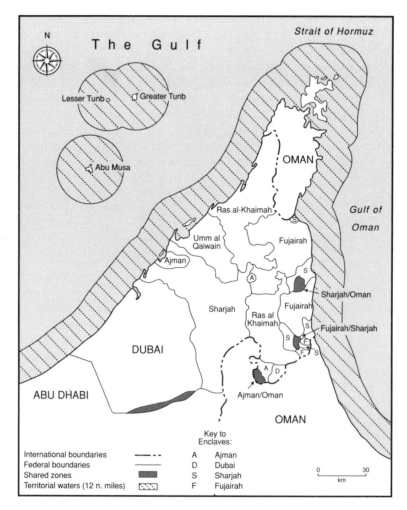

Figure 9.3 The United Arab Emirates showing shared territories.

have been equivalent to half or more of Bahrain's oil income, so they are of vital importance to the Bahraini economy. The importance of the Bu Saafah structure to Bahrain is, in early 1993, greater than ever, following Saudi Arabia's decision of late December 1992 to allow the island state to receive 70 per cent of all revenue from the field for a period of two years. This appears to be the only agreement in which a boundary line has been fixed but resources lying exclusively on one side of the line are shared between the two states.

Bahrain had long claimed the Bu Saafah area and the islands of Lubainah al-Saghirah (Bain al-Saghir) and Lubainah al-Kabirah (Bain al-Khabir; see

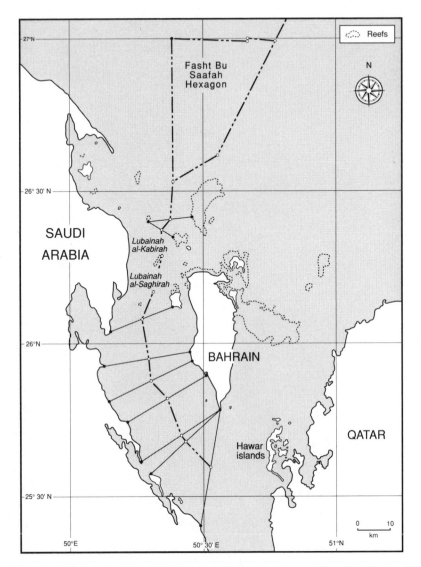

Figure 9.4 The Bahrain/Saudi Arabian maritime boundary and the Fasht Bu Saafah Hexagon.

Fig. 9.4). The Bahrain Petroleum Company (BAPCO) tried to operate in the region of these islands in 1941 but suspended its work after Saudi objections during 1949. By 1954 if not earlier the parties had agreed in principle to a division of the Bu Saafah area, but negotiations became deadlocked over the precise method of delimitation and the place of the seabed negotiations within the general rubric of the Anglo–Saudi frontier negotiations. Four

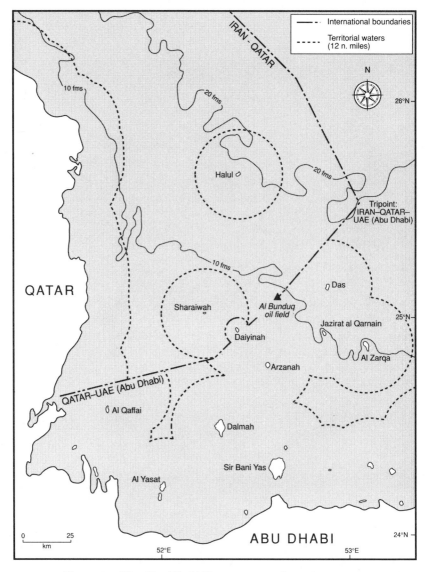

Figure 9.5 The Abu Dhabi/Qatar maritime boundary, 1969.

years later, during a state visit to Saudi Arabia, the Ruler of Bahrain
conceded Bu Saafah to Saudi Arabia in return for a permanent share of half
the oil revenues of the Fasht Bu Saafah oilfield. The technical management
of Bu Saafah was left entirely in the hands of the Saudis. According to some
British archival sources in 1957 the Saudis might have been willing for the
Bu Saafah hexagon to be divided equally between the parties.[8]

The Abu Dhabi / Qatar maritime boundary

Under the Abu Dhabi–Qatar continental shelf agreement of 20 March 1969, the parties agreed on the allocation of a number of disputed islands. Daiyinah island, which belongs to Abu Dhabi, was not given full effect in the alignment of the boundary line through the small Bunduq oilfield, whose revenues are shared equally between Abu Dhabi and Qatar (see Fig. 9.5), although Abu Dhabi is responsible for the exploitation of the Bunduq field. There are a number of examples in the Gulf of oilfields straddling international boundaries and creating problems for the parties concerned. This is believed to be the only case where a maritime boundary was deliberately located on a known oilfield as a solution to the problem.

Conclusion

The six examples cited above by no means exhaust the list of shared arrangements in the Gulf region. It is also worth noting that other kinds of territorial arrangement have been implemented in the region in an attempt to reduce the likelihood of conflict between neighbouring states. The Saudi Arabia / Iran continental shelf boundary of October 1968, for example, forbids drilling for oil within 500 metres of the maritime boundary, including directional drilling from beyond that limit. In four other Gulf agreements the prohibition on drilling was set at a distance of 125 metres (Iran–Qatar 1969; Iran–Bahrain 1971; Iran–Oman 1974; Iran–UAE 1974).[9] More recently, a UN-monitored demilitarized zone along the Iraq/Kuwait boundary has been established extending 10 km into Iraq and 5 km into Kuwait, as provided for under UN Resolution 687 (Article 5) of 3 April 1991 (see Fig. 9.2). Such provisions restrict the freedom of action of the states involved, but greatly enhance the prospects for peaceful co-existence. The territorial state, whose sovereignty is limited to its system of boundaries, will no doubt continue to be the basis of the political organization of space for the foreseeable future. Good government and good neighbourliness require that international boundaries are properly recognized and clearly delimited. On the other hand, alternative territorial strategies such as shared zones and zones of restricted activity have successfully provided temporary relief to potential flashpoints and perhaps deserve to be evaluated far more thoroughly than hitherto. Significantly, the United Nations Declaration of Human Rights makes it clear that rights and freedoms are an entitlement regardless of territorial status:

Furthermore, no distinction shall be made on the basis of the political, jurisdictional or international status of the country or territory to which a person belongs, whether it be independent, trust, non-self governing *or under any other limitation of sovereignty.*[10]

The use of shared political space in the Gulf region has arguably been effective, at least if judged by prevalence, variety and durability. Shared space on land and sea may yet prove to be a useful device in the quest for future regional peace.

Notes

1. E. Lauterpacht, C. J. Greenwood, Marc Weller, Daniel Bethlehem (eds), *The Kuwait crisis: basic documents*, 34 (Cambridge: Research Centre for International Law, Grotius Publications, 1991).

2. *Ibid*, 48.

3. H. M. al-Baharna, *The legal status of the Arabian Gulf states*, 1st edn (Manchester: Manchester University Press, 1968), 272.

4. Lauterpacht, et al., *The Kuwait crisis, op. cit.*, 57–8.

5. A. A. El-Hakim, *The Middle Eastern states and the law of the sea* (Manchester: Manchester University Press, 1979), 272.

6. H. R. P. Dickson, *Kuwait and her neighbours* (London: Allen & Unwin, 1956), 272–3.

7. US Department of State, *Limits in the sea* No. 108, *Maritime Boundaries of the World* (1990), 34.

8. Letter from the British Residency, 7 May 1957, FO *371/126934.* In R. N. Schofield & G. H. Blake (eds), *Arabian boundaries: primary documents 1853–1957,* vol. 10 (Farnham Common, England: Archive Editions, 1988), 129.

9. S. P. Jagota, *Maritime boundary* (Dordrecht, Netherlands: Martinus Nijhoff, 1985), 76-7.

10. United Nations General Assembly, *Universal Declaration of Human Rights*, Article 2, 10 December 1948.

CHAPTER TEN

Contemporary oil exploration and development policies in the Gulf region

PAUL STEVENS

Introduction

There is a circular relationship between territorial disputes on the one hand and hydrocarbon exploration and development activity on the other. Exploration and development can encourage such disputes for two reasons. First, the existence of subsurface hydrocarbon deposits (real or imagined) converts what would otherwise be worthless desert into a valued asset. Hence what may have been initial indifference over border delineation becomes a matter of urgency. Secondly, oil and gas both have the physical characteristic of being able to flow. Since they are no respecters of international boundaries, oil and gas discoveries straddling boundaries tend inevitably to lead to maximum production, for what is not produced by you will be produced by your neighbour. Recent developments in horizontal drilling allow producers to take even greater advantage of their neighbour's subsurface hydrocarbon deposits than was previously the case. Even if the field is to be unified, then the division, which is an essential prerequisite of any unification agreement, requires some agreement over the boundary delimitation.

In turn, territorial disputes can inhibit exploration and development activity. Oil operations represent long-lived, large and fixed investment projects. To ensure adequate financial return requires clear-cut property rights. If the region is the subject of a border dispute, such clear-cut property rights are not possible.[1]

This chapter concentrates upon the prospects for exploration and development activity in the Gulf region[2] during the 1990s. However, to provide a basis for analysis, an outline of the history of such activity is required. The analysis distinguishes between foreign oil companies and the national oil companies of the countries concerned. The distinction matters because the motivations and inhibitions frequently differ between the two types of company.

211

The history of exploration and development 1960–87

The foreign companies

During this period, with a few exceptions,[3] there was limited interest by foreign companies in either exploration or development in the Gulf. In support of this contention, Figure 10.1 shows the global capital expenditure in the Middle East[4] of a large sample of oil companies on geological, geophysical and leases, acting as a proxy for exploration. As is clear, the amount spent in the area is negligible. Figure 10.2 from the same sample shows expenditure on production, which acts as a proxy for development activity. The story of negligible activity is confirmed.

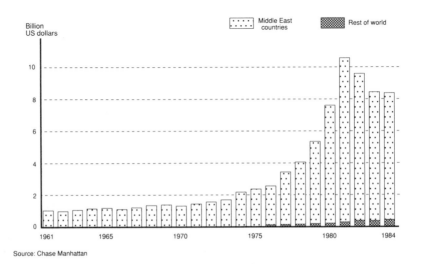

Source: Chase Manhattan

Figure 10.1 Company expenditure on geological, geophysical and leases in the Middle East, 1961–84.

During the 1960s, the reason for such limited interest from the foreign companies lay almost entirely in the fact that those operating in the region already had access to more oil than they could manage. Indeed, the history of the international industry during the 1960s can be written in terms of the struggle to protect the price structure from the excess capacity, which was largely concentrated in the Gulf.[5] Figure 10.3 illustrates the point with an estimate of the sources of excess capacity in the region for the main companies. In total, the four largest Gulf producers averaged some 3 million barrels per day (b/d) of excess capacity annually during the 1958–70 period. During the 1970s, the major companies lost their access to acreage in most of the Gulf either through a process of nationalization or through the "participation" negotiations of the first half of the decade.[6] The main exceptions to this were in Abu Dhabi and Oman. Where access remained

212

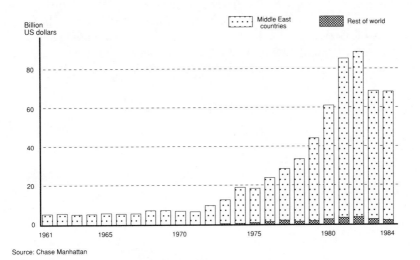

Source: Chase Manhattan

Figure 10.2 Oil company capital expenditure on production.

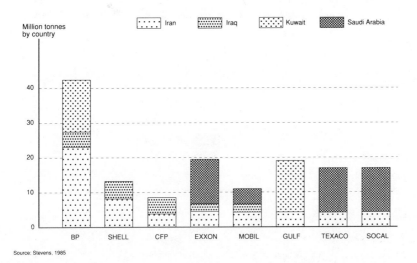

Source: Stevens, 1985

Figure 10.3 Average annual equity access to excess in the Gulf capacity by company, 1958–70.

feasible or subsequently developed, companies did express interest. However, during the 1970s and the first half of the 1980s, in many cases the terms demanded by governments for access to acreage were too difficult and inhibited interest.[7]

The national oil companies

In the main Gulf countries, exploration and development activity by the national oil companies in this period was relatively limited. Figure 10.4 illustrates well completion in the Gulf region, while Figure 10.5 gives some idea of the very small amount of exploration activity in the Gulf.

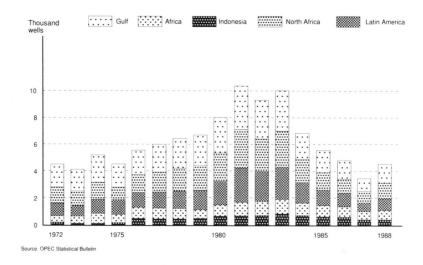

Figure 10.4 Wells completed in OPEC member countries by region.

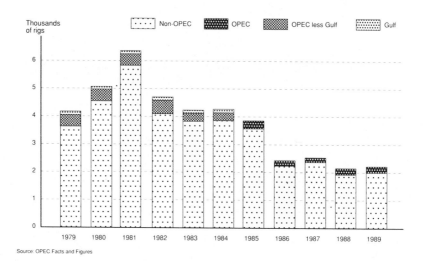

Figure 10.5 Active exploration rigs by region, 1979–89 (no Gulf split after 1985).

214

During the 1970s, the main reason for this relatively limited interest was that government revenues were not constrained by capacity. Most of the countries had surplus capacity and many were faced with more revenue than they could immediately use. Iraq was an exception to both these generalizations, but Iraq's constraint in the 1970s was that of export capacity rather than producing capacity.[8]

During the "second oil shock", there was renewed interest by national companies, as can be seen from Figure 10.4. However, it was short-lived for two reasons. The outbreak of the Iran–Iraq war in September 1980 meant that both combatants were more concerned with maintaining existing operations than with new development. Also the fact that the waters of the Gulf became a war zone inhibited many offshore developments. The second reason for the diminution of interest in exploration and development was the emergence of huge excess capacity in the international market, especially in the Gulf. Figure 10.6 illustrates the point clearly.

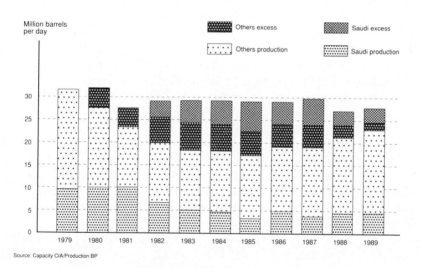

Figure 10.6 OPEC: production and excess capacity, 1979–89.

The reasons for the post-1986 revival of interest in exploration and development by the Gulf governments

The turning point in this situation was the oil price collapse of 1986.[9] After this there were clear signs of a renewal of interest in exploration and development, although in many cases even by mid-1990 this had not translated into actual drilling. So far the evidence for such a revival is rather *ad hoc* and anecdotal. The reason for this revival of interest in exploration and development lay in a coincidence of interest between the Gulf governments and the foreign oil companies.

There were three reasons for the governments' interest. The first was the fact that, as the 1980s proceeded, excess capacity began to erode, as can be seen from Figure 10.6. This was due to a rising call on Gulf production, the natural process of field depletion and the general lack of maintenance of the excess capacity that had developed earlier in the decade. The second reason for the renewed interest in exploration and development was the 1986 price collapse itself. In 1982, the Gulf Co-operation Council (GCC) countries' revenue from oil was $109 billion.[10] Between 1983 and 1985, the annual average oil revenue was $74 billion, but in 1986 this collapsed to $50 billion. The perception grew that the only insurance against lower prices was the offset of increased volume, which implied capacity expansion.[11] Lastly, during the later 1980s there was a growing view that the 1990s would see a tightening of the oil markets and hence prospects for higher prices.

However, despite the interest, many of the governments faced severe constraints on undertaking exploration or development, which in most cases was a prerequisite to capacity expansion.[12] There were three sources of constraint. First, many of the countries lacked the proven reserves.[13] Although many of the countries in the Gulf had posted significant improvements in reserves, most of the increases were a figment of some computer's imagination based upon changing assumptions.[14] This flurry of reserve changes in 1986–7 had in large part been triggered by the prospects that OPEC would use reserve size as a key variable in a formulae-based system for allocating quotas.[15] Secondly, many of the countries – especially Iran and Iraq – lacked access to the finance required for the necessary investment. Lastly, many of the countries lacked access to the technology, In particular, the 1980s had seen significant changes in exploration and drilling technology which presented new opportunities.[16]

The result of these constraints was a growing willingness to consider the entry of foreign companies back into the Gulf, a trend that was mirrored elsewhere in the world.[17] This was also accompanied by a general easing of terms of entry. In this environment, even countries such as Iraq were offering foreign companies terms,[18] while Iran was engaged in a series of informal and low-key meetings with the companies.

The reasons for the post-1986 revival of interest in exploration and development by the foreign companies

Evidence of a revival of company interest is difficult to determine. In part the picture is distorted by the observable fall in exploration budgets in response to the 1986 price collapse. However, this fall simply reflected the oil companies' urgent need to salvage their cashflow situation, where cutting back on drilling was the fastest and easiest route to reduce cash outflow. The companies' new interest stemmed from three factors. First, many areas of the world had been reassessed geologically and as a result had moved up in the league of prospective acreage. The southern Red Sea in particular had suddenly become a more interesting area. Secondly, many of the companies began to anticipate tighter oil markets in the 1990s compared with the 1980s.[19] Hence in many companies there was growing interest in securing access to crude in anticipation of both higher prices and the depletion of their existing reserves in the USA. Indeed, many companies began to adopt a policy of "frontier exploration", which involved trying to get acreage in areas that had previously been closed by either the limits of technology or politics. The Gulf was precisely such an area. Lastly, as the 1990s began, many of the oil companies began to talk in terms of developing strategic alliances. One such route would be the alliance of access to crude from governments with access to downstream facilities from companies.[20]

However, despite this interest, the companies faced some constraints in terms of the Gulf states. There were other attractive areas in which to direct resources – most obviously the Soviet Union and deeper offshore. Some companies with a long history in the region were still regarded with considerable suspicion by many in the local governments. Equally, some of the current senior oil company management had very negative experiences in the region during the "ejection" of the oil companies in the early 1970s and they had certain objections to renewing involvement. In any case, the Gulf was perceived by many within the companies as inherently unstable and an area to avoid.

Against this background of renewed interest by both governments and companies came the Gulf crisis – the invasion of Kuwait followed by US intervention. To consider the effects of this upon the future of exploration and development activity in the region it is necessary to disaggregate the analysis.

Saudi Arabia

Prior to the Gulf crisis, Saudi Arabia had outlined plans for capacity expansion.[21] These were intended to provide a gradual expansion to 10 million barrels per day (b/d) in order to meet the anticipated rising call for Saudi oil.

They were also to provide some degree of volume cushion, partially to provide market control but also as an insurance against further price collapses. Since this was the basis of the expansion, the timeframe was left deliberately vague.

The Gulf crisis created three new elements. The first was that the capacity plans were hurriedly accelerated.[22] Saudi ARAMCO claimed that, by the end of the war, sustainable capacity was 8.3 million b/d. Furthermore, it was announced that the 10 million b/d expansion would now be completed before 1995. Most of the immediate increase however had been as a result of de-mothballing and further expansion would require a significant drilling programme. The second impact from the crisis was that Saudi Arabia's financial situation deteriorated rapidly. Before the crisis there were already financial constraints, with the annual budget deficit running at some $6 billion.[23] Various estimates of the cost of the war have been floated but around $40 billion seems to be the modal average, with an offset of $14 billion due to windfall gains from higher oil prices and higher volume. Before the war there was talk in Saudi circles of getting Saudi ARAMCO to fund its capacity investments on the international capital markets. Such ideas will almost certainly now re-emerge. The third consequence of the crisis is that the ruling group within the Kingdom will now seek as many different ways as possible to try and reinforce the commitment to them by the USA, already greatly enhanced by the invasion and its aftermath. These last two consequences – financial constraints and need for US links – may well see a move to encourage foreign companies into the Kingdom. In particular, there is scope in the Red Sea that has been neglected in terms of exploration since the 1965 agreement with AUXIRAP (Société Auxiliaire de la Régie Autonome des Petroles).[24]

Iran

Before the Gulf crisis, Iran faced severe constraints on expanding capacity. There were considerable doubts about the state of the fields. In 1978, NIOC (National Iranian Oil Company) had drawn up a large investment programme for secondary recovery to offset the impending decline in what were generally very mature fields. This programme had been shelved by the revolution and the subsequent war. Iran was desperately short of finance, in particular the foreign exchange that would be a key input into any large-scale attempt to renew a programme of exploration and development. Lastly, although there were many extremely experienced and competent engineers in the Iranian oil sector, the post-revolutionary exodus had taken its toll. There were simply too few skills available. However, plans for expansion were afoot. Before the crisis, it was announced that capacity would be increased to 3.8 million b/d (from 3.3) within four months, rising to 4 million b/d in 1990 and 5 million b/d within five years.[25]

The main impact on this situation of the Gulf crisis was that the capacity expansion imperative was strengthened.[26] Attempts to increase production to take advantage of the higher price had illustrated the technical imperative to explore and develop. Equally, the possibility of a close alliance with Saudi Arabia to control the oil market jointly became a serious possibility. In such an alliance, the degree of Iranian influence would be very much determined by Iranian export capacity. The result has been announcements of capacity expansion plans and attempts to find acceptable ways to get the foreign oil companies involved as a means to offset some of the constraints outlined above.[27] In May 1991, an agreement with Totale was announced.[28]

Iraq

Before the invasion Iraq, like Iran, urgently sought capacity expansion.[29] The country was operating close to productive capacity and faced very large financial pressures. Increased capacity would give Iraq some influence in the corridors of OPEC and also provide a volume insurance against lower prices. The crisis made the financial pressures simply impossible. Although actual damage to oil production facilities is relatively limited,[30] UN sanctions remain in place and that will inhibit exports. Furthermore, Iraq now faces the familiar problem of constrained export capacity rather than production capacity.[31] The northern pipeline through Turkey with a design capacity of 1.65 million b/d goes through the Kurdish "safe haven" zone and is therefore vulnerable to interruption from the Kurds. The southern pipeline route through the IPSA network also has a design capacity of 1.65 million b/d. IPSA (Iraqi pipeline across Saudi Arabia) throughput is entirely at the mercy of Saudi Arabia, if only by its control of the storage and loading arrangements on the Red Sea. Lastly, the Mina al-Bakr export terminal, with its design capacity of 800,000 b/d, has been damaged to an unknown extent.

Iraq may well wish to carry out programmes of exploration and development. However, the existing constraints almost certainly will force it to accept foreign company involvement.[32] While the present regime remains, it is unlikely that oil companies would involve themselves both because of the probability of sanctions continuing[33] and because of the likely negative response from their Western shareholders.[34] In the event of a new regime, then it is quite likely that there would be a competitive scramble for acreage in Iraq by foreign oil companies. This could presage a significant period of exploration and development.

Kuwait

Before the crisis, Kuwait had rather vague plans for some capacity expansion within its borders[35] although the Kuwait Foreign Petroleum Exploration Company (KUFPEC) had a very active programme abroad as part of its general oil diversification strategy.[36] The crisis has dramatically changed that, with the virtual total destruction of Kuwait's above ground facilities together with unknown damage to the reservoirs as a result of uncontrolled flow. Clearly a massive redevelopment programme will be required in a situation where both finance and expertise may face constraints, especially given Kuwait's apparent policy of forcing out much of its expatriate labour.

Bahrain, Oman, Qatar and the UAE

Before the crisis, all four of these countries needed to expand their capacity.[37] Arguably, all four faced reserve constraints[38] and Bahrain, Oman and Qatar faced considerable financial constraints. In general, pre-crisis, all four had active programmes of exploration and development that also involved foreign oil companies since the sovereignty aspect presented much less of a constraint than in other countries of the Gulf. The outcome of the invasion of Kuwait has reinforced this need for extra capacity. The political situation gives the rulers a strong incentive to pump as much as possible. This is not only to secure revenue to try and enhance their legitimacy in such troubled times but also to enhance their own private wealth while they still may. It is therefore likely that the exploration and development plans that were in train before the crisis will be rapidly stepped up.

Conclusions

The analysis above argues quite strongly that the 1990s will see a considerable upturn in exploration and development in the Gulf, but in most cases only if there is considerable involvement by foreign companies. Most companies will be willing to engage in such involvement only if there is access to equity oil. For most governments this may not be a problem. However, if the term "territorial disputes" is widened to cover the general uncertainties and longstanding disputes that characterize the area, even such concessions may not be enough to attract large-scale foreign company involvement.

Postscript

This chapter was written and presented as a paper in May 1991. It is always tempting when asked to prepare for publication much later to make alterations to update the information. However, I have resisted this temptation, partly because the analysis has stood the test of time. For readers who would like an update there is P. Stevens, *Oil and politics: the post-war Gulf* (London: Royal Institute of International Affairs, 1992), which provides a detailed update on the capacity expansion plans of the Gulf countries and the oil market context in which it is taking place.

Notes

1. This is not strictly accurate since it is possible to reach an agreement enabling hydrocarbon activity in advance of any agreement on disputed borders. M. J. Valencia, "Joint development of petroleum resources in overlapping claim areas", in J. D. Lambert & F. Fesharaki (eds) *Economic and political incentives to petroleum exploration: developments in the Asia–Pacific region* (Washington DC: International Law Institute, 1990).

2. Defined as the Arabian peninsula countries (the Gulf Co-operation Council), Iran and Iraq.

3. The exceptions apply largely to Oman and Yemen, both of which were, as relative latecomers, outside the general trends of the region.

4. The Middle East, as presently defined here, also includes Syria, Lebanon and Jordan. Thus Gulf expenditure is overstated by the figures.

5. P. Stevens, "A survey of structural change in the international oil industry, 1945–84", in D. Hawdon (ed.), *The changing structure of the world oil industry* (London: Croom Helm, 1985), 18 1/n 51

6. P. Stevens, *Joint ventures in Middle East oil, 1957–75* (Beirut: Middle East Economic Consultants, 1976).

7. C. R. Blitzer et al., "An analysis of fiscal and financial impediments to oil and gas exploration in LDCs", *The Energy Journal* 6 (1985), 59–72 ; C. R. Blitzer et al., "Risk bearing and contract design: are stable contracts feasible?", in K. I. F. Khan (ed.), *Petroleum resources and development: economic, legal and policy issues for developing countries* (London: Pinter [Belhaven Press], 1987), 172–82; T. C. Lowinger, "Petroleum production in developing countries: problems and prospects", *Journal of Energy and Development* 7 (1982), 225–41 ; R. F. Mikesell, *Petroleum company operations and agreements in the developing countries: problems and prospects* (Washington DC: Resources for the Future, 1984).

8. Iraq was in fact relatively active in the field of exploration, although development lagged. E. Penrose & E. F. Penrose, *Iraq: international relations and national development* (Boulder, Colorado: Westview Press, 1978), 421–39.

9. Frequently referred to as the "third oil shock".

10. UPM Research Institute, *GCC main economic indicators 1976, 1986* (Dhahran: Economic and Industrial Research Division, King Fahd University of Petroleum and Minerals Research Institute, undated).

11. This is a classic example of the fallacy of composition since such a policy response by all would only aggravate the tendency to lower prices.

12. The only other route was de-mothballing existing capacity. Only Saudi Arabia had significant mothballed capacity that could realistically be retrieved. The apparently sharp increase in Saudi capacity during the recent Gulf crisis was almost entirely produced from de-mothballing.

13. Specifically – Abu Dhabi, Dubai, Bahrain, Oman and Qatar.

14. Most usually the recovery factor on the oil-in-place.

15. Some members actually adjusted their population figures since this too was to be a crucial input into the formula.

16. P. Jacquard & D. Champlon, "Impact of technological progress on oil supply", *Profils 90*(1), Mimeo, Centre de Geopolitique de l'Energie et des matières premières, University of Paris–Dauphine and Institut Français du Petrole 1990.

17. AMOCO, *Fiscal incentives and world petroleum exploration since 1986*. Report to the US National Energy Strategy hearings (1990); "Shift back to exploration highlights hot spots", *Petroleum Intelligence Weekly*, 16 July 1990; T. Walde, "Investment policies in the international petroleum industry: responses to the current crises", in J. D. Lambert & F. Fesharaki (eds), *Economic and political incentives to petroleum explortion: developments in the Asia–Pacific region* (Washington DC: International Law Institute, 1990), 9–37.

18. These were not taken up because the Iraqis were offering the companies only a contracting rôle.

19. M. C. Lynch, *Oil capacity costs and prices in the 1990s* (Washington International Energy Group, 1990).

20. This is in effect a resurrection of the ideas of Zaki Yamani, the former Oil Minister of Saudi Arabia, his so-called "catholic marriage", first developed in the late 1960s. Z. Yamani, "Participation versus nationalization: a better means to survive", In Mikdashi et al. (eds) *Continuity and change in the world oil industry* (Beirut: The Middle East Research and Publishing Center, 1970), 211–33.

21. *Middle East Economic Survey* [MEES], 20 November 1989.

22. MEES, 8 October & 22 October 1990.

23. This official figure is almost certainly an understatement since it fails to take account fully of either subventions to the Royal family or defence expenditure.

24. Stevens, *Joint Ventures in Middle East Oil*.

25. MEES, 2 July 1990.

26. MEES, 4 March 1991.

27. MEES, 26 March 1990.

28. MEES, 3 June 1991.

29. MEES, 26 March 1990.

30. Most of the damage upstream was done to specific key pumping stations which could be relatively easily repaired. The only exception to this was damage to the Mina al-Bakr export terminal in the Gulf. The extent of that damage has not yet been revealed.

31. MEES, 11 March 1991.

32. Before the invasion Iraq offered acreage to foreign companies but only on a contracting basis (MEES, 19 February 1990). The oil companies showed no interest, regarding the terms as too unattractive.

33. MEES, 20 May 1991.

34. An obvious exception to this could be oil companies from other Third World countries such as Petrobras of Brazil.

35. MEES, 12 February 1990.

36. MEES, 18 December 1989.

37. For details – Abu Dhabi: MEES, 4 June 1989; Bahrain: MEES, 6 August 1990 & 13 May 1991; Oman: MEES, 5 February 1990 & 12 November 1990; and Qatar: MEES, 9 April 1990.

38. The apparent reserve figures for Abu Dhabi suggest otherwise, but these official figures should be regarded with considerable circumspection.

CHAPTER ELEVEN

Hydrocarbons and Iranian policies towards the Gulf states
Confrontation and co-operation in island and continental shelf affairs

KEITH MCLACHLAN

Introduction

It is perhaps too easily forgotten that Iran and the Arabian peninsula states value territory highly for its endowment in crude oil and natural gas. This discussion will examine two convergent themes. First, that the Persian Gulf remains an inherently important geopolitical zone in an international context because of the concentration there of a high proportion of world hydrocarbon resources.[1] Second, that competition for oil and gas reserves has been an important influence on intra-Gulf relations and border arrangements since the British military withdrawal from its territorial base in the Gulf in 1971.[2]

Maritime territorial disputes, often affecting ownership of oil resources, continue to encompass both land areas, in the form of islands, and also parts of the shallow continental shelf of the Gulf.[3] The impetus to finalize land boundary delimitations, especially where they terminate on a sea coast, has often been the discovery of substantial hydrocarbon deposits in the offshore area, as for example was the case with the Oman–Ras al-Khaimah dispute of 1977 over Bakhah-Rims on the western flank of the Musandam peninsula. This discussion will examine the Iranian position on the exploitation of hydrocarbons and difficulties over international boundaries *vis-à-vis* that of the Arab states of the northeastern shore of the Arabian peninsula.

The particular context of the debate will be the interests of the developed world in the security of oil supplies from the Gulf in the 1980s and early 1990s. It will be argued that in the recent period, in effect since the allied defeat of Iraq in 1991, local conflicts, principally Irano–Arabian in origin but also underpinned by inter-Arab squabbles, continue to cause difficulties that the external powers, notably the USA, will find impossible fully to control.[4] Meanwhile, the latent problems of Iraqi territorial and other claims on its neighbours and not least the struggle for Gulf hegemony with Iran cast yet further uncertainty over security in the region.[5]

The rôle of hydrocarbons in the political geography of the Gulf

For the developed world the crucial consideration in the Gulf is the security of oil supplies from the region.[6] Although the Arab members of OPEC (Organization of Petroleum-Exporting Countries), mainly concentrated in the Gulf, have suffered severe reductions in production levels and revenues in recent years, largely in consequence of world economic recession,[7] there is an expectation that a decline in non-OPEC production and the growth in demand for oil in the years subsequent to the current reduction in world trade will change this situation.[8] The reliability of oil supplies from the Gulf has been a long-term concern for Europe, Japan and the USA.[9] Even during the recession of the early 1990s, the OECD (Organization for Economic Co-operation and Development) states remained heavily reliant on Gulf oil supplies, with the USA being 12 per cent, western Europe 33 per cent and Japan 64 per cent dependent on the Gulf area.[10] In 1991, the Gulf produced 16 million barrels per day (b/d) of crude oil (see Table 11.1) – approximately 42 per cent of the oil involved in international trade. The largest single producer, both in the Gulf and in OPEC, was Saudi Arabia with 8.5 million b/d, followed by Iran, Iraq and Abu Dhabi.[11]

Table 11.1 Oil production in the Gulf region, 1990 and 1991 ('000 b/d).

	1990	1991
Abu Dhabi	1,850	2,130
Dubai	450	490
Iran	3,125	3,260
Iraq	2,005	230
Kuwait	1,065	90
Neutral Zone	276	130
Oman	660	700
Qatar	455	440
Saudi Arabia	6,700	8,580
TOTAL	16,586	16,050

Source: Statistical review of world energy, British Petroleum, 1992.

In the late 1980s, OPEC as a whole emerged from a long and difficult period in which it had functioned as the residual producer or producer of last resort, supplying the market only after crude oil from elsewhere had been used up by consumers. Gulf oil producers were at that stage (and have been more or less continuously since then) subject to an OPEC quota, which placed upper ceilings on their output (see Table 11.2).

Table 11.2 OPEC quotas for Gulf producers, 1986–92 ('000 b/d.)

	1986	1988	1990	1992*
Iran	2,300	2,640	3,140	3,184
Iraq	1,200	2,640	3,140	505
Kuwait	900	1,037	1,500	1,180
Qatar	280	312	371	377
Saudi Arabia	4,353	4,524	5,380	8,000
UAE	950	988	1,500	2,244

Source: OPEC   *3rd quarter 1992.

In addition to the problems of the market place, the Gulf states faced specific difficulties arising from the effects of the Iranian revolution of February 1979 and the Iran–Iraq war that began in September 1980, affecting all oil exporters to a greater or lesser extent.[12] Iran had particular problems as a direct result of Iraqi air attacks on oil installations, especially on its Kharg island export terminals.[13] Iranian oil exports were dispatched to world markets through a complicated system of deliveries via temporary oil terminals to shuttle tankers which moved crude from Kharg island down to the lower Gulf. Makeshift oil storage and terminal installations were set up at both Sirri and Larak islands, using tankers as floating storage containers. Even these precautions were not always adequate to ensure that Iraqi air raids did not disrupt the flow of exports. Air strikes against tankers serving Iranian oil ports had affected a total of 123 vessels by June 1987. Nor were the distant terminals immune; Sirri was attacked repeatedly and, in a highly successful raid of mid-May 1985, five of the ten floating storage tankers at Larak were damaged, a feat repeated in December 1987.[14]

Iraq itself had to make do with exports via its oil pipelines to the Mediterranean coast at Dortyül and across Saudi Arabia to the Red Sea port of Yanbu. All of its Gulf terminals were put out of commission early on in the war. Other exporters were subjected to periodic attacks by Iranian forces. Kuwait was most affected by this activity and suffered reductions in its exports from time to time. Saudi Arabia also saw its ships attacked by Iran while the United Arab Emirates (UAE) suffered damage to its offshore oil facilities.

The Gulf crisis of 1990 following the Iraqi invasion of Kuwait brought short-term disruption to the region but deep damage to Iraqi oil production and export facilities.[15] Following the war in Kuwait, Iraq could export crude only under the control of the United Nations (see Table 11.2).

Table 11.3 Crude oil reserves, 1991.

	Volume (bn barrels)	Share (%)
North America	41.7	10.2
Latin America	119.8	12.0
Western Europe	14.5	1.5
Africa	60.4	6.0
Asia and Australasia	44.1	4.4
USSR, and non-OECD Europe	58.8	5.8
Middle East (outside Gulf)	5.8	0.6
Gulf region, of which:	*655.8*	*65.6*
Abu Dhabi	92.2	9.2
Dubai	5.9	0.6
Iran	92.9	9.3
Iraq	100.0	10.0
Kuwait	94.0	9.4
Neutral Zone	5.0	0.5
Oman	4.3	0.4
Qatar	3.7	0.4
Saudi Arabia	257.8	25.8

Source: British Petroleum 1992.

Table 11.4 Dependence on Gulf oil supplies 1991.

	Share of Gulf crude in total imports (%)	Volume imported from Gulf ('000 b/d)
USA	25.1	1,958
Latin America	73.9	317
Western Europe	38.3	3,878
Africa	57.7	368
Asia	78.9	3,357
Japan	66.9	3,298
Australasia	60.3	188
Rest of world	24.5	353
Other destinations	7.7	18
TOTAL	41.9	13,829

Source: British Petroleum 1992.

The Gulf's massive natural endowment of crude oil (see Table 11.3) – 65 per cent of the world's total proved reserves – has naturally made the question of its exports of intense interest to the West, especially during the periods of recent crisis, namely the 1980–8 Gulf War and the 1990–1 Kuwait Crisis.[16]

The Gulf region makes relatively little use of its own hydrocarbon resources and thus has considerable capacity for exports. The major multinational oil companies, the Japanese domestic suppliers and many other countries rely heavily on the Gulf for their oil. Every day, 14–15 million b/d of crude oil leave the Gulf, most of it in tankers sailing from terminals along its littoral and passing through the narrow Strait of Hormuz at the mouth of the Gulf. Although there has been diversification of sources of oil, some movement into other forms of energy and significant energy conservation in the developed world, oil from the Gulf remains a crucial component in global oil supply, particularly to Japan, the Pacific area and western Europe (see Table 11.4). Japan depends on the Gulf for 67 per cent of all the oil it uses, western Europe 38 per cent and the USA 25 per cent.

From sea routes to a territorial base: the rôle of pipelines

One fear in the past was the stranglehold over Gulf oil supplies that would result should the Strait of Hormuz be closed or if there were to be a general disruption of shipping in the Gulf at large. The assumption has been that Iran would use its geostrategic position to impose controls, since it was Iran that made threats of this kind during the Gulf war.[17] Even in the early 1990s, Iran has been most aggressive in developing its naval power, as exemplified by the purchase of ex-Soviet submarines in 1992.

Closure of the Strait of Hormuz is a less immediate threat to the stability of world oil supplies than was the case a decade ago. One of the few positive consequences of the Gulf war is that many regional oil exporters took the opportunity to diversify their means of crude transport to external markets. The principal vehicles in this switch were land-based oil pipelines.[18] Several major Gulf oilfield areas were also given terminals outside the Gulf, and by 1992 only the UAE, Bahrain and Qatar lacked any facilities to move crude by means other than tanker through the Gulf.

Use of land rather than sea routes by Arab exporters seeking sanctuary from the threat of Iranian intervention against sea traffic has not been without its cost. After several bitter experiences of arbitrary closures of the original Iraq Petroleum Company (IPC) pipeline by Syria (long before Iran made public its promises of disruption of oil export lines in the Gulf), the Iraqi authorities completed an alternative pipeline in 1977. This led from the northern oilfields into Turkey over a 980 kilometres route from Kirkuk to the

Mediterranean at Dortyül. The pipeline proved to be the saving grace of Iraq during the 1980–8 Iran–Iraq war since all its Gulf oil terminals were immobilized by the Iranians at the beginning of hostilities in late 1980, while the ex-IPC line through Syria was closed shortly afterwards. The 700,000 b/d capacity of the Turkish pipeline provided Iraq's only significant means of exporting oil. Throughput of the line was gradually increased towards 1 million b/d during the 1980s by the use of chemicals and improved pumping facilities. A parallel line was constructed and added a further 500,000 b/d to this export capacity by the end of 1987.

Iraqi determination to diversify its export outlets and to ensure that it would not fail in the Iran–Iraq war through loss of its oil exports and revenues led to other imaginative pipeline projects being adopted. A spur line, IPSA-1 (Iraqi pipeline across Saudi Arabia), was constructed in 1985 to carry Iraqi crude into Saudi Arabia where it linked up with the Saudi Petroline, which ran the width of the country from Abqaiq on the shores of the Gulf to Yanbu on the Red Sea coast.

A second phase of this scheme (IPSA-2) was confirmed in September 1987. With a length of more than 1,000 kilometres, the line was designed to provide a capacity of 1.65 million b/d by 1989. By the end of 1987, therefore, the new line lifted Iraq's export capacity to more than 3 million b/d by pipeline alone. The Iraqi Government also considered the feasibility of building a pipeline to the Jordanian port of Aqabah, and developed a useful capacity rated at 240,000 b/d for transporting oil and its products by road to Aqabah and to Turkish ports.

Iraq's long-established need for a defensible, deep water, export oil terminal site in the Gulf, together with a claim that Kuwait was exploiting Iraqi oil resources straddling the land border, were among the causes of the Iraqi invasion of Kuwait in 1990.[19]

Saudi Arabia constructed the Petroline in 1981 linking its oilfields to the Red Sea coast with a capacity of 1.85 million b/d. Oman exports all its oil via the Gulf of Oman and is not affected directly by events in the Gulf. Kuwait could theoretically make some use of the spur line that runs from Iraq through its territory to join the Saudi Arabian Petroline or it could lay a separate facility. Kuwait is also a member of the Gulf Co-operation Council (GCC), which has a contingency plan – so far not implemented – for a crude export line from Kuwait along the Arab coast of the Gulf to a location that by-passes the Strait of Hormuz, probably Salalah on the Arabian Sea coast. If the Gulf were closed to oil exports, there would be the opportunity for the construction of a shorter pipeline serving the UAE, Qatar and Bahrain.

In effect, the Arab states either have or could soon create export facilities to circumvent the waters of the Gulf.[20] Nonetheless, there would obviously be some immediate impact from an absolute stoppage of tanker traffic in the Gulf. Indeed, short-term problems would make the oil market nervous. But the medium-term outlook for oil supply is much less worrying, given the

228

alternative means of export that now exist. In fact, the threat of prolonged loss of oil output through closure of the Gulf would most affect Iran. Iran's problem, in the event of the closure of the Gulf, would be its lack of an alternative means of oil export. Iran's only export pipeline is the Iran Gas Trunkline (IGAT-1), which handles natural gas.

The National Iranian Oil Company (NIOC) toyed with the idea of constructing pipelines to augment its Gulf terminals for several years. There have long been discussions with the Turkish and Transcaucasian authorities on a proposal to construct a pipeline to western Europe, either for crude or for natural gas. In the mid-1980s, as a closure of the Gulf was thought to be a practical possibility, NIOC considered a project for the building of an emergency crude oil pipeline from the southern oilfields to a point in the lower Gulf or on the Sea of Oman. The most likely terminal has been thought to be near Bandar Taheri at Asaluyeh. To be of any real utility, an Iranian strategic export pipeline would have to offer a capacity of 2 million b/d or more to benefit from economies of scale. It was perhaps this basic consideration of geographical disadvantage in the oil war that most profoundly affected Iranian analyses of the Gulf situation in the closing months of the fighting with Iraq in 1988 and led to the acceptance of United Nations Resolution 598 in July of that year.

Territorial competition and oil: the Iranian position in the 1980s

Seen from the Arab side, there is a problem arising from what it has perceived as Iran's expansionist aims in the Gulf area. During the Iran–Iraq war, the geographic disposition of Iranian military forces indicated how close Iran could come to overrunning Iraq. After the January–February 1987 offensive in the Fish lake area adjacent to Basrah, Iranian front-line positions in the southwest sector were located only a few kilometres from the outskirts of the city. Basrah seemed at the time so vulnerable that a slight tactical defensive mistake by Iraq or a successful land campaign by Iranian forces could have dramatically changed the geopolitical pattern in the region. With hindsight we can now say that it was clear that Iran was ill equipped to end the war successfully by military means, but this was not the wisdom of the day.[21]

If, for example, Basrah had fallen as the result of military action, Iran would have obtained control of the southern Iraqi oilfields – Rumailah, Zubair, North Rumailah, Luhais, Nahr Umar, Abu Ghraib, Faqi, Buzurgan and the undeveloped areas around the Majnun structure taken by Iranian troops in the mid-1980s. While these were not the main Iraqi producing fields, their capture would have represented a significant gain for Iran. If Iran had taken over the entire Iraqi state, it would obviously have acquired control of the northern fields of Mawsul and Kirkuk as well.

There was an admittedly remote but real possibility that the Iranians, flushed with success and religious fervour in the wake of the fall of the Iraqi regime, might have turned their attentions to the Arabian peninsula. Until April 1988, Iranian bridgeheads in Iraq at Faw and around Basrah meant that their troops merely had to cross the narrow Khawr Abdallah sea inlet in order to enter Kuwaiti territory. An advance into Kuwait would have represented little difficulty from a military point of view. The Kuwaiti authorities had been at pains to create defences against any attack from the direction of Iraq but the Kuwaitis alone could not have held out against massed Iranian assaults. Although this danger receded as a result of Iraq's recapture of the Faw peninsula and a continuing ceasefire, Kuwait's internal political situation at the time provided very little basis for confidence that there would be a sustained defence.[22] Deep cleavages between Kuwaiti nationals and the majority immigrant community, between Sunni and Shi'i religious groups, between the ruling elite and those demanding a return to parliamentary government, and between Arabs and non-Arabs meant that there was little agreement or belief in common goals and shared national sentiments.[23] The invasion of Kuwait by Iraq in different circumstances in 1990 illustrated the ease with which Kuwait could be overrun.

In the 1980s, the problem as perceived by the oil consumers and the great powers was that, should Iran have managed to take control of Kuwait and southern Iraq, its ability to harass and pressure the Saudi Arabian authorities would have been considerable. Within OPEC, Iran would have become the dominant influence and it was difficult to imagine that Saudi Arabia would have been able to avoid co-operating with Iranian policies on oil production and price. This nightmare scenario was enough to hasten international action to assist the Iraqi defence effort in 1987 and 1988.[24]

The 1987 crisis, arising from the internationalization of the Iran–Iraq war, flared up because of perceptions in Europe and the USA that the way in which the war was developing was a threat to oil supplies and because of concern amongst the Western maritime nations over the freedom of navigation of shipping in the Gulf. The USA was apprehensive as recently as 1985–7 over what it saw as Soviet penetration of the area[25] in the guise of protector of the Arab states against Iranian naval aggression.[26] However, even though there were some geopolitical similarities, it must be borne in mind that the Iran–Iraq war and the Gulf crisis had separate causes and origins.

Territorial competition and oil: the Iraqi position in the 1990s

With the effective collapse of the Iranian military effort against Iraq in mid-1988, any danger to Kuwait and other Gulf states now came from Iraq. The Iraqi regime interpreted its narrow survival against the Iranians as a major victory. The attitude of the Iraqis in the immediate wake of their reoccupation of Faw, the Fish lake area, Majnun and other small enclaves formerly held by the Iranians was that "they had won the war". They also felt that the original aim of their attack on Iran in 1980 – an assertion of Iraqi dominance over the Gulf and especially the Arab areas of the Gulf – could now be realized since they were and certainly perceived themselves as the supreme military organization in the region, supported by enormous experience in battle and no longer faced with a powerful Iranian enemy. Given the fact that the Iraqis had never settled their territorial disputes with Kuwait, there was a real risk that Iraq's overweening sense of importance after 1988 could lead to action against neighbouring Arab states of the Gulf.[27] The Iraqi regime might have calculated that the USSR would be prepared to back Baghdad in a tacit way and the USA to stand aside if it were to resuscitate territorial claims to Kuwaiti territory and re-endorse its demands for the liberation of the Gulf islands of Abu Musa and the two Tunbs, previously made as Saddam decided to renounce the 1975 Algiers Accord in 1979.

The prospects of an ultimate *de jure* end to the main Iran–Iraq war did not guarantee, therefore, that the security of oil supplies from the main Gulf producers was permanently ensured. It could be argued with some merit that, on the contrary, the end of hostilities merely gave opportunity for the many suppressed conflicts within the Gulf to re-emerge, prompted mainly by Iraqi geopolitical pretensions, which manifested themselves far sooner than expected with the attack on Kuwait in August 1990. The events leading to the expulsion of Iraq from Kuwait had three significant and relevant effects. First, Iraq was reduced in military and political stature, with the regime of Saddam Husain isolated by post-war UN controls on oil exports and military imports. Secondly, the USA confirmed its continuing political and military primacy in the Gulf and Arabian peninsula, originally reinforced towards the end of the Iran–Iraq war in 1987–8. Thirdly, enhancing the security of oil supplies from the Gulf through conflict containment became an explicit regional policy of the OECD states led by the USA.[28]

Oil will be at the heart of the continuing struggle for hegemony in the Gulf and will underlie the motivations of most participants. The stakes are comparatively high. For Iran and Iraq there will be a reflection of the conflict of political interests in oil affairs. Iran will have to export its oil through the Gulf or not export in volume at all. It has no access to pipeline facilities that can circumvent the constraints of hostility in the Gulf, despite optimistic talk of the construction of new export pipelines. It has no other means of generating foreign exchange income of the amount needed by a 60 million population that must be kept fed and supplied by imported goods. On a number of occasions during the Iran–Iraq war the Iraqis succeeded in bombarding Iranian tanker traffic to a virtual standstill. Iranian energies will be directed towards ensuring this does not occur again, though the understandable Iranian aspirations to secure its position in the Gulf were systematically misinterpreted during the early 1990s.[29] Such US, European and Arab criticism of Iran for its rearmament programme in the early 1990s and for its policies designed to protect its regional interests in the Gulf indicated the large measure of their insensitivity to a valid Iranian desire for self-defence.

The OECD stance towards security of oil production and export in the Gulf

The objectives of the maritime powers became quite specific during the war in Kuwait. As indicated earlier, the petroleum reserves of the Gulf form an inescapable and integral part of future energy and chemical resources required by the members of OECD. Given that the industrialized states of the world will find themselves with a continuing dependence on oil from the Gulf into the 1990s and beyond, there is a strong argument for the maritime powers to maintain their positions in the Gulf to enforce freedom of navigation. Some OECD states, not least the USA itself and its oil multinationals, will need to service their international operations by purchasing expanding volumes of Gulf crudes and/or natural gas in the early 1990s. Shell and BP are important lifters of Gulf crudes and would not wish to be deprived of its considerable resources which supply their world markets both inside and outside the OECD group. In consequence, as events following the Iraqi invasion of Kuwait indicated, *ceteris paribus*, the OECD states will not be willing to see political changes adverse to their oil supply interests.

Symptoms of Irano–Arab confrontation

In the period immediately following the end of the Iran–Iraq war in 1988 and the death of Ayatollah Khomeini in 1989, Iranian policies towards the Gulf underwent marked change.[30] A convenient threshold was the November 1989 "Conference on the Persian Gulf" in Tehran at which President Hashemi Rafsanjani argued that Iran needed to established good relations with the states of the Arabian peninsula as a means of containing Iraq and ensuring the exclusion of non-regional countries from the area. The policies were prompted by dislike of the close alliance between the Arab states and the USA on the one hand and the growing pretensions of Iraq to be a regional leader of the Arabs against Iran on the other. An added bonus for Iran of a regional security arrangement with the peninsula states would have been mutual co-operation within OPEC and a greater opportunity for Iran to press OPEC members to achieve a relatively high oil price.

The Iranian Government adhered to a policy of alignment towards the peninsula states until 1992. By that time it was clear that the Arab states of the Gulf were making little effort to incorporate Iran within the regional security system and were continuing to build up their formal links with the USA and other Western powers. Iran also appeared to have accepted by 1992 its failure to make the point with its Arab neighbours that Iraq could be contained only by a joint Iranian–Arabian security initiative.[31]

The re-emergence of Irano–Arab territorial conflicts in the Gulf

Three specific areas of dispute arose between Iran and the Arab states of the peninsula to illustrate the lack of success enjoyed by Rafsanjani's initiative of November 1989. The first concerned the island of Abu Musa and the comparative degree of sovereignty and/or local control devolving upon Iran and Sharjah as a result of the 1971 joint administration agreement (the 1971 Memorandum of Understanding). The dispute spread to become one between Iran and the United Arab Emirates. It eventually led to a resuscitation of claims by the UAE to two other Gulf islands, the Greater and Lesser Tunbs, and constituted a second area of dispute. A third difficulty arose between Iran and Qatar over the development of gas resources in the North Dome – South Pars area of the continental shelf, which spanned areas claimed by both countries.

The problem of Abu Musa and the Tunbs

The crisis arose in April 1992 and soon became an obstacle to good Iranian relations with the states of the Arabian peninsula. The Iranian policy for creating an axis with the Arabian peninsula states was originally designed to give Iran an alliance with the states of the peninsula to hedge in Saddam Husain, make Western interference in the Gulf unnecessary and give some support to Iranian demands within OPEC for a \$21/barrel oil price.[32] Iran was disappointed by the lack of response from most Arab states to its radical scheme for local strategic management of the Gulf to the exclusion of foreign powers. Events surrounding the war in Kuwait and the marginalization of Iran in the subsequent peace settlement were an affront to both Iranian national pride and its policy. The intervention by the United Nations in southern Iraq[33] in September 1992, made without reference to Iranian sensitivities, emphasized Iran's exclusion from regional defence arrangements.

A small-scale local dispute in April 1992, in which a group of non-national employees of the emirate of Sharjah were expelled from Abu Musa island by the regional Iranian military commander occurred only a couple of

233

months after a visit to the island by the Iranian state president. The upset was dealt with by Iranian Foreign Minister, Ali Akbar Velayati. The Sharjah authorities were reassured that for practical purposes Iran was not proposing any changes in the status in the joint management of the island. In accordance with the 1971 agreement reached at the time of the British withdrawal, a *de facto* condominium would remain in force between Iran and Sharjah. However, the problem recurred in August, when returning school teachers and their families on contract to the government of Sharjah were forbidden landing rights by the Iranian military on the island. At this stage, the UAE, acting for Sharjah, appeared to challenge the very basis of the Iranian occupation of Abu Musa island.[34] By early September the UAE demanded that the status of the two Tunbs islands, forcibly occupied by Iran in 1971 and claimed by Ras al-Khaimah,[35] also be reconsidered.[36] Attempts at negotiating a settlement for Abu Musa on 27 September 1992 became entangled with the general problems of sovereignty over other disputed Gulf islands, at which point Iran refused to include the Tunbs on the agenda and broke off talks with the UAE.[37]

The Iranian Government was at pains to defuse the entire incident. President Rafsanjani repeatedly called for a peaceful settlement of the issue.[38] Iran had no wish to see the Abu Musa dispute taken to the UN Security Council, where Russia and possibly other powers would support the UAE. Initial discussions for a resolution of the dispute via the International Court of Justice at The Hague were examined. In November, Oman, which maintained good diplomatic relations with Iran in the period following the Gulf war, announced that a peaceful settlement was possible within a bilateral framework,[39] a route preferred by Iran.[40]

Iran had an imperative to trade with the Arab emirates both for its own imports and as entrepôts handling much needed Iranian exports. Any conflict with the peninsula states would be to risk making the return of the Gulf islands a pan-Arab issue. The breakdown of talks in late 1992 indicated that this latter damage had been done and that Iranian policy in the Gulf was in disarray. Iran was dismayed by the turn in events, which confronted it with a new geopolitical situation in which the Arabian peninsula states, with their external Arab and Western allies, became prepared to challenge Iran.[41] The Iranian Government was forced by this initiative to accept what had been true since the UN intervention in Kuwait – that it was no longer the dominant regional player even with Iraq under UN constraints.

Arabian suspicions of Iranian intentions in the Gulf were also seriously heightened by the Abu Musa dispute.[42] Any chance of Iran developing a diplomatic accord with the Gulf states for the exclusion of the USA and other external political interests was extinguished as was the opportunity for an Irano–Arab understanding on oil prices within OPEC. Such conclusions were reinforced by Iranian involvement during 1992 in an inter-GCC state dispute between Qatar and Saudi Arabia.

The Qatar affair

Beginning in 1990, Qatari–Iranian relations were affected by a dispute over ownership of the gas structures comprising the North Dome gasfield (known as the North field in Qatar and the South Pars field in Iran) on the continental shelf of the Gulf lying between the two countries. Qatar sought at first to ignore Iranian claims to gas reserves in that area. In August 1990, however, the Iranian oil minister, Gholamreza Aqazadeh, announced that he intended to visit Dawhah to arrange a "political accommodation" on the issue.[43] In November 1990 the official Iranian Republican News Agency[44] stated that plans had been drafted for "joint exploration with Qatar" of the gas structure in Iran named South Pars. An Iranian deputy oil minister, elaborating on the arrangement at that time, said that the field would be developed by 1994 at a cost of $3 billion. Qatari officials were slow to endorse Iranian claims that joint development would take place.

Qatar's view of Iran underwent noticeable change in 1990–1. Qatar, like Iran, had reservations on the use made of Arab territory by the UN coalition force against Baghdad for the liberation of Kuwait. Meanwhile, Qatar later experienced other difficulties with its Arab partners[45] in the GCC, which pushed it towards slightly greater alignment with Iran. Inter alia, an offshore boundary dispute with Bahrain, over the sovereignty of the Hawar islands and adjacent banks had exacerbated dynastic rivalries.[46] In another incident, Saudi Arabia built a road to by-pass Qatari territory on the coastal highway and made no effort to solve a boundary disagreement with Qatar on the southeastern rim of Qatar's border with the Kingdom.

On 10 November 1991 an agreement in principle was signed between Qatar and Iran for a feasibility study of a water pipeline to run from the Karun river in southwest Iran to Qatar.[47] The project, while technically possible, would be extremely costly and at greater political risk than gas-fuelled desalination inside Qatar. It was seen however as a demonstration of mutual goodwill. The axis between Tehran and Dawhah was enhanced in May 1992 by a visit to Iran of the Qatari Interior Minister, Shaikh Abdallah bin Khalifah al-Thani, and a return visit by Vice-President Habibi of Iran to Dawhah when matters relating to Gulf security and OPEC were discussed. Qatar's support for an Iranian rôle in joint Gulf security and the suggestion that Qatar had policies within OPEC in common with Iran were deeply encouraging for Iran, which had been excluded from these issues by all peninsula states other than Oman.[48]

The problems arising over Iranian actions on Abu Musa during the spring and late summer of 1992 highlighted the shift in Qatari policies towards tacit support for Iran in areas where it felt it could and would disadvantage its GCC partners. The attachment to Iran did not, however, prevent Qatar from signing a defence agreement with the United States in June 1992 for example, to the public annoyance of the Iranian Government.[49] Qatar played an ambivalent rôle in respect of Iran during the confrontation over

Abu Musa and the Tunb islands, when the Qatari ruler sent an official letter to the Iranian President praising Hashemi Rafsanjani's sagacious approach to border problems in the region.[50] In late October 1992, the Qatari deputy foreign minister visited Tehran, promising to promote further formal economic and regional ties with Iran[51] at the very time that Iran and the UAE were locked in a war of words over the disputed islands in the Gulf and Qatar was itself in the throes of a dispute over a border incident with Saudi Arabia.

Qatar appeared to be caught following a pro-Tehran policy for two reasons. First, there was a need to stabilize use of the important North Dome gasfield within the framework of technical co-operation with Iran rather than facing an international boundary conflict-cum-usufruct dispute over the issue. Second in importance and arising only because of the problem with Iran over development of the North Dome gasfield, Qatar could use alignment towards Iran as a lever to gain an advantage in its difficulties with its Arab neighbours.

Conclusions

The ownership of oilfields and control of oil transit routes remains a powerful factor influencing national policies towards Gulf regional affairs and bilateral relations between states. Far from abating, oil-related boundary and hydrocarbon exploitation issues increasingly complicate contemporary inter-state links. The strength and clarity of Western interests in freedom of navigation and security of access to oil in the region established during the Iran–Iraq and Kuwait wars have done little to eliminate underlying local disputes, which often hinge, *inter alia*, on the question of ownership of oil reserves. In some cases they might be regarded as temporarily submerged, as with the Iraq/Kuwait land boundary.[52] In other cases, disputes are finding new means of political expression (as in the instance of the Qatar–Iran alliance over the North Dome gasfield), or are manifest in nagging but damaging conflicts in law (as between Qatar and Bahrain) or in suppressed antagonism (as between Saudi Arabia and Qatar). The *Pax Americana* in the Gulf seems unlikely, indeed, to provide solutions to underlying local rivalries in oil affairs and elsewhere because it is biased towards Arab alliances solidified during the war against Iraq and because there is no evidence that the peace will or can be systematically upheld by the USA for other than a short period. In the interim, the regional states are entrenching their positions in support of their own interests, challenging the *status quo* where they feel able and storing up resentments for the future. The security of oil supply from the Gulf must appear therefore to be in the future, as in the past, a hostage to uncertain fortunes.

Notes

1. A. McLachlan & K. S. McLachlan 1988, *Oil and development in the Gulf* (London: John Murray), 7–9.
2. cf. G. Sick, "An American perspective", in *Great power interests in the Persian Gulf* (1988, New York: Council for Foreign Relations), 16–42.
3. G. H. Blake, "Maritime boundaries of the Middle East and North Africa", in G. H. Blake & R. N. Schofield (eds), *Boundaries and state territory in the Middle East and North Africa* (Wisbech, England: Menas Press, 1987), 123–8.
4. Economic Intelligence Unit (EIU), *Iran country report* 3 (London, 1991), 11.
5. L. Martin 1991. "Iran and the changing balance of power in the Persian Gulf", *Iranian Journal of International Affairs* 3 **(1991)**, 62–3.
6. E. Maechling 1982. "Security risks to energy production and trade: the problems of the Middle East", *Energy Policy* 10 (1982), 120–30.
7. See Chapter 10 by Paul Stevens.
8. Business International, *The postwar Gulf* (London, 1991–2), 142.
9. F. Fesharaki & D. T. Isaak 1983. OPEC, *the Gulf and the world petroleum market* Boulder: Westview, 249–50.
10. BP 1992. Statistical review of world energy. London: British Petroleum, 16.
11. BP 1992. Statistical review of world energy. London: British Petroleum, 5.
12. K. S. McLachlan & E. G. H. Joffé 1984. *The Gulf war*. London: EIU, 31–49.
13. E. G. H. Joffé & K. S. McLachlan 1988. *Building on the stalemate*. London: EIU, 34–5.
14. EIU 1988. *Iran country report* 1. London: Economic Intelligence Unit, 6.
15. N. Sarkis 1991. After the Persian Gulf war. *Iranian Journal of International Affairs* 3, 397.
16. BP 1992. *Statistical review of world energy*. London: British Petroleum, 2.
17. H. W. Maull 1989. "Alliance, co-operation and conflict". In H. W. Maull & O. Pick (eds), *The Gulf War* (London: Pinter, 1989), 116.
18. P. Mojtahed-Zadeh 1990. *The political geography of the Strait of Hormuz*. Occasional paper. Department of Geography, School of Oriental and African Studies, 65.
19. R. N. Schofield 1991. *Kuwait and Iraq: historical claims and territorial disputes*. London: Royal Institute of International Affairs, 126–8.
20. BP 1987–8. Document GF 16. Foreign Affairs Committee of the House of Commons.
21. G. Sick 1989. "The United States and the Persian Gulf". In Maull & Pick, 133.
22. K. S. McLachlan 1990. *Kuwait in the 1990s: a society under seige*. London: Business International, 21–44.
23. J. Bulloch 1984. *The Gulf*. London: Century, 93–113.
24. M. A. Hameed 1986. *Saudi Arabia, the West and the security of the Gulf*. London: Croom Helm, 35.
25. J. E. Peterson 1986. *Defending Arabia*. London: Croom Helm, 122–5.
26. R. F. Pajak 1988. "Soviet designs and dilemmas in the Gulf region". In *Crosscurrents in the Gulf region*, H. R. Sindelar III & J. E. Peterson (eds), 77–8. London: Routledge.
27. EIU 1990. *Iran country report* 1. London: Economic Intelligence Unit, 8.
28. Maull 1989, 161.
29. *International Herald Tribune* 1992. "Iran devours technology as Washington and allies differ on export controls", 11 November; *Le Monde* 1992. "Selon la CIA, Téhéran pourrait développer une arme nucléaire d'ici à l'an 2000", 2 December.
30. K. S. McLachlan 1992. Iran and the continuing crisis in the Persian Gulf. *GeoJournal* 28(3), 357–63.
31. B.I. 1991. *The postwar Gulf*. London: Business International, 142.
32. A. Velayati 1991. Speech delivered by H. E. Dr. Ali-Akbar Velayati to the "Third Conference on the Persian Gulf". *International Journal of Iranian Affairs* 3, 4.
33. Business International, *Iran Monitor* 8 (1992), 4.

34. *Financial Times* 1992. "Iran opens rift with Arabs over islands", 11 September.
35. A. H. Cordesman 1984. *The Gulf and the search for strategic stability.* Boulder: Westview, 416–8.
36. *Reuters* news service 1992. "Gulf states condemn Iranian action", 9 September.
37. *Mideast Mirror* 1992. *Asharq al Awsat*: "Iranian missiles on Abu Musa", 23 October, 17.
38. cf. *Tehran Times* 1992. "President on vital issues", 21 December.
39. Tehran Times 1992. UAE, "Iran can solve island dispute", 2 November.
40. EIU 1992. *Iran country report* 4. London: Economic Intelligence Unit, 8.
41. *Kayhan International* 1992. GCC policies heartening Zionists, West, 2 January.
42. *Mideast Mirror* 1992. GCC states at odds over Iranian rôle, 8 May, 12.
43. WGI 1990. *World Gas Intelligence*, August.
44. SWB 1990. Joint exploration of offshore gas field with Qatar. In *Summary of World Broadcasts*, 27 November, (9).
45. *Middle East Economic Survey* **36** (MEES) 1992. C1.
46. Hameed, 83.
47. Business International, *Iran Monitor* **9** (1991), 14.
48. SWB 1992. Visiting Qatari minister speaks on new phase in relations with Iran, 12 May. ME/1379 A/6.
49. SWB 1992. Radio condemns US–Qatari defence pact, 26 June, (7).
50. *Kayhan International* 1992. Qatar appreciates Iran stance, 14 October.
51. *Tehran Times* 1992. Qatar, Iran discuss key regional issues, 29 October.
52. Schofield, 130.

Index

'asabiya 86, 92
Abadan 163
Abdaly 170
Abdul Karim, Ibrahim 55
Abqaiq 198, 228
Abu Dhabi 17–20, 24, 27, 28, 30, 31,
  40, 41, 44, 51, 52, 56, 57, 84, 87–91,
  95, 101, 102–104, 106, 109, 114,
  179, 181, 182, 183, 185, 198, 201,
  205, 208, 209, 212, 216, 220, 224,
  226
  /Dubai boundary 30, 31, 179, 183
  /Dubai lateral boundary (1968
    agreement) 179, 181, 183
  –Dubai Neutral Zone 205, 206
  –Dubai war 114
  –Qatar agreement, maritime
    boundary 181, 185, 201
  Marine Areas Company 181
Abu Dhabi's 1952 claim 104
Abu Ghraib 229
Abu Musa island 2, 34–41, 59, 60,
  87, 180, 183–5, 196, 197, 201, 231,
  233, 234
  Iranian occupation (1971) 39–40,
    234
access to the Gulf 3–5, 13, 14, 28,
  33, 43, 56, 59, 60, 153, 154, 155,
  164, 169, 171, 172
Aden Protectorate 16, 19–21, 25, 26,
  33, 42, 95, 98, 100, 104
adjacent states 176, 181, 185
administration, joint 201, 204, 233
Aghassi, Hajji Mirza 35, 41
agnatic solidarity 86

air agreements 89
Ajman 28, 84, 114, 183, 197, 201
  –Oman boundary 28, 201
  –Oman neutral zone 28, 201
Al Bu Falah 103, 104
Al Bu Said 88
Al Bu Shamis 114
al-Ain 18
al-Ashat 181
al-Askari, Jaafar 162
al-Bakr, Ahmad Hasan 134, 219
al-Hajri, Abdallah 54
al-Hiti, Osama 192
al-Iryani, Abdul Karim 55, 194
al-Jalahimah 85, 119
al-Jana block 25
al-Khalifah 32, 33, 49–51, 55, 84, 85,
  119
al-Khalili 101
al-Manasir 32, 85
al-Qaisi, Riyadh 10
al-Qawi, Saad 195
al-Rashid 82
al-Sabah 44, 45, 53, 84, 85, 119–22,
  127, 134, 160–61, 166, 167, 172
al-Sabah, Shaikh Mubarak 42, 43,
  45, 89, 120, 121, 122, 156, 157, 158,
  159, 160, 172
al-Sabah, Shaikh Sabah al-Salim
  134
al-Said, Nuri 124, 131, 137, 155,
  162, 164, 167
al-Samarai, Ahmad Husain 192
al-Samtah 169
al-Saud 81, 82, 98, 105

al-Shaq 16
al-Suwaidi, Tawfiq 124, 155, 163
al-Thani 17, 32, 33, 44, 50, 51, 53, 85, 87, 100, 235
al-Thani, Shaikh Abdallah bin Khalifah 32, 53, 87, 235
al-Wadi'ah 25
al-Wajh 191
Alawi, Yusuf bin 57
Aleppo 82
Algiers Accord (March 1975) 4, 6, 60, 231
Ali, Muhammad 82, 87
Ali, Jawdat 163, 165
Allied Supreme Council 123, 129, 130
alluvial flats 154
Amarat 84, 205
ambassadorial exchange 135, 155
amir 79, 81, 98, 120, 179
Amir of Dariya 81
Amman treaty (Saudi/Jordanian 1965) 45
ams 113
Anaizah 81, 84
Ancel, J. 3, 4
anchorage facilities 42, 154, 157, 163, 167
Anglo
 –Iraqi Treaty of Alliance (1922) 123
 –Kuwaiti Secet Bond (1899) 43
 –Najdi
  Darin Treaty (1915) 20, 100
  Treaty of Jiddah (1927) 20, 53
 –Ottoman
  Convention (1913) 10, 15, 19–21, 26, 32, 43, 45, 53, 89, 91, 100–102, 121, 126, 136, 137, 160–162, 202
  Convention (1914) 94, 100–102, 104, 122
  status quo understanding respecting Kuwait (1901) 43, 156
 –Ottoman lines (1913–14) 19–21, 41, 42, 44, 47, 91, 107, 121, 160–62

Blue (1913) 19, 100, 102, 105, 107
Blue and Violet (1913–14) 20, 21, 24, 41, 42, 47, 91, 99, 101, 102
Green (1913) 43, 122, 136, 137, 161, 162, 202, 203
Red (1913) 24, 27, 43–5, 53, 90, 122, 161, 202
Violet (1914) 19–21, 25, 26, 42
 –Persian general treaty negotiations (1920s–30s) 34, 37
 –Qatari treaty (1916) 32, 90
 –Saudi
  Buraimi arbitration (1955) memorials 101
  claims 19–27
  Dammam conference (1952) 18
  frontier negotiations (1934–55) 16–20, 28, 45, 47, 53, 55, 207
  relations 34, 44–47
 –Yemeni Treaty of San'a (1934) 99, 100, 104
Aqabah 45, 56, 60, 228
Aqazadeh, Gholamreza 235
Arab League 3, 8, 9, 12, 13, 14, 31, 124, 125, 192
Arab League defence force (Kuwait 1961) 124
Arab League line (Kuwait–Iraq 1961) 13, 14, 192
Arabi island 179–181, 183, 185
Arabian Sea 19, 54, 228
Arabs 29, 119, 160, 230, 233, 234
arbitration 6, 11, 16, 20, 21, 24, 41, 42, 44, 47, 48, 51, 52, 100–102, 104, 109, 115, 117, 127, 177, 180, 183, 184
 awards 119, 132
 between the United Kingdom and France (English Channel, 1978) 180
 decisions 177
 proceedings 16, 20, 44, 104
 tribunal 131, 132, 135, 180
archival sources 37, 209
Arco (Atlantic Richfield Oil Company) 194, 195

Argentina 140, 187
Arif, President 125
Asaluyeh 229
Ashairij 32
Asir 54, 55, 94, 191
Asir coast 191
Asir Surat 54
asl 97
Australia 187
autonomy 27, 122, 127, 161, 202
Awamir 112
Awazim 42, 157, 159, 160
Awhah island 43, 122, 161
Aziz, Tariq 126

badu 81, 85, 102, 103, 113
Baggallay, L. 124, 162–4
Baghdad 3–6, 11, 13, 16, 17, 41, 45,
    55, 59, 82, 83, 88, 119–29, 131, 133,
    137, 153, 155, 157–9, 161–7, 171,
    172, 191, 192, 231, 235
    Pact 83
Bahrain 11, 17, 33, 34, 37, 41, 44,
    48–52, 55, 56, 59, 84, 85, 87–90, 94,
    95, 98–100, 113, 119, 168, 177, 179,
    181, 182–5, 188–90, 196, 200, 201,
    205–209, 216, 220, 227, 228, 235,
    236
    /Qatar seabed limit 48–50, 52
    /Saudi Arabia maritime boundary
        55, 181, 205
    –Qatar relations 50
    –Saudi seabed agreement (1958)
        55, 205
    Additional Area 49
    Hamad, Shaikh 50, 51
Bahraini coup (December 1981) 42
Baihan salient 104
Bainah islands 55
Bakhah-Rims 223
baklawah 27
Bandar Shuwaikh 121, 159
Bandar Taheri 229
Bani Kaab 114
Bani Khalid 84, 85, 119
Bani Qitab 110, 114
Bani Yas 84
Barents Sea 187

Basidu 35
Basrah 5, 82–4, 87, 119, 120, 122,
    124, 126, 128, 129, 136, 154–6, 158,
    161, 162, 163, 229, 230
Basrah Port Directorate 162
Batin 7, 12, 16, 17, 47, 56, 137, 138,
    141, 192
Baxter, C. W. 163
Bay of Biscay 179
bedouin 18, 21, 110, 112, 116
Belgrave, C. 50, 51
Bell, Sir Gawain 167
Beydoun, Z. R. 192
bilateral agreements 1, 11, 14, 24,
    34, 52, 53, 55, 169
Bin Mahfouz family 25
Bindagji, Hussein 24, 25, 104
Bini Hajar 32, 85
Bini Murra 32, 85
Bini Muslim 32, 85
Bithnah (Battle of 1902) 110
Boggs, S. W. 15, 19
Bombay 88
border post 11, 18, 49, 55, 57, 169,
    195
boundary,
    antecedent 15
    anthropogeographic 15, 27–9
    artificial 17
    colonial legacy 95, 96
    complex 15, 27–9
    cultural 29
    de facto 94, 96
    de jure 10, 13, 99, 104, 107
    delimitation 4, 9–11, 19, 45, 55,
        94, 109, 153, 154, 162, 171, 211
    geometric 15, 19–27, 29
    internal administrative 132
    linear 29, 30
    maritime *see* maritime
    natural 15
    physiographic 15, 17, 29
    pillar 2, 9, 11, 29, 39, 141
    pioneer 15
    points 7, 19, 21, 24, 141
        fixed 19, 21, 24
    permanent 105
    recognition, unilateral 135

relict 15
straight-line 19
treaties, abrogation 60
Boutros-Ghali, Boutros 9
Brazil 179, 219
breach of mandate 123, 129, 131
Britain 1, 2, 8, 11–13, 16–21, 24, 28–31, 33–9, 41–5, 47–57, 80, 82, 83, 85, 87–91, 94–6, 98–107, 118, 120, 122–4, 126, 129–33, 138, 153, 154–61, 163–8, 194, 196, 201, 202, 204
British
    Colonial Office 15, 21, 88, 136, 161, 162
    Foreign Office 9, 16–21, 32–4, 37, 38, 42–5, 49, 50, 51–5, 90, 91, 104, 106, 109, 112, 118–21, 124, 126, 129, 137, 138, 139, 156–9, 162–8
    government 4, 8, 16, 17, 20, 21, 24, 32, 47, 52, 55, 57, 90, 94, 99, 104, 105, 120, 121, 122, 133, 157, 163, 164
    High Commissioner for Iraq 123, 129, 136
    India Office 4, 17, 20, 35, 88, 91, 105, 118, 119, 124, 126, 158, 160, 162, 164
    Military Survey 8–10
    Petroleum (BP) 193–195, 224, 226 227, 228, 232
    Political Agency 33, 113, 121, 123, 137, 138, 167
    Residency in the Gulf 35, 83, 209
    treaty practice 133
    War Office 35
Bu Saafah field 55, 56, 189, 190, 205–209
Bu Saafah shoal 55
Bubiyan island 5, 7–9, 14, 42, 43, 45, 118, 120, 121, 122–125, 128, 136–140, 153, 154, 155–172
    cession or lease of 153, 154
    Iraqi claims 118
buffer zone 6, 7, 201
Bunduq oilfield 52, 181, 209

Buq'ah 55
Buraimi 16, 19–21, 24, 28, 44, 47, 55, 87, 91, 96, 100–104, 112
    arbitration (1955) 101, 103
    Arbitration Tribunal 20, 21
Buraimi-al-Ain 19
Burrows, Sir Bernard 51, 55, 167
Bushire 17, 35, 36, 38, 50, 83, 88, 160
Buzurgan oilfield 229

Cairo 20, 56, 129, 161, 196
Cairo Conference (1921) 129, 161
Calais 51
cantons 19, 42, 94, 100
Caribbean 185
Cayman islands 25
cession of territory 130, 131
China 124, 187
co-ordinates 19, 21, 27, 56, 57, 109, 138, 181
coasts,
    adjacent 179, 184
    features 179
    trade 86
colonies 95, 96, 132
Committee of Imperial Defence 118, 158, 159
communications 3, 88, 89
compensation 39, 163, 164
Constantinople 119, 126, 156, 157, 160
constitutional arrangements, internal 135
constitutional requirements 123, 132
constrained export capacity 219
consular representatives, exchange 125
continental shelf 41, 52, 176, 177, 179, 180, 184, 185, 205, 209, 223, 233, 235
conventions, international 134, 195
coral reefs 196
corridor of territory 56
Costa Rica 179
Cox, Sir Percy 16, 45, 102, 122, 123, 136, 137, 158, 160, 161
cross-border hydrocarbon reserves

187–91, 197
cultural landscape 15, 30, 32
currency 119, 120, 131
Curzon, Lord 14–16, 36, 42, 157,
167
Cyprus Buffer zone 201

Daiyinah 52, 181, 209
Damascus Declaration (6 March
1991) 2
Dammam 18, 101
Dammam Conference (1952) see
Anglo–Saudi
dar 29, 30, 55, 85
Darin treaty (1915) see Anglo–Najdi
Dariya 81
date palm 17
Dawasir 50
Dawhah 3, 18, 31–33, 44, 45, 48, 53,
85, 235
de Cuellar, Perez 7
defence agreement 236
delimitation 4–12, 16–19, 21, 26, 27,
29, 31, 45, 52, 54–7, 60, 94, 109,
118, 122, 125, 131, 132, 153, 154,
161, 162, 171, 176–85, 207, 211
   agreements 176, 177
   methods 177
demarcated boundary 2, 5, 7, 9, 20,
29
demarcation 2, 5, 7–14, 16, 17, 26,
31, 54, 55, 57, 59, 116, 118, 124,
136, 138, 141, 153, 165–9, 171, 184,
192
demilitarized zone 7–11, 45, 59,
171, 201, 203, 209
dependency 128, 129, 226
desert 15, 16, 18, 19, 26, 28, 30, 32,
45, 47, 53, 94, 97, 104, 107, 110,
112, 113, 114, 116, 166, 191, 198,
211
development zone, joint 177, 185
Dha'ain 32, 85
Dhahirah 101, 106
Dhaid 110
Dhank 28
Dhayah 111
Dibal shoal 3, 11, 48–50, 52

Dickson, H. 17, 44, 45, 123, 137,
205
dira 24, 30, 86
Directorate of Overseas Survey 111
disputes
   inter-state 126
   inter-Arab 224
disputed waters 196
dominion 118
Dortyül 225, 228
dredging 154, 157, 166
dry cargo port 154
Drysdale & Blake 31, 34, 45
Dubai 27, 30, 84, 88–92, 10, 111,
113, 114, 179, 181–4, 197, 201, 205,
216, 224, 226
Duhat as-Salwah 18
Duru 112, 114

East Africa 84
East India Company 88
Eastern province (of Saudi Arabia)
103, 190, 198
economic circulation 86, 97, 98
economic claim 140
economic recession 224
economic zone, exclusive 176, 185
Edmonds, C. J. 12, 165
Egypt 2, 95, 127, 196, 201
elections 193
Empty Quarter (Rub al-Khali) 99,
190
enclave 52, 180
territory, enemy-occupied 122
energy conservation 227
enhanced recovery project 197
equidistance 52, 177, 179–82, 185
   boundary 180
   line 52, 179–81
equitable principles 184
Erzurum, treaty (1823) 31
Erzurum, treaty (1847) 4
establishment of posts 159
Euphrates 82, 129
Europe 32, 60, 78, 123, 224, 226,
227, 229, 230
extraterritorial 48, 51

Fahad, Shaikh 167, 168
Failakah island 43, 122, 137, 161
Faisal, King 129
Falkland islands 140, 187
Farasan archipelago 54, 194
Fars province 35
Farsi island 179–81, 183, 185
Fasht al-Dibal 49, 50
Faw peninsula 4, 7, 14, 154, 166, 230, 231
federal state 200
federation 28, 30, 48, 84
Federation of Arab Emirates (proposed, 1968–71) 48
feudalization 105
First World War 37, 38, 89, 90, 94, 96, 99, 100, 102, 105, 106, 122, 127, 202
Fish lake area 229, 231
fishing 36, 42, 50, 157, 159, 160
flag 36, 37, 40, 119, 122, 127, 161
floating storage tankers 225
force majeure 195
foreign exchange 218, 231
France 1, 124, 131, 134, 179, 180, 193
freedom of navigation 230, 232, 236
frontier 5, 16–21, 24, 28–33, 43, 44, 45, 47, 53, 56, 57, 92, 94, 96, 98–107, 109, 110–116, 118, 123, 124, 127, 130, 132, 137, 138, 140, 141, 155, 162, 165, 166, 188, 190, 191, 193, 194, 195–8, 207, 217
  dispute (Burkino Faso/Mali case) 132
  settlement 47, 109, 110, 112, 115
Fujairah 84, 110, 114, 201
Fujairah–Sharjah shared zone 201

gas-fuelled desalination 235
gas–oil separation plants (GOSPs) 190
gasfield
  North Dome 233, 235, 236
  North Field 197, 235
  South Pars 197, 233, 235
General Treaty of Peace (1820) 88
Geneva 9, 20, 26, 44, 55

geographic co-ordinates 181
geographical contiguity 160
geographical disadvantage 4, 200, 229
geological surveys 90
geopolitical zone 223
Germany 11, 34, 42
Ghafiri 84
Government of India 14, 15, 18, 34, 37, 38, 42, 43, 50, 121, 122, 139, 154, 156–160, 164, 165, 172
government revenues 197, 215
grazing 24, 97, 110, 137, 160
Greater Oman 98
Greater Tunb island 36–38
Greater Yemen 54, 98
Guicciardi, V. 41
Guinea–Bissau/Senegal case 134, 135
Gulf Cooperation Council (GCC) 1–3, 41, 48, 49, 216, 228, 234–236
  Council of Ministers 48
Gulf, hegemony 231
Gulf of Aqabah 45, 56, 60
Gulf of Oman 228
Gulf security 235
Gulf states, Iranian policies 41, 223
Gulf War (1991) 6, 7, 11, 25, 31, 60, 153, 189, 191, 225-7, 234

Habarut (Yemeni concession block) 194, 196
Habibi, Vice President 235
hadar 85
Hadhramawt 16, 24–6, 30, 33
Hadhrami Bedouin Legion 21
Hafr al-Batin 56
Hajar mountains 28, 32, 85
Halaib triangle 196
Halifax, Lord 163–5
Halul island 51, 52, 182
Hamriyah 111
Hamzah line (1935) 20, 21, 24–6, 101
Hamzah, Fuad Bey 20, 21, 24–6, 101
Hanbalism 81
Hartshorne, R. (boundary definitions) 15, 29, 31

Hasa 47, 53, 99, 119, 190
Hasa mainland concession (1933) 47
Hashimite 56, 98, 123, 155
Hashimite Union of Iraq and Jordan
 155
Hawar islands 3, 11, 17, 33, 48–52,
 59, 184, 185, 196, 235
Hawar award (1939) 51, 52
Hendorabi island 182
Hijaz 82, 98
hijra 97
Hinawi 84
Hinawi–Ghafiri factionalism 84
historical claims 2, 3, 28, 42, 83, 99,
 117, 118, 155, 191, 192, 228
Holdich, Col. Thomas 16
Hormuz, Strait of 28, 36, 38, 84,
 183, 227, 228
Houston-Boswell 163
Hudaidah 54
Husain, Saddam 1, 3–6, 13, 40, 60,
 117, 125, 155, 231, 233
Husain–Rafsanjani correspondence
 (1990) 6
hydrocarbon 40, 187, 191, 195, 197,
 204, 211, 223, 227, 236
  allocation 190
  discoveries 195
  exploration 211
Hymans, M. 130

Ibadi 83, 84, 87, 98
Ibadi Imamate 98
Ibn Jiluwi 103
Ibn Khaldun 86
Ibn Muqrin, Saud ibn Muhammad
 81
Ibn Saud 1, 15, 17–21, 27, 32, 33,
 44, 45, 47, 53–5, 79, 81, 82, 85, 87,
 94, 98, 99–107, 161, 202
Ibn Thani 32, 85
Ibri 103
Iceland 179
Idrisi of Asir 54
ihram 92
Ikhwan 44, 82, 98
imam 24, 54, 55, 79–81, 83, 87, 94,
 98, 99, 100–104, 112

Imam al-Muslimin 98
Imam Ghalib (Oman) 112
Imamate 19, 54, 83, 95, 96, 98
independence 1, 15, 20, 29, 31, 41,
 91, 95, 99, 101, 104, 105, 110, 120,
 124–127, 131, 132, 139, 161, 168
India 4, 14, 15, 17, 18, 20, 34, 35,
 37, 38, 42, 43, 50, 78, 83, 84, 88,
 89, 91, 105, 107, 118, 119, 121, 122,
 124, 126, 139, 154, 156–60, 162,
 164, 165, 172
Indian Ocean 97
Indonesia 187
Indo–Persian Boundary Demarcation
 Commission (1890s) 16
International Court of Justice (ICJ)
 11, 48, 50, 94, 131, 132, 140, 176,
 177, 179, 180, 181, 184, 187, 234
international courts 17, 48, 49, 59,
 180
international guardianship 126, 128
International Labour Organization
 125, 136
International Straits Commission
 201
intra-Gulf relations 223
Iran 1–6, 14, 15, 18, 28, 29, 31,
 34–6, 38–41, 53, 59, 60, 78–81, 87,
 89, 90, 95, 96, 117, 125, 154, 163,
 168, 169, 176, 179–85, 188, 190,
 196, 197, 201, 209, 211, 215, 216,
 218, 219, 223–36
  /Abu Dhabi maritime boundary
   179, 181, 183
  /Bahrain maritime boundary 181,
   209
  /Iraq boundary 4–6, 27, 29, 31
  /Qatar maritime boundary 181,
   182, 209
  –Iraq war (1980–88) 1, 3, 4, 40,
   60, 154, 168, 169, 183, 215, 225,
   228–32
  –Saudi Arabia agreement (maritime boundary 1968) 180, 185,
   201
  –United States Claims Tribunal
   182
  and Dubai (maritime boundary

agreement 1974) 183
and Oman (maritime boundary
   agreement 1975) 183, 190
Council of the Islamic Revolution
   81
Gas Trunkline (IGAT–1) 229
Iranian
   –Arabian security initiative 233
   Foreign Ministry 37, 41, 42
   majlis 41, 169
   Republican News Agency 235
Irano–Arabian conflict 223
Iraq 1–17, 19, 27, 29–31, 34, 40–45,
   47, 53, 57, 59, 60, 78–83, 87, 89, 90,
   95, 98, 99, 117–19, 121–42, 153,
   154, 155–7, 160–72, 183–5, 188,
   191–3, 200–205, 209, 211, 215, 216,
   219, 223–34, 236
   /Kuwait boundary 2, 5, 7–11, 13,
      14, 42, 57, 59, 117, 118, 136,
      138, 140, 141, 153, 165, 171,
      184, 185, 191, 192, 209, 236
   /Kuwait exchange of correspond-
      ence (1932) 6, 7, 161, 171
   /Saudi Arabia border treaty
      (1981) 27
   /Saudi Arabia boundary 16, 19,
      27, 141
   –Kuwait agreement ("Agreed
      minutes", 1963) 7, 10, 117, 125,
      133, 153, 171
   –Saudi Arabia Neutral Zone 45,
      201, 204, 205
Iraq, King Faisal 129
Iraqi
   access to the Gulf 14, 59, 153,
      155, 172
   air attacks 225
   Constitution (1925) 133
   constitutional law 133
   Foreign Ministry 124, 162, 166,
      167
   House of Representatives 132
   invasion of Kuwait 1, 3, 5, 7,
      117, 135, 154, 165, 169, 225,
      228, 232
   National Assembly 11, 133, 134
   National Revolutionary Council
      132, 134
   Revolutionary Command Council
      27
   –Kuwaiti exchange of letters
      (1923) 89
   –Kuwaiti relations 133
Ireland 194
irrigation water 114
Islam 31, 79, 81, 86, 98
Islamic constitutional law 79, 86
Islamic constitutional theory 81
Islamic orthodoxy 79
Islamic state 79, 98
island 2, 3, 5, 7, 11, 17, 25, 33–43,
   48, 49, 50, 52, 55, 84, 87, 95, 118,
   120, 122, 123, 128, 136, 137, 139,
   140, 153, 154–6, 158–63, 165–71,
   176, 179–85, 187, 194, 196, 204–207,
   209, 223, 225, 231, 233, 234–6
   allocation 140, 209
Israel 25, 95

Jabal al-Thar 193
Jabal Naksh 17–19, 33, 91
Jabal Raiyan 21, 24
Jabal Sanam 17, 137
Jabal Shammar 82
Jahrah 1, 44, 53, 202
Jalloui, Ibn 32, 85
Janan island 48
Japan 11, 179, 224, 226, 227
Jaradah shoal 3, 48–50, 52
Jawf 30, 191, 193, 194
Jazirat al-Hamrah 111
Jiddah 20, 21, 24, 53, 54, 94, 100,
   105, 191
jihad 24, 105
Jiluwi, Ibn 103
Jizan 191
Jordan 44, 45, 56, 60, 80, 95, 98,
   155, 212
jurisdiction 34, 39, 48, 50, 51, 59,
   102, 103, 126, 159, 184, 204

Kadhamah (Kazima) Bay 159
Kalba 89
Karun river 235
Kedleston 15, 16

Kemp, Commander 157
Kerkennah islands 180
Khafji oilfield 189
Khafus 2, 18, 49, 57
Khaldun, Ibn 86
khalifa 79, 80
Kharg island 180, 181, 185, 225
Kharg island export terminals 225
Khawr Abdallah 5, 7, 9, 10, 14, 60,
   120, 124, 137, 138, 154, 157, 158,
   162–6, 171, 230
Khawr al Mahadnadah 33
Khawr al-Udaid 17–19, 33, 181
Khawr Bubiyan 43, 45, 154, 157,
   165
Khawr Maqtah 45, 204
Khawr Sabiya 12
Khawr Shetana 9, 12, 154, 165
Khawr Zubair 5, 7, 9, 12, 14, 17, 42,
   43, 120, 125, 138, 139, 154, 157,
   158, 162, 163, 164, 165
Khomeini, Ayatollah 80, 81, 232
Khosrovi 6
kingdom 18, 20, 24, 26, 47, 79, 80,
   82, 101, 124, 141, 180, 190, 193,
   218, 235
Kirkuk 227, 230
Kitchener, Lord 158
Knox, Major 159, 160
Kubr island 43, 122, 161
Kurdish rebellion 4
Kurdish safe haven 201, 202
Kurdistan 29
Kurds 6, 29, 219
Kuwait 1–17, 27, 31, 33, 42–5, 47,
   53, 57, 59, 60, 79, 82–5, 87, 89–91,
   94, 95, 99, 100, 102, 117, 118,
   119–42, 153–72, 183–5, 188, 189,
   191, 192, 200–205, 209, 217, 219,
   220, 224–8, 230–32, 233–6
   /Iraq boundary 5, 7, 16, 17, 59,
      136, 162, 165, 167, 168
   /Najd boundary 203
   /Saudi Arabia boundary 45
   Bay 43–5, 156, 157, 159, 162,
      163, 170
   crisis 6, 13, 118, 120–27, 129,
      131, 135, 137, 153, 169, 202,

204, 227
Kuwait,
   Department of Justice 135
   international status 155, 156
   oil-pricing policies 118
Kuwaiti
   –Najdi Neutral Zone 16, 43, 53,
      203
   –Saudi Neutral Zone 45, 185,
      203
   Ministry of information 170, 171

Lansdowne, Lord 120, 157, 158
Larak island 84, 183, 225
Latin America 140, 226
Lausanne treaty (1923) 83, 123, 127,
   128, 130
Lavan 182
law
   constitutional 79, 86, 133–5
   customary international 135,
      140, 176, 177
   European 115
   feudal 128
   international 2, 4, 11, 20, 21, 47,
      49, 57, 78, 79, 95, 96, 100, 102,
      104–107, 118, 122, 126–8, 131–5,
      140, 176, 177, 180, 184, 202,
      211, 216
   of treaties 131–5
   public international 126–128
League of Arab States 20, 56
League of Nations 37, 82, 123, 124,
   127, 129–31, 132, 133, 153, 162
   Council 123, 127, 130, 131
   Covenant 129
   mandate 123
Lebanon 40, 201, 212
   protected zone 201
legal
   advice 105
   personality 131, 136
   position 102, 106
   principles 78
legislative authority 133
legitimacy 32, 33, 41, 81, 92, 98, 99,
   220
Lesser Tunb island 34, 36, 41

Libya 177, 179, 180, 185
Libya–Tunisia continental shelf 180, 185
Lingeh 35, 36, 88
local conflicts 223
London 2, 3, 5, 7, 16, 18, 20, 30, 34–6, 38, 41, 45, 47, 51–3, 55, 60, 78, 79, 81, 83, 84, 87, 88,94, 112, 116, 118–20, 122, 134, 135, 155, 156, 159, 162, 170, 192, 205, 212, 213, 220, 223–5, 227, 228, 230, 231, 233, 234
Lorimer, J. G. 113, 118–20, 129, 159, 160
low-tide elevations 49, 50, 55, 177
Luce, Sir William 39
Lurs 29

Mahon, Captain 158
majlis 30, 41, 85, 155, 169
Majnun 229, 231
malik 79
mamlaka 79
Manamah 48, 114
Manasir 32, 33, 85
mandate 7, 9, 10, 13, 59, 82, 90, 123, 124, 128, 129–31, 190
mandated territory 129–32, 161
    A type 131
Mandates Commission 130, 131
Mandatory Power 124, 129, 132
manmade features 27
map 2, 4, 8, 9, 18, 20, 24, 25, 27, 30, 31, 35, 39, 43, 52, 57, 94, 96, 99, 100, 111, 113, 115, 116, 120, 121, 136, 138, 139, 141, 153, 161, 177, 192, 200, 201
Marib 30, 193, 194
Marib/Jawf concession (Yemeni) 193, 194
maritime
    boundary 34, 37, 52, 55, 56, 134, 179, 180, 181, 182, 183, 185, 190, 196, 201, 205, 207–209, 223
        Abu Dhabi–Qatar agreement (1969) 181, 185, 201
    delimitation 55, 132, 176, 178, 179, 184, 185

legislation 181
    trade 83, 85
    zones 185
Mashjan island 43, 122, 137, 161
Mawerdi, A-H. A. 80
Mawsul 82, 83, 122, 230
McCallum, Captain 161
Mecca 54, 79
median line 9, 21, 34, 138, 171, 177, 180–82, 185
    delimitation 9
mediation 48, 109, 115, 184
Medina 18, 79
Mediterranean 79, 225, 228
Memorandum of Understanding (Sharjah/Iran 1971) 39–41, 60, 233
Mesopotamia 85, 122, 123, 128–131
Mesopotamian
    mud 162
    plain 31, 164
Middle East global capital expenditure 212
Midhat Pasha 85, 119
Midi 54, 55, 193
Midyan 191
migration 12, 96, 116
military zones 49
Mina al-Ahmadi 167
Mina al-Bakr 219
mineral resources 24, 25, 179, 182, 185
Ministry of Petroleum and Mineral Resources (Saudi Arabia) 24, 25
Minto, Viceroy 158
More, Major J. C. 17, 161
Morocco 80, 131
Moss-Helms, C. (1981) 79, 80
mountains 16, 28, 31, 54, 55, 111–14, 116
Mubarak al-Sabah, Shaikh 42, 43, 45, 89, 120–22, 156, 157, 158–60, 172
Mubarak, Hosni 18
mudharabah 83
Muhammarah 80, 105, 202, 204, 205
mulk 79, 80
Murra 30, 32, 85
Musandam peninsula 28, 30, 48,

200, 223

Muscat 17, 20, 28, 29, 57, 84, 88, 91, 95, 98, 101, 102, 104, 106, 114, 118, 119
    and Oman 17, 20, 28, 101, 102, 104, 114, 118
Muscati Sultan 101, 104
    "no-claims" line (1937) 104

Na'im tribe 33, 50, 85
Nafud desert 191
Najd 27, 81, 82, 100, 102, 120, 123, 202, 203–205
Najd–Iraq Neutral Zone 27
Najd–Kuwait Neutral Zone 16, 27, 43, 203
Najran 20, 24, 25, 54, 55, 193
Najran 55
naqib of Basrah 156
National Commercial Bank of Saudi Arabia 25
natural
    anchorage 42, 154, 13, 167
    features 15–17, 21, 27
    gas 223, 229, 232
    resources 105, 181, 195
naval power 97, 227
navigation 5, 9, 18, 19, 154, 165, 230, 232, 236
    channel 9, 154
neutral zone 16, 27, 28, 43, 45, 56, 114, 189, 201, 203–205, 224, 226
    Ajman–Oman 28, 201
New York 7, 9, 15, 25, 27, 29, 31, 38, 41, 45, 55, 133, 155, 171, 200, 223
Newton, Sir Basil 164, 165
nomadic 16, 21, 29, 81, 85, 97, 98, 105, 204
North America 1, 32, 226
North Sea 177, 185
North Yemen 193
Norway 179, 187

O'Conor, Sir Nicholas 157, 158
oasis 16, 20, 24, 44, 87, 91, 97, 101, 103, 110, 112, 193
occupancy, effective 21, 26, 33, 60, 96, 105

occupation 3, 4, 6, 9, 25, 39, 41, 50, 79, 103, 106, 107, 120, 122, 155, 157, 159, 234
offshore
    development 187
    hydrocarbons 176
oil 11, 13, 17, 19, 25, 26, 32–4, 38, 40, 41, 43–5, 47, 49–54, 56, 57, 78, 83, 84, 85, 88–91, 96, 99, 103, 105, 106, 109, 111, 112, 114, 116, 118, 125, 131, 138, 140, 155, 163, 166, 167, 176, 180, 182, 183, 185, 187, 188, 189–98, 203–206, 208, 209, 211, 212–21, 223–33, 235–7
    company 26, 50, 51, 90, 106, 109, 176, 182, 193, 194–196, 211, 212, 214, 216, 217, 219, 220, 227
    American Independent Oil Company (AMINOIL) 189
    Anglo-Iranian Oil Company (AIOC) 90, 163
    Anglo–Persian Oil Company (APOC) 32, 54, 85, 90
    Arabian American Oil Company (ARAMCO) 21, 96, 106, 189–91, 198, 218
    Arabian Oil Company (AOC) 189
    Bahrain Petroleum Company (BAPCO) 49, 50, 196, 207
    Buttes Oil Company 40
    Crescent Petroleum Company 197
    development activity 211, 212, 214, 217
    Egyptian General Petroleum Corporation (EGPC) 196
    Elf Aquitaine 193
    Elf Petroland 193
    Exxon 193
    foreign 26, 90, 196, 211, 216, 219, 220
    Getty Oil Company 189
    Harken Energy Corporation 196
    Hunt Oil 193–5
    International Petroleum

Corporation 196
Iraq Petroleum Company 90,
99, 106, 167, 227, 228
Kuwait Foreign Petroleum
Exploration Company
(KUFPEC) 219
Kuwait Oil Company (KOC)
189
Mayfair Petroleum 195
National Iranian Oil Company
(NIOC) 218, 229
national 211, 214
Nimr Petroleum Company 25,
193, 195
multinational 227
nationalization 212, 217
Petro-Canada 194, 195
Petroleum Concessions Limited
49, 50
Petroleum Development
Trucial Coast Limited
(PD[TC]L) 111
Phillips Petroleum 194, 195
Saudi ARAMCO 189, 190, 198,
218
Shaibah 190, 191, 197, 198
Shell Oil Company of Qatar
52
Standard Oil Company of California (SOCAL) 44, 47, 53, 90,
99
Texaco 189
Tullow Oil 194
Turkish (later Iraq) Petroleum
Company (TPC) 90
concession 17, 19, 25, 32, 44, 53,
83, 91, 196
deposits 17, 33, 38
diversification strategy 219
drilling 25, 138, 182, 187, 190,
191, 193, 195, 196, 209, 211,
216–218
programme 218
installations 180, 183, 225
markets 216, 217
pipelines 225, 227
Iraqi Pipeline across Saudi Arabia (IPSA) 219, 228

ports, Iran 225
production 78, 193, 204, 219,
224, 225, 230, 232
and export facilities, Iraq 225
capacity expansion 190,
216–219, 221
quotas 182, 216, 225
reserves 18, 40, 49, 185, 187–199,
216, 217, 223, 226, 227, 232,
235, 236
revenues 96, 191, 205, 208
supply 227
security 223, 224, 231
tankers 225, 227
transit routes 236
wells 13, 192
Fateh 179
oil,
crude 84, 223–227, 229
diversification of sources 227
exploration 25, 56, 57, 90, 109,
176, 187–189, 190–193, 195, 196,
211–213, 214–220, 235
activity 214
and development (1960–87)
176, 187, 188, 190, 211, 212–15
budgets 217
export capacity 215, 219, 228
frontier exploration 217
offshore concessions 51
price collapses 218
proved reserves 216, 227
revenue, annual average 216
secondary recovery 218
"participation negotiations" 212
oilfield
development plans 190, 197, 220
Faqi 229
Hout 189
Lekhwair 56
Luhais 229
Mubarak 197
Nahr Umar 229
North Rumailah 192, 229
Ratgah 191, 192
Rumailah 13, 118, 125, 138, 192
Sassan 182
Zararah 190

Zubair 229
Oman 2, 17, 20, 24–31, 36, 44, 48,
  56, 57, 59, 81, 83–5, 87, 91, 94–6,
  98, 99, 101–104, 106, 109, 112–14,
  116, 118, 159, 183–5, 190, 195, 198,
  200, 201, 205, 209, 212, 216, 220,
  223, 224, 226, 228, 229, 234, 235
  /Saudi Arabia boundary 57
  /United Arab Emirates boundary
  27, 57
  /Yemen boundary 59
  –Ras al-Khaimah dispute (1977)
  223
  –Saudi agreement (1990) 20, 94
Oman,
  Ghalib, Imam 104, 112
  Imamate 96, 101
  Sultan Qabus 56
Oppenheim–Lauterpacht 126, 128
Organization for Economic
  Co-operatin and Development
  (OECD) 224, 226, 231, 232
  states 231, 232
Organization of Petroleum
  Exporting Countries (OPEC) 191,
  192, 214–216, 219, 224, 225, 230,
  233, 235
Orontes river 82
Ottoman
  Empire 2, 4, 14, 19, 26, 29, 31,
    34, 42, 43, 44, 53, 85, 88–90, 96,
    99, 100, 105, 118, 120–22, 126–8,
    155–7, 159–61, 164, 172, 202
  Grand Vizier 157
  Iraq 119
  territory 119, 127

Pahlavi, Shah Muhammad Reza 41
Panama 179
Partition agreement 45, 204
peacekeeping 5, 6, 14, 59, 171
pearling 33, 83, 85, 86
Pelly, L. 42, 119, 126, 154, 157, 163
People's Democratic Republic of
  Yemen 20, 25, 26, 56
Perpetual Maritime Truce (1853) 88
Persia 2, 4, 29, 34, 35, 37, 38, 44,
  84, 118, 164

Persian/Iranian claims to Bahrain 41
Perso–Ottoman boundary treaty,
  Kerden (1746) 31
  Hamadan (1729) 31
Philby line (conjectural
  Saudi/Yemen boundary) 194
Philby, H. St.John 194
pipeline 131, 166, 167, 198, 219,
  225, 227–9, 231, 235
piracy 35, 88, 89, 97
Pirie-Gordon, C. 109
Poe, Vice-Admiral 159
politics 29, 34, 48, 55, 60, 86, 104,
  120, 155, 217, 220
population 15, 33, 34, 78, 81, 85,
  86, 96, 119, 136, 200, 216, 231
Portugal 83, 84, 134, 187
  constitutional law 134
Principal Allied Powers 123, 129
principality 121–123
principles of delimitation 179, 184,
  185
Prior, Charles 2, 49, 75, 163
protectorate 16, 19–21, 25, 26, 33,
  36, 42, 54, 88, 89, 95, 98, 100, 104,
  120, 122, 123, 127, 131, 132, 156
province of Basrah 119, 124, 126,
  128, 155
Provisional Free Kuwaiti
  Government (PFKG) 125
Public Record Office 4, 94, 118, 119,
  157
Pusht-i-Kuh 29

qadha 16, 89, 122, 126, 160, 202
qaimmaqam 119, 120, 122, 161
Qais island 182
Qajar 41
Qaru island 3, 42, 121, 136, 203
Qasim, General 124, 125, 133, 155,
  168
Qasimi 28, 34–41, 84, 87
  shaikhdoms (of Sharjah and Ras
  al-Khaimah) 34, 39
Qatar 2, 11, 15, 17–20, 24, 29, 32,
  33, 41, 44, 45, 48–54, 56, 57, 59, 84,
  85, 87, 88, 90, 91, 94, 95, 99–101,
  119, 155, 181–5, 188, 191, 196, 197,

198, 200, 201, 208, 209, 216, 220,
224–8, 233, 235, 236
  /Abu Dhabi maritime boundary
    51–2, 182
  /Bahrain boundary dispute
    48–50, 182
  –Abu Dhabi maritime boundary
    agreement (1969) 52, 185
  –Iran alliance (over the North
    Dome gasfield) 236
  General Petroleum Corporation
    196
  Khuff–4 structure 197
  oil concession 44, 53
  peninsula 17–20, 29, 32, 33, 44,
    45, 48–54, 56, 85, 95, 119
  seabed 52
Qatari
  –Iranian relations 235
  Foreign Ministry 49
Qatif 81, 126
Qawasim 28, 36, 35, 84, 88, 110
Qeshm island 84
Qit'at al-Jaradah 50
Quraish 80

Rafsanjani, Ali Akbar Hashemi 3, 6,
  40, 41, 169, 232–4, 236
railway 27, 42, 43, 88, 120, 121, 127,
  128, 131, 154, 157–9, 162, 163
  Baghdad 88, 120, 121, 127, 157–9
  terminus 42, 120, 121, 154, 157
  trans-continental system 158
Raiyan 16, 21, 24, 101
Rams 111
Ras al-Khaimah 28, 34–9, 84, 87, 88,
  90, 109, 110, 114, 183, 223, 234
Ras al-Qaid 156–9, 161
Ras Hasian 109, 179
Ras Tanurah 198
Ras Tanurah export terminal 198
ratification 20, 54, 124, 133
Razouki, Tariq A. 12
recognition 2, 7, 21, 25, 33, 34, 38,
  39, 52, 80, 82, 94, 99, 111, 116,
  121–3, 124, 125, 128, 131, 133, 135,
  136, 139, 140, 155, 160
Red Sea 20, 54, 94, 129, 191, 193,

194, 196, 217–19, 225, 228
  coast 191, 193, 194, 228
  exploration blocks 196
Republic of Turkey 127, 128
Republic of Yemen 20, 24–6, 56, 60,
  194
resource 30, 98, 167, 188, 201
Reza Shah 80
river 3, 4, 6, 15, 16, 29, 60, 82, 128,
  129, 235
Riyadh 2, 10, 16, 18–21, 24–7, 44,
  54, 56, 57, 81, 101, 104, 189, 190,
  193, 194, 195, 198
  line (1935) 16, 20–21, 24–7, 44,
    56, 101, 104
    modified (1937) 20, 21, 25, 44,
      56, 104
Rouhani, Ayatollah 41
Royal Geographical Society 111
Royal Institute of International
  Affairs 2, 3, 7, 118, 155, 192, 220,
  228
Ru'us Abu Adh Dhuhif 33
Ru'us al-Jibal 28
Rub al-Khali 16, 19, 21, 27, 30, 99,
  100, 111, 190
Rumailah 10, 13, 118, 125, 138, 191,
  192, 229
  –Ratgah area 192
Russia 29, 31, 34, 42, 187, 234
Ryan line (1935) 101; see also Riyadh
  line (1935)
Ryan, Sir Andrew 21, 24, 54, 107

Sabiyah 170
Sabkhat Matti 19
Safavid 31, 80
safe haven 201, 202, 219
Safwan 8, 9, 12, 17, 122, 137, 138,
  141, 142, 156, 157, 192
Saiar tribe 25
sakham 114
Salalah 56, 228
Salazar, President 134
Salih, Ali Abdallah 26
Salisbury, Lord 36
Salwah 18
San Remo conference (1920) 123

San'a 2, 30, 55, 94, 99, 100, 104,
  193, 195
Sanaw 21, 194
sanjaq 100, 102, 119
Saud, Abdul Aziz Ibn 81
Saud, Ibn 1, 15, 17–21, 27, 32, 33,
  44, 45, 47, 53–5, 79, 81, 82, 85, 87,
  94, 98, 99–107, 161, 202
Saud, Muhammad Ibn 81
Saudi Arabia 2, 3, 16–21, 24–9,
  31–4, 41–5, 47–9, 53–7, 59, 60,
  78–83, 87, 89–91, 94–6, 100, 101,
  103, 104–107, 141, 177, 179–81,
  182–5, 187–90, 193–8, 201, 203–206,
  208, 209, 216–18, 219, 224–6, 228,
  230, 235, 236
  /Bahrain boundary 55–6, 179
  /Kuwait, divided zone 189
  /UAE boundary 188
  –Bahrain agreement (1958) 55,
    179, 185, 201
  –Kuwait partitioned zone 201,
    204
  King 'Abd al-'Aziz 55
  King Fahd 48, 56, 216
  Kingdom 18, 82, 193
Saudi
  /Jordanian boundary 45
  /Oman boundary agreement
    (1990) 20
  /Yemen boundary 19, 20, 24, 25,
    42, 54, 94, 194
  –Idrisi agreements of 1926 and
    1930 54
  –Jordanian landswap (1965) 45
  –Qatar boundary agreement
    (1965) 56, 57
  –South Yemen, independence
    line 20
  –Wahhabi state 105
  –Yemeni relations 54, 55
  –Yemeni Treaty of Taif (1934) 54
  –Zaidi war (1934) 54
  Economic and Development
    Company (SEDCO) 25
  Foreign Ministry 21, 24, 54, 94
  government 24–26, 47, 56, 104
  Kingdom 20, 80

military survey map (1986) 20,
  24, 25
Scilly islands 180
Second World War 17, 33, 87, 91,
  96, 99, 103, 106, 138, 165
Secret Additional Protocol
  (Anglo–Ottoman 1913) 127
seismic studies 190, 191
self-defence 140, 232
semi-enclosed sea 200
Senegal 134, 135
Sèvres, treaty of (1920) 83, 123, 127,
  130
Shabwah concession 193
shaikh 17, 30, 32, 35, 37, 38, 42–5,
  49, 50, 51–3, 81, 87, 89–91, 98, 100,
  103, 106, 109, 114, 119–23, 126,
  127, 134, 137, 154, 156–68, 172,
  202, 203, 235
shaikhdom 18, 35, 39, 55, 80, 122,
  124, 127, 156, 161, 198
  of Muhammarah 80
Shakhbut, Shaikh (Abu Dhabi) 52,
  90, 91, 109
Shar' 81
shared zones 45, 200, 209
sharia law 86
Sharjah 28, 34–6, 38–41, 60, 84,
  87–9, 92, 110, 114, 183, 184, 196,
  197, 201, 233, 234
  –Iran Memorandum of Under-
    standing (1971) 39
  –Oman shared zone 201
Shatt al-Arab 3–6, 14, 29, 34, 40, 60,
  119, 120, 122, 125, 126, 154, 158,
  162–4, 166–8, 171, 184
  water carrier scheme 166–168
shi'i 29, 31, 230
Shi'ite 11
shipping lanes 197
shoal 3, 11, 48–50, 52, 55, 177, 184,
  185, 189
Shuraiwah island 181
Sirri island 35, 36, 38, 183, 185, 225
siyada 79
smuggling 30
Société Auxiliare de la Régie Auto-
  nome des Petroles (AUXIRAP) 218

South Yemen 20, 25, 94, 95, 187, 193
sovereign state 105, 124, 126
sovereignty 2, 3, 5, 6, 21, 31, 32, 34, 36–41, 43–5, 48, 50–52, 59, 60, 78, 79, 80–83, 86–9, 91, 92, 96, 98, 99, 101, 102, 104–106, 110, 114, 116, 117, 118–20, 124–8, 136, 139, 140, 154–6, 160–66, 169–71, 177, 179, 180, 183–5, 189, 190, 193, 196, 200–202, 204, 209, 210, 220, 233–5
  European notions 105
  restricted state 201, 202
Soviet Union 124, 125, 217
Spain 179
spatial organization 19, 29
sphere of influence 19, 99, 105, 107, 121
Spratly islands 187
state practice 128, 132, 176, 177, 179–181, 185
statement of frontier (Saudi 1949) 101, 103
Stavrides 119
Stobart incident (1949) 101, 103
straight-line segments 16, 21, 24, 27, 29
Strait of Hormuz 28, 36, 38, 183, 227, 228
succession 80, 126–128, 131, 132
successor state 2, 80, 100, 102, 105
Sudan 196
Suez Canal zone 201
sultah 79, 80
Sultan of Muscat 20, 28, 29, 98, 101, 102, 104, 106, 114
sunni 31, 79, 230
survey 2, 4, 6, 8–10, 19–21, 24, 25, 30, 54, 94, 111, 141, 157, 158, 163, 189, 190, 212, 217, 235
suzerainty 85, 87–9, 114, 126–8
Syria 2, 82, 131, 212, 227, 228

Taif 20, 24, 26, 54, 55, 60, 94, 193, 194
  line (Saudi/Yemeni 1934) 24, 54, 55, 60, 194
  Treaty of 1934 20, 54

Taimourtache, M. 37, 38
Tehran 35–9, 41, 232, 234–6
territorial
  arrangements 44, 53, 57
  claims 6, 20, 21, 24, 25, 30, 37, 42, 47, 56, 60, 91, 96, 101, 104, 106, 118, 139, 191, 193, 202, 205, 231
    maximum 44, 53
    minimum 21
  concessions 4, 162–4, 166
  consciousness 169
  enclaves 201
  organization 95, 97
  rights 97, 105
  sea 9, 39, 180, 181, 183, 185, 204
  settlement 6, 11, 167
  sovereignty 45, 78–80, 83, 86–8, 91, 92, 110, 116, 126, 127, 140, 200
    Western concept 116
  space 97
  understandings 57
  units 97
  waters 9, 44, 49
territoriality 1, 29
territory 2, 3, 5, 7, 11, 13–15, 17–19, 21, 24, 25–34, 37, 42–5, 50, 51, 53, 54, 56, 57, 59, 60, 78, 83, 86, 90–92, 94, 96, 99–102, 105, 107, 110, 113, 114, 115–17, 119–23, 125, 127, 128, 129–32, 136, 138, 140, 155, 156, 159, 161–6, 168, 169, 181, 183, 184, 190–93, 198, 201–203, 210, 223, 228, 230, 231, 235
  of Kuwait 122
territory,
  alienation 130
  annexation 45, 54, 79, 102, 125, 140
thalweg 4, 6, 12, 16, 60, 138, 141
Thanaw 21
Thar 55, 193
The Hague 11, 48, 50, 94, 182, 234
  Tribunal 182
Tigris 129
Tihamah plain 54
Tihamat Asir 54

Timor Gap 187
Tonkin Gulf 187
Totale 219
trade 30, 38, 83, 85, 86, 96, 97, 109,
  153, 224, 234
Treaty
  between Iraq and Britain (1930)
  82
Treaty of
  Alliance (Anglo-Iraqi 1922) 123,
    128, 129, 131, 133
  Islamic Friendship and Brother-
    hood (Taif; Saudi-Yemeni 1934)
    54
  Jiddah (Anglo-Najdi 1927) 53,
    100, 105
  peace and demarcation of
    frontiers (Zohab:
    Perso-Ottoman 1639) 31
  Sib (Anglo-Muscati 1920) 99,
    101, 103
tribal 18, 21, 24, 25, 27, 28, 30, 33,
  45, 80, 81, 83-7, 89, 97, 98, 102,
  105, 109, 110, 119, 187, 193, 204,
  205
  allegiance 45, 205
  confederation 28, 81, 87
  divisions 28
  grounds 21, 24
  migrations 33
  territories 25, 28
tribe 16, 17, 24, 25, 30, 32, 33, 35,
  36, 42, 45, 53, 56, 85-7, 90, 94,
  97-9, 101, 105, 110, 111, 114, 119,
  122, 157, 159, 202, 204, 205
tribunal 20, 21, 47, 104, 106, 131,
  132, 134, 135, 180, 182
tribute 35, 50, 119, 126, 161
Trucial Coast 18, 28, 30, 31, 38, 84,
  87-91, 103, 109, 111, 112, 116
Trucial Oman Scouts 112
Tunb islands 2, 34-41, 59, 60, 87,
  180, 183-185, 231, 233, 234, 236
Tunisia 179, 180, 185
Turco-Persian boundary commission
  (1914) 29
Turkey 29, 118, 123, 124, 127, 128,
  130, 131, 160, 219, 227

Turkish nationalists 123
Turkish Straits zone 201

Umm al Maradim island 3, 43, 44,
  122, 204
Umm al-Qaiwain 84, 109, 110, 183,
  197
Umm al-Samim 21
Umm al-Samim/Raiyan line
  (Saudi/Aden 1949-54) 21
Umm al-Zamul 29, 56
Umm Qasr 5, 7, 9, 12, 13, 17, 42,
  59, 120, 122, 125, 138, 141, 142,
  154, 156, 157, 158-60, 163-9, 192
  lease agreement 167
  scheme (1954-55) 166, 167
Umm Said 52
umma 79, 80
United Arab Emirates (UAE) 19,
  27-31, 33, 38, 40, 41, 44, 48, 57, 84,
  91, 94, 95, 109, 116, 124, 181, 183,
  185, 188, 190, 191, 196-8, 200, 205,
  206, 209, 220, 225, 227, 228, 233,
  234, 236
United Nations (UN) 2, 3, 4-14, 16,
  20, 27, 38, 39, 41, 53, 57, 59, 79,
  87, 117, 119, 124-6, 134, 135,
  139-41, 153, 171, 176, 179, 181,
  184, 185, 187, 191-195, 201, 203,
  209, 210, 219, 226, 229, 231, 233-5
  Charter 79, 139, 140
  Convention on the Law of the
    Sea 176, 181, 184, 185
  General Assembly 126, 133, 139,
    140, 210
  Iran-Iraq Military Observer
    Group (UNIIMOG) 5, 6, 59
  Iraq-Kuwait Boundary Demarca-
    tion Commission (UNIKBDC) 2,
    7-15, 171, 192
  Iraq-Kuwait Observation Mission
    (UNIKOM) 5, 7-11, 59, 171
  Resolution 598 229
  Security Council 2, 7, 9, 11, 13,
    16, 38, 39, 41, 87, 117, 124-6,
    139-42, 192, 234
    Resolution 678 117
    Resolution 687 16, 87, 192

Resolution 773 9, 10, 142
Resolution 833 2
Treaty Series 134
United States of America (USA) 1,
26, 36, 45, 52, 124, 133, 135, 182,
229, 236
Universal Transverse Mercator (UTM)
111
Uqair 16, 27, 43, 45, 53, 87, 89, 99,
100, 102, 105, 123, 161, 203, 204
Protocol (1922) 16, 27, 43, 45, 53,
87, 89, 99, 123, 161, 203
protocols 100
Uruguay 179
US
Nationals in Morocco 131
Navy 183
State Department 9, 24, 26, 27,
45, 52, 177, 180, 182
Utub 85, 119

velayat-e faqih 80
Velayati, Ali Akbar 41, 233, 234
Versailles, treaty of (1919) 4, 129
Viceroy of India 15, 122
Vienna Convention on the Law of
Treaties 131–5
Vietnam 187

wadi 7, 12, 19, 25, 28, 81, 94, 100,
114, 137, 141
Wadi
al Batin 141
Bana 19, 94, 100
Hadf 28, 114
Hanifah 81
Wafrah field 189
Wahhab, Muhammad Ibn Abdul 81
Wahhabi 29, 32, 79–82, 87, 88, 98,
99, 105, 106
–al-Saud state 98, 105
imamate 79, 80, 82
movement 79, 81, 82
Wakrah 33, 85
Walker, Julian 27, 28, 30, 31, 47, 48,
109, 116
Warbah island 5, 7–9, 14, 42, 43,
45, 118, 120, 121, 122–125, 128,

136–140, 153, 154, 155–172
Warbah and Bubiyan islands
cession or lease of 153, 154
Iraqi claims 118
Ward, Sir John 162, 163
wells 13, 20, 30, 97, 112, 114, 116,
137, 138, 179, 190–92, 204, 205, 214
wilayat 19, 42, 54, 94, 100, 119, 124,
128, 161
of Basrah 124, 128
of Yemen 19, 42, 54, 94, 100
Wilkinson, John 47
Williamson, Hajji Abdallah 17, 32,
33, 54, 85
Wilton, John 109
Wright, Sir Michael 166, 167

Yanbu 225, 228
Yemen 2, 11, 19, 20, 24–7, 30, 34,
42, 53, 54, 56, 59, 60, 81, 94–6,
98–100, 101, 102, 104, 105, 129,
187, 188, 191, 193–6, 212
/Omani boundary 94
Arab Republic 25, 30, 54
Yemen, Imamate 19, 24, 54, 98, 99,
102
Yahya, 55, 100
Zaidi 54, 98
Yemeni
Boundary Demarcation
Committee 26
concession block
central highlands 194
North Sanaw 194
Sirr Hazar 194
Zaidiah 194
mashriq 24, 25, 30
oil concessions 26
Antufash 193, 195
Yemeni unification (May 1990) 20,
25, 26, 55

Zagros 29, 31
Zaidi 54, 98
zakat 24, 86, 87, 103, 105, 114
Zakhnuniyah island 19, 100
Zohab 31
Zubarah 48, 50, 51, 84, 85, 88, 89, 119